The Rohingya Crisis

This edited volume addresses the broader aspects of the political and social landscape, human rights violations, accountability and advocacy efforts, and humanitarian challenges faced by the Rohingya from Myanmar.

The work brings together different voices of legal, policy, and international affairs experts to construct a framework which addresses the complex and nuanced issues comprising the Rohingya crisis. Although there is recognition that international legal mechanisms are moving forward more quickly than anticipated, these processes do not constitute standalone, sustainable solutions. Myanmar's myriad political, social cohesion, development, and security challenges are likely to persist even as justice and accountability processes move forward. Thus, this book project is premised on the consensus that the international community should complement international justice mechanisms by looking towards creative and multi-faceted approaches, in addition to justice and accountability.

This timely contribution will be of interest to academics, researchers, development practitioners, and human rights organizations.

Manzoor Hasan is Executive Director at the Centre for Peace and Justice, Brac University, Bangladesh.

Syed Mansoob Murshed is Professor of the Economics of Conflict and Peace at the International Institute of Social Studies (ISS), Erasmus University Rotterdam, the Netherlands and Professor of Economics at Coventry University in the UK.

Priya Pillai is Head of the Asia Justice Coalition Secretariat.

Routledge Research in Human Rights Law

International Human Rights Law and Crimes Against Women in Turkey
Legislation on So-Called Honour Killings
Ayşe Güneş

Rights of the Child, Mothers and Sentencing
The Case of Kenya
Alice Wambui Macharia

Capturing Caste in Law
The Legal Regulation of Caste Discrimination
Annapurna Waughray

The Workings of Human Rights, Law, and Justice
A Journey from Nepal to Nobel Nominee
Surya P Subedi

Civilian Drones, Visual Privacy and EU Human Rights Law
Girish Agarwal

International Human Rights Law and Destitution
An Economic, Social and Cultural Rights Perspective
Luke D. Graham

The European Convention of Human Rights Regime
Reform of Immigration and Minority Policies from Afar
Dia Anagnostou

Decisional Privacy and the Rights of the Child
Georgina Dimopoulos

The Rohingya Crisis
Humanitarian and Legal Approaches
Edited by Manzoor Hasan, Syed Mansoob Murshed and Priya Pillai

For more information about this series, please visit: www.routledge.com/Routledge-Research-in-Human-Rights-Law/book-series/HUMRIGHTSLAW

The Rohingya Crisis

Humanitarian and Legal Approaches

Edited by
Manzoor Hasan,
Syed Mansoob Murshed and
Priya Pillai

Routledge
Taylor & Francis Group
LONDON AND NEW YORK

First published 2023
by Routledge
4 Park Square, Milton Park, Abingdon, Oxon OX14 4RN

and by Routledge
605 Third Avenue, New York, NY 10158

Routledge is an imprint of the Taylor & Francis Group, an informa business

British Library Cataloguing-in-Publication Data
A catalogue record for this book is available from the British Library

ISBN: 978-1-032-28821-5 (hbk)
ISBN: 978-1-032-30393-2 (pbk)
ISBN: 978-1-003-30488-3 (ebk)

DOI: 10.4324/9781003304883

Typeset in Galliard
by Deanta Global Publishing Services, Chennai, India

Contents

Contributors

Aakash Chandran is an international lawyer and researcher based in New Delhi, and the Communications, Advocacy, and Campaign Fellow at the Asia Justice Coalition.

Michelle Foster is Professor and Director at the Peter McMullin Centre on Statelessness, Melbourne Law School, Australia. Michelle has published widely in the field of international refugee law, human rights, and statelessness.

Quazi Omar Foysal is an international law researcher and Bangladesh-qualified lawyer. Currently, he is pursuing an Advanced Master's degree in International Law at Université Catholique de Louvain, Belgium. Earlier, he completed LLM in International Humanitarian Law and Human Rights from the Geneva Academy of International Humanitarian Law and Human Rights, Switzerland and LLB (Honours) from the University of Dhaka, Bangladesh. Mr Foysal has taught international law in several Bangladeshi universities and worked with several national and international organizations. He was a part of the *amicus curiae* submission submitted by Bangladeshi Non-Government Representatives to the ICC in support of the Prosecutor's Request on the Jurisdictional Ruling over the Rohingyas Deportation dated 18 June 2018.

Brian Gorlick is Senior Research Associate, Course Convenor and Tutor at the Refugee Law Initiative, School of Advanced Study, University of London. Previously, he worked with the Office of the High Commissioner for Refugees (UNHCR) and the UN Secretariat for twenty-seven years.

Manzoor Hasan is the Executive Director of the Centre for Peace and Justice of Brac University. He was instrumental in establishing the Institute of Governance Studies in 2005. Previously he was the Deputy Executive Director of BRAC, Regional Director (Asia-Pacific) of Transparency International, Berlin, Germany and the founding Executive Director of Transparency International Bangladesh. Her Majesty Queen Elizabeth II awarded the Officer of the Most Excellent Order of the British Empire to Mr. Hasan in 2003 for his promotion of transparency in Bangladesh. He was called to the English Bar in 1985 and practised as a Barrister in England and Bangladesh.

Ahmed Shafquat Hassan is a Research Associate at the Centre for Peace and Justice, BRAC University, Bangladesh. Shafquat is a constitutional law and international law scholar, who has been working on the Rohingya refugee situation for the past two years. He is a qualified barrister, and, prior to joining BRAC University, had practiced law as a pupil lawyer in Bangladesh with Probir Neogi and Associates. Shafquat also boasts a number of publications and has lectured on numerous forums on issues relating to constitutional law and minority protection.

Helen Hintjens is Assistant Professor in Development and Social Justice, International Institute of Social Studies, Erasmus University, the Hague, the Netherlands. She has worked for more than 20 years in online role- play simulations. She specializes in research on genocide and post-genocide politics, asylum advocacy, and post-colonial relations.

Sadaf Noor Islam, PhD, is a Post-doctoral Research Associate in the Department of Anthropology at Durham University, UK. Islam is a British Academy/ Leverhulme postdoctoral scholar and a medical anthropologist with extensive ethnographic research experience through her Wellcome Trust-funded PhD on the biomedicalization of death in Bangladeshi hospitals. Her research interests are in the fields of health, biomedical technology, death and end-of-life care, hope and health, gender and social inequalities, and hospital and ethnographic research.

Jennifer Keene-McCann is Senior Legal Fellow with the Asia Justice Coalition. She is an international lawyer and solicitor admitted to the Supreme Court of Victoria and the High Court of Australia.

Tonny Raymond Kirabira is a PhD researcher at the University of Portsmouth, UK. Tonny R. Kirabira is a legal practitioner, socio-legal researcher and academic, focusing on transitional justice and international criminal law. He is also a Visiting Fellow at the Firoz Lalji Institute for Africa, London School of Economics and Political Science.

Ron Linser is Simulation Consultant and Coordinator at SimPlay.NET. Ron is a former Lecturer in Political Science, has an MA in Educational Technology, and has been a simulation designer and administrator for more than 30 years. He co-authored the Fablusi simulation software, and authored numerous role-play research publications in journals, conferences, and book chapters.

Brian McGarry is Assistant Professor of Public International Law at the Grotius Centre for International Legal Studies, Leiden Law School, the Netherlands. Prior to joining Leiden University, Brian McGarry held teaching and research appointments at Sciences Po Law School (Paris), the Graduate Institute of International and Development Studies (Geneva), and the University of Cambridge. Dr. McGarry's first monograph, *Intervening in International Justice: Third States Before Courts and Tribunals*, will be published in early 2023.

Nayanika Mookherjee is Professor in Political Anthropology in the Department of Anthropology at Durham University, UK. Mookherjee is the author of The *Spectral Wound. Sexual Violence, Public Memories, and the Bangladesh War of 1971* (2015 Duke University Press; 2016 Zubaan), editor of the *Journal of Royal Anthropological Institute* special issue 'On Irreconciliation' (2022), and co-authored/co-directed a graphic novel and animation film: *'Birangona and Ethical Testimonies of Sexual Violence During Conflict'*, (2019) which received the 2019 Praxis Award. She has published extensively on anthropology of violence, ethics, and aesthetics and has expertise in political anthropology, genocide, migration and state violence, gendered violence in conflicts, (ir) reconciliation, and adoption.

Syed Mansoob Murshed is the Professor of the Economics of Conflict and Peace at the International Institute of Social Studies (ISS) of the Erasmus University of Rotterdam. He is also Professor of Economics at Coventry University in the UK.

Emma Palmer, PhD, is a Senior Lecturer at Griffith Law School in Australia and is a member of the Griffith Asia Institute, Law Futures Centre, and Disrupting Violence research beacon. Her work addresses international criminal law and human rights law in the Indo-Pacific.

Priya Pillai, PhD, currently heads the Asia Justice Coalition secretariat, which is focused on justice and accountability in Asia. Priya Pillai is an international lawyer, with two decades of expertise in the areas of international justice, international human rights, transitional justice, peace and conflict, and humanitarian issues.

Md Mizanur Rahman is Assistant Professor at the Department of Anthropology, Jagannath University, Dhaka-1100, Bangladesh. He is currently doing a PhD at the University of Melbourne, Australia. His research interests include statelessness, forced migration and refugee studies, and development.

Jade Roberts (BA/LLB, University of Western Australia; Master's in International Law, Graduate Institute of International and Development Studies) is a PhD candidate in the Peter McMullin Centre on Statelessness at the Melbourne Law School. Her doctoral research explores alternative approaches to statelessness in international law.

Acknowledgements

The edited volume, *The Rohingya Crisis: Humanitarian and Legal Approaches*, emerged from the 2019 Hague Conclave organised by the Centre for Peace and Justice (CPJ) of BRAC University, Bangladesh, the Asia Justice Coalition (AJC), and the International Institute of Social Studies (ISS) of Erasmus University Rotterdam, to bring focus back to the humanitarian challenges and issues of justice and accountability for the Rohingya.

The edited volume addresses the broader aspects of the political and social landscape, human rights violations, accountability and advocacy efforts, and humanitarian challenges faced by the Rohingya from Myanmar. It brings together different voices of legal, policy, and international affairs experts to construct a framework which addresses the complex and nuanced issues comprising the Rohingya crisis.

Many people have contributed to shaping and designing the project, in small and big ways. It would be difficult to name everyone here, and we are grateful to many of those whom we cannot list here. We thank Professor Inge Hutter, Rector ISS, for her continued support since 2019 to the cause of justice and accountability and for generously hosting the Hague Conclave at the ISS. We are grateful to the Vice Chancellor of BRAC University, Professor Vincent Chang, for his kind support and for his gracious presence at the 2019 conclave. Special thanks go to M. Badiuzzaman and Ziauddin for their brilliant organisation and management that led to the successful culmination of the 2019 Hague Conclave. We owe our gratitude to the rapporteurs (Lize Swartz and Mahardhika S. Sadja) and editorial staff (Jessica Olney, Brian Gorlick, and M. Badiuzzaman) for their skilful and technical presentation of the 2019 meeting report.

We must thank the administrative and financial teams of AJC and CPJ for all their work in the background, ensuring that the edited volume project has been completed and faced no logistical impediments.

Tremendous thanks also go to Jennifer Keene-McCann, Rachel Khoo, and Ruwadzano Makumbe of the Asia Justice Coalition secretariat for steering the project since its inception. We would also like to thank our publisher, Routledge, and Ms. Alison Kirk for believing in our project and working with us through the midst of the global pandemic.

Many individuals have contributed to bringing this project to fruition. We cannot fail to mention the editorial support and oversight rendered by Aakash Chandran and Ahmed Shafquat Hassan. We owe our sincere gratitude to the contributors to the edited volume. Their continuous support, dedication, and patience have brought a diverse and rich flavour to the book. Each contributor brings a fresh legal and policy perspective to the issue at hand.

This book is dedicated to the thousands of Rohingya within and without Myanmar, whose voices have been incorporated and echoed in the chapters. The editors and contributors have attempted to amplify the voices of the Rohingya and call for international action and attention to the mass atrocities committed which are continuing against the Rohingya.

Introduction

The complex Rohingya humanitarian crisis

Manzoor Hasan, Syed Mansoob Murshed, and Priya Pillai

Rohingya Muslims from the Northern Rakhine (formerly Arakan) State of Myanmar (Burma)[1] find themselves in a predicament which is one of the world's most complex humanitarian disasters, involving, as it does, insurgency, civil war, genocide, politicide, internally displaced persons (IDP), as well as an international refugee crisis, the latter placing burdens on the international community and the neighbouring state of Bangladesh. It is, therefore, of interest to a multitude of actors and stakeholders situated broadly within the international development and human rights communities. The Rohingya people are considered distinct from the majority in Burma, being Muslim and more South Asian (although there is considerable ethnic diversity elsewhere in Myanmar). Historically, Arakan (present-day Rakhine State) is at the cross-roads between South and East Asia. Rohingya inhabitants of Northern Rakhine State in Myanmar are denied citizenship within the nation-state where they traditionally reside, being considered to be Bangladeshis. The laws governing freedom to marry are also constrained by restraints on inter-faith unions. There is a growing literature on the Rohingya crisis; this volume represents a collection of papers which mainly focuses on the human rights, legal, and international relations surrounding this complex humanitarian crisis, the enormity of which cannot be overemphasized.

No crisis occurs in a socio-economic and historical vacuum. There is now a considerable literature on the topic of the Rohingya crisis,[2] but a few stylized facts about the conflict need to be stated at this juncture. There is a long history of Buddhist–Muslim tensions in the history of Buddhist majority[3] in Burma, predating the British colonial period in Burma (1824–1948).[4] Towards the end of British rule in the 1930s, serious inter-communal riots erupted, between 'indigenous' Buddhist Burmans and Indians, including with Muslims. British rule facilitated and encouraged the emigration of South Asians (chiefly from Bengal) into Burma. Historically, Arakan has had considerable interaction with South Asia, being the Burmese province adjacent to South Asia (present-day Bangladesh); parts of Bangladesh, such as Chittagong, were in Arakanese kingdoms; Arakanese rulers were also vassals of the Muslim Bengal Sultanate (fourteenth to sixteenth centuries);[5] during the reign of Emperor Aurangzeb, the Mughal Governor of Bengal (Shaista Khan) expelled the Arakanese from Chittagong. Within the Northern segment of the Rakhine State, separatist movements can be traced

DOI: 10.4324/9781003304883-1

back to the inter-ethnic (indigenous Burman versus Indian) riots in the 1920s and 1930s, as well as the separatist movement in Arakan in the aftermath of the Second World War and independence in 1948.[6] The present-day armed struggle for the Muslim Rohingya is conducted under the banner of the Arakan Rohingya Salvation Army (ARSA).

In February 2021, the Burmese Army staged a coup, declared a state of emergency, and imposed martial law across the country. The nullification of the November 2020 election result and the replacement of the civilian government with the 'State Administration Council' (SAC) sparked nationwide protests by millions of people calling for democracy and the restoration of the civilian government. The Burmese Army responded to the peaceful protests with excessive and lethal force.[7] Widespread, systematic attacks against civilians, including forcible transfer, enslavement, torture, rape, sexual violence, enforced disappearances, among others, constitute crimes against humanity. The brutal crackdown by the military has resulted in the killing of over 1,906 people, the arrest of 14,032 people, and the detention of 10,976 individuals.[8] The ongoing non-international armed conflict and the commission of war crimes by the military junta, including indiscriminate aerial attacks on villages and towns, destruction of civilian and cultural property, using a 'scorched-earth' policy, violates international law. According to the UN Office for the Coordination of Humanitarian Affairs (OCHA), there are over one million people (including 70,000 since the military coup) who are internally displaced in Myanmar[9] and 14.4 million people are in dire need of humanitarian aid.[10] The continuous attacks against civilians and violence perpetrated by the Myanmar military have pushed over 60,000 people to take refuge in neighbouring countries.[11]

The citizenship laws of Myanmar are heavily discriminatory against non-Burman minorities, particularly Muslims, and, since 1982, the Rohingyas of Rakhine State have had their citizenship revoked; this process can be dated back to 1962 when attempts were made to deprive them of their identity and ration cards.[12] The mistreatment of the Rohingya people by the military commenced in Burma in 1962, and encompasses both the concept of structural violence developed by Johan Galtung[13] to describe systematic discrimination, as well as the outright genocidal violence and ethnic cleansing of recent years. There is a history of religious strife in Rakhine State, as is the case in the rest of Burma/Myanmar.[14] In Rakhine State, some 30% of the population are Muslim; its poverty rate is 43.5% compared to the Myanmar average of 25.6%. Although traditional agriculture and fishing continue to play an important role in the region's income generation, the region is rich in natural resources, oil, and gas, and a special economic zone is being developed in Kyaukpu.[15] In addition, Amnesty International has reported on the re-development of Rakhine land abandoned by Rohingyas.[16] Much of the evidence gathered by them amounts to systematic evidence of ethnic cleansing, with the bulldozing of vegetation and farmland with a view towards re-settlement by other groups and re-development for mining and other economic activities.

The post-colonial independent nation-state of Burma is one of the world's prime examples of development failure, both in terms of its polity and its economic development record.[17] The nation-state of Burma, later Myanmar, has seen the highest incidence of civil wars, measured by a metric defined as civil war years, since the end of the Second World War.[18] This high number of civil war years is also due to the multiplicity of ethnic conflicts that have been ongoing in Burma. Its recent record in terms of democracy and freedom of expression is abysmal. The VDEM (varieties of democracy) Institute's estimate of liberal democracy places it as a poor performer since 1962 (the year of the Ne Win military coup), even relative to other countries in South-East Asia, a region not noted for its exemplary democratic credentials.[19]

In addition to being a resource-rich country, Burma was also the rice bowl of the region and has also been an exporter of oil, precious gems, and teakwood since the nineteenth century. Burma can be classified as an economic growth failure, at least until recently, when the growth rates picked up after the partial restoration of democracy post-2011. The growth projection for the year to September 2022 is a meagre 1%, according to the World Bank, whereas the military coup from 1 February 2021 may result in further economic setbacks.[20] Besides having the dubious distinction of hosting the greatest number of civil wars on its territory, the Myanmar polity has been classified as a closed autocracy, following the coup of 1 February 2021 and a phase of democratization after 2011. A closed autocracy is the most autocratic regime type, as classified by the VDEM Institute.[21] The period between 1962 and 2011 was also an extremely undemocratic era of military rule. In terms of freedom of expression, after a recovery since the country's democratization in 2011, it has again declined markedly following the military coup of 1 February 2021.

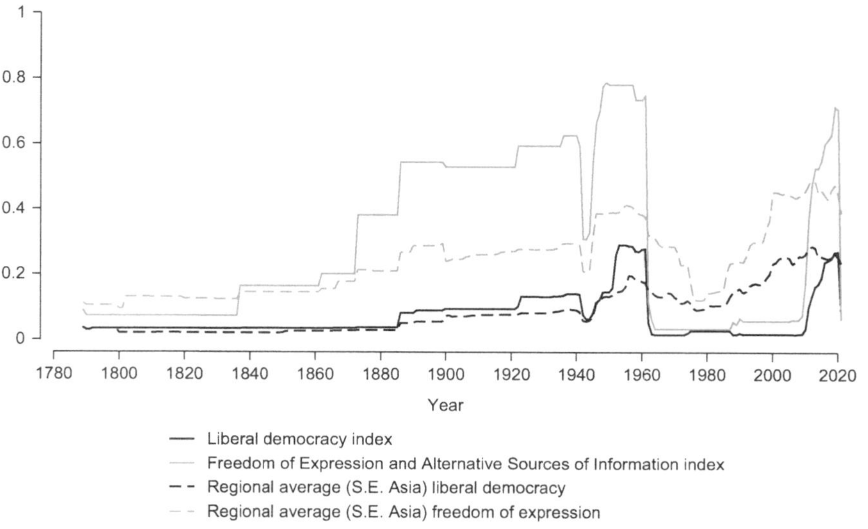

Figure I.1 Trends in democracy and freedom of expression in Burma. Source: VDEM Institute, https://www.v-dem.net/data_analysis/CountryGraph/.

The post-independence development trajectory of Burma, and later Myanmar, can be characterized as exhibiting the most acute form of the resource curse, causing a downward development spiral, in contrast with resource-abundant neighbouring states like Thailand or Malaysia, which have been relatively successful. In a nutshell, the resource curse works[22] by distorting economic signals that are harmful to the economy and its growth prospects. It is also argued to have negative effects on political institutions and channels of governance by encouraging more rent-seeking behaviour. Equally, the converse is true. It is argued that there will be no resource curse when good institutions are already present, and are resilient to the nefarious influences, if any, of resource rents as is so often cited to be the case for oil-rich Norway. An abundance of natural resources also led to the widely believed claim that it was a major cause of civil war.[23] Even if they are not identified or believed to be the major cause of civil war, they certainly perpetuate its duration[24], as is the case in the drug- and gemstone-fuelled civil wars in Burma. The existence of a narco-economy, as in Myanmar (also in Colombia and Afghanistan), is a major perpetuator of internal armed conflict. Thus, there is both an economic and political (institutional) resource curse. Yet, politics and economics are inseparably connected.

It is worthwhile noting the kleptocratic nature of Myanmar's military regime. It has been alleged that, since the military coup of 2021, the economy shrank and the poverty head count doubled to 46%.[25] The Burmese drug golden triangle is well known, but the Myanmar military is said to siphon off approximately US$900 million from a variety of shadowy economic activities and trade.[26] Besides drugs, the shadowy trade in jade is an important source of illicit revenue, Myanmar being a major exporter of jade to China. All in all, this means that the military junta is unlikely to easily loosen its iron grip on power. This feature, coupled with the rich pickings that a de-populated Rakhine province offers and the narrow nationalistic ethnic identity politics favoured by the military, does not bode well for the Rohingya population who, until recently, inhabited Northern Arakan (Rakhine) State.

Buddhism and the Theravada variety of Burmese Buddhism has shaped the ethno-politics and the ethnic conflict and tensions between the majority of Burmans and those whose ethnicity is more South Asian in Burma.[27] The role of Theravada Buddhism in shaping Burmese politics and the political rhetoric in that country is well documented.[28] It has also been pointed out that, since the beginning of political liberalization in 2011, there has been a toxic mixture of hate and insecurity shaping Buddhist Burman nationalism with violence and vitriol directed against Muslim inhabitants of Burma, the Rohingyas bearing the brunt of this tendency. Buddhist monks, like their counterparts in Sri Lanka (*Bodu Bala Sena*), are increasingly politicized and militant, viewing their religion (in reality, their Theravada variant of Buddhism) as being under threat from global Islam. Of course, these illiberal developments are not exclusive to Myanmar; the tide of nationalistic populism is on the rise universally, set in the particular contexts of diverse cultures across Asia, Europe, and Latin America. In Myanmar, there are two noteworthy dangerous developments. The first is the

969[29] movement, with a view to boycotting commerce with Muslims. The other is known by the Burmese acronym *MaBaTha*, denoting a Patriotic Association of Burma, formed by Buddhist monks, another right-wing nationalist organization targeting Muslims. Interestingly, these extremist ethno-religious organizations emerged during an era of relative political liberalization. With the return of direct military rule in 2021 and economic developments in Rakhine State, conditions do not bode well for either the return or the reconciliation with Rohingya refugees.

The anti-liberal environment pervading Burma is not exclusive to that country. There is the growth of populist nationalism in developing Asia, especially in India, in Latin America, and even in the staunchly democratic West (Poland, Hungary, even in the UK and the USA). In the democratic, developed countries of the West, populism is driven by the recent growth in income and wealth inequality, which has particularly disadvantaged the working and even middle classes of those countries.[30]

A liberal society is one where there is respect for minority rights, constraints on the executive (and legislature), with an independent judiciary, and there is respect for the rule of law. In a democracy, there is an electoral process in place. A purely electoral process can, and does, elect populist/autocratic dictators or parties with scant respect for liberalism.[31] More often than not, they represent a toxic mixture of populist nationalism[32] and plutocratic motives. They despoil their poorer followers, who are duped by their nationalistic rhetoric.

The maintenance of a liberal order requires not only institutionalized checks on the exercise of power but also vigilance from society at large. These avenues of vigilance are along a narrow corridor, according to some scholars.[33] The state can be viewed as a Leviathan in the sense developed by Thomas Hobbes.[34] The Leviathan is a necessary evil which citizens must subject themselves to, in order to receive security[35] and the myriad public goods that modern life demands. But it also needs to be checked so as to remain a shackled Leviathan in a liberal society; otherwise it can transform itself into a despotic Leviathan. Some despotic Leviathans are capable of some benevolence, providing some public goods, as in China, whereas other despotic Leviathans are mainly paper Leviathans as they provide their citizenry with little, despite being despotic, as in many developing countries.[36] In recent years the despotic Leviathan appears to be emerging in more nations. According to the latest reports of the VDEM Institute, autocracy throughout the world is very much on the increase. This trend can be described as the third wave of autocratization following in the wake of the third wave of democratization immediately after the end of the cold war in 1991.[37] Furthermore, a prominent feature of the growing autocracy in recent years is the curtailment of the freedom of expression and the viral spread of misinformation, utilizing social media, by the autocratic rulers of the world.

In summary, Burma (Myanmar) is a case of development failure, rife with civil war, cursed by its natural resource abundance, where illiberal forces are forming at both the societal and state levels. Be that as it may, there is always light at the end of the tunnel.

Plan of the volume

The rest of this collection of papers concerning the Rohingya refugees is organized as follows. The chapter by Brian Gorlick looks at the conditions enhancing the risk of civil war and the escalation of the conflict, regional issues, including those in Bangladesh, and operations by the United Nations and other actors. It argues for a broader view of solutions for this crisis, where voluntary return may be ruled out, which will require significant shifts in thinking about policy and operations by the major actors in this tragic drama. The chapter by Sadaf Noor Islam and Nayanika Mookherjee explores the protracted refugee situation and the conditions in the Rohingya refugee camps in Bangladesh's Cox's Bazar. In particular, it examines the impact of the absence of the formal right to work, the absence of institutional schooling, and the absence of freedom of movement and information.

The next set of chapters deals with justice and accountability. The chapter by Quazi Omar Foysal applies two principles of international law in obtaining justice for crimes committed against the Rohingyas. The chapter explores the role of the principle of objective territoriality and the principle of *erga omnes partes* in advancing international justice and accountability for crimes against humanity and genocide. The chapter by Brian McGarry argues that there is a need to reconcile twenty-first-century principles of justice and accountability with twentieth-century limitations on access to international courts, essentially the sovereignty of the Westphalian state. In particular, it explores the potential for the third-state intervention in contentious cases before the International Court of Justice in the light of The Gambia's institution of proceedings in connection with crimes against the Rohingya and the joint statement of Canada and the Netherlands of their intention to intervene. The chapter by Michelle Foster and Jade Roberts looks at the scope of crimes against the Rohingya to be investigated and tried before the International Criminal Court (ICC). It particularly examines Myanmar's discriminatory laws and practices, especially its citizenship laws, and argues that arbitrary deprivation of nationality is to be treated as crimes against humanity and apartheid. Priya Pillai's chapter on fact finding and international accountability assesses the various initiatives undertaken based on the Rohingya crisis. This includes an examination of the Independent International Fact-Finding Mission on Myanmar (IIFFMM) and the Independent Investigative Mechanism for Myanmar (IIMM), as well as the two international courts—the International Court of Justice and the International Criminal Court. The chapter addresses the interlinkages and relationships between these myriad proceedings viewed from the lens of fact finding and the impact on the quest for accountability for atrocity crimes. The chapter by Jennifer Keene-McCann and Aakash Chandran explores the principle of universal jurisdiction in the context of crimes against the Rohingya as one of the means to advance justice. In particular, it examines the 2019 case brought by the Burmese Rohingya Organisation UK (BROUK) in Argentina under the principle of universal jurisdiction. The chapter considers variables that could be used to identify other favourable jurisdictions in which to bring further universal jurisdiction cases. It then uses these variables to consider the viability of three potential Forum States–India, Australia, and Turkey.

The final set of papers explores sustainable solutions to the problem. The chapter by Helen Hintjens, Mizanur Rahman, and Romi Lenser examines ethical dilemmas in the Rohingya crisis through role play by students at the International Institute of Social Studies (ISS) of the Erasmus University Rotterdam. This simulated situation was conducted in the classroom in late 2019, involving scenarios of suffering and individual, as well as collective, trauma. In particular, it examines whether these simulations lead to the creative search for solutions, as well as the defining of the Rohingya as passive victims and the handling of vicarious trauma by the participants. The chapter by Tonny Kirabira and Emma Palmer looks at the role of non-governmental organizations (NGOs) in achieving transitional justice for the Rohingya. International NGOs are sometimes regarded as intermediaries facilitating Western hegemony. It argues that NGOs can play a potentially constructive role in achieving transitional justice in localized situations like for the Rohingya. The paper by Ahmed Shafquat Hassan analyzes the concept of the responsibility to protect. He argues that the responsibility to protect needs to incorporate mechanisms of redistributing responsibility throughout the international community, unburdened from the political shackles of administrative barriers. He argues that the existing mechanism is cumbersome and that, by expanding the principle to include protection mechanisms for the Rohingya in host countries and relocation policies, the principle will be more readily invoked and implemented. Drawing on other international examples, like the Darfur and Kosovo, he argues that the responsibility to protect has to be utilized as the reason for intervening in this crisis.

Biographical notes:

Manzoor Hasan is a public policy reform specialist with nearly three decades of experience in capacity building and institutional strengthening aimed at strengthening governance in Bangladesh and globally. Mr Hasan graduated from the London School of Economics & Political Science in 1979 and was called to the bar of England and Wales in 1985. Since being called, Mr Hasan practised in both England and Bangladesh for many years.

Mr Hasan is currently serving as the Executive Director of the Centre for Peace and Justice, BRAC University. He was instrumental in establishing BIGD (formerly the Institute of Governance Studies) in 2005, of which he was the Founding Director. Previously, he worked as the Deputy Executive Director of BRAC, the largest NGO in the world. He was also the founding Executive Director of Transparency International Bangladesh and was subsequently the Regional Director (Asia-Pacific) of Transparency International, Berlin, Germany.

Her Majesty Queen Elizabeth II awarded the Officer of the Most Excellent Order of the British Empire to Mr Hasan in 2003 for his promotion of transparency in Bangladesh. Mr Hasan currently serves as the chairperson for the Asia Justice Coalition, and for ActionAid Bangladesh. He also serves as a board member for ActionAid Australia. He previously chaired the UN Convention Against Corruption Coalition.

Mr Hasan is also a published author, having written multiple reports and articles, published across various platforms. His book entitled *The Real Politics of Bangladesh—The Inside Story of Local Power Brokers* remains to date one of the best descriptions of Bangladesh's informal political scape.

Syed Mansoob Murshed is Professor of the Economics of Peace and Conflict at the International Institute of Social Studies (ISS), Erasmus University in the Netherlands and is also Professor of Economics at Coventry University in the UK. He was the first holder of the rotating Prince Claus Chair in Development and Equity in 2003. He was a Research Fellow at UNU/WIDER in Helsinki, where he ran projects on Globalization and Vulnerable Economies and Why Some Countries Avoid Conflict, While Others Fail. He also ran a project on The Two Economies of Ireland, financed by the International Fund for Ireland at the Northern Ireland Economic Research Centre (NIERC), Belfast. He is the author of nine books and over 160 refereed journal papers and book chapters. His latest monograph, published in 2018, is on the Resource Curse. He is an Associate Editor of the *Journal of Peace Research* and is on the editorial boards of *Peace Economics, Peace Science and Public Policy* (PEPS), as well as *Civil Wars.* He was also recently a principal researcher on a QNRF-(Qatar) funded research project on food insecurity and conflict. His research interests are in the economics of conflict, resource abundance, aid conditionality, political economy, macroeconomics, and international economics.

Priya Pillai is an international lawyer, with two decades of expertise in the areas of international justice, international human rights, transitional justice, peace and conflict, and humanitarian issues. She currently heads the Asia Justice Coalition secretariat, which is focused on justice and accountability in Asia.

Priya has worked in national and international institutions, including at the United Nations International Criminal Tribunal for the Former Yugoslavia (ICTY), relating to trials in the aftermath of the conflict in the Balkans, and on various humanitarian issues globally while at the International Federation of Red Cross and Red Crescent Societies (IFRC) headquarters in Geneva. She has been involved in different aspects of peace and transitional justice initiatives, in South and South East Asia. She is a contributing editor at the international law blog *OpinioJuris* and is on the editorial board of the *Indian Society of International Law Yearbook of International Humanitarian and Refugee Law.*

Priya holds a PhD in international law from the Graduate Institute, Geneva, an LL.M from New York University School of Law as a Global Public Service Scholar, and obtained her first law degree from the National Law School of India University, Bangalore.

Notes

1 We shall use Burma and Myanmar inter-changeably.
2 See, for example, Anthony Ware and Costas Laoutides, *Myanmar's Rohingya Conflict*, Oxford University Press, 2018.
3 The variant of Buddhism followed in Burma is Theravada Buddhism, as in Sri Lanka, and, in both countries, there is a tendency towards mili-

tant Buddhist politics; see International Crisis Group, *Buddhism and State Power in Myanmar*, 2017, https://www.crisisgroup.org/asia/south-east-asia/myanmar/290-buddhism-and-state-power-myanmar, accessed 13 May 2022. Also Matthew J Walton, *Burmese Buddhist Politics*, Oxford Handbooks online, 2017, https://www.oxfordhandbooks.com/view/10.1093/oxfordhb/9780199935420.001.0001/oxfordhb-9780199935420-e-21, accessed 6 May 2022.

4 Roman Husarski, 'Buddhist Nationalism and Islam in Myanmar', *Acta Asiatica*, Varsoviensa, no 30, 2017, https://core.ac.uk/download/pdf/154361336.pdf, accessed 9 May 2022.

5 Suthachai Yimprasert, 'The Portuguese in Arakan in the Sixteenth and Seventeenth Centuries', *Manusya, Journal of Humanities* 7.2, 2004, https://brill.com/downloadpdf/journals/mnya/7/2/article-p66_5.pdf, accessed 10 May 2022.

6 Moshe Yeagar, *The Muslims of Burma: A Study of Minority Group.* Otto Harrassowitz: Wiesbaden, 1972.

7 'Myanmar: Protesters Targeted in March Massacre' (*Human Rights Watch*, 2 December 2021) < https://www.hrw.org/news/2021/12/02/myanmar-protesters-targeted-march-massacre > accessed 8 June 2022; 'Myanmar: New Evidence and Findings of Post-Coup d'État Crimes Against Humanity' (*Fortify Rights*, 24 March 2022) < https://www.fortifyrights.org/mya-inv-2022-03-24/ > accessed 8 June 2022.

8 https://aappb.org/?p=21733

9 'Myanmar Humanitarian Update No. 18' (*UN Office for the Coordination of Humanitarian Affairs*, 31 May 2022) < https://reliefweb.int/report/myanmar/myanmar-humanitarian-update-no-18-31-may-2022 > accessed 8 June 2022.

10 'Myanmar Humanitarian Response Plan 2022 (January 2022)' (*UN Office for the Coordination of Humanitarian Affairs,* 31 January 2022) < https://reliefweb.int/report/myanmar/myanmar-humanitarian-response-plan-2022-january-2022 > accessed 8 June 2022.

11 'Myanmar Emergency Update' (*UNCHR Regional Bureau For Asia And Pacific*, 1 June 2022) < https://reporting.unhcr.org/document/2501 > accessed 8 June 2022.

12 Haradhan Kumar Mohajan, History of Rakhine State and the Origin of the Rohingya Muslims, MPRA Paper No. 88186, 2018, file:///C:/Users/44796/Documents/Mansoob's%20Documents/CONFLICT/BURMA/MPRA_paper_88186.pdf, accessed 9 May 2022.

13 Johan Galtung, 'Violence, Peace and Peace Research, *Journal of Peace Research*, 6 (3): 167–191, 1969.

14 Adam Burke, New Political Space, Old Tensions: History, Identity and Violence in Rakhine State, Myanmar, *Contemporary Southeast Asia* 38 (2), August 2016): 258–283.

15 Shagun Gupta, Development in Times of Transition: The Socio-Economic Status of Rakhine State, Myanmar, 2020,https://www.researchgate.net/publication/340076537_The_Socio_Economic_Status_of_Rakhine_State_Myanmar, accessed 13 May 2022.

16 Amnesty International, Remaking Rakhine State, 2017, https://www.amnesty.org/en/wp-content/uploads/2021/05/AA1680182018ENGLISH.pdf, accessed 18 May 2022.

17 Anne Booth, 'The Burma Development Disaster in Comparative Historical Perspective,' *South East Asia Research*, 11:2, 141–171, 2003, DOI: 10.5367/000000003101297179.

18 Syed Mansoob Murshed, The Conflict–Growth Nexus and the Poverty of Nations in *Growth Divergences: Explaining Differences in Economic*

Performance, edited by Jose Antonio Ocampo, Jomo, KS and Rob Vos, London: Zed Books, 324–351, 2007.

19 See the VDEM report, https://v-dem.net/media/publications/dr_2022.pdf. Liberal democracy is a hybrid of multi-party elections, the degree of its fairness as well as liberal values of tolerance, respect for human rights, separation of powers, and constraints on the executive.

20 https://www.worldbank.org/en/country/myanmar/publication/myanmar-economic-monitor-january-2022-economic-activity-in-myanmar-to-remain-at-low-levels-with-the-overall-outlook-blea, accessed 18 May 2022.

21 The other regime types are electoral autocracies, which can be improved upon by electoral democracies, where constraints on the executive are weak or non-existent, and further improved upon by full liberal democracies. See, https://v-dem.net/media/publications/dr_2022.pdf.

22 Syed Mansoob Murshed, *The Resource Curse*, Newcastle: Agenda Press, 2018.

23 Paul Collier and Anke Hoeffler 'Greed and Grievance in Civil Wars', *Oxford Economic Papers* 56(4): 563–595, 2004.

24 See chapter 3 of Syed Mansoob Murshed, *Explaining Civil War: A Rational Choice Approach*, Cheltenham: Edward Elgar, 2010

25 Daniel Combs, Guns, gems and drugs: One year after Myanmar's coup, how the generals hold power, 2022, https://www.grid.news/story/global/2022/01/28/guns-gems-and-drugs-one-year-after-myanmars-coup-how-the-generals-hold-power/, accessed 13 May 2022.

26 Combs, ibid.

27 As indicated, even among the Buddhist majority, there are differences between the Burman majority and other East Asian/Buddhist ethnicities, such as Karen and the Shan.

28 See, for example, the work of Matthew Walton and the International Crisis Group Report of 2017, op.cit.

29 969 symbolizes Buddha's virtues.

30 Branko Milanovic, *Global Inequality: A New Approach for the Age of Globalization*, Cambridge: Harvard University Press, 2018.

31 See Syed Mansoob Murshed, Globalization and the Twin Scourges of Illiberalism and Inequality in Fayyaz Baqir and Sanni Yaya (eds), *Beyond Free Market: Social Inclusion and Globalization*, May 2021, 44–56, Abingdon, Oxford: Routledge.

32 See, for example, Cas Mudde 'The populist zeitgeist'. In: *Government and Opposition* 39.4, pp. 541–563, 2004.

33 Daron Acemoglu and James A Robinson, *The Narrow Corridor: States, Societies and the Fate of Liberty*, New York: Penguin Press, 2019.

34 Thomas Hobbes, *Leviathan*, originally published in 1651, reprinted 1998, Oxford: World Classics.

35 To prevent *bellum ominium contra omnes* (war by all against all) in the state of nature.

36 Acemoglu and Robinson, op.cit., describe this as the Red Queen effect, a simile drawn from Lewis Carroll's Through the Looking-Glass, and What Alice Found There, where Alice and the Red Queen run vigorously but do not move at all; this futile running can even take us backwards.

37 See VDEM reports, op.cit. Each of the three waves of rising autocracy follow waves of rising democracy: the first wave of democracy follows the First World War, followed by rising autocracy in the 1930s; the second wave of democracy is after the Second World War and decolonialization, followed by the rise in autocracy from the 1960s.

Theme 1

The Rohingya crisis and Myanmar's social and political landscape

1 Political-legal considerations of the Rohingya refugee situation

Seeking accountability, relief, and solutions

Brian Gorlick[1,2]

Introduction and political context

The latest chapter of the Rohingya saga, which began on 25 August 2017 with the influx of several hundred thousand refugees from Myanmar to Bangladesh, the day after the release of the Advisory Commission report chaired by late United Nations (UN) Secretary-General Kofi Annan,[3] remains an enormous challenge. Not only is neighbouring Bangladesh under the strain of hosting close to one million of Myanmar's would-be citizens, but long-term solutions are not forthcoming.

The *coup d'état* executed by the Myanmar military (known as the Tatmadaw) on 1 February 2021, amongst other factors, has effectively shut down national efforts towards a return solution for the Rohingya.[4] These dramatic events and renewed incidents of civil conflict and increased militarism, public demonstrations, and security crackdowns have created new movements of internally displaced persons[5] as well as cross-border arrivals of asylum seekers and refugees and other individuals fleeing the country.

Despite continuing pressure by Bangladesh, with support from the international community, inaction by the UN Security Council, uneven support from ASEAN,[6] and the notable failure of powerful neighbours like China to pressure the Tatmadaw to put down their guns and accept the Rohingya back permits yet another military junta in Southeast Asia to exercise unbridled power and authority against its own people.[7] As a result, there is negligible progress in the creation of the conditions required to promote safe, dignified, and sustainable refugee returns. Although the responsibility to create these conditions lies squarely with the Myanmar authorities, the Tatmadaw have no interest to permit the Rohingya to repatriate.[8] Despite this current reality, the Bangladesh government continues to push for repatriation as the only viable long-term solution for the Rohingya who they refuse to formally recognize as 'refugees'.[9]

At the time of writing, thousands of individuals, including state counsellor Aung San Suu Kyi and several other elected politicians and civil servants have been arrested, detained, and criminally convicted,[10] with many others being held incommunicado. Hundreds of thousands of Myanmar citizens have courageously taken to the streets to demonstrate against the imposition of military rule and

DOI: 10.4324/9781003304883-3

suspension of parliament. In response, large numbers of civilians and demonstrators, including children, have been shot and killed.[11] In a country teeming with arms, trained militia, and the legacy of decades of internal armed conflict, the risk of full-blown civil war in Myanmar is real.[12]

On 26 February 2021, in an extraordinary display of diplomatic courage, the Myanmar Permanent Representative (PR) to the United Nations in New York addressed a special session of the UN General Assembly. The Myanmar diplomat identified himself as speaking for the Committee Representing Pyidaungsu Hluttaw (CRPH) (now part of the National Unity Government (NUG)[13]), which, at that time, was a self-declared parliamentary committee led by the National League for Democracy (NLD). In his address to the gathered diplomats, the PR condemned the military takeover and called on UN member states to use 'any means necessary' to restore peace and democracy in Myanmar. Without specifically mentioning the Rohingya, he detailed the use of neutering techniques and 'unspeakable violent methods' by the Tatmadaw to attack ethnic minorities in the border areas and he lamented the continuing immunity for such horrendous crimes.[14]

Although this extraordinary intervention brought applause from the gathered UN ambassadors, the next day the PR was officially sacked from his position by the Tatmadaw leadership.[15] Although remaining at the Myanmar UN Mission in New York, the Tatmadaw continues to challenge the PR's continuation as the government representative. The UN Credentials Committee is now addressing the matter, apart from formal recognition of one party or another, the current option to defer the decision allows the NUG-supported PR to continue in his current role.[16]

Given what the PR revealed on the world stage, he and his family and other officials aligned with the opposition will be unable to safely return to Myanmar if the Tatmadaw remain in power.[17] It is not unlikely that the PR and his family may even be compelled to seek international protection through asylum if their diplomatic immunity and privileges were to end. Many individuals are fleeing Myanmar because of the *coup*, only this time they include ethnic Bamar members of the police and army who refuse to follow orders,[18] Myanmar diplomats, government officials,[19] and civilians.[20]

The UN Refugee agency, UNHCR, has called on neighbouring Asian countries to protect those forced to flee.[21] In addition to individuals able to leave, there are an estimated 223,000 internally displaced persons, including 165,000 in the southeast of Myanmar. Some 144,000 Rohingya are still confined to camps and similar settings in the country and over 100,000 persons have been forcibly displaced in the Kachin and Shan States. The UN humanitarian chief has advised that some three million persons require assistance due to the deteriorating situation inside Myanmar.[22]

The Tatmadaw leadership including Myanmar's supreme military commander-in-chief, Min Aung Hlaing, are the principal architects of the 2017 counter-insurgency campaign against the Rohingya in Rakhine State. Well before the *coup*, General Hlaing's presidential ambitions were well known and, having lost the 2020 election, a military takeover was not unexpected.[23] Over decades, the Tatmadaw has long employed fear mongering of Islamist terrorism and the growing Rohingya population, and the Tatmadaw's role as the guardian of the Buddhist majority population to drive a wedge between certain ethnic minorities and religious groups. According to Dr K Yhome: 'The regime has been able to create a very systematic division between the majority Burmans and the "others"—which includes other ethnic minority communities and the Rohingya [...] there is a huge [number of] Burman Buddhists that believe what Min Aung Hlaing and the Tatmadaw is doing is for the good of the Burman society'.[24]

This paper reviews the evolving political situation in Myanmar and the regional, political, and operational limitations, including within the UN, with a specific focus on how it impacts Rohingya refugees and their search for solutions. I argue for expanding the scope of solutions while continuing to explore the full breadth of accountability measures. The humanitarian and political situation in Bangladesh and Myanmar will continue to evolve, but there is a risk of waning international interest and support for another protracted refugee situation. Other global crises, of which there is no shortage, could eclipse the Rohingya refugee situation as a priority. This could result in reduced donor contributions and increasingly frayed generosity on the part of the Bangladesh authorities and public. Although diplomatic efforts and international and domestic leveraging of the Myanmar junta, including through the imposition of sanctions, will continue, there is little hope that the situation for forcibly displaced Rohingya, both within Myanmar and externally, will ever permit safe and sustainable repatriation and long-term protection of their human rights if the Tatmadaw remain in power.

The phenomenon of forced migration and refugee flows out of Myanmar is nothing new. However, the current situation is destined to fester and become more entrenched unless we can move on new approaches and shifts in policy. It is unacceptable from a human rights, humanitarian, and international law perspective to permit an enormous refugee population to languish for years in sprawling, overcrowded closed and island camps where regular acts of violence, limitations on rights, and other deprivations occur.[25] As argued in this paper, other solutions, relief, mitigation, and accountability efforts should be urgently implemented in a coordinated manner.

Challenges in advancing international and domestic justice measures

Although international justice and accountability measures concerning the Rohingya situation have made considerable strides, proceedings before the International Court of Justice (ICJ) and the International Criminal Court (ICC)[26] will take years to conclude.[27] Even then, findings of responsibility by these eminent Courts will not create pathways for voluntary repatriation.[28]

The Myanmar situation and related international support for justice and accountability measures before the ICJ[29] and ICC have to date been steady and relatively swift,[30] with The Gambia initiating the ICJ application[31] on behalf of the 57-nation Organisation of Islamic Cooperation, supported by Canada, the Netherlands[32] and the Maldives.[33] Separate and complementary legal proceedings have commenced in other jurisdictions, notably Argentina.[34]

The Gambia's application under the 1948 *Genocide Convention*[35] and other measures of pursuing criminal investigations by the ICC and other legal proceedings[36] make finding a return solution more challenging by creating contradictory pressures on the Tatmadaw.[37] There is no political advantage or interest for the Tatmadaw in permitting the Rohingya to repatriate. On the contrary, pressure from these initiatives will likely motivate the Myanmar generals to hang on to power. In this connection, and as noted by the Independent International Fact-Finding Mission (IIFFM),[38] the Tatmadaw's domination in Myanmar politics is absolute:

> Under the [Myanmar] Constitution, 25% of the seats in each house of parliament and in the state and regional assemblies belong to unelected members of the military, who are appointed by the Tatmadaw. This is significant because the Constitution requires 75% of votes in both houses of parliament for a constitutional amendment to be adopted, giving the Tatmadaw, through its appointed members of parliament, effective veto power. Furthermore, Parliament elects the President from among three proposed candidates, one nominated by each legislative body and the third by the military- appointed members of parliament. This effectively guarantees the Tatmadaw at least one vice-presidential position. Additionally, *the Tatmadaw selects candidates for (and effectively controls) three key ministerial posts: Defence, Border Affairs, and Home Affairs. This is sufficient to control the National Defence and Security Council and the entire security apparatus.*[39]
>
> (emphasis added)

During oral proceedings before the ICJ in early 2020, the issue of refugee return was specifically addressed by the Court. The Myanmar government submitted that it was engaged in initiatives to facilitate the return of the Rohingya, noting that it intended to promote ethnic reconciliation, peace, and stability in Rakhine State and make the military accountable for violations of international law. The ICJ rejected this plea, and, in its Order on provisional measures, noted that Myanmar had not presented 'any concrete measures aimed specifically at recognizing and ensuring the right of the Rohingya to exist as a protected group under the *Genocide Convention*'. Citing a UN General Assembly resolution, the Court highlighted that 'the situation has not improved in Rakhine State to create the conditions necessary for refugees and other forcibly displaced persons to return to their places of origin voluntarily, safely, and with dignity'.[40]

The same ICJ Order obliges Myanmar to take 'all measures within its power' to prevent acts of genocide in relation to members of the Rohingya group in its territory and to ensure that its military as well as any irregular militia which may be subject to the 'control, direction, or influence' of the state do not commit such acts. Myanmar is further ordered to 'take effective measures to prevent the destruction and ensure the preservation of evidence related to allegations of acts within the scope of the [*Genocide Convention*]' and is required to submit a report to the Court on all measures taken to give effect to the order within four months, and thereafter every six months until a final decision is rendered.[41]

While a forceful judicial order by the world's highest court is encouraging, it does not bring the Rohingya any closer to repatriation. On the contrary, it suggests that the evidence before the ICJ is sufficiently compelling that the Judges were unanimously concerned for the welfare of the remaining Rohingya in Myanmar. Expecting the Tatmadaw to preserve evidence of potential genocide, as ordered by the Court, while now required by law, is politically naïve. Former villages and communities from where Rohingya fled for their lives have been razed to the ground,[42] with the systematic destruction of villages continuing.[43] What can be expected is that much physical evidence in Myanmar is missing, destroyed, tainted, or otherwise unreliable. In the absence of cooperation by the Tatmadaw, key territory, documents, and other sources of evidence in Myanmar remains inaccessible to investigators.

Despite the views of some military experts that the 2017 attacks against the Rohingya were planned and not militarily justified or proportionate in responding to acts by opposition militants, learning from the errors of other regimes engaged in genocidal behaviour, the Tatmadaw may take precautions to avoid leaving an evidentiary trail with their imprimatur. Even with these challenges, thousands of pages of evidence have reportedly been brought out of the country to support ongoing accountability initiatives. The flight or capture of ex-Tatmadaw soldiers who, like the refugees they helped create, are an additional source of potential evidence, which may be used in legal proceedings.[44] Of course the testimony of thousands of Rohingya refugees is an important evidentiary base, as are the statements of military, human rights, and other experts.

Not surprisingly, international accountability measures identifying senior Tatmadaw officers for allegedly committing atrocity crimes in expelling the Rohingya are not recognized by the junta.[45] Although the Myanmar authorities must now engage with the ICJ, the Tatmadaw have to date preferred to rely on domestic commissions of inquiry[46] and court martial measures[47] to deal with accountability issues. This is not surprising as it permits any process to be controlled, managed, and manipulated. As noted by legal scholar Yazuki Nagakoshi, under the Myanmar Constitution 'the decision of the Commander-in-Chief of the Defence Services [in the adjudication of military justice] is final and conclusive'.[48] As a result, 'genuine prosecution of the persons responsible for mass atrocities is unlikely, considering the Commander-in-Chief himself is likely liable for them as well'.[49]

Even before the February 2021 *coup*, a prime example of the Myanmar government averting responsibility is reflected in it establishing the Myanmar Independent Commission of Enquiry (ICOE). The ICOE, a domestic body with international members established by the Myanmar authorities, was to investigate the attacks that began in August 2017 and resulted in mass displacement to Bangladesh. After conducting its work, which included some Myanmar junta-led field visits, the ICOE released its report on 20 January 2021. The ICOE's findings and conclusions are so far removed from documented statements and the testimony of thousands of Rohingya refugees and others as to make them wholly unreliable.

The ICOE was comprised of four members including ex-UN officials and diplomats from the Philippines and Japan. The ICOE chairperson was a former expert of the UN Committee on the Elimination of All Forms of Discrimination Against Women (CEDAW), and another member was the former UN under-secretary general for humanitarian affairs. The presence of these ex-senior UN officials makes the Commission's conclusions particularly shocking. Even the number of Rohingya the ICOE noted as having fled Myanmar following events in 2017 differs by over 400,000 individuals. Furthermore, the ICOE members made no findings of rape or serious sexual assault or torture by the Myanmar authorities or agents in their report, and it appears that they relied almost exclusively on government sources and chosen witnesses while conducting field visits.[50] In brief, the report is a deliberate whitewash.

Advancing credible justice measures requires long-term support, sustained resources, and political commitment to make them work. Whereas ending impunity for atrocity crimes is the overall objective, whether the various initiatives underway will reach that goal is uncertain. Meanwhile, members of the Tatmadaw leadership will be considered international pariahs by responsible UN member states. In that status, they may be unable to leave the territory of Myanmar to avoid the risk of arrest for atrocity crimes, ironically trapped in an authoritarian state of their own making.

Surveying the accountability landscape

The international community cannot overlook the serious violations of human rights and alleged criminal conduct experienced by the Rohingya and there is a need to ensure accountability. Within the UN, the establishment of the IIFFM by the Human Rights Council (HRC) was far reaching and remarkably efficient. The IIFFM investigated and prepared extensive detailed reports on the events which gave rise to the 2017 refugee exodus based on interviews with hundreds of survivors, government officials, UN, and NGO staff, in addition to conducting field visits and obtaining forensic and other evidence collected and vetted by a team of experts. The IIFFM's voluminous report released in September 2018[51] and its subsequent reports,[52] provide an unprecedented amount of information, including names of individuals alleged to have committed the most serious crimes and human rights violations against Rohingya men, women, and children which established a roadmap for advocates and international investigators.[53] As concerns the possibility of refugee returns, in May 2019 the IIFFM concluded 'that the government [of Myanmar] has not taken steps necessary to put the requisite conditions for the return of the refugees in place'.[54]

The IIFFM's findings fed into another mechanism established by the HRC, the Independent Investigative Mechanism for Myanmar (IIMM), tasked with 'collecting, consolidating, preserving, and analyzing evidence of the most serious crimes and violations of international law committed in Myanmar since 2011',[55] and its findings will eventually feed in to ongoing processes before the ICC and ICJ to assist the judges, as well as other international or domestic courts of law or tribunals with requisite jurisdiction.[56] The IIMM has reportedly collected over two million pieces of evidence and, since the February 2021 *coup*, has received 200,000 communications from individuals and organizations concerning alleged crimes in Myanmar. Distilling, verifying, and organizing this massive amount of evidence is an arduous task which will take skilled human resources to do well.

The IIMM is required to prepare evidence and files leading to eventual criminal prosecutions employing a criminal law standard of proof. Getting to the point where prosecutions can be brought could once again take years. The global COVID-19 pandemic, rampant throughout Myanmar, has only complicated this work[57] in addition to negatively impacting the humanitarian situation in the country.[58]

An important group of potential witnesses to an eventual criminal process are the Rohingya themselves. Refugees who provide evidence to a criminal investigation or related human rights process may never be able to safely repatriate as they risk being identified, sought after, harmed, or even killed. The physical protection of individual witnesses including family members, some of whom remain in Myanmar or Bangladesh, is a sensitive issue rightly identified by the IIMM.[59] Despite the many challenges, the IIMM is, according to its head, making important progress.[60]

Even while waiting for these international mechanisms to bear fruit, some states have imposed sanctions against individual Tatmadaw officers[61] and their family members, including those residing abroad.[62] Moreover, virtually all nations can deny access to their territory by undesirable individuals by refusing to issue visas, or to allow study, work, or visitation privileges. This has an immediate impact. Identifying and seizing hidden assets outside Myanmar linked to corrupt officials and the illicit drug trade[63] is another area the international community through national departments of justice should and can explore.

Distinct from individual and state accountability as part of eventual criminal processes and other proceedings before international tribunals, the IIFFM has suggested that states divest and embargo Myanmar business interests and impose sanctions against companies tied to the Tatmadaw. This would cut off financial and other support to Myanmar's armed forces which have used 'its own businesses, foreign companies, and arms deals to support brutal operations against ethnic groups that constitute serious crimes under international law, bypassing civilian oversight, and evading accountability'.[64] Since that prescient call, numerous countries including the United States, Canada, and the European Union have imposed targeted sanctions and embargos against Myanmar.[65]

In addition to formal sanctions, there have been extensive calls by human rights groups for foreign companies to sever ties and close operations in Myanmar.[66] Multinational corporations (MNCs) are being pressured to divest in Myanmar and take human rights responsibility as corporate entities.[67] One

MNC, Telenor, the Norwegian-government-backed telecommunications enterprise, in trying to divest in Myanmar, has struggled to identify buyers with responsible human rights records that have resulted in calls for the Norwegian government to stop any sale.[68]

Private social media companies like Facebook (as Meta) and Twitter and the individuals who run these corporations also bear the responsibility to ensure their platforms are not used for harmful or unlawful purposes, including propagation of hate speech which has played out horrifically in Myanmar and throughout Southeast Asia.[69] Calls for accountability measures and claims of civil liability[70] against these affluent and influential corporations, including demands that they respect human rights in their business operations,[71] and, at another level, cooperate with sanctioned international investigations, are not misplaced.[72]

Facebook has for years struggled to be a responsible corporate player in Myanmar and elsewhere in the Asia region. It is incapable of monitoring its use in countries where it neither has a presence nor the expertise or capacity to monitor the use of the platform.[73] As one measure, taking down the Facebook pages of the Tatmadaw commander-in-chief and other senior military officials[74] and eventually banning the Tatmadaw *in toto*[75] was long overdue. How long these bans will continue is unknown.

If these companies and the individuals who lead them are serious about being good corporate citizens and supporting human rights defenders and principles, universally worthy goals, in addition to complying with reasonable demands for disclosure of records in the face of allegations of serious criminal conduct, other decisive steps must be taken.[76] Relying on self-regulation and internal oversight[77] with teams of well-paid experts, algorithmic or other technical 'solutions', is a seemingly impossible task given the tens of millions of subscribers and volume of messages posted daily around the globe. Furthermore, any true incentive to limit outrageous or extremist postings may be lacking as that is precisely the sort of information which goes 'viral' and increases revenue and may be especially difficult to curb and control.[78]

There is a strong case for human rights and legal oversight and accountability of this commercial 'online' domain, with some commentators suggesting strong legislation and regulation or possibly banning particular social media services altogether due to the range of harm they cause.[79] Establishing in-house vetting and content monitoring capacity is taking place in larger entities like Facebook (Meta),[80] but that poses challenges of its own including to employees engaged in this burdensome, endless work.[81] Naturally, attempting to do this work has its own limitations due to the risk of human error and negligence.

Inaction by the UN Security Council and neighbouring Asian states

Why the events of August 2017 and the mass exodus of close to a million ethnic Rohingya have not prompted decisive Security Council (SC) action in what should be considered a textbook case envisioned by the Responsibility to Protect

(R2P)[82] doctrine can be summed up in a few words: lack of collective political will. Although the ability to seek 'asylum' in Bangladesh arguably satisfies one of the requirements of the R2P regime,[83] the principle of 'responsibility sharing' has otherwise failed to take root.

Approved by most UN member states who supported the adoption of the non-binding *Global Compact on Refugees* and *NY Declaration*,[84] that includes the concept of 'responsibility sharing', to date this has failed to materialize to the benefit of the Rohingya. On the contrary, there are disturbing reports of Asian states, some of whom are hosting significant numbers of displaced Rohingya, engaging in illegal measures including pushbacks of boats filled with asylum seekers and refusing disembarkation, putting passengers, including women and children, at serious risk. These same states, including Indonesia, Thailand, and Malaysia, with negative policy transfer and material support from western governments like Australia,[85] systematically use long-term immigration detention as a deterrent measure. Malaysia also shockingly entered into an agreement to return asylum seekers and refugees to Myanmar, including some Rohingya, with the assistance of the Tatmadaw[86] and it has refused to grant UNHCR access to Rohingya and other refugees sitting in detention.[87] These examples demonstrate a distressing tendency of not adhering to international refugee and human rights law standards including universally binding principles of *non-refoulement* and freedom from torture, that the UN and international community should denounce.

Practices are often led by example, and, whereas it was hoped that the UN's highest body would substantively engage on Myanmar, given the international outcry and sustained political pressure for the Security Council to take action,[88] this has not happened.[89] The Council's formal engagement has been to issue a series of non-binding statements including press releases, the lowest level of 'action', such as one from 10 November 2021 that *inter alia* calls for a cessation of hostilities, unhindered humanitarian access, support for ASEAN's Five Point Consensus,[90] and reaffirming their strong commitment to the sovereignty, political independence, territorial integrity, and unity of Myanmar.[91]

Permanent Council member China, supported by the Russian Federation,[92] along with some other non-permanent Council members, consistently refuses to take decisive action on Myanmar and does not hesitate to use its veto power to avoid substantive Council engagement or condemnation.[93] In light of the war in Ukraine and aggression by Russia, there are renewed calls to reform the Council and in particular the veto, including its abolishment.[94] Beyond geo-political considerations and while waiting for much-needed UN reform, there is also a historical reluctance to set a precedent by addressing 'refugee crises' which fail to serve the interests of powerful states.

Despite the current standstill, international law is clear. As an executive organ with authority to act under Chapter VII of the *UN Charter*, the Council is obliged to act when credible allegations of genocide or crimes against humanity are brought before it.[95] Some commentators and political leaders have suggested UN peacekeepers or international observers or monitors be deployed to Myanmar as the situation jeopardizes regional safety and security. With credible claims of genocide and increasing conflict and militarization in Rakhine, Kachin, Shan, and Chin States and other parts of the country, a military *coup*, risk of civil war, and continuing outflows of refugees, this is a reasonable proposal. However, such a decision can only happen with agreement of all permanent Security Council members. Regrettably, the governing Tatmadaw and its supporters in the Council make reaching that decision impossible given the current structure.

Questions of state sovereignty and non-interference aside, honoured principles in the ASEAN context, perceived international interference in the treatment of religious and ethnic minorities in the territory of UN member states is at play. A related concern is ASEAN's close ties to the Myanmar junta, especially those member states that share similar ideologies and military-controlled government structures.[96] The importance of maintaining positive bilateral and economic relations and trade, including large-scale arms sales and transfers,[97] further tends to trump protection and human rights considerations.[98] The political-economic ambitions of the People's Republic of China are especially apparent. China wants access to the Bay of Bengal as part of its Belt and Road Initiative (BRI), and a direct line to this strategic maritime route is through Myanmar.

A country's domestic policies and treatment of its own religious and ethnic minorities can reflect how it reacts to similar behaviour by other states. China's human rights record with its own Turkic Muslim minority, the Uyghurs, is a relevant consideration. More than one million ethnic Uyghurs have been imprisoned or interned by the Chinese authorities.[99] Precise figures may never be known. Although China's mistreatment of the Uyghur populations has been internationally condemned,[100] there are credible reports of crimes against humanity, including forced labour, use of torture, forced sterilization, and shaving the heads of women prisoners to produce hair pieces for export.[101] Added to the regional ethos of non-interference, this creates a toxic mix of indifference and impunity which leads to severe violations of human rights, religious intolerance, and racism. One should not expect the Chinese government to care about Myanmar's mistreatment of the Rohingya any more than it cares for the welfare of the Uyghurs. This attitude can be reflected in a state's relations and positions taken with UN institutions, which can help explain why China continues to stymie the Security Council concerning the Rohingya situation.[102]

Despite ongoing conflict in Northern Rakhine and several other states in Myanmar, a largely empty geography can facilitate infrastructure development and security while serving an interest in repopulating Rakhine with Bamar Buddhists. With China's economic power, military might, and regional presence, one can expect that any future development of Myanmar will experience its continued engagement and dominant influence. Although the BRI may eventually be of economic benefit to Bangladesh, the regional interest and net gain to Myanmar is more prominent.[103]

Japan, another influential country in Asia, although showing strong support for Bangladesh and the humanitarian plight of the Rohingya as a donor country for humanitarian response, has consistently supported Myanmar, including in the ICJ genocide case. In 2019 in Yangon, the Japanese ambassador to Myanmar stated in a press conference that 'his government firmly believes that no genocide was committed in the country' and prays and hopes that the 'ICJ will not issue a ruling for provisional measures' against Myanmar.[104] Japan was among a handful of states, including India, that abstained during voting on UN General Assembly[105] and Human Rights Council[106] resolutions concerning the human rights situation in Myanmar. Although abstaining is neither voting for nor against a resolution, this was not appreciated by Bangladesh, amongst others. Japan's enduring interest 'to promote foreign business opportunities in war-torn Rakhine State' has been strongly criticized.[107]

India has similarly ambitious economic interests in Myanmar as a part of its Act East policy and potential land bridge into Southeast Asia. Notwithstanding pre-Myanmar-*coup* high-level diplomacy seeking agreement for the 'safe, speedy, and sustainable' repatriation of the Rohingya,[108] the Hindutva-movement and view of the Indian authorities concerning the national security implications of Rohingya residing in their territory have resulted in deportations to Myanmar.[109] For both India and Japan, Myanmar is a bridge country for their regional ambitions. The geo-political and economic interests of these countries certainly help explain why regional responses and powers remain lukewarm, at best, to pressuring Myanmar.

Another factor which inhibits finding a solution for the Rohingya is a chauvinistic attitude towards Bangladesh. Economic exchange between Myanmar and Bangladesh is not particularly high when compared to other regional partners, and the Rohingya refugee situation has made the trade picture less favourable.[110] Politically and existentially, Bangladesh is viewed as a predominantly Islamic country which threatens Buddhist-dominant Myanmar. The Rohingya exodus repeating itself since before the formation of the People's Republic of Bangladesh only aggravates bilateral relations. National security concerns regarding the Rohingya have been raised by Bangladesh *and* Myanmar, although the evidence suggests such worries are unjustified.[111]

Another consideration is the long history of conflict in Myanmar which relies on contraband trade to finance both state and non-state actors.[112] Widespread corruption and militant and criminal enterprises operating at borders throughout South and Southeast Asia and China contribute to the trade in illegal arms, narcotics, and humans.[113] There are regular reports from national human rights bodies, NGOs, and the media on these issues and, in some instances, criminal convictions of government officials engaged in these activities have been issued.[114] These activities and lack of government control further limit the possibility of safe refugee return. Even before the *coup*, conditions for voluntary repatriation were not present. With military rule now in place, barring international and domestic pressure to convince the Tatmadaw to step down, an unlikely scenario,[115] or the junta's defeat following a civil war, any opening for safe return has now vanished.

Limitations of UN operations and influence in Myanmar

In Myanmar, UN entities have for decades been operating in a country which imposes firm controls. UN personnel have limited freedom of movement and access to senior government personnel. Post-*coup*, the situation has worsened with senior officials and envoys of the UN Secretary-General being largely unable to even visit the country. Official and private communications and movements of staff, which include humanitarian operations and other interventions, are all closely monitored. For the average UN official who may be someone at the middle or beginning of their professional career, living, and working with the concern of being made *persona non grata* due to perceived overstepping of limits restricts one's appetite for risk taking and exposure. And if a UN staff member does get into trouble, even if what they did is principled and upholding the UN's mandate, it is not a given that the organization will be supportive. As a result, limited engagement and risk taking is the norm. This leads to an unhealthy degree of bureaucratic secrecy and self-censorship within offices and between colleagues. Regrettably, lack of sharing information is the way some UN agencies like UNHCR have operated for years in Myanmar. 'Delivering as One' and transparency are nice mantras, but they are often not reflected in practice.

In fairness, constraints by the Myanmar authorities severely impinge on the UN's capacity to conduct needs assessments and to plan, deliver, and monitor humanitarian assistance and promote human rights. Engagement in meaningful political dialogue is also difficult if decision makers refuse to meet you. Despite these limitations, several donor countries continue to fund UN operations in Myanmar in circumstances of questionable effectiveness.[116] Rather than engage in calculated downsizing or mission withdrawal, it is considered more important and strategic to support the UN as the 'eyes and ears' of the international community. Trying to contribute and mitigate whatever harm it can through delivery of humanitarian assistance and continued presence are considered satisfactory objectives. Influencing the political landscape, admittedly a complicated task, is well beyond what the UN funds and programmes and respective envoys can hope to deliver in Myanmar.

Limitations on the UN's operational presence and scope of activities nevertheless compromise its ability to fulfil mandates. This can result in the adoption of negative coping strategies.[117] Pressure from the UN General Assembly[118] and the policy imperative of the Human Rights Up Front mandate (and sequel 'A Call to Action for Human Rights') demands that the UN improve its track record on ensuring robust operational human rights focus. Courageous and capable leadership and a coordinated game plan are key factors.[119] Although the UN country team has a mandate to improve the situation in Myanmar and ultimately move on the recommendations of the Annan Advisory Commission Report, serious limitations on its ability to shift policy and operate must be acknowledged.

Regarding any potential repatriation of the Rohingya, the reality on the ground is that restrictions on UN personnel in Myanmar make it impossible to effectively monitor refugee return, and working through partners and local actors poses similar challenges. Given the UN's inability to provide sufficient relief or solutions for several hundred thousand internally displaced persons in Myanmar, the continued call for Rohingya repatriation is perplexing.

Following the release of the report by Guatemalan Ambassador Gert Rosenthal into the UN's involvement and operations in Myanmar from 2010 to 2018,[120] in a joint letter to the UN Secretary-General (SG), a group of prominent human rights NGOs made the following recommendations:[121]

- Implement reforms to prevent the recurrence of the 'systematic' failures and 'obvious dysfunctional performance' and ensure accountability for those failures as required;
- Re-energize the Human Rights Up Front Initiative (HRUF) prompted by the Charles Petrie [re Sri Lanka[122]] report;
- Return to the SG's office a senior staff member dedicated to ensuring the HRUF is fully implemented throughout the UN system;
- Take steps to hold accountable those UN officials responsible for failures before, during, and since the 2017 ethnic-cleansing campaign;
- Support the UN Resident Coordinator to ensure that they have authority to implement a comprehensive HRUF strategy that considers the views of national and international NGOs, community-based organizations, and the human rights community, and is reflected and implemented at country level;
- Show leadership to take concrete steps to improve coordination at all levels of the UN on the situation in Myanmar;
- Commit to publishing annual updates on progress in adopting the recommendations of the Petrie and Rosenthal reports until they are fully implemented;
- Formally submit Rosenthal's report to the Security Council and invite Rosenthal to brief the Council, the UN General Assembly, and non-governmental organizations.

Some recommendations focus on internal processes and shortcomings, including lack of coordination of UN operations, that reportedly remain relevant today. Although some action has since been taken,[123] implementation of several recommendations requires follow up. Better coordination, courageous leadership, and a common human rights direction by UN entities present in Myanmar have been legitimately called for. Unfortunately, these same agencies have no discernible leverage or political engagement with the Tatmadaw. Whereas the long-term political future of Myanmar is difficult to predict, what seems clear is that the Tatmadaw have no intention of retreating or giving up power and, in that context, the UN will continue to struggle and have limited impact.

A legacy of discrimination, displacement, and impossibility of safe return

The mass influx of some 866,000 Rohingya refugees from Myanmar to Bangladesh, which began in August 2017, was shocking and dramatic but not unprecedented. Significant numbers of ethnic Rohingya fled to Bangladesh in 1942, 1978, 1991, 2012, and 2016. Over many years, thousands of individual

Rohingya managed to travel to Bangladesh for medical treatment and studies or other reasons prior to the most recent mass influx. Some never returned home.

In the 1990s, because of closed camp settings and the absence of long-term integration prospects, a repatriation exercise based on a memorandum of understanding (MOU) between the Bangladesh government and UNHCR took place in 1993–97, with some 230,000 Rohingya returning to Myanmar. Sub-standard living conditions, the absence of legal and human rights protection, political exclusion, and questionable voluntariness resulted in this operation being soundly criticized.[124] The intimidating presence of a large number of armed Bangladesh police engaged in an earlier repatriation exercise in the 1970s is well known.[125] Earlier attempts at repatriation of Rohingya refugees in the 1970s and 1990s were regarded as low points in UNHCR's operational history in Asia,[126] something the High Commissioner's office should not wish to repeat.

The ongoing conflict in Rakhine State creates a dynamic of both external and internal displacement and precarious living conditions.[127] The estimated few hundred thousand ethnic Rohingya remaining in Rakhine have a dire existence. Aggressive and ethnocentric attitudes towards the Rohingya by the Arakan Army[128] and militant Buddhist nationalists who support the Tatmadaw[129] multiplies the unlikelihood of long-term safety and human rights protection for the Rohingya. As if the *coup* and systemic discrimination against the Rohingya were not difficult enough, the COVID-19 pandemic severely limits humanitarian access and delivery of assistance.[130] There are reports the Tatmadaw is weaponizing the pandemic, and ongoing conflict has blocked an international plan to administer vaccines to civilians by civil society organizations. Myanmar is reported to have hundreds of thousands of COVID-19 cases which its barely functioning health care system is unable to manage.[131]

The Rohingya are not unique in terms of protection needs as some other ethnic groups, who previously fled Myanmar and sought asylum, also remain outside the country, with UNHCR calling for their continued protection.[132] The fundamental commitments, human rights protection, and political will required to instil confidence in safe, dignified, and sustainable refugee returns are simply not in place. Arguably, the level of protection guarantees required by the Rohingya is heightened given their experience as victims of extreme human rights violations,[133] earlier flawed repatriation attempts, and other deprivations. While there was some hope that the 2020 national elections, which restored Aung San Suu Kyi and her party to power, would gradually change the political landscape,[134] the particularities of constitutional power sharing and vested interests of the Tatmadaw and lack of genuine accountability measures make opportunities for political reform remote.[135] The *coup* sealed that fate.

Another obstacle to creating an inclusive democratic society in Myanmar is the political creation of a national race identify, or *taingyintha,* of which the Rohingya are distinctly considered not a part. The concept of *taingyintha*,[136] in addition to decades-long internal conflict, has given an outsized role to the Tatmadaw to shape Myanmar as a military-driven and conflict-ridden state. One of the few issues where there appears to be near-national consensus is that the

Rohingya, despite having lived in Myanmar for generations, are foreigners who do not belong.[137] There is nothing to suggest that this attitude amongst the Tatmadaw and the governing elite will change.

The systematic discrimination and absence of human rights protection of the Rohingya, one of over one hundred and thirty ethnic groups of diverse religions (89% of Myanmarese identify as Buddhist) residing in the territory of Myanmar since the twelfth century[138] has been extensively documented.[139] As much as any territory, the Republic of the Union of Myanmar can be considered the Rohingya's country of origin and homeland. Although some Rohingya refugees have naturally expressed a desire to return 'home', among other reasons that is unconscionable in light of the ICJ's findings of 'plausible' genocide having taken place and the significant risks of harm remaining.[140]

Even if repatriation was an option, or, less likely, a decision to apply the cessation clause was taken, what the vast majority of Rohingya refugees experienced and suffered 'arising out of previous persecution', including widespread sexual violence and state-sponsored terror, would exempt them from returning under principles of international refugee law.[141] Those Rohingya who fled Myanmar following the events of 2017 have been granted *prima facie* refugee status in Bangladesh, but if individual status determination was undertaken, they would be considered refugees under international refugee law, including large numbers on gender-related grounds.

The continuing focus on repatriation by Bangladesh, other governments, and the UN is at odds with the status of the Rohingya as refugees under international law. Beyond the thousands of women and girls and others who experienced extreme violence and may never wish to return, they are perfect candidates for *non-refoulement* and complementary protection under provisions of international human rights law.[142] This is another important consideration, seemingly missing from discussions concerning a return solution.

The urgency of solutions for Rohingya refugees

Although safe and voluntary repatriation may be considered the most apposite solution, that can only happen with adequate and sustainable state-supported human rights protection in the country of origin. The situation of the Rohingya is no different. Although there are calls and a desire by members of the Rohingya refugee community to eventually return to Myanmar, many refugees and activists living abroad have voiced opposition to such a move. Whatever way forward, refugees should have legal empowerment and a voice in seeking access to durable solutions and options,[143] both to their benefit and that of the host or receiving communities.

Several options can be considered, including: (i) local integration in Bangladesh and a gradual end to encampment; (ii) providing economic support to host communities; (iii) regional responsibility sharing through resettlement in neighbouring Asian countries under a managed scheme; (iv) permitting third-country resettlement; (v) granting formal protection status to Rohingya residing in Asian countries; (vi) ensuring safe passage and reception of Rohingya refugees who risk travelling from Bangladesh; (vii) ensuring access to public education, health services, and work rights wherever Rohingya refugees are located; and (viii) promoting and securing reparations.

- ***Local integration and international protection through asylum***

The budgetary requirement for UN operations in Bangladesh is approximately US$1 billion per annum. Sustained funding for the current operation remains a serious challenge. Although lack of funding should not detract from developing and attempting to implement an ambitious humanitarian agenda, it poses a limitation and reality check in terms of solutions. A humanitarian funding shortfall can result in pressuring the Rohingya to prematurely return to Myanmar. Another scenario is that they will continue to live as refugees with even fewer resources. Neither option is desirable.

Despite these obstacles, the position of donor states should not be limited to supporting humanitarian operations but also linked to engaging with Myanmar and other states and regional actors to take responsibility and implement solutions. The government of Bangladesh has resisted the idea of permitting local integration and long-term development assistance to support the Rohingya. It is time to face the reality that the Rohingya refugees are unable to return to Myanmar. Short of using coercive measures or permitting conditions in the camps to become unbearable, or simply continuing encampment which adds to the Rohingyas alarming levels of mental health disorders[144] and violence against women and girls,[145] the Bangladesh government should take meaningful steps to permit long-term local integration.

Diplomatic support from donor countries should likewise shift to advocating for appropriate policy changes by the Bangladesh authorities. Development actors including the UN should robustly support this narrative with long-term assistance contingent upon commitment of Bangladesh to permitting local integration. The *coup* and renewed internal conflict and displacement has resulted in new arrivals of Rohingya refugees and other ethnic groups to Bangladesh and neighbouring countries. Under provisions of customary international law, these individuals must be able to access international protection through asylum. Respect for the universally binding principle of *non-refoulement* is paramount. Provisions of international and domestic human rights law granting protection to all persons must also be assured and respected.[146]

- ***Promoting regional responsibility sharing and third-country resettlement***

While limited movement of Rohingya refugees from Myanmar and Bangladesh to third countries is taking place, this is often through informal channels and at great personal risk.[147] Managed migration *via* third-country resettlement, family reunification, or educational sponsorship schemes offered by some countries[148] are all options. For example, in the absence of a national refugee law or clear policy, Malaysia *de facto* permits an estimated 150,000 Rohingya to reside in the country, and the Malaysian authorities permit UNHCR and IOM to arrange third-country resettlement for UNHCR-recognized refugees. Over the past decade, several thousand Rohingya refugees have benefitted from being resettled from Malaysia to several countries, including the United States, Canada, Japan, and New Zealand. This durable solution should be scaled up. Some countries have offered to resettle Rohingya refugees from Bangladesh. Canada has communicated this interest at the highest level of government.[149] A properly managed resettlement programme, including a private or community sponsorship component,[150] can avoid or mitigate any risk of 'pull factors' or fraud.

Resettlement from Bangladesh should prioritize individuals with urgent protection needs, such as victims of violence, in particular the thousands of Rohingya women and girls who survived sexual assault,[151] the medically at-risk, and separated family members.[152] It is not unrealistic that a few hundred thousand Rohingya refugees could be resettled from Bangladesh over the next several years.[153] Long-term resettled refugees may be able to sponsor family members under provisions of immigration law. Opportunities for refugees to study as part of a resettlement scheme can also be promoted.

Resettlement opportunities are not just to the advantage of the lucky few; it also benefits resettlement countries through developing job and leadership skills,[154] human capital, and providing life-saving remittances. Support from the Rohingya diaspora is already taking place, and privately generated funds are reaching refugees in Bangladesh, which helps them survive and manage their lives.

As a country that has benefitted enormously from its own nationals working abroad, there is an irony in the Bangladesh government not permitting third-country resettlement, essentially a migration option, for the Rohingya. The Bangladesh authorities should change their stance and permit managed third-country solutions. Countries with traditional resettlement programmes, such as the United States and Canada, both strong supporters of Bangladesh and the humanitarian response, should continue to advocate with the government and the UN (notably UNHCR, IOM, and the Secretary-General). If the widespread support of states in the international system can manage a large-scale response for other refugee groups with robust third-state options, there is no reason why the same should not be made available for the Rohingya. Notwithstanding the limited global space available for this durable solution, the Rohingya should not be treated any differently.

Resettlement and other stay arrangements can also be promoted in Asia. There are economic advantages and political opportunities for successful regional resettlement or temporary stay arrangements. Thailand, Malaysia, Indonesia, and other Southeast Asian states currently provide work opportunities for many refugees and migrants, often in the informal labour sector. Some Gulf states host several hundred thousand Rohingya as migrant workers, so any additional arrivals would have an immediate community support network. Regional support and solidarity through a managed programme of moving Rohingya from Bangladesh to neighbouring countries in Asia would be a positive example of global responsibility sharing envisioned by the *Global Compact on Refugees*.[155]

ASEAN and the OIC can choose to support and advocate for these third-country regional approaches, but political leadership and courage is required to push the narrative. Continuing to exploit the Rohingya in the labour context while keeping them in legal limbo is as objectionable as it is unhelpful. Taking inspiration from the Comprehensive Plan of Action previously adopted for Indo-Chinese refugees that was considered a success in the Asian region, similar schemes for the Rohingya, including the grant of temporary protection; temporary protection and stay with eventual resettlement; and eventual repatriation (if and when conditions permit) under international supervision, with an option of applying for asylum when it is required, can be organized.[156] Asian states should live up to their political statements and commitments to supporting the Rohingya in their time of need and decidedly move away from burden-shifting and promoting deterrence and external immigration controls.

- ***Access to education, work rights, and other services with government support***

Bangladesh and other countries hosting Rohingya refugees should grant access to public schools and work rights in addition to ensuring public health care, including psycho-social support and family planning and reproductive health services.[157] Bangladesh is permitting some of this assistance to the Rohingya as UN agencies and dozens of domestic and international NGOs[158] are working on a range of programmes in the areas of health, education, and protection. Of particular importance is access to education for children and young adults, as this could prevent another lost generation, given current figures of 70% of the Rohingya being illiterate and innumerate.

Permitting access to these public services would permit more individuals to benefit and the quality of education and health care could significantly improve. Commitments from the World Bank,[159] UN development actors, and, crucially, donors[160] to support and upscale the welfare and economic absorption and co-existence of the Rohingya with local communities should be welcomed. With government support at all levels, this can help develop and finance plans to help refugees and host communities alike.[161] Establishing and sustaining programmes requires continued commitment from the Bangladesh government and local authorities and institutions. Engagement in a range of humanitarian programmes, including training, capacity building, community development, and outreach delivered by staff on the ground, requires a huge input of resources.[162] Critically, the required billions of dollars could be utilized to improve public services for refugees *and* host communities and raise living standards for all in a sustainable way.[163]

Apart from providing services, refugees want to work and help themselves and many refugees have skills. While the refugee community in Bangladesh may be able to find limited work in the informal economy, the absence of legal protection makes them vulnerable to exploitation and abuse. Refugees may be willing to work in sectors considered undesirable by locals, and permitting the Rohingya to legally work in areas with labour needs, including seasonal engagement, would be a step forward. Such arrangements would support the refugee population to become more self-reliant and is a win-win approach for both refugee and local communities.[164] Engagement of the International Labour Office (ILO) in supporting job skill training and job opportunity creation for the Rohingya, like initiatives for Syrian refugees in Jordan, can be promoted in Bangladesh and throughout Asia.[165]

- ***Reparations and restitution***

The International Independent Investigative Mechanisms for Syria and Myanmar established by the UN General Assembly and Human Rights Council provided mandates that extend traditional human rights monitoring, documentation, and reporting to include the preparation of files to be used in national, regional, and international criminal processes. The creation of these mechanisms has led to calls for similar structures to look at other atrocity crimes in countries such as Sri Lanka.[166] The importance of ensuring international and national accountability, justice, and reparations to victims of serious human rights violations, including refugees,[167] cannot be overstated. Failure to act sends a signal that such events can happen with impunity. In addition to directly impacting victims, accountability provides psychological closure for families and communities. Different approaches, including establishing truth-and-reconciliation commissions and even amnesties, may provide an effective route to healing and accountability.

Article 75 of the *International Criminal Court* (ICC) *Statute* recognizes the need to establish principles relating to reparations to victims including 'restitution, compensation, and rehabilitation'. This provision permits the Court, on its own initiative or upon request, to 'determine the scope and extent of any damage, loss, and injury to, or in respect of, victims and will state the principles on which it is acting'.[168] Apart from the *ICC Statute*, there is a significant body of jurisprudence based on international civil liability and other international law which provides reparations and damages for injury to aliens and others as a result of wrongful acts by states or state agents.[169] There is also scope to seek reparations from the International Court of Justice.[170]

In the refugee context, there are some historical examples of UNHCR administering indemnification funds to refugees who were victims of the German national socialist regime as well as to British citizens of Asian origin who were expelled from Uganda.[171] The UN-based compensation commission for Iraqi nationals who lost property and fled as refugees is another example.[172] Despite earlier attempts at the former UN Commission on Human Rights[173] (now Human Rights Council) to develop the right to restitution, compensation, and rehabilitation for victims of gross violations of human rights and fundamental freedoms, sporadic development of regional principles,[174] and academic contributions,[175] there is limited discussion in international fora including within UNHCR, on developing a universal scheme to provide reparation or compensation to refugees.

For the Rohingya, similar compensation arrangements have been proposed,[176] with some addressing the phenomenon of 'land grabbing', which took place before and in the aftermath of the 2017 refugee exodus.[177] Moving such initiatives forward will take a significant diplomatic drive to engage and harness international support.

Finally, individuals may seek reparations and restitution through domestic schemes, as in the case of Colombia,[178] or by petitioning domestic courts or national human rights commissions. One example is the case of a Rohingya widow who has 'requested $2 million in compensation from the Myanmar government for its gross failure to meaningfully address the 'Inn Din massacre' during which her husband was killed by the Tatmadaw'. The complaint was filed at the Myanmar National Human Rights Commission (MNHRC) with support from Legal Action Worldwide, an NGO, and a UK law firm.[179] While it is unlikely the Myanmar Commission will satisfactorily address the complaint, it remains an interesting example of how individuals can potentially pursue justice and raise awareness in a domestic context.

Conclusion

Some of these proposals for solutions are being actively discussed and promoted by governments, within the UN, by members of civil society, and the human rights community, while others need to be kickstarted. There is no easy road ahead. There needs to be a coordinated response to promote and implement protection, including rights-based protection and solutions, in the medium to long term. No one knows what may happen if the Rohingya are left without a future. Resentment and anger can only lead to greater hardship, difficulties, and risks. Refugees themselves are not a security concern but failing to find solutions can lead to security concerns at various levels. In this regard, we need to redress the imbalance between national interests and protecting humanity.

Regional solutions can be advanced to promote human rights protection and responsibility sharing. Playing the long game of 'wait and see' at the expense of the Rohingya is not an option. The world cannot afford another protracted encamped refugee population losing their heart and soul when attainable solutions are present. Collective, coordinated, international, and regional pressure and support is required with the immediate track to ensure support for humanitarian assistance while diplomatic efforts continue. To this end, inclusive and systematic refugee representation in decisions which affect them is key. Failure to directly involve the Rohingya will limit or prevent buy-in to whatever is negotiated on their behalf. As with other refugee groups, the Rohingya in all their diversity need to be a part of and own any solutions which impact them.

Solutions for refugees are never easy to come by, but the international community should not fail the Rohingya. There is too much at stake and too much to lose. It will take mobilization and consolidation of the collective political good will and commitment of governments and international and regional institutions and bodies, and, crucially, civil society organizations and the Rohingya themselves to have any hope of success and ensure that their rights and dignity are respected and upheld.

Notes

1 https://rli.sas.ac.uk/about-us/senior-research-associates/brian-gorlick.

2 Several ideas in this paper were presented at The Hague Conclave on Justice and Accountability for the Rohingya co-convened by the Centre for Peace and Justice, BRAC University, partnered with the International Institute for Social Sciences (ISS) and Asia Justice Coalition on 18 October 2019. Subsequent dramatic events have taken place in Myanmar, notably the February 2021 *coup* and renewed internal conflict and forced displacement. This paper draws on further research and exchanges with colleagues working in the field. I wish to acknowledge the generous support of academic, UN, and legal experts who provided comments and shared insights and information. They are, however, not responsible for the views expressed and any errors are my own. I would like to dedicate this work to the Rohingya refugees and activists in Bangladesh and abroad who continue to work for a better future and the many individuals who provide front-line support and assistance to refugees worldwide. I further wish to honour the contributions to refugee studies, human rights advocacy, humanitarian work and diplomacy of the following colleagues who left us too soon: Professor Gil Loescher, Ambassador Augustine Mahiga, Professor David Petrasek, and Dr Gary Troeller.

3 'Towards a Peaceful, Fair, and Prosperous Future for the People or Rakhine: Final Report of the Advisory Commission on Rakhine State' (August 2017): http://www.rakhinecommission.org/app/uploads/2017/08/FinalReport_Eng.pdf.

4 Twitter feed: https://twitter.com/pyaezone/status/1356242402764181504/photo/1

The *coup* was the result of the Tatmadaw's dissatisfaction with the results of the multi-party general election held on 8 November 2020 which returned the then-National League for Democracy (NLD) to power. Official notification of the *coup* was issued by the Myanmar Office of the Commander-in-Chief of Defence Services on 1 February 2021 and *inter alia* notes: '[…] The Union Election Commission will be re-constituted to continuously take appropriate measures including checking the voting lists in accord with the law […]. Emphasis will be made to recover as much as possible on restoring eternal peace all over the country in accord with the National Ceasefire Agreement. […] When these tasks have been completed in accord with the provisions of the State of Emergency, a free and fair multi-party general election will be held and then State responsibilities will be handed over to the winning party meeting norms and standards of democracy'.

5 'The UN's Response to the Human Rights Crisis after the *Coup* in Myanmar: Destined to Fail?', International Peace Institute (IPI) (June 2021): https://www.ipinst.org/wp-content/uploads/2021/06/The-UNs-Response-Coup-in-Myanmar-Final.pdf.

Hundreds of thousands of individuals have been displaced due to armed conflict and countless others have fled within the country because of the security crackdowns against public protests in Yangon and other urban areas.

6 ASEAN Parliamentarians for Human Rights, 'ASEAN's Rakhine Crisis: Assessing the regional response to atrocities in Myanmar's Rakhine State' (October 2020): http://aseanmp.org/wp-content/uploads/2020/11/ASEANs-Rakhine-Crisis_-APHR-Report-1.pdf; 'ASEAN: Overhaul Regional

Response to Rohingya Crisis', *Human Rights Watch* (26 June 2020): https://www.hrw.org/news/2020/06/26/asean-overhaul-regional-response-rohingya-crisis; also Security Council Report (SCR), 'Myanmar – Private Council Meeting' (16 August 2021): https://www.securitycouncilreport.org/whatsinblue/2021/08/myanmar-private-council-meeting-2.php; Daniel Sullivan, 'ASEAN Has Failed on Myanmar: What Next?', *Just Security* (27 October 2021) https://www.justsecurity.org/78772/asean-has-failed-on-myanmar-whats-next/

In August 2021, after several months delay, ASEAN announced the appointment of Dato Erwyan bin Pehin Yusof of Brunei as Special Envoy for Myanmar. The Special Envoy's work was focused on 'building trust and confidence with full access to all parties concerned and providing a clear timeline on the implementation of the five-point consensus which include: cessation of violence; dialogue between the parties; the appointment of a special envoy to facilitate mediation of the dialogue process; a visit of the ASEAN special envoy to Myanmar; and the provision of humanitarian aid by ASEAN'. (SCR, 2021).

7 David Hutt, 'The Staying Power of SE Asia's political militaries', *Asia Times* (Richmond, BC, Canada, 27 February 2021): https://asiatimes.com/2021/02/the-staying-power-of-se-asias-political-militaries/.

8 'Trilateral Talks on Rohingya Repatriation Resume', *Radio Free Asia* (Washington, DC, 19 January 2021): https://www.rfa.org/english/news/myanmar/talks-01192021191027.html

Diplomatic discussions brokered by China with Bangladesh and Myanmar, concerning Rohingya repatriation, took place on 19 January 2021 with reportedly Myanmar and Bangladesh agreeing to attempt repatriation in the second quarter of 2021, after two earlier repatriation attempts failed. To date, no organized repatriation of Rohingya refugees from Bangladesh to Myanmar has taken place.

9 'Foreign Minister Momen: Bangladesh against any idea leading to Rohingya integration', *Dhaka Tribune* (Dhaka, 31 July 2021): https://www.dhakatribune.com/bangladesh/rohingya-crisis/2021/07/31/fm-momen-bangladesh-against-any-idea-leading-to-rohingya-integration.

10 'Myanmar's generals want Aung San Suu Kyi locked up forever' *The Economist* (11 December 2021): https://www.economist.com/asia/2021/12/11/myanmars-generals-want-aung-san-suu-kyi-locked-up-forever

On 6 December 2021, Aung San Suu Kyi was sentenced to four years in prison. Although the sentence was later reduced to two years it is the first in a series of verdicts that could keep the 76-year-old Nobel laureate imprisoned for the rest of her life.

11 The Assistance Association for Political Prisoners (Burma), a human rights organization based in Mae Sot, Thailand and Rangoon reports on these numbers: https://aappb.org.

12 'The Cost of the Coup: Myanmar Edges Toward State Collapse', *International Crisis Group* (April 2021): https://www.crisisgroup.org/asia/south-east-asia/myanmar/b167-cost-coup-myanmar-edges-toward-state-collapse; Poppy McPherson and Shoon Naing, 'The young generation risking all to topple the Myanmar junta', *Reuters* (10 November 2021): https://www.reuters.com/investigates/special-report/myanmar-politics-youth-resistance/; Sui-Lee Wee, 'As Soldiers Abandon Notorious Myanmar Army, a Morale Crisis Looms', *The New York Times* (21 November 2021): https://www.nytimes.com/2021/11/21/world/asia/myanmar-defectors-coup.html.

13 Website of the National Unity Government of the Republic of the Union of Myanmar: https://nugmyanmar.org/en/.

14 'Myanmar envoy Kyaw Moe Tun breaks ranks, urges 'strongest possible' UN action against military coup' (26 February 2021): https://www.youtube.com/watch?v=G-YepXLfPZc.

15 'Myanmar coup: UN ambassador fired after anti-army speech', *BBC News* (28 February 2021): https://www.bbc.com/news/world-asia-56222987.

16 'The UN General Assembly must reject Myanmar Junta's Attempts to Grab Envoy Seat', *Pass Blue: Independent Coverage of the UN* (New York, 26 July 2021): https://www.passblue.com/2021/07/26/the-un-general-assembly-must-reject-myanmar-juntas-attempts-to-grab-envoy-seat/; Special Advisory Committee for Myanmar (SAC-M)(11 August 2021): https://spcialadvisorycouncil.org/wp-content/uploads/2021/08/SAC-M-Briefing-Paper-Recognition-of-Governments-ENGLISH.pdf; Catherine Putz, 'Afghanistan's Taliban, Myanmar's Tatmadaw Denied UN Seats, For Now', *The Diplomat* (Arlington, VA, USA, 3 December 2021): https://thediplomat.com/2021/12/afghanistans-taliban-myanmars-tatmadaw-denied-un-seats-for-now/.

17 'Myanmar duo arrested in New York over plot to kill UN ambassador', *The Guardian* (London, 6 August 2021): https://www.theguardian.com/world/2021/aug/06/myanmar-arrests-plot-ambassador-united-nations-kyaw-moe-tun.

18 Anupam Nath, 'Fleeing Myanmar police: We defied orders to kill protesters', *Associated Press* (19 March 2021): https://apnews.com/article/myanmar-india-asia-asia-pacific-southeast-asia-7054a0f5671a2a8e8dde33c720c436cc.

19 On 12 March 2021, the US Secretary of Homeland Security designated Burma (Myanmar) for Temporary Protection Status (TPS) for eighteen months. This enables Myanmar nationals and those individuals without nationality who last resided in Myanmar (viz. the Rohingya) and are currently in the United States to file an application for TPS, and asylum, or both: https://www.reuters.com/article/us-myanmar-usa-diplomat/myanmar-envoy-seeks-asylum-u-s-pressure-on-rulers-idUSTRE76471120110705.: https://www.dhs.gov/news/2021/03/12/secretary-mayorkas-designates-burma-temporary-protected-status; https://www.federalregister.gov/documents/2021/05/25/2021-11075/designation-of-burma-myanmar-for-temporary-protected-status.

20 'Avoid Pushing Back Refugees from Thailand to Myanmar, says Save the Children', Save the Children (30 March 2021): https://www.savethechildren.net/news/avoid-pushing-back-refugees-thailand-myanmar-says-save-children.

21 Gillian Triggs, 'News comment: UNHCR calls on Myanmar's neighbours to protect people fleeing violence' UNHCR (31 March 2021): https://www.unhcr.org/news/press/2021/3/60648c304/news-comment-unhcr-calls-myanmars-neighbours-protect-people-fleeing-violence.html.

22 'Statement from UN Emergency Relief Coordinator Martin Griffiths regarding the increasing violence and humanitarian need in Myanmar', *Reliefweb* (8 November 2021): https://reliefweb.int/sites/reliefweb.int/files/resources/ERC%20Myanmar%20Statement%20_%2008112021.pdf

23 Zaheena Rasheed, 'Why Myanmar's military seized power in a coup', *Al Jazeera* (1 February 2021): https://www.aljazeera.com/news/2021/2/1/who-is-min-aung-hlaing.

24 Paul Millar, 'Meet one of the main architects behind the bloody crackdown against the Myanmar's Rohingya', *Southeast Asia Globe* (8 January 2018):
https://southeastasiaglobe.com/min-aung-hlaing/?utm_source=newsletter&utm_medium=email&utm_campaign=TheDigest_20210212&utm_content=MeetOneOfTheMainArchitectsBehindTheBloodyCrackdownAgainstTheMyanmarsRohingya

In a remarkable passage in his book, Thant Myint-U references an event which took place in 2020 when the Myanmar consul general in Hong Kong, Ye Myint Aung, wrote a letter to all heads of foreign missions, refuting allegations of discrimination against the Rohingya. In his letter, the consul general suggested that the Rohingya were 'not one of "Myanmar's ethnic groups" and compared their "dark brown" complexion to that of the Burmese, which was "fair and soft, good-looking as well". For good measure, he noted that his own complexion was a "typical genuine one" for Burmese "gentlemen". "You will accept how handsome your colleague Mr Ye is". The Rohingya, by contrast, were "as ugly as ogres". Mr Ye was never reprimanded. Instead, he was promoted'. Myint-U, Thant, *The Hidden History of Burman: Race, Capitalism, and the Crisis of Democracy in the 21st Century,* 128 WW Norton & Co NY (2020).

25 'UN expert wants scrutiny of conditions at Bhasan Char', *Al Jazeera* (11 December 2020): https://www.aljazeera.com/news/2020/12/11/myanmar-rohingya; Verena Hölz, 'As violence soars in refugee camps, Rohingya women speak up', *The New Humanitarian* (2 August 2021): https://www.thenewhumanitarian.org/news/2021/8/2/as-violence-soars-in-refugee-camps-rohingya-women-speak-up; Jeff Crisp, 'Bhasan Char: Prison island or paradise? Are Rohingya refugees being denied their right to freedom of movement?', *Lacuna Magazine* (12 May 2022): https://lacuna.org.uk/migration/are-rohingya-refugees-being-denied-their-right-to-freedom-of-movement/.

26 'Bangladesh/Myanmar, Situation in the People's Republic of Bangladesh/Republic of the Union of Myanmar ICC-01/19 – Investigation', International Criminal Court (14 November 2019): https://www.icc-cpi.int/bangladesh-myanmar.

27 Each case brought before the ICJ and ICC raises unique facts and legal issues that must be addressed within the Courts respective jurisdictional and procedural standards. As one benchmark, the last case involving the *Genocide Convention* at the ICJ in the case of *Bosnia Herzegovina v Serbia and Montenegro* took fourteen years to conclude, while the case of *Croatia v Serbia*, which was eventually dismissed, took sixteen years.

28 Yazuki Nagakoshi, 'The Scope and Implications of the International Criminal Court's Jurisdictional Decision over the Rohingya Crisis', 43 *Human Rights Quarterly* 259–289 (2021).

A detailed review of international and domestic legal proceedings concerning the Rohingya situation and Myanmar is beyond the scope of this paper, but some excellent scholarship and reports are available. Moreover, dozens of international symposia on the topic of justice and accountability for the Rohingya continue to take place. See, for example, Priya Pillai, 'Symposium on The Impact and Implications of International Law: Myanmar and the Rohingya – An Introduction' *Opinio Juris* (24 August 2020): https://opiniojuris.org/2020/08/24/symposium-on-the-impact-and-implications-of-international-law-myanmar-and-the-rohingya-an-introduction/; and Kriangsak Kittichaisaree, *The Rohingya, Justice and International Law* (Routledge, November 2021), and the related discussion sponsored by Oxford Law Faculty: https://www.youtube.com/watch?v=uX-WqXyUafI;

29 International Court of Justice (ICJ), Application of the Convention on the Prevention and Punishment of the Crime of Genocide (The Gambia v Myanmar): https://www.icj-cij.org/en/case/178.

30 'Gambia's foreign minister says Rohingya issue to be taken to the ICJ' *Dhaka Tribune* (17 May 2019): https://www.dhakatribune.com/bangladesh/2019/05/17/gambia-s-foreign-minister-says-rohingya-issue-to-be-taken-to-icj.

Also, Priya Pillai 'The ICJ and the Rohingya: The Long Road Ahead for Accountability' *Opinio Juris* (6 November 2019): http://opiniojuris.org/2019/11/06/the-international-court-of-justice-and-the-rohingya-the-long-road-ahead-for-accountability/; John Packer, 'Genocide is an act of state, and demands a response by other states' (24 April 2019) *Open Global Rights*: https://www.openglobalrights.org/genocide-is-an-act-of-state-and-demands-a-response-by-other-states/.

31 'Q & A on the ICJ and Genocide in Myanmar', *Global Justice Center Blog* (11 November 2019): https://www.globaljusticecenter.net/blog/19-publications/1147-q-a-the-international-court-of-justice-the-genocide-of-the-rohingya?utm_source=Global+Justice+Center&utm_campaign=bb2ef627cc-EMAIL_CAMPAIGN_2017_11_06_COPY_02&utm_medium=email&utm_term=0_1d25714382-bb2ef627cc-56664303.

32 Priya Pillai, *Opinio Juris* (3 September 2020): http://opiniojuris.org/2020/09/03/canada-and-the-netherlands-new-intervention-in-the-gambia-v-myanmar-at-the-international-court-of-justice/; Global Affairs Canada, 'Joint Statement of Canada and the Kingdom of the Netherlands regarding intention to intervene in *The Gambia v Myanmar* case at the ICJ' (2 September 2020): https://www.canada.ca/en/global-affairs/news/2020/09/joint-statement-of-canada-and-the-kingdom-of-the-netherlands-regarding-intention-to-intervene-in-the-gambia-v-myanmar-case-at-the-international-cou.html; Kingdom of the Netherlands (2 September 2020): https://www.government.nl/documents/diplomatic-statements/2020/09/02/joint-statement-of-canada-and-the-kingdom-of-the-netherlands-regarding-intention-to-intervene-in-the-gambia-v.-myanmar-case-at-the-international-court-of-justice.

33 'Maldives to intervene at ICJ in support of Rohingya' *The Edition* (Malé, 25 February 2020): https://edition.mv/covid_19/15185; 'Maldives, Gambia discuss case against Myanmar at ICJ' *The Edition* (25 March 2020): https://edition.mv/news/15727.

34 Tun Khin, 'Universal Jurisdiction, the International Criminal Court, and the Rohingya Genocide' *Opinio Juris* (23 October 2020): https://opiniojuris.org/2020/10/23/universal-jurisdiction-the-international-criminal-court-and-the-rohingya-genocide/; Burma Campaign UK, 'Historic decision by Argentinian Courts to take up Genocide Case against Myanmar' (28 November 2021): https://burmacampaign.org.uk/historic-decision-by-argentinian-courts-to-take-up-genocide-case-against-myanmar/.

35 The Gambia's submission to the ICJ filed on 11 November 2019 provides a detailed summary of key facts with references making out the claim of acts of genocide having been committed by the Myanmar government. Full text is available at: https://www.icj-cij.org/files/case-related/178/178-20191111-APP-01-00-EN.pdf.

36 Priya Pillai, 'Three Complementary Legal Strategies for Accountability: A Momentous Week for the Rohingya' *Opinio Juris* (19 November 2019): http://opiniojuris.org/2019/11/19/three-complimentary-legal-strategies-for-accountability-a-momentous-week-for-the-rohingya/?utm_source=feedburner&utm_medium=email&utm_campaign=Feed%3A+opiniojurisfeed+%28Opinio+Juris%29.

37 An interesting perspective on the quest for retributive justice in Myanmar is offered by Morten Pedersen:

> "… herein lies the ultimate paradox in the push for criminal prosecution. By putting not only the Commander-in-Chief but any military officer who served in Rakhine State during the violence on notice that they could someday be held accountable for their crimes, we have essentially ensured that

the military-as-an-institution cannot risk letting go of control of the state. *They will be well aware of what happened, for example, to General Pinochet of Chile and that the only way for them to remain safe is to be in power.*" (emphasis added).

Morten B Pedersen, 'The ICC, the Rohingya and the limitations of retributive justice', 73 *Australian Journal of International Affairs* 12 (2019); Kyaw Phyo Tha, 'Analysis: History Suggests International Targeting of Tatmadaw over Rohingya is Misguided', *The Irrawaddy* (Yangon, 28 September 2018): https://www.irrawaddy.com/news/burma/history-suggests-intl-targeting-tatmadaw-rohingya-misguided.html

38 Independent International Fact-Finding Mission on Myanmar: https://www.ohchr.org/en/hrbodies/hrc/myanmarffm/pages/index.aspx.

39 IIFFM Report, *op cit* (A/HRC/39/CRP.2, 17 September 2018), para 81, p 24; Melissa Crouch, *The Constitution of Myanmar: A Contextual Analysis*, Hart Publishing (2019): https://www.bloomsburyprofessional.com/uk/the-constitution-of-myanmar-9781509927364/.

40 ICJ Order of 23 January 2020, para 73: https://www.icj-cij.org/public/files/case-related/178/178-20200123-ORD-01-00-EN.pdf; UN General Assembly resolution 'Situation of human rights of Rohingya Muslims and other minorities in Myanmar' (December 2019): https://digitallibrary.un.org/record/3841021.

41 ICJ Order, *ibid.*

42 'Everything is gone': satellite images in Myanmar shows dozens of Rohingya villages bulldozed', *The Guardian* (23 February 2018): https://www.theguardian.com/world/2018/feb/24/myanmar-rohingya-villages-bulldozed-satellite-images.

43 'Myanmar: Villages burned, civilians injured and killed as Rakhine State conflict escalates', *Amnesty International* (12 October 2020): https://www.amnesty.org/en/latest/news/2020/10/myanmar-villages-burned-civilians-injured-rakhine-state-conflict/.

44 Hannah Beech, Saw Nang, Merlise Simons, ''Kill All You See': In a First, Myanmar Soldiers Tell of Rohingya Slaughter' *The New York Times* (19 October 2021): https://www.nytimes.com/2020/09/08/world/asia/myanmar-rohingya-genocide.html; 'International Criminal Court: Prosecute and Offer Witness Protection to Myanmar Army Deserters', *Fortify Rights* (8 September 2020): https://www.fortifyrights.org/mya-inv-2020-09-08/.

45 'Myanmar says International Criminal Court has no jurisdiction in Rohingya crisis', *Reuters* (7 September 2018): https://www.reuters.com/article/us-myanmar-rohingya-icc/myanmar-says-international-criminal-court-has-no-jurisdiction-in-rohingya-crisis-idUSKCN1LN22X; Marlise Simons, 'International Criminal Court Opens Door to a Rohingya Inquiry', *The New York Times* (6 September 2018): https://www.nytimes.com/2018/09/06/world/asia/rohingya-myanmar-international-criminal-court.html.

46 'Executive Summary of [Myammar] Independent Commission of Enquiry-ICOE', *Reliefweb* (22 January 2020): https://www.icoe-myanmar.org/.

47 'Myanmar military demands return of two soldiers who confessed to Rohingya atrocities', *The Irrawaddy* (Yangon, 14 September 2020): https://www.irrawaddy.com/news/burma/myanmar-military-demands-return-two-soldiers-confessed-rohingya-atrocities.html.

48 Constitution of the Republic of the Union of Myanmar 343(b)(2008): https://www.burmalibrary.org/docs5/Myanmar_Constitution-2008-en.pdf?__cf_chl_jschl_tk__=pmd_b357eba4e8f4b8764a00f5cd489fdaa1aeb0b97c-1628686901-0-gqNtZGzNAfijcnBszQZO.

49 Nagakoshi, *op cit* (2021) 274.

50 The executive summary of the ICOE report, *op cit*, under 'causalities and damages' notes: 'There are very significant inconsistencies in the victimization figures provided by different actors. According to the ***data provided by the Government [of Myanmar]*** to the ICOE, human fatalities were 376 ARSA members, and 133 civilians with 181 missing. More than 40,000 houses were destroyed and 410,000 persons, mostly Muslims, fled into Bangladesh ….' (emphasis added, 4).

Concerning incidents of 'rape' the report concludes: 'There were no credible statements of allegations of gang rape committed by Myanmar's security forces. Although some interviewees mentioned rape cases, these were all second-hand information heard from someone else. Additionally, some female witnesses noted that they were searched by male Myanmar's Defence Services personnel as part of the operations. This behaviour may constitute sexual violence'. (*ibid*, 6).

Under 'torture', the Commissioners noted that: 'Some witnesses recalled seeing Myanmar's Defence Services personnel beat Muslim villagers for the purpose of intimidating them to make them follow orders, such as forcing them to move to a specific place of the village as ordered'. (*ibid*).

51 UN doc ref: A/HRC/39/64, (18 September 2019): https://www.ohchr.org/en/hr-bodies/hrc/myanmar-ffm/index.

52 Sexual and gender-based violence in Myanmar and the gendered impact of its ethnic conflicts (UN doc ref: A/HRC/42/CRP.4, 22 August 2019) available at: https://www.ohchr.org/EN/HRBodies/HRC/MyanmarFFM/Pages/sexualviolence.aspx; Economic interests of the Myanmar military, A/HRC/42/CRP.3 (5 August 2019): https://www.ohchr.org/EN/HRBodies/HRC/MyanmarFFM/Pages/EconomicInterestsMyanmarMilitary.aspx.

53 Guy Goodwin-Gill and Jason Poboy, 'Joint Legal Opinion on the Government of Myanmar's Compliance with the Convention on the Rights of the Child in the Context of the Treatment of Rohingya Children Following the Events of 25 August 2017', *Save the Children* (12 June 2018): https://resourcecentre.savethechildren.net/library/joint-legal-opinion-government-myanmars-compliance-convention-rights-child-context-treatment

54 A/HRC/42/50, *op cit*, paras 76 & 85.

Seehttps://reliefweb.int/report/myanmar/statement-42nd-session-human-rights-council-marzuki-darusman-chair-independent; also the August 2019 report of the UN Secretary General at paras 29–32: https://undocs.org/A/74/311.

55 UN Independent Investigative Mechanism for Myanmar: https://iimm.un.org/.

56 Yannick Pasquet, 'In landmark trial, Germany convicts Syrian agent of state-sponsored torture', *The Times of Israel* (Jerusalem, 24 February 2021: https://www.timesofisrael.com/germany-convicts-syrian-agent-of-state-sponsored-torture-in-landmark-trial/; and Loveday Morris and Sarah Dadouch, 'German court convicts Syrian ex-intelligence office in historic torture trial', *The Washington Post* (24 February 2021): https://www.washingtonpost.com/world/europe/in-first-ever-trial-over-the-syrian-civil-war-german-court-convicts-a-former-intelligence-officer/2021/02/24/8032ef28-7681-11eb-9489-8f7dacd51e75_story.html; Bethan McKernan, 'Germany convicts former Assad regime agent in historic Syrian torture verdict', *The Guardian* (24 February 2021): https://www.msn.com/en-gb/news/world/germany-convicts-former-assad-regime-agent-in-historic-syria-torture-verdict/ar-BB1dYeuv;

57 Statement to the Human Rights Council by Nicholas Koumjian, Head of the IIMM, on the 45th Regular Session of the Human Rights Council (14 September 2020): https://iimm.un.org/statement-to-the-human-rights-coun-

cil-by-mr-nicholas-koumjian-head-of-the-independent-investigative-mechanism-for-myanmar-on-the-45th-regular-session-of-the-human-rights-council/;

58 Rebecca Ratcliffe, 'Myanmar could become Covid 'super-spreader' state, says UN expert', *The Guardian* (28 July 2021): https://www.theguardian.com/world/2021/jul/28/myanmar-could-become-covid-super-spreader-state-says-un-expert.

59 IIMM Annual Reports: https://iimm.un.org/annual-reports/.

60 UN News Interview with IIMM Head Nicholas Koumjian (15 October 2021): https://news.un.org/en/audio/2021/10/1103212.

61 Chris Sidoti, 'Beyond the *Coup* in Myanmar: The Tatmadaw Must Be Hit Where it Hurts: Its Wallet', *Just Security* (14 July 2021): https://www.justsecurity.org/77424/beyond-the-coup-in-myanmar-the-tatmadaw-must-be-hit-where-it-hurts-its-wallet/.

62 *The Global Magnitsky Human Rights Accountability Act* in the United States and other legislation passed in Canada and the United Kingdom, and several other countries is applicable and has been applied to members of the Tatmadaw and Myanmar government officials: https://crsreports.congress.gov/product/pdf/IF/IF10576; https://www.humanrightsfirst.org/sites/default/files/hrf-global-magnitsky-faq.pdf; https://laws.justice.gc.ca/eng/acts/J-2.3/FullText.html.

63 'Fire and Ice: Conflict and Drugs in Myanmar's Shan State', *International Crisis Group* (8 January 2019): https://www.crisisgroup.org/asia/south-east-asia/myanmar/299-fire-and-ice-conflict-and-drugs-myanmars-shan-state.

64 IIFFM press release (5 August 2019): https://www.ohchr.org/en/press-releases/2019/08/un-fact-finding-mission-myanmar-exposes-military-business-ties-calls; IIFFM report on the economic interests of the Myanmar military (UN doc ref: A/HRC/42/CRP) (16 September 2019):
https://www.ohchr.org/EN/HRBodies/HRC/MyanmarFFM/Pages/EconomicInterestsMyanmarMilitary.aspx.

65 For an overview of sanctions against Myanmar, see: 'Sanctions: Law, Practice and Guidance' https://www.europeansanctions.com/region/burma/; FACT SHEET: Biden-Harris Administration Actions in Response to the Coup in Burma (11 February 2021): https://www.whitehouse.gov/briefing-room/statements-releases/2021/02/11/fact-sheet-biden-harris-administration-actions-in-response-to-the-coup-in-burma/; US House Foreign Affairs Committee (5 October 2021): https://foreignaffairs.house.gov/2021/10/chairman-meeks-senator-cardin-and-rep-chabot-introduce-burma-act; Canadian Sanctions Related to Myanmar: https://www.international.gc.ca/world-monde/international_relations-relations_internationales/sanctions/myanmar.aspx?lang=eng;

66 'Myanmar: Groups call on more companies allegedly linked to military to sever ties', Business and Human Rights Centre (6 April 2021): https://www.business-humanrights.org/en/latest-news/myanmar-groups-call-on-more-companies-allegedly-linked-to-military-to-sever-ties/

67 'Cut the Cash', Special Advisory Council–Myanmar (SAC-M): https://specialadvisorycouncil.org/cut-the-cash/

The extent of foreign economic and commercial interests operating in Myanmar either directly or through subsidiaries is vast. Chris Sidoti, amongst others, has called for sanctions and disengagement with commercial enterprises supporting the Myanmar regime.

68 'Junta Cronies Eye Telenor's Myanmar Business', *The Irrawaddy* (11 November 2021): https://www.irrawaddy.com/news/burma/junta-cronies-eye-telenors-myanmar-business.html; 'Myanmar: Investors Should Act to Halt Funds to Junta: Revenues from Foreign Companies Keep Military in Power', *Human*

Rights Watch (19 November 2019): https://www.hrw.org/news/2021/11/19/myanmar-investors-should-act-halt-funds-juntad; 'Norway freezes Norwegian Kronors (NOK) 65 million bilateral aid to Myanmar', *ScandAsia* (21 February 2021): https://scandasia.com/norway-freezes-nok-65-million-bilateral-aid-to-myanmar/.

69 Jack Brook and Govi Snell 'Facebook remains a centre of authoritarianism and hate in Southeast Asia', *Southeast Asia Globe* (13 December 2021): https://southeastasiaglobe.com/facebook-authoritarianism-hate-in-southeast-asia/.

70 Rebecca Klar, 'Rohingya refugees sue Facebook for $150 billion', *The Hill* (6 December 2021): https://thehill.com/policy/technology/584472-rohingya-refugees-sue-facebook-for-150b; https://edelson.com/wp-content/uploads/doevmetacomplaint.pdf.

71 'The role of the private sector in protecting civic space', *Chatham House* (February 2020): https://www.chathamhouse.org/sites/default/files/2021-01/2021-01-29-private-sector-protecting-civic-space-freeman-et-al.pdf.pdf.

72 Jenny Domino, 'Crime as Cognitive Constraint: Facebook's Role in Myanmar's Incitement Landscape and the Promise of International Tort Liability', 52 *Case Western Reserve Journal of International Law* 142 (2020); Jenny Domino, 'How Facebook is Reconfiguring Freedom of Speech in Situations of Mass Atrocity: Lessons from Myanmar and the Philippines', *Opinio Juris* (1 January 2019): https://opiniojuris.org/2019/01/01/how-facebook-is-reconfiguring-free-dom-of-speech-in-situations-of-mass-atrocity-lessons-from-myanmar-and-the-philippines/; Francisco Javier Zamora Cabot and Maria Chiara Marullo, 'El Conflicto Rohingya y sus Proyecciones Juridicas: Aspectors Destacados', *Ordine internazionale e diritti umani* 461–484 (2020). Accessed at: www.ssrn.com.

73 Steve Stecklow, 'Hatebook: Inside Facebook's Myanmar Operation – A Reuters Special Report', *Reuters* (15 August 2018): https://www.reuters.com/investi-gates/special-report/myanmar-facebook-hate/.

74 Timothy McLaughlin, 'Facebook blocks accounts of Myanmar's top general, other military leaders', *The Washington Post* (27 August 2018): https://www.washingtonpost.com/world/asia_pacific/facebook-blocks-accounts-of-myan-mars-top-general-other-military-leaders/2018/08/27/da1ff440-a9f6-11e8-9a7d-cd30504ff902_story.html.

75 Antoni Slodkowski, 'Facebook bans Myanmar army chief, others in unprecedented move' *The Reuters* (27 August 2018): https://www.reuters.com/article/uk-myanmar-facebook-idUKKCN1LC0RG

76 Matthew Smith, 'Facebook Wanted to Be a Force for Good in Myanmar. Now It Is Rejecting a Request to Help with a Genocide Investigation', *Fortify Rights* (18 August 2020): https://www.fortifyrights.org/mya-inv-oped-2020-08-18/.

77 Evelyn Douek, '"What Kind of Oversight Board Have You Given Us?"', *The University of Chicago Law Review Online* (11 May 2020): https://lawreview-blog.uchicago.edu/2020/05/11/fb-oversight-board-edouek/; https://www.justsecurity.org/70035/the-republic-of-facebook/.

78 Steve Rathje, Jay Van Bavel, Sander van der Linden, 'Why Facebook really, really doesn't want to discourage extremism', *The Washington Post* (13 July 2021):https://www.washingtonpost.com/politics/2021/07/13/why-face-book-really-really-doesnt-want-discourage-extremism/.

79 The scholarship and writing of Shoshana Zuboff of Harvard Business School makes this point: https://shoshanazuboff.com/book/recent-work/; 'The *Coup* We Are Not Talking About', *The New York Times* (29 January 2021): https://www.nytimes.com/2021/01/29/opinion/sunday/facebook-surveil-lance-society-technology.html; Christino Lima, 'A whistleblower's power: Key

takeaways from the Facebook papers', *The Washington Post* (26 October 2021): https://www.washingtonpost.com/technology/2021/10/25/what-are-the-facebook-papers/.

80 David Kaye, 'The Republic of Facebook', *Just Security* (6 May 2020): https://www.justsecurity.org/70035/the-republic-of-facebook/.

81 Alex Hern, 'Revealed: catastrophic effects of working as a Facebook monitor', *The Guardian* (17 September 2019): https://www.theguardian.com/technology/2019/sep/17/revealed-catastrophic-effects-working-facebook-moderator?fbclid=IwAR2aT25EOeSgT-kgIJ80ybLu6VjqDzc8ZuFkq8-E6s4-mZwwTgB-gJA7wP30.

82 Phil Orchard, 'Making States Accountable for Deliberate Forced Displacement', *World Refugee Council Research Paper No 17* (June 2019): https://www.cigionline.org/publications/making-states-accountable-deliberate-forced-displacement; Simon Adams, 'If Not Now, When?: The Responsibility to Protect, the Fate of the Rohingya and the Future of Human Rights', *Global Centre for the Responsibility to Protect* (January 2019): https://www.globalr2p.org/publications/if-not-now-when-the-responsibility-to-protect-the-fate-of-the-rohingya-and-the-future-of-human-rights/.

83 Brian Barbour and Brian Gorlick, 'Embracing the 'Responsibility to Protect': A Repertoire of Measures Including Asylum for Potential Victims', 20(4) *International Journal of Refugee Law* (December 2008); *UNHCR New Issues in Refugee Research* paper no 159 (July 2008): https://www.unhcr.org/research/working/487b619b0/embracing-responsibility-protect-repertoire-measures-including-asylum-potential.html.

84 https://www.unhcr.org/new-york-declaration-for-refugees-and-migrants.html.

85 Amy Nethery and Carly Gordyn, 'Australia-Indonesia cooperation on asylum-seekers: a case of 'incentivised policy transfer', 68(2) *Australian Journal of International Affairs* 177–193 (2014)

Following Australia's long-standing example of off-shore deterrence, detention, and processing of asylum seekers who arrive "spontaneously", a practice that has been internationally condemned, Denmark recently amended its domestic law and procedure to permit off-shore asylum processing, and the UK has proposed similar changes. See: Nikolas Feith Tan, 'Denmark's Extraterritorial Asylum Vision', School of Advanced Study, University of London, *Refugee Law Initiative (RLI) Blog* (19 April 2021): https://rli.blogs.sas.ac.uk/2021/04/19/denmarks-extraterritorial-asylum-vision/; Nikolas Feith Tan, Elizabeth Mavropoulou, David Cantor and Marian Gkliati, 'Offshore Asylum Processing: The Future of Asylum in the UK or Dead Letter?', *RLI Blog* (6 April 2022): https://rli.blogs.sas.ac.uk/2022/04/06/offshore-asylum-processing-the-future-of-asylum-in-the-uk-or-dead-letter/.

86 Rozanna Latiff, 'Malaysia to hand 1,200 Myanmar detainees to country's navy', *Reuters* (11 February 2021): https://www.reuters.com/article/us-myanmar-politics-malaysia/malaysia-to-hand-1200-myanmar-detainees-to-countrys-navy-idUSKBN2AB1T4; Scott Neuman, 'Myanmar Nationals Deported from Malaysia Despite Outcry from Rights Groups', *National Public Radio* (NPR) (23 February 2021): https://www.npr.org/2021/02/23/970470873/myanmar-nationals-deported-from-malaysia-despite-outcry-from-rights-groups.

87 Jason Thomas, 'Malaysia can do more to protect refugees, say activists' *Free Malaysia Today* (Selangor, Malaysia, 22 August 2021): https://www.msn.com/en-my/news/national/malaysia-can-do-more-to-protect-refugees-say-activists/ar-AANBvwr.

88 Jan Egelund, Secretary-General of the Norwegian Refugee Council and former UN Under-Secretary-General for Humanitarian Affairs expressed criticism on

the Council's inaction concerning impeded humanitarian access to Tigray by saying: '*It's not rocket science. I would like to see the Security Council act like a Security Council*'. The same can be said regarding the Council's inaction on Myanmar: *The New York Times*, p A6 (US print version, 12 June 2021).

89 While the Security Council has held several meetings and invited UN and other experts for briefings on Myanmar since August 2017, and some Council ambassadors were able to visit Myanmar and Bangladesh in 2018, no formal resolution has yet been adopted, and efforts by Council members for substantive action have been consistently blocked or ignored by China and Russia. For an overview of Council activities on Myanmar see *Security Council Report*: https://www.securitycouncilreport.org/myanmar/.

90 ASEAN Chairman's Statement on the ASEAN Leaders' Meeting, ASEAN Secretariat, Jakarta (24 April 2021): https://asean.org/wp-content/uploads/Chairmans-Statement-on-ALM-Five-Point-Consensus-24-April-2021-FINAL-a-1.pdf.

91 Security Council Press Statement on Myanmar (SC/14697) (10 November 2021): https://www.un.org/press/en/2021/sc14697.doc.htm.

92 Russia and China remain major arms exporters to Myanmar. By contrast, the European Union has maintained a broad arms embargo against Myanmar since the early 1990s: 'EU arms embargo on Myanmar (Burma)' Stockholm International Peace Research Institute (SIPRI): https://sipri.org/databases/embargoes/eu_arms_embargoes/myanmar.

93 Shamala Kandiah, Karin Landgren and Paul Romita, 'The United Nations in Hindsight: Challenging the Power of the Security Council Veto', *Just Security* (28 April 2022): https://rli.blogs.sas.ac.uk/2021/04/19/denmarks-extraterritorial-asylum-vision/;

94 Augusto Lopez-Claros, 'The Origins of the UN Veto and Why it Should be Abolished', *Global Governance Forum Blog* (28 April 2022): https://globalgovernanceforum.org/origins-un-veto-why-it-should-be-abolished/

95 'Beyond Killing: Gender, Genocide and Obligations under International Law', Chapter VI on 'Genocide and International Organizations', *Global Justice Center* (December 2018): http://www.globaljusticecenter.net/files/Gender-and-Genocide-Whitepaper-FINAL.pdf.

96 'ASEAN Risks Flouting All Humanitarian Principles', Special Advisory Council-Myanmar Statement (9 May 2022): https://specialadvisorycouncil.org/2022/05/asean-risks-flouting-all-humanitarian-principles/; 'ASEAN's Plan to Deliver Aid to Myanmar via Junta Condemned', *The Irrawaddy* (11 May 2022): https://www.irrawaddy.com/news/burma/aseans-plan-to-deliver-aid-to-myanmar-via-junta-condemned.html.

97 The Arms Transfer Programme database maintained by SIPRI tracks transfers of major arms that have been supplied to or are on order by different 'suppliers' to 'recipient' countries. A search of the period 2016 to 2020 reveals that China, Russia, India, and Israel, and others, provided a wide range of weaponry and military supplies to Myanmar estimated at hundreds of millions of dollars. Picture evidence revealed that Myanmar has several Russian and Israeli armoured vehicles in use that were likely delivered in 2020 or earlier but were not known from any source until the first day of the *coup*: https://armstrade.sipri.org/armstrade/page/trade_register.php.

98 Chan Mya Htwe, 'Myanmar–China border trade in focus', *Myanmar Times* (Yangon, 7 December 2018): https://www.mmtimes.com/news/myanmar-china-border-trade-focus.html

Myanmar enjoys a trade surplus with China, and in 2018 it was reported that largely border-area exports from Myanmar to China totaled US$2.4 billion, whereas imports from China totaled US$900 million. It is expected this trade surplus has only increased.

99 Ben Mauk and Matt Huynh, 'Inside Xinjiang's Prison State', *The New Yorker* (28 February 2021): https://www.newyorker.com/news/a-reporter-at-large/china-xinjiang-prison-state-uighur-detention-camps-prisoner-testimony?utm_source=nl&utm_brand=tny&utm_mailing=TNY_Daily_022621&utm_campaign=aud-dev&utm_medium=email&bxid=5be9cea82ddf9c72dc18b9c5&cndid=51183252&hasha=1acb1ba6d54d64414c5d00d556531e0c&hashb=9d11c9a67a9a0fe82488596d4a314c3a26aead66&hashc=8f05e230f89aa7eb3e574969637f7a68f17b845e372f2fecdb1d7ebc4e090e52&esrc=profile-page&utm_term=TNY_Daily.

100 Joint statement on the human rights situation in Xinjiang delivered by the Canadian Permanent Representative of Canada, Ambassador Leslie E Norton, to the UN in Geneva on behalf of more than 40 countries (21 June 2021): https://ishr.ch/wp-content/uploads/2021/06/HRC47_Canada-JST-on-China.pdf

101 Sophie Ryan, 'Atrocity Crimes in Xinjiang: Moving beyond Legal Labels', 13(1) *Global Responsibility to Protect* 20-23 (16 February 2021): https://brill.com/view/journals/gr2p/13/1/article-p20_20.xml; Adrian Zenz, 'China Didn't Want Us to Know. Now Its Own Files Are Doing the Talking', *The New York Times* (24 November 2019): https://www.nytimes.com/2019/11/24/opinion/china-xinjiang-files.html; 'Submission to the UN Committee on Economic, Social and Cultural Rights (66th Pre-sessional Working Group), *Uyghur Human Rights Project* (December 2020): https://docs.uhrp.org/pdf/CESCR_Submission_FINAL_2020-12-18.pdf; 'The Xinjiang Data Project', *Australian Strategic Policy Institute (ASPI)*: https://xjdp.aspi.org.au/; Rebecca Wright, Ivan Watson, Zahid Mahmood and Tom Booth, "Some are just psychopaths': Chinese detective in exile reveals extent of torture against Uyghurs', *CNN* (5 October 2021): https://www.cnn.com/2021/10/04/china/xinjiang-detective-torture-intl-hnk-dst/index.html.

102 An opportunity for substantive UN Security Council action on Myanmar followed the 1 February *coup*, but the only outcome taken after closed consultations was a 'press statement' which, in diplomatic terms, is the lightest touch. The statement shared by the rotating (UK) Council president expressed 'deep concern at the declaration of the state of emergency imposed in Myanmar by the military … and the arbitrary detention of members of the government, including state counsellor Aung San Suu Kyi and president Win Myint and others'. It called for their immediate release and the 'need for the continued support of the democratic transition in Myanmar [and] the need to uphold democratic institutions and processes, refrain from violence, and fully respect human rights, fundamental freedoms and rule of law […] the members of the Security Council reiterated the need to address the root causes of the crisis in Rakhine State and to create conditions necessary for safe, voluntary, sustainable and dignified return of displaced persons'. The Council also 'reaffirmed their strong commitment to the sovereignty, political independence, territorial integrity and unity of Myanmar'. (emphasis added): https://www.un.org/press/en/2021/sc14430.doc.html.

At a Special Session of the UN Human Rights Council held on 12 February 2021, the US State Department Representative used stronger language: 'The United States condemns the military's February 1 coup against the democratically-elected government of Myanmar. We stand with the people of Myanmar in calling for the immediate restoration of the country's democratic institutions. We ask all Council members to join the United States and others to: 1. Urge the military to immediately release all those unjustly detained, including politicians, civil society representatives, journalists, foreign nationals, and human rights defenders; 2. Urge the military and police [... to] refrain from further violence against peaceful protesters; 3. Urge the military to lift all restrictions on access to information, including by maintaining telecommunications and internet access; and 4. Join us in promoting accountability for those responsible for the coup, including through targeted sanctions. (emphasis added): https://geneva.usmission.gov/2021/02/12/us-statement-at-the-hrc-special-session-on-the-human-rights-implications-of-the-crisis-in-myanmar/.

103 Jinny Yan, 'The Belt and Road Initiative in Southeast Asia', in *China's BRI and Southeast Asia, LSE !deas* (October 2018): www.lse.ac.uk/ideas; *CIMB ASEAN Research Institute*: www.cariasean.org;

The Belt and Road, A Quarterly Magazine, Issue 1, Centre for East Asia Foundation (April–June 2019): www.ceafasia.org.

104 Yazuki Nagakoshi, 'Japan and Myanmar's Toxic Friendship', *The Diplomat* (15 January 2020): https://thediplomat.com/2020/01/japan-and-myanmars-toxic-friendship/.

105 'The situation in Myanmar', UN General Assembly resolution (18 June 2021): https://undocs.org/en/A/RES/75/287;

106 'The situation of human rights in Myanmar', UN Human Rights Council resolution (19 March 2019): https://reliefweb.int/report/myanmar/situation-human-rights-myanmar-ahrc40l19.

107 'UN resolution on Myanmar: Abstention from voting doesn't mean opposing Bangladesh, Japan says', *bdnews24.com* (Dhaka, 19 November 2017): https://bdnews24.com/bangladesh/2017/11/19/un-resolution-on-myanmar-abstention-from-voting-doesnt-mean-opposing-bangladesh-japan-says; Teppel Kasai, 'Japan's Cold-Blooded Approach to the Rohingya Crisis', *Human Rights Watch* (20 June 2019): https://www.hrw.org/news/2019/06/20/japans-cold-blooded-approach-rohingya-crisis.

108 'Hasina, Modi for expediting efforts for sustainable Rohingya repatriation', *Dhaka Tribune* (5 October 2019): https://www.dhakatribune.com/bangladesh/foreign-affairs/2019/10/05/hasina-modi-for-expediting-efforts-for-sustainable-rohingya-repatriation.

109 Tapan Bose, 'Rohingyas: Pawns on the Geopolitical Chessboard', Chapter 11, *The Rohingya Refugee Crisis: Towards Sustainable Solutions*, Imtiaz Ahmed (editor), Centre for Genocide Studies, University of Dhaka (2019)

110 'Rohingya crisis hits Bangladesh's exports to Myanmar, *Dhaka Tribune* (12 July 2018): https://www.dhakatribune.com/business/commerce/2018/07/12/rohingya-crisis-hits-bangladesh-s-exports-to-myanmar.

111 Christine Fair, a political scientist and terrorism expert, has produced rich scholarship on issues concerning radicalization and the Rohingya. A series of papers including 'The Making of the Genocide and Myanmar's Impunity' (2019), and 'Rohingya: Victims of a Great Game East' (2018) are available at: [http://www.christinefair.net/html_pages/journal_articles.html].

Regarding the Arakan Rohingya Salvation Army (ARSA) and its alleged connection to the Rohingya refugee population, Dr Fair has written that:

> "'spite of the grotesque brutalities the Rohingyas have endured, they have not articulated an Islamist or separatist demand. Their demand is simply to return to Myanmar with citizenship and, problematically, with government recognition as a distinct ethnic group. The Rohingya have not given rise to many violent non-state actors claiming to represent them. One of the few violent groups that has emerged in recent years is ARSA. While many in the "Islamist terrorism" industry have been quick to paint ARSA

> with the jihadi brush, I am skeptical of ARSA's Islamist *bona fides.* ARSA has assiduously rejected Islamist appeals. However, other Islamist groups in the region have identified the Rohingya as a *cause celebre*, including the Pakistan-based Lashkar-e-Taiba (LeT), the Islamic State, and al-Qaeda Indian Subcontinent. The longer the Rohingya remain cramped in inadequately appointed camps in Bangladesh or countenance ongoing ethnic cleansing in Myanmar, the more probable it becomes that either the nature of ARSA will bend towards Islamism and/or Islamist militant groups will conduct violence on their behalf'.

See: https://www.lawfareblog.com/arakan-rohingya-salvation-army-not-jihadis-you-might-expect; https://www.irrawaddy.com/in-person/interview/no-evidence-arsa-links-isis-terrorism-expert.html.

112 Bertil Lintner, *Burma in Revolt: Opium and Insurgency Since 1948*, Silkworm Books (1999); Michael RJ Vatikiotis, *Blood and Silk: Power and Conflict in Modern Southeast Asia*, Weidenfeld & Nicolson (2018); 'Shan state drug blitz nets big haul', *The Bangkok Post* (15 June 2019): https://www.bangkokpost.com/thailand/general/1695792/shan-state-drug-blitz-nets-big-haul.

113 'Analysis – Arakan Army – A Powerful New Threat to the Tatmadaw', *Reliefweb* (8 January 2019): https://reliefweb.int/report/myanmar/analysis-arakan-army-powerful-new-threat-tatmadaw; and

114 'Sold Like Fish": Crimes Against Humanity, Mass Graves, and Human Trafficking from Myanmar and Bangladesh to Malaysia from 2012 to 2015', *Human Rights Commission of Malaysia (SUHAKAM)* and *Fortify Rights* (March 2019): https://www.fortifyrights.org/downloads/Fortify%20Rights-SUHAKAM%20-%20Sold%20Like%20Fish.pdf.

115 Concerning mass protests in Myanmar, Swe Win, a celebrated and courageous Myanmar journalist and co-founder of the news service *Myanmar Now* [www.myanmar-now.org], when asked 'Do you think the protests will make a difference against coup?', offered this perspective: 'I don't think so at all. The military knew how to deal with these protests, how to deal with public opposition. They have already started big-time information warfare, psychological warfare against the public. They have cut off all the internet. Yesterday [i.e. 9 February 2021], the vigilante groups hired by the military, they went around a neighbourhood in trucks saying Aung San Suu Kyi was already released. People flooded the street to celebrate the rumour of the release; they lit firecrackers. So I'm not hopeful about these ongoing protests, even though I congratulate [the people], even though I feel emotional about the bravery of the youth'. Interview available at: https://www.cjr.org/special_report/swe-win-journalism-in-myanmar-the-coup-and-what-comes-next.php.

116 OCHA Financial Tracking Service – Myanmar: https://fts.unocha.org/appeals/934/donors?order=total_funding&sort=desc.

Several donors including the US, the UK, the European Commission, Australia, and Japan appreciate this role and continue to fund the UN agencies and operations in Myanmar to the tune of US$200 million dollars per annum.

117 Liam Mahoney, 'Time to Break Old Habits: Shifting from Complicity to Protection of the Rohingyas in Myanmar', *Fieldview Solutions* (June 2018), p 26: https://www.fieldviewsolutions.org/2-uncategorised/64-time-to-break-old-habits-groundbreaking-new-study-on-the-rohingya-crisis-in-myanmar.

118 UN General Assembly resolution on the 'Situation of Human Rights in Myanmar' (UN doc ref: A/RES/73/264) para 6, p 5 (2018): http://undocs.org/en/A/RES/73/264

119 Jennifer Norris, 'Given UN failings in Myanmar, where is Human Rights Up Front?', *Universal Rights Group* (30 October 2019): https://www.universal-rights.org/blog/given-un-failings-in-myanmar-where-is-human-rights-up-front/; IPI Report (June 2021), *op cit*, 21–23.

120 Gert Rosenthal, 'A Brief and Independent Inquiry into the Involvement of the United Nations in Myanmar from 2010 to 2018' (29 May 2019): https://www.un.org/sg/sites/www.un.org.sg/files/atoms/files/Myanmar%20Report%20-%20May%202019.pdf.

121 'Myanmar: Joint open letter to the UN Secretary-General on the inquiry into UN operations in Myanmar', Amnesty International (5 September 2019): https://www.amnesty.org/en/documents/asa16/1003/2019/en/.

122 Charles Petrie, 'Report of the Secretary-General's Internal Review Panel on United Nations Action in Sri Lanka' (2012): https://digitallibrary.un.org/record/737299.

123 António Guterres, 'The Highest Aspiration: A Call to Action for Human Rights', United Nations Secretariat (2020): https://www.un.org/sg/sites/www.un.org.sg/files/atoms/files/The_Highest_Asperation_A_Call_To_Action_For_Human_Right_English.pdf.

124 David Petrasek, 'Through Rose-Coloured Glasses: UNHCR's Role in Monitoring the Safety of the Rohingya Refugees Returning to Burma' 114-136, *Human Rights and Forced Displacement*, AF Bayefsky and J Fitzpatrick (eds) Kluwer Law International (2000).

125 Ziauddin Choudhury, 'The intractable Rohingya repatriation', *Dhaka Tribune* (4 September 2019) See: https://www.dhakatribune.com/opinion/op-ed/2019/09/04/the-intractable-rohingya-repatriation.

The former deputy commissioner for Chittagong noted that, during the 1978 repatriation exercise, the government of Bangladesh: '… deployed one full battalion of armed police around the camp [of Rohingya refugees], which we revealed after we took back control of the camp. It was easy later to transport the selected repatriates to another camp and take them from there to the designated repatriation outpost. I myself took them across the border and handed them to the Myanmar authorities'.

126 For an overview of Rohingya forced displacement to Bangladesh see: 'Historical Review—Rohingya influx since 1978': https://reliefweb.int/report/bangladesh/historical-review-rohingya-influx-1978; CR Abrar, *Repatriation of Rohingya Refugees*, Dhaka University (date unknown): https://www.burmalibrary.org/docs21/Abrar-NM-Repatriation_of_Rohingya_refugees-en.pdf; Mohfidul Hoque (ed), 'The Rohingya Genocide: Compilation and Analysis of Survivors' Testimonies', *Centre for the Study of Genocide and Justice,* Liberation War Museum, Dhaka (September 2018): www.liberationwarmuseumbd.org; Gil Loescher and James Milner, 'Burmese refugees in South and Southeast Asia: A comparative regional analysis', in *Protracted Refugee Situations: Political, Human Rights and Security Implications,* Loescher, Milner, Newman, Troeller (eds), *United Nations University* (Tokyo, 2008); 'Independent evaluation of UNHCR's response to the Rohingya refugees influx in Bangladesh, August 2017–September 2018', para 31–32 UNHCR (December 2018): https://www.unhcr.org/en-us/research/evalreports/5c811b464/independent-evaluation-unhcrs-l3-emergency-response-bangladesh.html.

127 ACAPS Website (Myanmar): https://www.acaps.org/country/myanmar/crisis/rakhine-conflict.

128 David Scott Mathieson, 'The Arakan Army in Myanmar: Deadly Conflict Rises in Rakhine State' 15–17, *United States Institute of Peace* (2 November 2020):

https://www.usip.org/publications/2020/11/arakan-army-myanmar-deadly-conflict-rises-rakhine-state.

129 Brenna Artinger and Michael Rowand, 'When Buddhists Back the Army', *Foreign Policy* (16 February 2021): https://foreignpolicy.com/2021/02/16/myanmar-rohingya-coup-buddhists-protest/.

130 'Human Rights Watch Statement: Impacts of Covid-19 on Internally Displaced People in Myanmar', *Human Rights Watch* (14 December 2020): https://www.hrw.org/news/2020/12/14/human-rights-watch-statement-impacts-covid-19-internally-displaced-people-myanmar#.

131 Edith M Lederer, 'Britain urges halt to Myanmar clashes to allow vaccination', *Associated Press* (17 August 2021): https://apnews.com/article/health-coronavirus-pandemic-myanmar-united-nations-f655875325ee016d1b349877363d26b7.

132 'UNHCR Myanmar Operational Update, 1–30 November 2020', *Reliefweb* (11 January 2021): https://reliefweb.int/report/myanmar/unhcr-myanmar-operational-update-1-30-november-2020; 'UNHCR says ethnic Chin refugees may require continued international protection as security situation worsens in Myanmar', UNHCR (14 March 2019): https://www.unhcr.org/news/press/2019/3/5c8a31984/unhcr-says-ethnic-chin-refugees-require-continued-international-protection.html; 'Asia Justice Coalition Condemns the Escalating Military Abuses in Chin State and Neighbouring Regions', *Reliefweb* (12 November 2021): https://reliefweb.int/report/myanmar/asia-justice-coalition-condemns-escalating-military-abuses-chin-state-and.

133 'Documenting Atrocity Crimes Committed Against the Rohingya in Myanmar's Rakhine State: Factual Findings Report', and compendium 'Factual Findings & Legal Analysis Report', *The Public International Law & Policy Group (PILPG)* (September & December 2018): https://www.publicinternationallawandpolicygroup.org/rohingya-report.

134 Hannah Beech and Saw Nang, 'Myanmar Election Delivers Another Decisive Win for Aung San Suu Kyi', *The New York Times* (4 December 2020): https://www.nytimes.com/2020/11/11/world/asia/myanmar-election-aung-san-suu-kyi-results.html

135 'Myanmar army warns against changing constitution', *The ASEAN Post* (24 February 2019): https://theaseanpost.com/article/myanmar-army-warns-against-changing-constitution-0

The IIFFM's September 2019 Report to the UN Human Rights Council concluded that:

> The mission found a near-complete absence of accountability at the domestic level for gross violations of international human rights law and serious violations of international humanitarian law. The Prosecutor of the International Criminal Court, in her request for authorization of an investigation […] concluded much the same. The government of Myanmar is simply unwilling to end impunity for these violations, especially those committed by security forces. Impunity is also structural; it is built into the legal framework and the system of governance, including the *Constitution*, article 343 (b) of which stipulates those decisions of the Commander-in-Chief concerning military justice matters are 'final and conclusive', with no right of appeal. The government's outright rejection of the mission's findings is also indicative of its unwillingness to pursue accountability at the domestic level.

A/HRC/42/50, para 95: https://documents-dds-ny.un.org/doc/UNDOC/GEN/G19/236/74/PDF/G1923674.pdf?OpenElement.

136 Nick Cheesman, 'How Myanmar "National Races" Came to Surpass Citizenship and Exclude Rohingya', 14(3) *Journal of Contemporary Asia* 461–483 (2017)

137 Niloy Ranjan Biswas: 'Myanmar's military and the garrison state: State-military relations in Myanmar and their influence in the [re]production of violence against minorities', 5(2) *Asian Journal of Comparative Politics* 158-173 (Sage 2020).

The article discusses Myanmar as a so-called garrison state. In a particularly telling passage, the author references a meeting which took place in 2012 between then-Myanmar President Thein Sein and former UNHCR Head (now UN Secretary-General Guterres): 'Even after the revival of the so-called civilian government in 2010, the influence of the Tatmadaw remained significant. It had banked on the idea of *taingyintha* in dealing with the issue of the Rohingyas in the state of Arakan … in his meeting with the visiting head of UNHCR, [the Myanmar President] clearly mentioned that, regarding people who had fled from attacks into Bangladesh, his government would 'take responsibility for our *taingyintha,* but under no circumstances would accept illegally entering non-*taingyintha* "Rohingya"', p. 166.

138 Melissa Crouch, 'Myanmar's Muslim Mosaic and the Politics of Belonging', Chapter 1, in M Crouch (ed), *Islam and the State in Myanmar*, Oxford University Press (2016).

139 Imtiaz Ahmed (ed), *The Plight of the Stateless Rohingyas: Responses of the State, Society and the International Community,* The University Press Limited, Dhaka (2014); Francis Wade, *Myanmar's Enemy Within: Buddhist Violence and the Making of the Muslim 'Other'*, Zed Books (2017).

International human rights organizations notably Human Rights Watch, Amnesty International, and Fortify Rights have documented and published numerous reports on the plight and human rights situation of the Rohingya.

140 International Court of Justice, 'Application of the Convention on the Prevention and Punishment of Genocide' (*The Gambia v Myanmar*), Request for the Indication of Provisional Measures, Order of 23 January 2020: https://www.icj-cij.org/public/files/case-related/178/178-20200123-ORD-01-00-EN.pdf.

141 James Hathaway notes that the intention of the drafters of the 1951 *Refugee Convention* concerning exemption to cessation was twofold: 'first, to recognize the legitimacy of the psychological hardship that would be faced by the victims of persecution were they to be returned to the country responsible for their maltreatment; and second, to protect the victims of past atrocities from harm at the hands of private citizens, whose attitudes may not have reformed in tandem with the political structure […] Atle Grahl-Madsen suggests that the existence of a psychological distance between the refugee and her former home, the continued unpopularity in the country of origin of the views or personal characteristics of the refugee, or the severing of familial, social and other linkages between the refugee and her state or origin are the sorts of concerns which warrant exemption from return'. James Hathaway, *The Law of Refugee Status*, 203–204, Butterworths, Toronto (1991); David Milner, 'Exemption from Cessation of Refugee Status in the Second Sentence of Article 1(C)(5)/(6) of the 1951 Refugee Convention', 16(1) International Journal of Refugee Law (2004).

142 On the link between international human rights law and refugee protection see Guy Goodwin-Gill and Jane McAdam, *The Refugee in International Law*, Chapter 7, 'Protection under Human Rights and General International Law' (4th ed) Oxford University Press (2021); Ruma Mandal, 'Protection Mechanisms Outside of the 1951 Convention ("Complimentary Protection"), *Legal and Protection Policy Research Series*, UNHCR (June 2005): https://www.refworld.org/docid/435e198d4.html; https://www.unhcr.org/research

/working/3ae6a0cf4/human-rights-refugees-enhancing-protection-international-human-rights-law.html; Brian Gorlick, 'Human Rights and Refugees: Enhancing Protection through International Human Rights Law', *New Issues in Refugee Research Working Paper no 30*, UNHCR (October 2000): https://www.unhcr.org/en-us/publications/legal/45a7acb72/self-study-module-5-vol-human-rights-refugee-protection.html.

Myanmar is state party to the following UN human rights treaties: *Convention on the Rights of the Child*, *Convention on the Elimination of All Forms of Discrimination against Women*, and the *International Covenant on Economic, Social and Cultural Rights*. Bangladesh is state party to the above treaties in addition to the *Convention Against Torture*, *International Covenant on Civil and Political Rights*, and the *Convention on the Protection of the Rights of All Migrant Workers and Members of Their Families*.

143 Anna Lise Purkey, 'The dimensions of legal empowerment in protracted refugee situations', Chapter 4, *Refugee Dignity in Protracted Exile: Rights, Capabilities and Legal Empowerment*, Routledge, New York (2020).

144 'The Torture in My Mind: The Right to Mental Health for Rohingya Survivors of Genocide in Myanmar and Bangladesh', *Fortify Rights* (December 2020): https://www.fortifyrights.org/mya-inv-rep-2020-12-10/.

145 Natasha Yacoub, Nikola Errington, Wai Nu & Alexandra Robinson, 'Rights Adrift: Sexual Violence Against Rohingya Women on the Andaman Sea', 22 *Asia-Pacific Journal on Human Rights and the Law* 96–114 (2021).

Verena Hölz, *op cit* (2 August 2021).

146 Jane McAdam and Tamara Wood, 'The Concept of "International Protection" in the Global Compacts on Refugees and Migration', *Interventions: International Journal of Postcolonial Studies*, Routledge (January 2021): https://papers.ssrn.com/sol3/papers.cfm?abstract_id=3779077; and Ruma Mandal, *op cit* (June 2005).

147 '84 Rohingya stopped from boat journey to Malaysia', *The Star* (Dhaka, 19 May 2019): https://www.thestar.com.my/news/regional/2019/05/19/84-rohingya-stopped-from-boat-journey-to-malaysia/; 'Police rescue dozens of Malaysia-bound Rohingyas on boat', *The Daily Star* (Dhaka, 15 May 2019) https://www.thedailystar.net/backpage/news/police-rescue-dozens-malaysia-bound-rohingyas-boat-1743880.

148 World University Service of Canada (WUSC) Student Refugee Programme: https://srp.wusc.ca/students/.

149 '"Tell them we're human" What Canada and the World can do about the Rohingya Crisis', Government of Canada (2018): https://www.international.gc.ca/world-monde/issues_development-enjeux_developpement/response_conflict-reponse_conflits/crisis-crises/rep_sem-rap_esm.aspx?lang=eng#a5.

150 https://www.humanrightsfirst.org/resource/private-sponsorship-refugee-resettlement-united-states; Guide to Private Sponsorship of Refugees Programme, Government of Canada: https://www.canada.ca/en/immigration-refugees-citizenship/corporate/publications-manuals/guide-private-sponsorship-refugees-program.html.

151 Data on cases of sexual violence which Rohingya were exposed to at the time of flight in 2017 and beyond, is a challenge to collect. Some UN entities and NGOs, including *Médecins Sans Frontières* (MSF) are making efforts through contact with individual refugees. It is not uncommon these cases are under-reported and men and boys who experienced sexual violence may not come forward due to feelings of shame, fear of retribution, risk of being ostracized by the community, and further victimization. See for example ''No one was left' – Death and Violence Against the Rohingya', MSF (9 March 2018): https://www

.msf.org/myanmarbangladesh-%E2%80%98no-one-was-left%E2%80%99-death-and-violence-against-rohingya.

152 'UNHCR's Assistant High Commissioners conclude four-day visit to Bangladesh', UNHCR (June 2021): https://www.unhcr.org/news/press/2021/6/60b7a1d94/unhcrs-assistant-high-commissioners-conclude-four-day-visit-bangladesh.html.

During a visit by the two UNHCR Assistant High Commissioners (namely for Protection and Operations), for the first time UNHCR publicly mentioned the possibility of other "alternative" solutions besides voluntary repatriation for the Rohingya through introducing 'resettlement to third countries for the most vulnerable with specific protection needs, as well as complementary pathways overseas, which could include employment and educational opportunities'.

153 By analogy, starting in 2008, over 100,000 Bhutanese refugees, whose plight was not dissimilar to the Rohingya in terms of being denied citizenship by the Bhutanese government, were resettled over several years with support by UNHCR and IOM from Nepal. In 2006, the United States made an offer to settle 60,000 Bhutanese refugees. As another example, between 4 November 2015 and 29 February 2016, in only four months, Canada resettled more than 25,000 Syrian refugees: https://bhutaneserefugees.com/resettled; https://www.canada.ca/en/immigration-refugees-citizenship/services/refugees/welcome-syrian-refugees.html.

154 Lise Martin, 'Tampa refugee taken in by New Zealand wins Fulbright Scholarship', *The Guardian* (2 June 2021): https://www.theguardian.com/world/2019/jun/18/tampa-refugee-taken-in-by-new-zealand-wins-fulbright-scholarship.

155 https://www.unhcr.org/the-global-compact-on-refugees.html; https://www.unhcr.org/gcr/GCR_English.pdf (para 90-100); T Alex Aleinikoff, '*From Dependence to Self-Reliance: Changing the Paradigm in Protracted Refugee Situations*', *Migration Policy Institute* (May 2015): https://www.migrationpolicy.org/research/dependence-self-reliance-changing-paradigm-protracted-refugee-situations.

156 Peter H Schuck, 'Refugee Burden Sharing: A Modest Proposal', *Yale Law School Legal Scholarship Repository* (1997): https://digitalcommons.law.yale.edu/cgi/viewcontent.cgi?article=2691&context=fss_papers; 'Refugee Burden-Sharing: A Modest Proposal Fifteen Years Later?', *Yale Law & Economics Research Paper No 506* (2014): https://papers.ssrn.com/sol3/papers.cfm?abstract_id=2478844; Meltem Ineli-Ciger, 'The Global Compact on Refugees and Burden Sharing: Will the Compact Address the Normative Gap Concerning Burden Sharing?', 38(2) *Refugee Survey Quarterly* (June 2019): https://academic.oup.com/rsq/article/38/2/115/5474959.

157 Porimol Palma, 'Family Planning: Too important, yet ignored', *The Daily Star* (Dhaka, 3 November 2017): https://www.thedailystar.net/frontpage/family-planning-too-important-yet-ignored-1485694; 'Finding Reproductive Healthcare in the World's Biggest Refugee Camp', *Reliefweb* (5 April 2019): https://reliefweb.int/report/bangladesh/finding-reproductive-healthcare-world-s-biggest-refugee-camp; Liesel Schnabel and Cindy Huang, 'Removing Barriers and Closing Gaps: Improving Sexual and Reproductive Health and Rights for Rohingya Refugees and Host Communities', *Center for Global Development* (5 June 2019): https://www.cgdev.org/publication/removing-barriers-and-closing-gaps-improving-sexual-and-reproductive-health-and-rights?mkt_tok=eyJpIjoiTldRelpESXhNREEyWlRoaiIsInQiOiJsXC91djZ1V0lRRUx3V3Q3cFVKcU05VVwvdjRzTlVYSVwvVExXZzFtSjh6NlVNR0pSVUFmMzErSHhcL1oyQTVYUEVnZWpKRXRzT1VcL3hoOVlXWm8rclZ

4TjNYNzBIVVI0Y3RRUGJ3YmFCZk9tTmdHd2VKckNMM0lwMmwyNzZOTWJVbEdnIn0%3D.

158 Bangladesh has many skilled individuals and experienced organizations contributing to humanitarian work in the Rohingya camps. For example: https://bracusa.org/rohingya-refugee-crisis/.

159 Lauren Post, Rachel Landry, Cindy Huang, 'Moving Beyond the Emergency: A Whole of Society Approach to the Refugee Response in Bangladesh', *Centre for Global Development/International Rescue Committee* (October 2019): https://www.rescue.org/report/moving-beyond-emergency-whole-society-approach-refugee-response-bangladesh; 'Bangladesh: Emergency Multi-Sector Rohingya Crisis Response Project', The World Bank (7 March 2019): http://www.worldbank.org/en/news/loans-credits/2019/03/07/bangladesh-emergency-multi-sector-rohingya-crisis-response-project.

160 Under an agreement between the government of Norway and the UN Development Programme (UNDP), Norway supports work aimed at 'fostering peace and harmony in Rohingya camps and host communities in Cox's Bazaar': https://www.thedailystar.net/city/news/undp-norway-sign-747306-agreement-1744648.

161 Post, Landry, Huang, *op cit* (October 2019).

162 Fahmida Khatun, 'Addressing the Rohingya crisis: whose responsibility is it?', *The Daily Star* (13 May 2019): https://www.thedailystar.net/opinion/macro-mirror/news/addressing-the-rohingya-crisis-whose-responsibility-it-1742485.

The Dhaka-based Centre for Policy Dialogue estimates that if the Rohingya stay in Bangladesh for five years from 2018–19 onwards, the cost to maintain them will be US $7.046 billion until 2023. With population growth and inflation adjustments, this cost will continue to increase and, over 10 years, will rise to US $17.204 billion.

163 A thoughtful analysis of the humanitarian challenges facing the Rohingya in Bangladesh is offered by Ipshita Sangupta and Brian Barbour, 'An Agenda for a Dignified and Sustainable Rohingya Refugee Response in Bangladesh', *Act For Peace* (May 2021): https://reliefweb.int/report/bangladesh/agenda-dignified-and-sustainable-rohingya-refugee-response-bangladesh-may-2021.

164 Melati Nungsari and Sam Flanders, 'A Comprehensive Study of Rohingya Construction Works in Peninsular Malaysia and Recommendations for a Future Work Pilot Program', Asia School of Business, Kuala Lumpur, and MIT Sloan School of Management, Boston (13 August 2018): http://www.melatinungsari.com/uploads/2/3/6/3/23631450/finalreport-mnsf.pdf.

There are an estimated 175,000 ethnic Rohingya from Myanmar residing in Malaysia, with the majority being currently registered with UNHCR. Being registered permits access to UN-issued identity documents that can assist an individual to avoid arrest and legal process for illegal entry and stay. Although UNHCR registration does not provide legal work rights, it can offer a degree of protection as the police, prosecution service, and courts often appreciate what it means to be a refugee and they can exercise their discretion and authority accordingly. Many Malaysian employers are willing to hire refugees, but domestic law does not permit it. Efforts by UNHCR to promote a 'work rights' scheme with the Malaysian government have failed to advance.

165 'Programme of Support to the Jordan Compact: ILO Response to the Syrian Refugee Crisis in Jordan, International Labour Organization (2018): https://www.ilo.org/wcmsp5/groups/public/---arabstates/---ro-beirut/documents/briefingnote/wcms_670182.pdf; Cindy Huang and Kate Grough, 'The Jordan Compact: Three Years On, Where Do We Stand?', *Center for Global Development*

(11 March 2019): https://reliefweb.int/report/jordan/jordan-compact-three-years-where-do-we-stand.

Some 10 million Bangladeshi citizens work outside their home country and contribute US$1.2 billion in monthly remittances, making it one of the largest and most important contributions of direct capital. Many Bangladeshi migrant workers eventually return home with new skills, including languages, networks, and the ability to manage a business. Remittances are an invaluable source of income for many families, and, by example, they permit children to pursue a better standard of education that directly impacts future opportunities. Permitting refugees to legally work would provide similar benefits.

166 Kingsley Abbott and Sam Zia-Zarifi, 'Is It Time to Create a Standing Independent Investigative Mechanism (SIIM)? Part 1, *Opinio Juris* (10 April 2019): http://opiniojuris.org/2019/04/10/is-it-time-to-create-a-standing-independent-investigative-mechanism-siim/; and Part 2 (11 April 2019):

http://opiniojuris.org/2019/04/11/is-it-time-to-create-a-standing-independent-investigative-mechanism-siim-part-ii/.

167 Bernadette Ludwig, 'Reparations and Refugees' in I Ness (editor) *Encyclopedia of Global Human Migration*, 2566–2570, Wiley-Blackwell, New Jersey (2013).

168 http://legal.un.org/icc/statute/99_corr/cstatute.html.

169 Dinah Shelton, *Remedies in International Human Rights Law* (3rd ed), Oxford University Press (2015); Steven Ratner, Jason Abrams, James L Bischoff, *Accountability for Human Rights Atrocities in International Law: Beyond the Nuremburg Legacy* (3rd ed), Oxford University Press (2009); Nina Jorgensen, *The Responsibility of States for International Crimes* 192–207, Oxford University Press (2009; John Murphy, 'Civil Liability for the Commission of International Crimes as an Alternative to Criminal Prosecution', 12 *Harvard Human Rights Law Journal* 28–56 (1999); Christian Tomuschat, 'State Responsibility and the Country of Origin', *The Problem of Refugees in Light of Contemporary International Law Issues*, Vera Gowland Debbas (ed) Martinus Nijhoff Publishers (1995); David Matas, *No More: The Battle against Human Rights Violations*, Chapter 12 on 'Compensation', Dundurn Press Limited, Toronto (1994); Luke Lee, 'The Right to Compensation: Refugees and Countries of Asylum', 80 *American Journal of International Law* (1986); Payam Akhavan and Morten Bergsmo, 'The Application of the Doctrine of State Responsibility to Refugee Creating Situations', 58 (3-4) *Nordic Journal of International Law* 253-254 (1989).

170 See Packer, *op cit* (24 April 2019); Michael A Becker, 'The Situation of the Rohingya: Is there a Role for the International Court of Justice?, Gonville and Caius College, Cambridge (14 November 2018): https://www.ejiltalk.org/the-situation-of-the-rohingya-is-there-a-role-for-the-international-court-of-justice/.

171 Luke Lee, 'Questions of Responsibilities and Reparations', 16(3) *Refugee Survey Quarterly* (1997).

172 United Nations Compensation Commission: https://uncc.ch/.

173 Theo van Boven, 'Study concerning the right to restitution, compensation and rehabilitation for victims of gross violations of human rights and fundamental freedoms: final report', United Nations (1993): https://digitallibrary.un.org/record/172321.

174 Principle 4 of the Cairo Declaration of Principles of International Law on Compensation to Refugees: https://www.cambridge.org/core/journals/american-journal-of-international-law/article/cairo-declaration-of-principles-of-international-law-on-compensation-to-refugees/6BB54211294E; and Article VIII of the Asian-African Legal Consultative Organisation (AALCO) 1996

'Bangkok Principles' on the Status and Treatment of Refugees: http://www.aalco.int/Final%20text%20of%20Bangkok%20Principles.pdf.

175 'Special Issue: Accountability and Redress for the Injustices of Displacement', Vol 27, Issue 2, *Journal of Refugee Studies*, Oxford University Press, June 2014.

176 Farhaan Uddin Ahmed, 'Myanmar should pay reparations to the Rohingya', *The Daily Star* (13 May 2018): https://www.thedailystar.net/opinion/human-rights/myanmar-should-pay-reparations-rohingyas-1575334; Afrose Jahan Chaity, 'Myanmar should pay $6 billion in compensation for Rohingya crisis, study finds, *Dhaka Tribune* (12 February 2019): https://www.dhakatribune.com/world/south-asia/2019/02/12/myanmar-should-pay-us-6-billion-in-compensation-for-rohingya-crisis-study-finds; Christine A Jubb, Mohsin Habib, Salahuddin Ahmad, 'Rohingya mass exodus: Who should pay compensation and how much?', Conference paper, ResearchGate (December 2018): https://www.researchgate.net/publication/329362946_Rohingya_mass_exodus_Who_should_pay_compensation_and_how_much/download.

177 'Land Grabbing as an Internationally Wrongful Act: A Legal Roadmap for Ending Land Grabbing and Housing, Land and Property Rights Abuses, Crimes, and Impunity in Myanmar', Displacement Solutions (October 2019): https://issuu.com/displacementsolutions/docs/dis6171_land_grabbing_as_an_internationally_wrongf.

178 David James Cantor, 'Restitution, compensation and satisfaction: transitional reparations and Colombia's Victims' Law', UNHCR New Issues in Refugee Research, Paper No 215, (August 2011): https://www.unhcr.org/en-us/4e423f6c9.pdf.

179 'Rohingya widow seeks compensation from Myanmar government for death of her husband', Reuters/NBC News (11 December 2020): https://www.nbcnews.com/news/world/rohingya-widow-seeks-compensation-myanmar-government-death-her-husband-n1250913.

2 The double burden of lives in camps

Stateless Rohingya communities in Bangladesh and their multiple displacements

Sadaf Noor E Islam and Nayanika Mookherjee

Introduction: Rohingya—A stolen citizenship

Musammet Ara,[1] a respondent in Bhashan Char,[2] told me over a WhatsApp call:

> Our accommodation in the Bhashan Char is better than Cox's Bazar's Rohingya camp housing. But look at this bunk bed; it seems like a prison bed. We get enough rations. But we don't have freedom; we cannot meet our relatives at Cox's Bazar. It's restricted. We are deeply concerned about children's education. There is no formal Myanmar curriculum for children. We are not happy here; we don't have freedom. We cannot move freely. There is no referral system for the treatment. The graveyard is getting bigger.

This narrative expresses the stateless Rohingyas' seemingly insoluble tensions raised after their multiple displacements, juxtaposed with distress, insecurity, and vulnerabilities. The life of the Rohingya people in exile and their urge for freedom of movement are comparable to the essentials of life. In the host country, displaced Rohingya people receive food, necessities, and shelter. Yet, they don't have the assurance of good education for their children and freedom of movement. These restrictions were already in place in Myanmar (formerly known as Burma) before they fled. In Myanmar, they lack citizenship status, which exacerbates their insecurity and vulnerabilities which are embedded in their long, politically oppressive past and the denial of refugee status by the host country, Bangladesh- that we are referring to as the 'double burden'. Therefore, we argue that securing the quality of life for Rohingya people by eradicating the double burden of stereotyping the Rohingyas is only possible by understanding the perspective from their political history.

This paper highlights the historical trajectory through which the Rohingya people have been rendered stateless in a context of discrimination, citizenship denial, exclusion, and extermination, based on their 'rootedness', which has been interrogated by Burmese rulers for many decades. Understanding this process is essential to bringing justice and accountability to the situation of the Rohingyas. In this context, it is essential to highlight that the Bangladesh government has

DOI: 10.4324/9781003304883-4

not recognized the Rohingyas as refugees because Bangladesh is not a signatory to the Refugee Convention or Statelessness Convention. To understand the Rohingya predicament, between the pressures from the Myanmar and Bangladeshi governments, we aim to explain the term 'refugee' in the historical context and explore the reticence of the Bangladeshi authorities to use the term 'refugees' for the Rohingyas.

Refugees in a historical context

In the context of world history, the concept of a 'refugee' is a relatively recent phenomenon having emerged from a specific global situation following the First World War. This is not to say that there were never any refugees previously; people have always looked for safety from outer world. After the Russian, Austro-Hungarian, and Ottoman empires collapsed, the new Peace Treaties created on the nation-state model brought an intense change in Central Europe that led thousands of Russians, Armenians, Bulgarians, Greeks, Germans, Hungarians, and Romanians to leave their countries. After a few years, another two major incidents, propagation of the racial law in Germany and the civil war in Spain, caused further outflows of refugees.[3] Thousands of people were forced to flee their homes because they did not fulfil the criteria of the nationalist principle of 'one state, one culture' and thus could not be accommodated within European nation-state borders.[4]

Nevertheless, this was the period when 'the refugee' emerged globally as a specific, social, political, and legal problem. In Europe, the Second World War began with replacing the old multi-ethnic European empires with the new world order of sovereign nation-states.[5] Liisa Malkki notes that, towards the end of the Second World War, refugee camps became a standardized, generalized technology of power.[6] Through the process of organizing mass displacement, post-war refugees emerged as a knowable, nameable figure and an object of social-scientific knowledge. The refugee problem was deemed to be arising as a result of war and it was increasingly anticipated that, upon victory, the masses uprooted during the war would become a bigger problem. However, Agamben reminds us of the differences between refugees and stateless people, creating a complex phenomenon which continues today.[7] Whereas politically persecuted refugee people cannot return to their country for their lives are at risk, there is another way of denaturalization and denationalization of their own citizens by creating new laws. This happened in Soviet Russia and Turkey. In the context of the stateless Rohingyas, we see both exclusionary processes of mass killing and state-created denationalization laws.

However, Siddiqi suggests that the denationalization of the Rohingyas is not particularly a Burmese problem but is an extreme version of the post-colonial predicament of nation-states at the present time.[8] She adds that, despite the restoration of formally democratic politics, the state did not take any initiative to change the existing discriminatory and violent policies which provoked the Rohingya's sufferings. She identifies how the problematic idea of ethnic or racial purity lies in imagining and unifying the national community and constructing a minority of 'others'. Thereby, Siddiqi understands the Rohingya genocide as an extreme outcome of the imperative of exclusion at the heart of all nation-making processes and other contextualized factors.[9] In the context of discovering the Rohingya's 'authentic' history, she finds it problematic to tie citizenship to ethnicity or indigeneity. She appeals to us to rethink the question of belonging and citizenship and to reject these current exclusionary frameworks.

Many voluntary agencies, such as the Red Cross, began to plan for the refugee problem, although it was still considered the military's responsibility. In fact, the concentration camps were often modelled on military barracks. In 1951, when the United Nations High Commissioner for Refugees (UNHCR) was established, refugees began to emerge as a global, social, and humanitarian problem. The Universal Declaration of Human Rights was adopted in 1948, as was the Genocide Convention. Since then, refugee law has been an inseparable part of human rights. The principal elements of this law and the relevant legal instruments grew out of the aftermath of the war in Europe, which had produced a strong sense of post-war shame and responsibility regarding the predicament of people who had fled from their own countries. One of the critical components of this law was the provision of a legal definition of refugee status. Refugees are often conceptualized with certain essential traits, such as being stateless or displaced. Researchers and policymakers often tend to attach specific general characteristics to refugees, as if all refugees share a common experience and legal, to overcome the 'refugee issues', which often exacerbated the sufferings of refugee life.

Another tendency has been to treat refugees as a political problem, a historical problem, and a psychological problem due to the displacement distress they suffer.[10] Refugees are also seen as a mobile, unstable social phenomenon. The essentializing of problems in this way can be compared with the category of 'tribe' in anthropology, which treats all tribes as if they are the same. Discussions of rootedness within the study of refugees bring in another significant dimension—that of culture and its various constituents, which are seen to be territorialized (Mallki 1995). Marrus (1985) states that uprooted refugees are seen as having been 'torn loose from their culture'.[11] In the context of the Rohingya ethnic group, they have been denied their citizenship by the Burmese rulers for not having the 'rootedness' in the Burmese culture, as they are allegedly considered to be 'seasonal migrant workers' from other parts of the subcontinent. However, internal ethnic conflicts, ethnocentrism, political and religious biases, and labelling them as Islamic terrorists were embedded in this ethnic categorization that has been used to exclude them from their country. This shows that the 'purity and security of Burmese state and nationalism' were at the heart of the exclusionary process.

The Rohingya exodus and the history of ethnic oppression

Before 2012, there were only a few illustrations of anthropological or social science research on the Rohingya, their exodus, and persecutions (Leider 2018).[12] However, since the massive Rohingya displacement, the level of anthropological interest in these issues is increasing. There are two tendencies that can be found in the prevalent literature: one describes the recent Rohingya exodus in the context of history, whereas the other tends to focus on the formation of Rohingya identity in exile and focuses on their resilience and activities after their recent exodus.

In exploring the scholarship which focuses on the Rohingya exodus on the basis of history, it primarily identifies the Rohingya as being predominantly Muslim and living mainly in the northern Arakan State.[13] According to the Myanmar census of 2014, the estimated total number of Rohingyas was more than one million, living in Maungdaw, Buthidaung, and Rathedaung along the border with Bangladesh.[14] The language, culture, and religion of Rohingyas are seen as different from the mainstream Burmese identity in Myanmar. This has been used to exclude the Rohingya from being citizens of Myanmar. The Myanmar state authority has discriminated against, marginalized, and persecuted Rohingyas for many years, dating back to colonial times. The Rohingya exodus has complex and lengthy historical roots, during which time there have been severe tensions among different ethnic groups.

The Rohingya people's citizenship and sense of belonging have been systematically eroded for decades through the elimination, destruction, and the systematic non-issuance of documents that could prove their citizenship. Slowly but steadily, Rohingyas have been reduced to a position where their citizenship has been denied by enforcing the state narrative that they are 'foreigners' or 'Bengalis'. Even to obtain national verification cards, they were forced to accept the label of Bengali. Furthermore, since 1980, Myanmar's military and authoritarian state governments have described Rohingyas as a political and security threat and have increasingly taken away the citizenship rights of Rohingyas. However, the dehumanization of the Rohingya people as a threat to the nation was evident many decades before. The Rohingya people's denationalization and persecution can be understood in the context of Rakhine Buddhist nationalism and nation-state-building attitude. On the contrary, since post-colonial times, Rohingya people have been raising their pre-colonial history to support their ethnic claims. Still, they could not prevent the oppression, conflicts, and impoverishment that continuously hampered their lives.[15]

While presenting the pre-colonial history of Arakan, Alam mentions that, in 1784 AD, the Burmese king Boddawphaya sent soldiers to take control over Arakan.[15] The soldiers returned with the Arakanese royal family one year later, along with 20,000 inhabitants as prisoners. However, thousands of Arakanese Muslims and Arakanese Buddhists were killed, and mosques, temples, shrines, seminaries, and libraries, including the Mrauk-U Royal Library, were destroyed by the Burmese king. In addition, the Mahamuni Image of Lord Buddha was taken to Burma. Muslims were devastated by the fall of the Mrauk-U Empire, and everything that was materially and culturally Islamic was demolished and razed to the ground. During the 40 years of Burmese rule (1784–1824 AD), two-thirds of Rohingya and Rakhine inhabitants of Arakan were believed to have fled to Bengal (India).

When the British took control of Burma, it became a province of British India. The British rulers brought migrant labourers, traders, and various groups of people to Burma from India. A deep dissatisfaction steadily grew up among the Burmese people, who were the majority during that time. In 1826 AD, Arakan was invaded by British India, and there was a population of thirty thousand Muslims, which represented 30% of the total demography of Arakan. Eventually, the British separated Burma from India and made Arakan a part of Burma in 1937.

In 1942, the Japanese occupation began, pushing the British away from Burma. Burmese nationalists (Buddhists) attacked Muslims, killing up to 40,000 people, and many more fled to neighbouring countries. The Buddhist Rakhine persecuted Rohingyas for the first time because the Burmese believed that Muslims took advantage of British colonial rule. The Japanese government supported the Arakan massacre of 1942 (Crouch 2016;Alam 1999). Since then, the Rohingya people have had their citizenship repeatedly denied due to their religious claims and ethnic identity. It was stated that the Rohingyas were 'illegal migrants from East Pakistan'. (now known as Bangladesh after independence in 1971).

In 1945, the British Army, alongside the Burma Independence Army (BIA), led by Bo Rang Aung, and Rohingya fighters, took back control of Burma from the Japanese occupation. The British colonial rulers persuaded the Burmese government to give the Rohingya the right to vote and participate in elections. However, the Rohingya felt betrayed as the British did not keep their promise to grant full autonomy to the Arakan region. However, in 1947, the Rohingyas were given the right to vote and contest the 1947 Constituent Assembly Election through the influence of the British prime minister, Clement Attlee.[17] Beginning in 1947, the leaders of active political and religious Muslim organizations started demanding from the authorities that the northern Arakan State should be a separate Muslim zone.[18] These calls were denied on the grounds that there was no historical evidence of Muslim Rohingyas in the pre-state formation of Burma.

In 1948, the ethnic tensions between Muslims and Buddhists intensified when the newly independent Burmese government claimed the Arakan State to be their own. In contrast, the Rohingya wanted Arakan to join with Pakistan.[19] Rohingya resistance, known as the 'Mujahid movement', gained impetus soon after Burma's independence in 1948 when the Rakhines (Burmese Buddhists) formed a group against the Rohingya. They burnt down Rohingya villages and killed many.

In 1959, the first president of Burma, Sao Shwe Thaike, a Shan, claimed that the 'Muslims of Arakan' certainly belonged to the indigenous races of Burma.[20] The Rohingya people were given citizenship/ID cards (Islam, 2020) and granted the right to vote under Burma's first post-independence prime minister, U Nu. Rohingyas held important positions in the civil service.[21] In the 1960s, the official Burma Broadcasting Service (BBS) relayed a Rohingya-language radio programme three times a week as part of its minority language programming, and the term 'Rohingya' was used in journals and school textbooks until the late 1970s (Macmanus et al. 2015).[22]

After the military takeover in 1962, the Rohingyas were systematically excluded from the nation-building process. The level of deprivation was aggravated during the socialist era of General Ne Win, during which several reforms were introduced in the period from 1962 to 1974.[23] He removed the parliamentary system and this impacted the Rohingya severely.

The Rohingyas' citizenship and rights were continuously denied and deprived in all respects. The citizenship status of all Rohingya Muslim residents in Burma has repeatedly been called into question, particularly when military governments were in power. Burmese authorities have periodically positioned themselves against 'illegal immigrants', challenging the Rohingyas to prove their citizenship. Prime Minister Ne Win introduced the most oppressive three-tier form of citizenship in 1982: citizenship, associate citizenship, and naturalized citizenship, which entirely excluded the Rohingya. Under the Burmese Socialist Programme Party (BSPP), 1962–88, policies were enacted that provoked more conflict, based on ethnic, religious, cultural, and linguistic assimilation. Insecurity among Muslims and other non-indigenous populations increased as a result of the new citizenship law that took effect in 1982 and demanded confirmation of lineage from an 'indigenous race;' those who could not do so would not be granted citizenship status. Myanmar's ethnocentric and exclusionary 1982 Citizenship Law and the arbitrary implementation of citizenship rules implemented structured discrimination, persecution, and expulsion. The Rohingya population was denied citizenship and rights by the Myanmar government, which also reinforced the State's official narratives that Rohingyas were foreigners—'illegal immigrants'—unworthy of state protection. This, in turn strengthened narratives that threatened the Rohingya people's entire identity. The dominant State's voices proclaimed that 'there is no ethnic group called Rohingya' and that 'they are Bengali', which caused the Rohingya lose its identity, dignity, and rights. The purpose of the Citizenship Act was to deprive the Rohingyas of their citizenship. Thus the new immigration law redefined people who migrated during British colonial rule as illegal migrants and[24] and did not recognize the Rohingya as one of the nation's 135 ethnic groups. Defending this exclusion, General Ne Win's government argued that the citizenship law recognized those persons as citizens whose families had settled in the country before 1948.[25] Rohingya babies were no longer given birth certificates.

In 1970, General Ne Win's discriminatory policies towards the Rohingya ensured that the National Registration Cards (NRCs) were revoked from them. From 1977 to 1978, a junta operation known as Nagamin ('the Dragon King') took place, conducted by the Burmese immigration and military authorities and aimed at screening and registering citizens, and removing minorities and foreigners from Burma (Alam 1999; Islam 2020).[26] This led to the Rohingya losing their official documentation, thus making them stateless, with over 200,000 fleeing to Bangladesh. However, the Bangladeshi government negotiated with the Burmese government for Rohingya repatriation through the UN.[27] It is widely believed among the Rohingya that Operation Nagamin was designed to remove the Rohingya from Burma.

There were at least two waves of ferocity between Rohingyas and majority Buddhists in Rakhine State took place in 2012.[28] In retaliation for past brutalities, the Arakan Rohingya Salvation Army (ARSA)[29] is reported to have attacked border guard posts, killing 12 Myanmar security personnel in 2017. Retaliation from the Myanmar forces was vicious and gruesome and involved the brutal killing of thousands, which forced around one million Rohingya out of Myanmar.

There was ongoing oppression against Muslim Rohingyas. The UNHCR reaffirmed in 1995 that most of the Muslims of Rakhine State were not able to claim their citizenship under Myanmar's citizenship laws. The Rohingya Muslims were not only refused citizenship but also suffered from economic discrimination, targeted harassment, and persecution. Human Rights Watch's Asia Division[30] mentioned in their report in 1996 that 'they [Rohingyas] are always ready to flee if there is an option open to them to avoid suffering further abuse'. The Myanmar government has not recognized the Rohingya as citizens, and the issues surrounding their circumstances remain unresolved. In the exodus, most people moved to the Middle East and the countries bordering Myanmar, with major movements taking place in 1978, 1991–92, 2007, and 2012. Thus, Rohingyas are now scattered today within South Asia and the Middle East—in Bangladesh, India, Pakistan, and Saudi Arabia—and within Southeast Asia—Thailand, Indonesia, and Malaysia, among others. They are also in the USA, Canada, Australia, the UK, and various European countries. Unresolved Rohingya issues have additionally resulted in a recent massive exodus in 2017, following major military atrocities.

Long-time Burmese human rights activist Maung Zarni has, together with Natalie Brinham, reported two similar issues that have emerged historically in *Reworking the Colonial-Era Indian Peril: Myanmar's State-Directed Persecution of Rohingyas and Other Muslims* (2017).[31] These researchers argue that successive Burmese governments carried out organized violence against Muslims all over the country, as well as officially sanctioning violence against the Arakanese Muslims, popularly known as the Rohingya. The writers argue that the Burmese army, as the most powerful institution in the country, has always seen Muslims and Rohingyas through the lens of security. The army continued the legacy of popular, historical, and official discourses about Indian ancestry that existed in the colonial era—the fear of inter-racial marriage between Burmese women and Indian men, who were seen as predatory and abusive. Similar discourses were used to frame Rohingyas and have depicted them as 'a new threat to national security' since 1966. Even in recent times, by referring to the Rohingya as '*jihadis*'—or Islamic extremists—the Myanmar government frames them using the same lens of threat, and legitimizes their persecution, deeming them to be 'illegal citizens of Myanmar'. According to Nurul Islam (2020)[32]:

> The Rohingya have mixed more with Indian people than with the Burmese. Being an ethnic mix of native Indo-Aryan, Bengalis, Persians, Moghuls, Turks, and Pathans, they have evolved distinct ethnic characteristics over the

> past several centuries and developed a culture and language which is unique to the region and different from other people.
>
> (p. 3)

Jacques Leider has presented an extensive historical account of the Rohingya crisis from the pre-colonial period to recent times in *Rohingya: The History of a Muslim Identity in Myanmar*.[33] Considering the historical context, he recognizes the Rohingyas as an ethnopolitical-religious identity. Leider disputes the monolithic Rohingya identity; instead, he sees the Rohingyas as a transnational group of communities, who have reinvented their lives in varied geographical and political contexts. We can compare this situation with that described in Malkki's work *Purity and Exile* (1995b), which is based on the Hutus' exile in Tanzania, but in an urban setting.[34] She finds that the Hutus wanted to assimilate with the majority population rather than holding on to their 'Hutu' identity. Arnab Roy Chowdhury argues that the emergence of the Rohingya identity has been encouraged by state formation, war, and power shifts in Myanmar during pre-colonial, colonial, and post-colonial times.[35] He showed how 'Rohingya Muslims' were depicted as the enemy 'Other' by the post-coup state of Myanmar, along with religious civil society and the Buddhist Burmese. While Arnab Roy identifies religious and exclusivist nationalism as provoking the construction of the 'Muslim Other', this construction has poignantly worsened since the democratization of Myanmar, for Rohingya as a Muslim ethnic group remained as a marginal group compared with the dominant Buddhist ethnic community. Furthermore, the Rohingya, who have become alienated from their own national space, have become politicized and their identity reified, while their resilience has been transformed into the identity of victimhood.

Md Khan (2018) pursues an anthropological exploration of the global response to the recent atrocities and examines whether the Islamic *ummah* (the collective community of Islamic people) has played any role in the formation of group identity among the displaced Rohingyas. He finds that the religiopolitical context triggered the construction of a shared group identity between the Rohingyas and other Muslims. Through imagination, other Muslims perceive the Rohingyas' experiences and feel united with them. Sayema Khatun (2019) explores the resilience of the Rohingya in the US. Her empirical research contributes to understanding the Rohingya's marginal life at the edge of persecution and maps the human agency Rohingya employ to survive and recreate their society and identity. Khatun finds that the Rohingya communities keep moving from country to country to make their own life and identity.

Similarly, Shucharita Sen (2020) shows how, despite their experience of persecution, the stateless Rohingyas transform their identity through exclusion, counter-resistance, and self-resilience. Sen looks beyond the Rohingya's victimization and anthropologically explores their survival strategies through their economic activities and the transformation of their identity over time and in different contexts.[36]

Bhatia (2018) carried out a study of the Rohingya camps in Cox's Bazar, in which they conducted a rapid needs assessment of recently arrived Rohingya and host community households.[37] They found high levels of mortality among young Rohingya men, alarmingly low levels of vaccination among children, poor literacy, and rising poverty. This study also found that, because the Rohingyas are denied formal refugee status, they cannot access complete protection and thereby find themselves in a state of insecurity, in which they are unsure of their future and unable to seek work or formally send their children to school.

The Rohingya people's double burden in the camp

The doubling of the world is occurring among the Rohingya people as they leave their families and village to escape the atrocities in Myanmar. Given that the Bangladesh government had insufficient resources to support such a massive displacement of Rohingya people from Myanmar in 2017, the support of national and international non-governmental organizations (NGOs) was essential. The Bangladesh Refugee Relief and Repatriation Commissioner (RRRC) and numerous NGOs have been working together to provide services in response to the emergency since the Rohingya people began to cross the border and flee to Bangladesh. Furthermore, various local, national, and international NGOs already working in this area began helping the Rohingyas as soon as they reached the site, with whatever resources they had.[38] Anthropologist David Lewis (2019) explains the humanitarian responses to the massive Rohingya influx into Bangladesh's territory through the concept of performance.[39] In the early days of their arrival in the southern part of Bangladesh, he finds that various actors and activities have shaped humanitarian responses to the Rohingya victims. These activities generated a varied and complex set of local, national, and international humanitarian responses. He found acts of piety by local people and a combination of religious and secular attitudes in the humanitarian responses to the Rohingyas. He also added that sometimes a person-to-person humanitarian response is changed by market processes and is transformed into a charitable organization. Lewis states that the way the Bangladesh government has responded to save the displaced Rohingya can be linked to the country's own experiences of the Bangladesh Liberation War of 1971.

However, despite being provided with various forms of developmental and humanitarian assistance in the world's largest refugee camp in Cox's Bazar, the difficulties of the Rohingyas continue. Their lives are impacted by the lack of both the right to work, and the right to formal institutional education (including higher education); there is no freedom of movement, and information among the stateless Rohingyas is lacking. In addition, mistrust and dissatisfaction about health services (Islam and Mookherjee 2022), health and safety issues after the fire, gunfights, abductions, killings, and various other forms of violence hugely burden their lives in the camp.[40]

Since 2017, the stateless Rohingyas have lived in inhumane conditions under roofs made of polythene sheets. Most of them have settled in the Cox's Bazar region of Bangladesh, living in crowded camps, either UNHCR-managed camps or unofficial settlements. The Rohingya camp, with almost one million inhabitants, is the largest in recent history. According to the UNHCR, as of 30 September 2021, there were 902,947 individuals (190,662 families) residing in these camps in Bangladesh.[41] The average family comprises 4.7 people. These mega-camps are overcrowded; e the average amount of space per person is 10.7 square meters, whereas the recommended international standard for refugee camps is 45 square meters per person. Inevitably, crowded camps expose refugees to the heightened risk of communicable diseases, fires, community tensions, and domestic and sexual violence.[42] Although the families have been provided with food, liquefied petroleum gas (LPG), and other resources and facilities, Rohingya children do not receive a formal education; instead, children learn at temporary learning centres run by facilitators. There is no education at all for adolescents or adults. Only one-quarter of school-age children attend temporary learning centres, which means that nearly 400,000 children and young people are not receiving formal education. After three years of living in the camps, the Rohingya community is deeply concerned about their children's future and education.[43]

Several fires in the camps have caused fatalities and destruction, and led to fears that there is an attempt to push residents to Bhashan Char. Furthermore, the fire incidents have rendered these already 'homeless' people homeless again. The fire on 22 March 2021 spread through the Balukhali camp and two other camps. It destroyed 500 acres and 10,000 camp shelters, leaving 45,000 people homeless. At the same time, an estimated 600 were injured and 15 killed.[44] A barbed-wire security fence surrounding the camps prevented the Rohingyas from fleeing quickly and effectively trapped them in the fire.

The relocation of the stateless Rohingyas to the island of Bhashan Char, a form of incarceration, was another burden added to the Rohingyas' already overburdened circumstances (Bhuiyan, 2020). Despite the 'safe, secured and well-arranged shelter, food supplies, health services and aid', the use of this island initially sparked debate because of its location in the path of cyclones. The remote island is also detached from the mainland and abides by stringent security measures, giving limited scope for meeting friends and family in the Cox's Bazar camp, and leaving their lives burdened with more captivity and insecurity and fear of another forced displacement. The Rohingya people have already experienced massive violence that compelled them to flee their country and position themselves as vulnerable communities. Furthermore, they face negative stereotyping by the Bangladeshi media's anti-Rohingya attitude, reflected in their representation of Rohingya people as traffickers of Yaba (an illegal stimulant drug), and as criminals and weapon carriers.

The situation described above explains why the label 'protracted refugee situations' has highlighted this problem (Loescher and Milner 2005; Loescher et al. 2008). These situations have been created as a result of the stateless Rohingyas having to live in exile for five years or more, often in an indefinite, intermediate state over which they have no control, and they may continue to remain without a homeland for decades. This situation results in the denial of both the right to work and the freedom of movement to the displaced, sometimes leaving entire generations of people indefinitely confined to these camps. Ranging from the Dadaab camps in Kenya to the Nyarugusu camp in Tanzania and the position of many Palestinians throughout the Middle East, such situations have been described as a 'denial of rights and a waste of humanity'.[45]

This conventional approach to refugee assistance is unsustainable. With the recent mass displacements worldwide, such as those from Syria or Somalia, host countries are becoming less willing to accommodate large numbers of people indefinitely. Several states have closed their borders entirely to refugees. International donors are also increasingly unwilling to support large numbers of refugees within camps indefinitely, given the restrictions of their finite humanitarian budgets. Furthermore, without adequate protection and assistance within their region of origin, increasing numbers of refugees are forced to move to urban areas—sometimes illegally—or to commence dangerous journeys to other parts of the world in search of freedom, rights and dignity, a situation which also applies to the stateless Rohingya people.

Clearly, there need to be alternative ways to think about refugee rehabilitation. Existing ways of thinking about Rohingya refugee issues too often ignore the fact that these refugees have a prolonged history of experiencing deprivation, oppression, and contempt. Yet refugees have capabilities as well as vulnerabilities. They need not inevitably be a 'burden' on host states: they have the potential to contribute economically and socio-culturally. However, they concurrently have an unjust history of political persecution and the urge to survive, with the hope of a secure future. By viewing the stateless Rohingyas only as a humanitarian issue, their lives will never be eased, and dissatisfaction, scepticism, and mistrust will continue to grow, leading to an 'uncomfortable' situation for the host country.

Relief and aid are essential for the displaced Rohingya people to survive, but they also need freedom of movement, freedom to educate their children, freedom to take their own life decisions. However, the Rohingya problems have generally been conceived of in an aid-centric way, relying upon the presumption that donor agencies, NGOs, and other countries will assist host states in ensuring long-term local integration for refugees. Perhaps this attitude also assumes that there will be a 'magic moment' when the displaced will return to their own country. Meanwhile, one or maybe several generations will waste their lives in the protracted refugee situation. Instead, there are opportunities to look at the problem as being grounded in the Rohingya peoples' political history, which will ensure justice and accountability.

We argue that an understanding of the lives of stateless communities after their displacement can provide the building blocks for understanding the lived experiences of Rohingya communities and others forcibly displaced in the Global South. This alone can engender multi-faceted engagements for concrete action and provide sustainable solutions, which are essential in searching for justice and accountability. Moreover, through this approach, it may be possible to take a broader view of the political history that shapes the possibilities for refugees' self-reliance, while also recognizing them as refugees to give them access to their internationally prescribed rights. By integrating them into policymaking, we can maximize opportunities for their protection and assistance, along with their autonomy and their capability of flourishing, which can lessen the burden of their displaced lives.

Acknowledgements

We would like to thank the respondents for their participation in the study and for sharing their experiences with us. We are indebted to Professor Veena Das for her stimulating discussion during the fieldwork for this article, which greatly inspired us to explore the Rohingya experiences in the context of the COVID-19 pandemic. We also thank the editors of this volume for inviting us to contribute. This chapter is part of a project funded by the British Academy/Leverhulme Research Grant (2020–2022) (SRG20\201602): 'Household Dynamics under Crisis: COVID-19 Policies and its Implications for Bangladeshis at Home and in the Diaspora (UK)', PI Professor Nayanika Mookherjee (Durham University).

Notes

1 Pseudonym.
2 Bhasan Char is an island 37 miles away from the Bangladesh mainland, located in the Bay of Bengal. As an extension project of Ashrayan, the Bangladesh Government decided to build 10,000 homes in Bhashan Char in 2019 to relocate Rohingya people from Cox's Bazar. Despite the opposition of Rohingya leaders and human rights activists, the Bangladesh Government started relocating Rohingya communities in January 2020. It was not easy to contact displaced Rohingya people living in the Bhashan Char as the internet network was not always in our favour. We were introduced to Musammet Ara through one of our other research interlocuters.
3 Giorgio Agamben, *Means without End: Notes on Politics* (Cesare Casarino and Vincenzo Binetti ed, 2nd vol, University of Minnesota Press 2000).
4 Ernest Gellner, *Nations and Nationalism* (2nd ed, Cornell University Press 2008).
5 Liisa Malkki, 'National Geographic: The Rooting of Peoples and the Territorialization of National Identity among Scholars and Refugees' (1992) 7 (1) Cultural Anthropology <www.jstor.org/stable/656519> accessed 24 April 2022.
6 Ibid.
7 cf Agamben (n 3).
8 Dina M Siddiqi, 'Weaponising Paperwork: Rohingya Belonging and Statelessness' *The Daily Star* (6 May 2019) <www.thedailystar.net/in-focus/news/weaponising-paperwork-rohingya-belonging-and-statelessness-1739416> accessed 24 April 2022.
9 cf Siddiqi (n 8).
10 Liisa H. Malkki, *Purity and Exile* (University of Chicago Press 1995).
11 Michael R. Marrus, 'The Unwanted: European Refugees in the Twentieth Century' (1985) 81 (1) American Journal of International Law <www.cambridge.org/core/journals/american-journal-of-international-law/article/abs/the-unwanted-european-refugees-in-the-twentieth-century-by-michael-r-marrus-new-york-and-oxford-oxford-university-press-1985-pp-xii-414-index-2495/D53824C0629AD5781B67A8D58481CE22> accessed 24 April 2022.

12 See Jacques P. Leider, 'History and Victimhood: Engaging with Rohingya Issues' (2018) 20 (1) Insight Turkey <www.jstor.org/stable/26301070> accessed 24 April 2022; Jacques Leider, 'Rohingya: The History of a Muslim Identity in Myanmar' (2018) Oxford Research Encyclopedia of Asian History. <www.networkmyanmar.org/ESW/Files/Leider-ORE.pdf> accessed 24 April 2022.

13 Arakan was a sovereign and independent state and became one of the states of the Myanmar, now known as Rakhine State. At different points in history, Arakan had been an independent and sovereign monarchy ruled by Hindus, Buddhists, or Muslims. Arakan, in fact, is a continuation of the Chittagong Plain and was neither a Burmese nor an Indian territory until the eighteenth century.

14 Cf Leider, n (12).

15 Cf Leider, n (12).

16 Mohammed Ashraf Alam, *A Short Historical Background of Arakan* (Arakan Historical Society 1999).

17 Nurul Islam, 'Rohingya: A People Under Endless Tyranny' (2020) 48(1) Asian Affairs An American Review <www.researchgate.net/publication/343085154_Rohingya_A_people_Under_Endless_Tyranny> accessed 24 April 2022.

18 Cf Leider, n (12).

19 AKM Ahsan Ullah and Diotima Chattoraj, 'Roots of Discrimination Against Rohingya Minorities: Society, Ethnicity and International Relations' (2018) 26 (2) Intellectual Discourse. <www.law.ox.ac.uk/sites/files/oxlaw/oscola_4th_edn_hart_2012quickreferenceguide.pdf> accessed 24 April 2022

20 Nay San Lwin,'Making Rohingya statelessness' (*New Mandala*, 29 October 2012). <www.newmandala.org/making-rohingya-statelessness/> accessed 24 April 2022.

21 Cf Ullah and Chattoraj, n (19).

22 Cf Ullah and Chattoraj, n (19).

23 Lindsay Maizland, '*Myanmar's Troubled History: Coups, Military Rule, and Ethnic Conflict*' (Council on Foreign Relations, 31 January 2022) <hwww.cfr.org/backgrounder/myanmar-history-coup-military-rule-ethnic-conflict-rohingya> accessed 25 April 2022

24 Cf Ullah and Chattoraj, n (19).

25 See A.K. M. Ahsan Ullah, '*Rohingya Crisis in Myanmar: Seeking Justice for the "Stateless"*' (Rohingya Khobor) <https://rohingyakhobor.com/mdocs-posts/rohingya-crisis-in-myanmar-seeking-justice-for-the-stateless/> accessed 24 April 2022.

26 See Human Rights Watch, 'Historical Background' (Human Rights Watch) <www.hrw.org/reports/2000/burma/burm005-01.htm> accessed 24 April 2022.

27 Akm Ahsan Ullah, 'Rohingya Refugees to Bangladesh: Historical Exclusions and Contemporary Marginalization' (2011) 9 (2) Journal of Immigrant & Refugee Studies <www.tandfonline.com/doi/abs/10.1080/15562948.2011.567149> accessed 24 April 2022.

28 See 'Why is there communal violence in Myanmar?' *BBC* (3 July 2014) <www.bbc.com/news/world-asia-18395788> accessed 24 April 2022.

29 ARSA is a Rohingya insurgent group active in northern Rakhine State, Myanmar, where mostly Muslim Rohingya people have faced persecution.

30 Human Rights Watch is a non-profit organization which works for people's human rights in 90 countries all over the world. The link is last accessed on 20/09/2022. https://www.hrw.org/reports/1996/WR96/Asia-01.htm#P93_25085

31 Maung Zarni and Natalie Brinham, 'Reworking the Colonial-Era Indian Peril: Myanmar's State-Directed Persecution of Rohingyas and Other Muslims' (The Brown Journal of World Affairs) <https://bjwa.brown.edu/24-1/reworking-the

-colonial-era-indian-peril-myanmars-state-directed-persecution-of-rohingyas-and-other-muslims1/> accessed 24 April 2022.

32 Cf Islam, n (17).

33 Cf Leider, n (12).

34 cf Makki, n (10).

35 Arnab Roy Chowdhury, 'An 'Un-Imagined Community': The Entangled Genealogy of an Exclusivist Nationalism in Myanmar and the Rohingya Refugee Crisis' (2020) 26 (50) Social Identities <www.researchgate.net/publication/342478555_An_'un-imagined_community'_the_entangled_genealogy_of_an_exclusivist_nationalism_in_Myanmar_and_the_Rohingya_refugee_crisis> accessed 24 April 2022.

36 Sucharita Sengupta, 'Being Stateless and Surviving: The Rohingyas in Camps of Bangladesh' in Nasreen Chowdhory and Biswajit Mohanty (eds), *Citizenship, Nationalism and Refugeehood of Rohingyas in Southern Asia* (Springer 2020).

37 Abhishek Bhatia and others, 'The Rohingya in Cox's Bazar: When the Stateless Seek Refuge' (2018) 20 (2) Health and Human Rights <www.researchgate.net/publication/329988225_The_Rohingya_in_Cox's_Bazar_When_the_Stateless_Seek_Refuge> accessed 24 April 2022.

38 David Lewis, 'Humanitarianism, civil society and the Rohingya refugee crisis in Bangladesh' (2019) 40 Third World Quarterly <www.tandfonline.com/doi/abs/10.1080/01436597.2019.1652897> accessed 24 April 2022.

39 Ibid.

40 Sadaf Noor E Islam, Nayanika Mookherjee, Naveeda Khan, 'Medicine in Name Only': Mistrust and COVID-19 Among the Crowded Rohingya Refugee Camps in Bangladesh. Medicine Anthropology Theory 9 (2): 1–32 (2022); ISSN 2405-691X, https://doi.org/10.17157/mat.9.2.5424.

41 'Joint Government of Bangladesh - UNHCR Population Factsheet' (Reliefweb) <https://reliefweb.int/sites/reliefweb.int/files/resources/GoB%20UNHCR%20Population%20Factsheet%20-%20Sep%202021.pdf> accessed 24 April 2022.

42 Human Rights Watch, 'Bangladesh Is Not My Country' (Human Rights Watch, 5 August 2018) <www.hrw.org/report/2018/08/05/bangladesh-not-my-country/plight-rohingya-refugees-myanmar> accessed 24 April 2022.

43 CDP, 'Rohingya Refugee Crisis' (*CDP*, 13 January 2022) <https://disasterphilanthropy.org/disasters/rohingya-refugee-crisis/> accessed 24 April 2022.

44 Jon Emont and Krishna Pokharel, 'Fire in Rohingya Refugee Camp Leaves Hundreds Missing' *The Wall Street Journal* (23 March 2021) <www.wsj.com/articles/fire-in-rohingya-refugee-camp-leaves-hundreds-missing-11616521768> accessed 24 April 2022.

45 U.S. Committee for Refugees and Immigrants, 'Lives in Storage: Refugee Warehousing and the Overlooked Humanitarian Crisis' (US Committee for Refugees and Immigrants, 2019)<https://reliefweb.int/sites/reliefweb.int/files/resources/USCRI-Warehousing-Dec2019-v4.pdf> accessed 24 April 2022.

Reference

Abhishek Bhatia and others, 'The Rohingya in Cox's Bazar: When the Stateless Seek Refuge' (2018) 20 (2) Health and Human Rights <www.researchgate.net/publication/329988225_The_Rohingya_in_Cox's_Bazar_When_the_Stateless_Seek_Refuge> accessed 24 April 2022

David Lewis, 'Humanitarianism, Civil Society and the Rohingya Refugee Crisis in Bangladesh' (2019) 40 Third World Quarterly <www.tandfonline.com/doi/abs/10.1080/01436597.2019.1652897> accessed 24 April 2022.

Dina M Siddiqi, 'Weaponising Paperwork: Rohingya Belonging and Statelessness' *The Daily Star* (6 May 2019) <www.thedailystar.net/in-focus/news/weaponising-paperwork-rohingya-belonging-and-statelessness-1739416> accessed 24 April 2022.

Ernest Gellner, *Nations and Nationalism* (2nd edn, Cornell University Press 2008).

Giorgio Agamben, *Means without End: Notes on Politics* (Cesare Casarino and Vincenzo Binetti ed, 20nd vol, University of Minnesota Press 2000).

Helal Mohammed Khan, 'Becoming Rohingya: Group Formation and Global Imaginaries' *Panel Paper IAPSS World Congress* (Paris, 24 April 2018).

Jacques Leider, 'Rohingya: The History of a Muslim Identity in Myanmar' (2018) Oxford Research Encyclopedia of Asian History <www.networkmyanmar.org/ESW/Files/Leider-ORE.pdf> accessed 24 April 2022.

Jacques P. Leider, 'History and Victimhood: Engaging with Rohingya Issues' (2018) 20 (1) Insight Turkey <www.jstor.org/stable/26301070> accessed 24 April 2022.

Liisa Malkki, 'National Geographic: The Rooting of Peoples and the Territorialization of National Identity among Scholars and Refugees' (1992) 7 (1) Cultural Anthropology <www.jstor.org/stable/656519> accessed 24 April 2022.

Liisa H. Malkki, *Purity and Exile* (University of Chicago Press 1995).

Gil Loescher, James Milner, and Edward Newman. Protracted refugee situations: Political, human rights and security implications. (2008).

Gil Loescher, and James Milner. *Protracted refugee situations: Domestic and international security implications.* (Routledge), 2013.

T. Macmanus, P. Green, and Alicia De la Cour Venning. *Countdown to annihilation: Genocide in Myanmar.* (International State Crime Initiative 2015).

Melissa Crouch, 'Myanmar's Muslim mosaic and the politics of belonging.' *Islam and the state in Myanmar: Muslim-Buddhist relations and the politics of belonging* 6: 45–66; (2016).

Michael R. Marrus, 'The Unwanted: European Refugees in the Twentieth Century' (1985) 81 (1) American Journal of International Law <www.cambridge.org/core/journals/american-journal-of-international-law/article/abs/the-unwanted-european-refugees-in-the-twentieth-century-by-michael-r-marrus-new-york-and-oxford-oxford-university-press-1985-pp-xii-414-index-2495/D53824C0629AD5781B67A8D58481CE22> accessed 24 April 2022.

Mohammed Ashraf Alam, *A Short Historical Background of Arakan* (Arakan Historical Society 1999).

Nurul Islam, 'Rohingya: A people Under Endless Tyranny' (2020) 48(1) Asian Affairs An American Review <www.researchgate.net/publication/343085154_Rohingya_A_people_Under_Endless_Tyranny> accessed 24 April 2022.

Sadaf Noor E. Islam, Nayanika Mookherjee, Naveeda Khan, 'Medicine in Name Only': Mistrust and COVID-19 Among the Crowded Rohingya Refugee Camps in Bangladesh. *Medicine Anthropology Theory* 9 (2): 1–32; (2022) ISSN 2405-691X; https://doi.org/10.17157/mat.9.2.5424.

Sayema Khatun, '"We Had Been Just Like Animals to Them": Life Histories from the Rohingya Diaspora in Wisconsin' In *Nribiggyan Potrika*, Vol 24: 111–150 (2019).

Sucharita Sengupta, 'Being Stateless and Surviving: The Rohingyas in Camps of Bangladesh' in Nasreen Chowdhory and Biswajit Mohanty (eds), *Citizenship, Nationalism and Refugeehood of Rohingyas in Southern Asia* (Springer 2020).

Theme 2

Justice and accountability

3 A tale of two international law principles

Ensuring justice and accountability for the Rohingya

Quazi Omar Foysal

Introduction

The International Court of Justice (ICJ), in its judgment of the *Armed Activities* (*Democratic Republic of Congo v. Rwanda*) case, highlighted the fact that the lack of jurisdiction of the international adjudicative bodies does not necessarily imply that there is no violation of obligations under international law.[1] The same is equally valid for other international judicial institutions, including the International Criminal Court (ICC). The consent-based international adjudicative system made the initial impression that the events of large-scale atrocity crimes and gross violation of human rights allegedly committed against the Rohingya are out of the ambit of both the ICC and the ICJ.

Several reasons contributed to this conjecture. First, Myanmar is not a Party to the Rome Statute of the International Criminal Court.[2] In addition, given the political allies of Myanmar, a United Nations Security Council (UNSC) resolution is highly unlikely. Second, though Myanmar did not make any optional clause declaration of the ICJ Statute, Bangladesh—the directly affected State following the Rohingya exodus—made a declaration for Article IX of the Convention on the Prevention and Punishment of the Crime of Genocide.[3] Moreover, the fact that the alleged violation of the Genocide Convention took place in the territory of Myanmar[4] rendered the possibility of an inter-State adjudication further challenging. At this juncture, the application of two principles of international law—the principle of objective territoriality at the ICC and the principle of obligation *erga omnes partes* at the ICJ—paved the way for ensuring accountability and justice on the international plane.

This chapter will first explain the concept of jurisdiction of international courts, focusing on the ICC and the ICJ. Then, it will shed light on the concept of the principle of objective territoriality, its application to the proceedings of the ICC, and the challenges of the application of the principle in future ICC proceedings. Moving to the next section, this chapter will elucidate the concept of the principle of *erga omnes partes*, its application to the Provisional Measures hearing of the ICJ, and the challenges of the application of the principle in future ICJ proceedings. This chapter will end with the general impact made by the application of the above-mentioned principles on the protection of the Rohingya.

DOI: 10.4324/9781003304883-6

Jurisdiction of international courts

The jurisdiction of international courts and tribunals is entirely dependent on the consent of the State in question.[5] As international governmental organizations, including international courts and tribunals, are the creation of the States, their powers and functions depend on their constituent instruments and to what extent the Member State accepts those jurisdictions over certain subject matters by compromising its sovereignty.[6]

The Rome Statute contains several jurisdictional aspects. These are (1) Jurisdiction *ratione temporis* or temporal jurisdiction, i.e., no offence committed before 1 July 2002 in general and the date when the Rome Statute entered for a State Party in particular;[7] (2) Jurisdiction *ratione personae* or personal jurisdiction, i.e., jurisdiction to try and prosecute a natural person who is a national of a State Party;[8] (3) Jurisdiction *ratione materiae* or subject-matter jurisdiction, i.e., jurisdiction over genocide, crimes against humanity (CAH), war crimes, the crime of aggression and offences against the administration of justice;[9] and (4) Jurisdiction *ratione loci* or territorial jurisdiction, i.e., territory of a State Party or of a State that accepted the jurisdiction of the Court on an *ad hoc* basis by lodging an application pursuant to Article 12(3) of the Rome Statute or where the Security Council authorised the investigation under Article 13(b) of the Rome Statute.[10]

The jurisdiction of the ICC is triggered in three ways: (1) State-Party Referral, i.e., where a State Party of the ICC refers any situation (including its own situation) to the ICC;[11] (2) Security Council Referral, i.e., where the UN Security Council refers a situation of a Non-Party to the Rome Statute to the ICC;[12] and (3) *Proprio Motu* investigation of the Prosecutor, i.e., where the Prosecutor of the ICC initiates the investigation on the basis of information on crimes within the jurisdiction of the Court.[13] Being a creation of a multilateral treaty, the jurisdictional ambit of the Rome Statute over crimes is extremely limited to the acceptance of the jurisdiction of the Court. Of the five principles of the jurisdiction of a State under international law,[14] the drafters of the Rome Statute in the Rome Conference in 1998 accepted only the principles of territoriality and active personality or nationality.[15] Currently, 123 States are Parties to the Rome Statute.[16] The list of non-Parties to the Rome Statute includes many populous and powerful States, including India, Russia, and the United States of America, and many States having serious allegations of commission of atrocity crimes, including Myanmar, Syria, and North Korea. The political nature of the UNSC referrals appears to be another limitation of ICC's extended jurisdictional reach. This limited count of the State Parties to the Rome Statute and the political nature of the UNSC referrals put the ICC in a challenging situation to exert its jurisdiction over many situations involving egregious crimes, including Myanmar.

The jurisdiction of the ICJ[17] is contingent upon, in addition to its membership, whether the State in question has accepted jurisdiction over a particular subject matter.[18] States confer consent to the jurisdiction of the ICJ in four different ways: (1) Special Agreement or *Compromis*, i.e., two or more disputant States refer their dispute to the Court by mutual agreement;[19] (2) Compromissory Clause, i.e., the provision of a treaty that provides the ICJ with the jurisdiction to adjudicate any dispute arising out of that treaty;[20] (3) *Forum Prorogatum*, i.e., when one State Party initiates an Application Instituting Proceedings without any jurisdictional basis and another State Party accepts it;[21] and (4) Optional Clause Declaration, i.e., when a State accepts the compulsory jurisdiction of the ICJ envisioned in Article 36(2) of the ICJ Statute.[22] In several instances, the existence of the jurisdiction of the Court was questioned. Generally, there can be no presumption on the existence or non-existence of the jurisdiction of the Court.[23] In the case of uncertainty, the Court may exercise its power, i.e., *la compétance de la compétance*, to settle its jurisdictional contour.[24] Nevertheless, fulfilment of the issue of jurisdiction gives rise to the question of standing. The competence to stand before the Court complements the issue of jurisdiction in a given case. Generally, injured States with appropriate jurisdiction are entitled to stand before the Court. Nevertheless, standing before the Court may extend beyond the traditional construction of injured States in certain cases.

The principle of objective territoriality

Conceptual framework and its development in international law

Among the principles of jurisdiction, territoriality is the most basic and prominent in international law.[25] If an action takes place wholly within a territory, the question of exercise of jurisdiction on behalf of the territorial State is undeniably absolute.[26] However, when a legal situation arises, having the nexus with several States, the exercise of jurisdiction based on territorial grounds appears to be the decisive factor.[27] In such situations, comparative criminal law offers ‘the constituent elements’ approach as a viable solution to determine the suitability of the application of this principle.[28] As per this approach, the territoriality principle may be applied if an essential element of crime occurs within the territory of a State.[29] This principle has also been accepted in international economic[30] and environmental law.[31] Though the rule of the territoriality principle is universally recognized, its exact contents have been constantly challenged by the lack of uniformity in the application of the general principles of law in different systems and the imperatives of sovereignty.[32] The increasing number of crimes with transborder elements is considered to be another challenging factor.[33] This contributed to the development of the subjective and objective aspects of the principle of territoriality.[34]

The conceptual distinction between subjective territoriality and objective territoriality first appeared in Moore’s Report on Extraterritorial Crime and the Cutting Case.[35] Harvard Draft Convention on Jurisdiction with Respect to Crime 1935 also upheld the distinction.[36] As mentioned earlier, the question of subjective and objective aspects of the principle of territoriality only arises in the context of cross-border crimes.[37] In those situations, the exact determination of jurisdiction depends on where different elements of a certain criminal activity are said to have taken place.[38] The subjective territoriality denotes 'to prosecute and punish for crimes commenced within the State but completed or consummated abroad'.[39] This proposition has been recognized beyond any controversy.

On the other hand, objective territoriality 'establishes the jurisdiction of the State to prosecute and punish for crime commenced without the State but consummated within its territory'.[40] In other words, when crimes were completed on a State's territory but commenced in another State's territory, the former State may exercise its jurisdiction upon that crime by applying the principle of objective territoriality.[41] Both principles are based on the 'constituent elements' approach,[42] contrasted with the 'effects' approach.[43] The latter approach gives rise to the 'effects doctrine'.[44] Many consider the 'effects doctrine' to be an extended form of the objective territoriality principle.[45] Evidently, this is more linked with the 'protection principle' than the objective territoriality.[46]

In the *Lotus case* decided by the Permanent Court of International Justice,[47] the principle of objective territoriality gets its endorsement in public international law.[48] The *Lotus case* does not identify the qualification of the constitutive elements of this principle, which were left to domestic or international legislation.[49] This principle has been incorporated in several international treaties enjoying wider ratifications and adopted in national legislation in different countries.[50] On 6 September 2018, the Pre-Trial Chamber I of the International Criminal Court (PTC I) upheld the principle in its Decision on the 'Prosecution's Request for a Ruling on Jurisdiction under Article 19(3) of the Statute' (Decision).[51] The following sub-section will deal with the application of the principle in the ICC.

Application in the Rohingya situation

As Myanmar was not a Party to the Rome Statute[52] and a UN Security Council referral was very unlikely,[53] the avenue for accountability for crimes allegedly committed against the Rohingya appeared to lead to a *cul-de-sac*. However, the Prosecutor's Request for a Ruling on Jurisdiction under Article 19(3) of the Statute (Prosecutor's Request) dated 9 April 2018 was a unique approach to ensure access to justice for the Rohingya before the ICC. In this innovative application, the Prosecutor requested the ICC to clarify its jurisdictional extent under Article 19(3) of the Rome Statute.[54] The Prosecutor's Request used the principle of objective territoriality to claim jurisdiction over the CAH of deportation (deportation) allegedly committed against the Rohingya.[55] To be precise, the Prosecutor's Request sought the exercise of jurisdiction based on the principle of objective territoriality only if crimes within its subject-matter jurisdiction contain elements that may fit within the framework of the principle of objective territoriality.

The Prosecutor's Request was based on two specific provisions of the Rome Statute, both relying on the principle of objective territoriality. The underlying object of the Prosecutor's Request was to have a judicial determination of the nature of deportation under Article 7(1)(d) of the Rome Statute and that of its territorial jurisdiction under Article 12(2)(a) of the Rome Statute. In factual terms, the then-Prosecutor intended to ascertain whether 'the Court has territorial jurisdiction when persons are deported from the territory of a State which is not a Party to the Statute [Myanmar] directly into the territory of a State which is a Party to the Statute [Bangladesh]'.[56]

First, it sought to clarify that 'deportation' under Article 7(1)(d) of the Rome Statute is a distinct crime from 'forcible transfer of population', which is only completed when the victim has been forced across an international border rather than within the country of origin. Article 7(1)(d) of the Rome Statute incorporates '[d]eportation or forcible transfer of population'. Though Article 7(2)(d) of the Rome Statute provides an explanation of '[d]eportation or forcible transfer of population', it leaves room for further clarification.[57] The corresponding part of the Elements of Crimes of the Rome Statute (EoC) provides further clarification.[58] In many cases, the EoC made separate sets of crimes for more than one crime contained in the same provision.[59] However, this was not the case for Article 7(1)(d) of the Rome Statute. The Prosecutor's Request asserted that 'deportation' and 'forcible transfer of population' are two separate crimes, and the former takes place where the forcibly displaced persons cross the international territory of their State of origin where the latter becomes complete within the State of origin of the displaced persons. In other words, the 'crossing of international frontier' is the defining element of deportation.[60] The Prosecutor's Request resorted to both judicial practice and academic commentaries to show the distinctiveness of deportation.[61] In particular, it provided three alternative interpretations of the Rome Statute: first, disjunctive nature of 'or' between 'deportation' and 'forcible transfer of population' throughout the Rome Statute;[62] and second, contextual reading of 'deportation' and 'forcible transfer',[63] and object and purpose of the Rome Statute.[64]

In response to the claims of the Prosecutor's Request, the PTC I upheld positively that 'Article 7(1)(d) of the Statute sets forth two separate crimes, namely deportation and forcible transfer'.[65] The PTC I reached the decision primarily on the basis of the ordinary meaning of 'or' between 'deportation' and 'forcible transfer of population' throughout the Rome Statute and its contextualization with the EoC.[66] It held that 'the displacement of persons lawfully residing in an area to another State amounts to deportation, whereas such displacement to a location within the borders of a State must be characterized as forcible transfer'.[67] The PTC I also gave weight to the teleological interpretation of the Rome Statute,[68] the case laws of different international criminal courts and tribunals,[69] and the jurisprudence of the ICC itself.[70] In addition, the PTC I upheld the rationale of CAH of deportation equally applies to (1) persecution linked with deportation and (2) other inhumane acts of a similar character that involve border crossing.[71] This pronouncement of the Chamber paves the way for the application of the principle of objective territoriality in appropriate instances.

The second assertion of the Prosecutor's Request relates to the interpretation of 'conduct in question' of Article 12(2)(a) of the Rome Statute in the context of territorial jurisdiction of the ICC.[72] The Prosecutor's Request sought the confirmation of the Chamber that the ICC may exercise its jurisdiction over a situation under Article 12(2)(a) where at least one legal element of a crime has occurred on the territory of a State Party. First, the Prosecutor's Request, having highlighted the practice of the ICC, deduced that the 'conduct' requirement denotes the commission of 'at least one legal element of an Article 5 crime' in the territorial jurisdiction of the Court.[73] It moved to contextualize the crime of deportation and claimed that 'when a person is deported directly into the territory of a second State ... the Court may exercise jurisdiction under Article 12(2)(a) either if the originating State is a State Party to the Court or if the receiving State is a State Party to the Court'.[74] Moving from the framework of the Rome Statute, the Prosecutor's Request resorted to general international law to justify its claim on the 'conduct' requirement.[75] It started with the conceptual dimensions of the principle of territoriality in international law[76] and the origin and development of the principle of objective territoriality in practice, particularly the *Lotus* case and Harvard Draft Convention.[77] It then showed that the principle of objective territoriality has gained a noticeable status in positive international law[78] and entered into domestic legislation of an overwhelming number of states.[79] The Prosecutor's Request took the aid of rules of treaty interpretation to clarify that the principle of the objective territory is inherent in the Rome Statute.[80]

In response to the propositions contended in the Prosecutor's Request, the PTC I took

> the view that acts of deportation initiated in a State not Party to the Statute (through expulsion or other coercive acts) and completed in a State Party to the Statute (by virtue of victims crossing the border to a State) fall within the parameters of article 12(2)(a) of the Rome Statute.[81]

It first made it clear that 'preconditions for the exercise of the Court's jurisdiction pursuant to Article 12(2)(a) of the Rome Statute are, as a minimum, fulfilled if at least one legal element of a crime within the jurisdiction of the Court or part of such a crime is committed on the territory of a State Party'.[82] It came to a conclusion on the basis of contextual interpretation of Article 12(2)(a) of the Rome Statute made with reference to general international law.[83] Moving to the teleological interpretation, the PTC I stated that the intention of the drafters of the Rome Statute was to allow the ICC to exercise its territorial jurisdiction over crimes in which a State Party would be permitted to exercise domestic jurisdiction over the same crimes, and a restrictive interpretation of Article 12(2)(a) of the Rome Statute would be contrary to the 'object and purpose' of the Rome Statute.[84] Subsequently, the Bangladesh/Myanmar Authorisation Decision, the Pre-Trial Chamber III of the ICC (PTC III) recognized the principle of objective territoriality, but from the viewpoint of customary international law.[85] In the Authorisation Decision, the PTC III went on to explore the relevant state practices and *opinio juris* relevant to the principle of objective territoriality and concluded that the principle in question exists in customary international law.[86] This formulation of the principle of objective territoriality as a norm of customary international law provides additional legal authority in the realm of International Criminal Law.

The challenges of the application of this principle

Though the confirmation of the principle of objective territoriality received a positive reception in the legal fraternity, it nonetheless attracted some criticisms regarding its applicability and its prospects.

First, the ICC has been criticized for its judicial incoherence and the question of legitimacy has been raised in several stances.[87] There is a general fear among international criminal law practitioners that the ICC may change its approach to the principle of territoriality in other cases.[88] The author argues that the principle of objective territoriality has already attained additional support within and beyond the ICC. The PTC III reconfirmed the principle of objective territoriality on a different ground in the Authorisation Decision.[89] The first full Report of the UN Independent International Fact-finding Mission on Myanmar (UNFFMM) relied on the principle of objective territory to interpret the crimes of deportation and persecution.[90] The above-mentioned confirmations appear to fill up the legitimacy incompleteness of the principle of objective territoriality.

Second, the confirmation of broader jurisdictional scope following the objective territoriality principle broached the question of whether the State Parties to the Rome Statute delegated the same to the ICC.[91] In particular, the negotiation of the aggression amendment to the Rome Statute may imply that acceptance of broader territorial jurisdiction would be contrary to the intention of the States. This issue invites two responses. First, the territorial dimension of the crime of aggression required re-negotiation since its jurisdictional feature was different from that of the rest of the crimes under the Rome Statute. Second, no State Party to the Rome Statute protested either the Prosecutor's Request or the Decision on the Prosecutor's Request.[92] If the decision were contrary to the position of State Parties to the Rome Statute in relation to the territorial principle, it would attract voluminous responses in the form of *amicus curiae* submissions from different States. The absence of any persistent objection from the State Parties may be construed in favour of the principle of objective territoriality.

Third, as the application of the principle of objective territoriality may involve any non-Party State (here, Myanmar), the co-operation of territorial governments is a crucial issue in investigating and prosecute alleged offences.[93] Though State co-operation of the forum State of the crime is crucial, it is not a panacea for the ICC. In most cases of active State cooperation, the crimes of the rebels have been seen as the focus of the activities of the Court.[94] It is always challenging to investigate crimes in a hostile State by the ICC. It is not only true for a Non-Party (e.g., Sudan); it is equally valid for a State Party (e.g., the Philippines). Nevertheless, this argument misses the incidental impact of an ICC investigation. The ICC investigation has impacts on the continuity of the atrocities. The Northern Uganda situation illustrates it well.[95] From a non-legal point of view, the luck of the tyrant leaders does not remain so throughout their lifespans.

Slobodan Milošević is a very handy example. Or who could imagine ten years ago that Omar al-Bashir would risk ending up in ICC detention one day?[96]

Fourth, in the situations of transboundary civilian displacement, there may be a temptation to use (or misuse) the principle of objective territoriality. It is feared that wholesale resort to this principle may do 'more harm than good to the credibility and legitimacy' of the ICC; thus, it invites the strict interpretation of the principle to preserve its legitimacy.[97] This assumption solidified when a group of lawyers filed an Article 15 Communication to the ICC on the crimes committed against Syrian civilians relying on the Bangladesh/Myanmar precedent.[98] As per the Report on Preliminary Examination Activities 2020 prepared by the Office of the Prosecutor (OTP), this issue is still under consideration.[99] Nonetheless, the Report expressed its caution by stating that the OTP will not look at crimes other than deportation and give due consideration to the gravity and the intention.[100] Relying on the principle of objective territoriality, several exiled Uighur leaders filed another Article 15 Communication regarding the crimes allegedly committed against Uyghurs in China having transboundary nature on 6 July 2020.[101] Eventually, the OTP declined to proceed with the investigation and stated that 'it does not appear that such conduct would amount to the crime against humanity of deportation under Article 7(1)(d) of the Statute within the jurisdiction of the Court'.[102] Hence, it appears that the ICC is already cautious about confronting any injudicious application of this principle in apparently similar situations.

Fifth, the principle of objective territoriality presents a challenge regarding the application of the Rome Statute to a non-Party.[103] In the present case, the ICC is not investigating the crimes committed in Myanmar but on the territory of Bangladesh.[104] It is unequivocally accepted that when a crime is adjudicated on the basis of territoriality, the nationality of the offender becomes irrelevant.[105] Thus, the delicate line between 'jurisdiction over the third State' and 'jurisdiction over nationals of the third State for crimes committed in its territory' should not be confused. Thus, the application of the principle of objective territoriality can hardly be discredited with reference to the principle of *pacta tertiis nec nocent nec prosunt*. If the Rome Statute were meant only to be applied within the limit of the State Party, there would be no provision conferring jurisdiction based on nationality. Moreover, the ability of the Non-Party State to challenge the admissibility of a case implies the ICC's applicability beyond the State Parties.[106]

Finally, the Government of Myanmar contended that, as a non-Party, it is not bound by the Rome Statute.[107] Myanmar's assertion invoked the question of legality. The international criminal tribunals since Nuremberg frequently encounter the principle of legality.[108] This principle is expressed in Latin as *nullum crimen sine lege,* which means nothing is a crime except as provided by the Rome Statute.[109] This principle has been adopted in the Rome Statute with a different construction.[110] However, the challenge of overcoming the question of legality can be debunked in two ways. First, the crimes against humanity as defined in Article 7 of the Rome Statute reflects customary international law.[111] Thus, the customary law may dismantle the legality question.[112] Therefore, the defence of legality may hardly find its position against the customary construction of the crime of deportation. Second, Article 22(1) of the Rome Statute can be interpreted to overcome the challenge of the legality principle. It says: 'A person shall not be criminally responsible under this Statute *unless the conduct in question constitutes, at the time it takes place, a crime within the jurisdiction of the Court*' (emphasis added). If we interpret 'crossing of the international border by the deported persons' as 'the conduct in question', the deportation is said to be within the jurisdiction of the Court. Therefore, the principle of legality cannot find a ground for a dispute in the current situation.

The principle of obligation *erga omnes partes*

Conceptual framework and its development in international law

In the traditional fabric of international law, the international obligations spanning from international treaties, whether bilateral or multilateral, are generally bilateral or *inter partes* in nature.[113] Furthermore, the international obligation springing from customary international law is also bilateral in nature.[114] The strict, bilateral nature of international law began to change in the first half of the twentieth century, giving rise to 'collective interest' or 'concerns of the international community as a whole' in international legal order.[115] The jurisprudence of the ICJ and the works of the International Law Commission (ILC) solidified the paradigm shift on the nature of international obligation, leading to the emergence of two comparable principles of international law, i.e., the principles of *erga omnes* and *erga omnes partes.*[116] For the convenience of conceptual clarity, both principles will be discussed together, although giving emphasis to the latter.

The principle of *erga omnes* was first introduced in the *Barcelona Traction* case.[117] The principle of obligation *erga omnes* was further reaffirmed by the Court on a number of occasions, especially in the *East Timor* case,[118] the *Wall* opinion,[119] and the *Chagos* opinion.[120] In the meantime, the work of ILC on the state responsibility provides an additional layer of authority to the principle of obligation *erga omnes.*[121] At the same time, the principle of obligation *erga omnes partes* developed out of the works of the ILC on state responsibility.[122] Article 48 of the Articles on the Responsibility of States for Internationally Wrongful Acts (ARSIWA) deals with the '[i]nvocation of responsibility by a State other than an injured State', as contrasted with Article 42 of ARSIWA that deals with '[i]nvocation of responsibility by an injured State'. Article 48(1) of ARSIWA defines obligation *erga omnes* and obligation *erga omnes partes* in two separate sub-paragraphs.[123] It states as follows:

> 1. Any State other than an injured State is entitled to invoke the responsibility of another State in accordance with paragraph 2 if:
>   (a) the obligation breached is owed to a group of States including that State, and is established for the protection of a collective interest of the group; or
>   (b) the obligation breached is owed to the international community as a whole.

Though the text of Article 48(1) does not provide any further indication, the ILC Commentary on ARSIWA clarifies that Article 48(1)(a) denotes obligation *erga omnes partes*[124] while Article 48(1)(b) denotes obligation *erga omnes*.[125] Institut de Droit International also took the issue of '[o]bligations and rights erga omnes in international law', and it adopted the Resolution on Obligations *Erga Omnes* in International Law in its 2005 Krakow Session.[126] Article 1 of the Resolution incorporated a broad understanding of obligation *erga omnes* and put obligation *erga omnes partes* within the same heading. It stipulates as follows:

> For the purposes of the present articles, an obligation *erga omnes* is:
>
> (a) an obligation under general international law that a State owes in any given case to the international community, in view of its common values and its concern for compliance, so that a breach of that obligation enables all States to take action; or
>
> (b) an obligation under a multilateral treaty that a State party to the treaty owes in any given case to all the other States parties to the same treaty, in view of their common values and concern for compliance, so that a breach of that obligation enables all these States to take action.[127]

The fundamental difference between the two principles is that the former derives its obligation from general international law, whereas the latter derives its authority from the treaty law regime. In the *Belgium v. Senegal* case, the ICJ confirmed the principle of obligation *erga omnes partes* in relation to the Convention against Torture and Other Cruel, Inhuman or Degrading Treatment or Punishment 1984 (UNCAT).[128] It held that:

> 68. … The States parties to the Convention have a common interest to ensure, in view of their shared values, that acts of torture are prevented and that, if they occur, their authors do not enjoy impunity … That common interest implies that the obligations in question are owed by any State party to all the other States parties to the Convention. All the States parties 'have a legal interest' in the protection of the rights involved … These obligations may be defined as 'obligations *erga omnes partes*' in the sense that each State party has an interest in compliance with them in any given case.

Furthermore, In the *Whaling in the Antarctic* case, although Australia did not base its claim on the principle of the *erga omnes partes*, the subject matter of the dispute was not bilateral in nature.[129] Though the Court did not explicitly mention the principle of *erga omnes partes* in its Judgment, the rationale employed by the Court implicitly confirmed the principle.[130] The ICJ also applied the principle of obligation *erga omnes partes* in *The Gambia v. Myanmar* (Provisional Measures Order) case on a *prima facie* basis in relation to the Genocide Convention.[131] The next sub-section of this chapter will scrutinize the issue.

The extension of the nature of the obligation to certain multilateral treaty regimes or customary international law also paves the way for the resort by third States to initiate international adjudication by broadening the concept of *locus standi* before the international courts.[132] This extended formulation of *locus standi* gives rise to the concept of '*actio popularis*' in international law.[133] With the obligation *erga omnes partes* being towards all the parties of a treaty, any breach of any obligation *erga omnes partes* contained in the treaty in question will entitle any State, in addition to the injured State, to invoke the international obligation of the defaulter State.[134] There is no need for the existence of 'special interest' owed to a litigating State that invokes the principle of obligation *erga omnes partes*,[135] while neither does the litigating State in question need to prove to be a 'specially affected' State to bring the dispute before the ICJ.[136] The development of the International Human Rights Law presents a potential opportunity for implementation through inter-State dispute settlement mechanisms following the infliction of serious human rights violations by a State on its own citizens.[137] This is primarily due to the fact that such violations take place in the territory of the deviant State involving its own citizens. At this juncture, the principle of obligation *erga omnes partes* becomes more relevant in cases involving human rights obligations.[138] International litigation stemming from the Genocide Convention and the UNCAT solidifies this assertion.

Application in The Gambia v. Myanmar case

Though many persons and institutions termed the atrocities against the Rohingya as genocide, the first report of the UNFFMM created momentum. After analysing the available evidence, the UNFFMM 'concludes, on reasonable grounds, that the factors allowing the inference of genocidal intent are present'.[139] It led to the possibility of bringing Myanmar before the ICJ for its state responsibility to prevent and punish the genocidal acts under the Compromissory clause of Article IX of the Genocide Convention.[140]

Though Myanmar was not a Party to the Rome Statute, it ratified the Genocide Convention on 14 March 1956 with no reservation or declaration to Article IX of the Convention.[141] Due to a declaration on Article IX of the Genocide Convention, Bangladesh, the most affected country following the Rohingya deportation, cannot bring a case before the ICJ.[142] Eventually, this resulted in The Gambia—a West African State 7000 miles away from Myanmar—filing an application before the ICJ against Myanmar to ensure accountability, relying on the principle of obligation *erga omnes partes*.[143] The Gambia filed an Application Instituting Proceedings on 11 November 2019 with a Request for Provisional Measures.[144] The Court has already delivered its Order Indicating Provisional Measures on 23 January 2020.[145] As of 20 March 2022, the ICJ heard the preliminary objections of Myanmar, and it is due to deliberate its Decision.[146]

The moment The Gambia moved to initiate the ICJ proceedings against Myanmar, the ICJ had already applied the *erga omnes partes* in the *Belgium v. Senegal* case, though in relation to CAT. In the Application Instituting

Proceedings, The Gambia claimed that 'the prohibition of genocide has the character of a peremptory norm and the obligations under the Convention are owed *erga omnes* and *erga omnes partes*'.[147] As regards the applicability of the principle of *erga omnes partes* to the Genocide Convention, it first referred to the *dicta* of the *Belgium v. Senegal* case and claimed that the same rationale applies to the Genocide Convention *mutatis mutandis*.[148] It further pledged that 'The Gambia also seeks to protect the *erga omnes partes* rights it has under the Convention, which mirror the *erga omnes* obligations of the Convention with which it is entitled to seek compliance'.[149]

The pleading of The Gambia in the Provisional Measures hearings also included arguments based on the principle of *erga omnes partes*. Myanmar did not contest the *erga omnes partes* character of the obligations of the Genocide Convention and The Gambia's entitlement of interest in the compliance of such obligations by Myanmar.[150] However, Myanmar contested that The Gambia should be 'specially affected' to invoke Myanmar's responsibility before the ICJ.[151] The Gambia responded that there is no need to provide such a 'special interest' to invoke such responsibility.[152] It further contended that 'if a special interest were required with respect to alleged breaches of obligations *erga omnes partes*, in many cases no State would be in a position to make a claim against the perpetrator of the wrongful act'.[153] The Court, recalling its Advisory Opinion on *Reservation to Genocide Convention*, concluded that 'all the States parties to the Genocide Convention have a common interest to ensure that acts of genocide are prevented' and such common interests 'implies that the obligations in question are owed by any State party to all the other States parties to the Convention'.[154] The Court then moved to find the similarities between the obligations under the Genocide Convention and those under CAT in the light of the *Belgium v. Senegal* case and concluded that 'any State party to the Genocide Convention, and not only a specially affected State, may invoke the responsibility of another State party with a view to ascertaining the alleged failure to comply with its obligations *erga omnes partes*'.[155]

The challenges of the application of this principle

Unlike the principle of objective territoriality, the principle of obligation *erga omnes partes* was an established principle in the international realm before the commencement of the ICJ proceedings. Instead, the actual challenge appears to be its application to the Genocide Convention. In addition, there are some challenges ancillary to its application to the present case.

First, Myanmar has argued about the requirement of 'special interest' or a 'specially affected' State. The ICJ did not deal with the obligation *erga omnes partes* of the Genocide Convention earlier. However, it has already declared the *erga omnes* character of the prohibition of genocide since the Barcelona Traction case.[156] Notably, in the *Belgium v. Senegal* case, Senegal pleaded that there is a requirement for the existence of a 'special interest' to bring a case under the UNCAT.[157] Nevertheless, the ICJ held that there is no such requirement.[158] The cardinal purpose of the obligation *erga omnes partes* is to enable the non-injured Parties to a treaty to invoke the responsibility of the non-compliant State Party without being specially affected. In the language of the ICJ, '[i]f a special interest were required for that purpose, in many cases no State would be in the position to make such a claim'.[159] Moreover, the ICJ has already upheld on *prima facie* basis that a litigating State relying on obligation *erga omnes partes* does not need to be a 'specially affected' State.[160] Unsurprisingly, Myanmar raised this issue in the Preliminary Objections hearing.[161] This issue is subject to ICJ's deliberation of the Preliminary Objections decision. It is implausible that the Court will depart from its earlier positions unless Myanmar shows that 'there is cause not to follow the reasoning and conclusions of earlier cases'.[162]

Second, the question of the nature of remedies is deemed to be a paramount challenge in an inter-State dispute based on the obligation *erga omnes partes*. In the Application Instituting Proceedings, The Gambia has four different remedies.[163] The nature of the remedies appears to be more than declaratory remedies. The jurisprudence and practice of the Court on the entitlement of the third State regarding the nature and extent of the remedies to be sought is as yet unsettled, and the present proceeding poses a novel question before the Court.[164] In the Provisional Measures hearing, Myanmar contested the customary law status of the provisions of Article 48(2), which entitles the third States to seek remedies on the basis of obligation *erga omnes partes*, asserting that it was *lex ferenda* at the time of its adoption by ILC.[165] Though the Court did not deal with this question during the deliberation of the Provisional Measures Order, this contention will lead to a heated debate in the subsequent stages of the proceedings. At this juncture, it remains to be seen how the Court, subject to the outcome of the Preliminary Objections of Myanmar, deals with the customary status of Article 48(2) of ARSIWA after the *Belgium v. Senegal* case and 20 years of development. The Court's determination on this contention may also impact the nature and extent of remedies sought by The Gambia.

Third, since the obligation *erga omnes partes* arises outside of a bilateral treaty transaction, the identification of a dispute appears to be very challenging. It can be partly explained by the fact that the Party invoking the obligation *erga omnes partes*, not being a directly interested and specially affected State, may not be involved with the subject matter from the very beginning.[166] In the Provisional Measures hearing, Myanmar strongly challenged the existence of a dispute between the Parties.[167] Though the Court ruled positively on the existence of dispute on a *prima facie* basis, the Court will need to address the issue in the Preliminary Objections stage on a higher standard of evidence.[168]

Fourth, when the subject matter of the dispute takes place in the territory of a non-cooperative disputant Party, the collection of evidence is always a challenge for the opposite Party. It is evident in *The Gambia v. Myanmar* case. In response to international reaction towards Myanmar's alleged atrocities against the Rohingya, Myanmar has not only denied the occurrence of such events but has also disallowed international investigating agencies, including UNFFMM.[169] Though The Gambia sought access to the territory of Myanmar for collecting evidence in its Provisional Measures Request, the Court did not entertain the request, stating that 'indication is necessary in the circumstances of the case'.[170] In the Provisional Measures hearing, The Gambia relied heavily on the reports of FFMM.[171] The evidence has been collected on 'reasonable grounds' that appeared to be compatible with the *prima facie* basis.[172] In the earlier cases, the ICJ accepted the 'beyond reasonable ground' as the standard for proving the crime of genocide.[173] In relation to the standard of proof, Judge Xue commented that '"the weight" of the UNFFMM reports "cannot be ignored"'.[174] Now, it remains to be seen how The Gambia and the ICJ will deal with the evidence at the subsequent stages of the proceedings.[175]

Finally, in a proceeding based on the obligation *erga omnes partes*, both applicants and potential intervening States are non-injured States, and consequently, the demarcating lines between the disputing States and intervening States become very blurred.[176] In *The Gambia v. Myanmar* case, the Maldives, the Netherlands, and Canada showed their intention to intervene.[177] In this case, the application of general rules for accepting (or rejecting) the intervening States would be challenging to apply. Moreover, the Court may encounter extra-legal considerations like the judicial economy.[178]

Conclusion

The Rohingya situation presents demonstrable challenges and opportunities to the realm of international law and international institutions. On the one hand, the consent-based fabric of international law and the restricted treaty obligations assumed by Myanmar advance the seemingly unassailable limits of the application of international law in the Rohingya crisis. On the other hand, the progressive interpretation of international law, coupled with the development of favourable principles of international law, provide armour in the arsenal of idealistic international lawyers to attack such legal hurdles with utmost success. The application of the principle of objective territoriality at the ICC and the principle of the obligation *erga omnes partes* demonstrate the humanizing tendency of international law departing from its positivistic character. Despite the theoretical and practical challenges of the application of these principles in their respective forums in the subsequent stages of proceedings, their immediate political impact on the protection of the Rohingya in Myanmar cannot be simply overlooked. Both the Bangladesh/Myanmar situation before the ICC and *The Gambia v. Myanmar* case before the ICJ are in their initial stages. But the prospects of the proceedings in ensuring accountability and justice for the crimes allegedly committed against the Rohingya remain crucial in the coming days. The application of these principles does not remain limited solely to the Rohingya situation. Rather, the Rohingya experience encourages international human rights lawyers to seek justice in situations with similar legal perplexities.[179] Hence, the successful application of the principle of objective territoriality and the principle of the obligation *erga omnes partes* in the Rohingya situation will certainly contribute to the protection of vulnerable communities elsewhere in the world.

Notes

1 *Armed Activities on the Territory of the Congo (New Application: 2002) (Democratic Republic of the Congo v. Rwanda)*, Jurisdiction and Admissibility, Judgment, ICJ Reports 2006, 6, §127. The ICJ took this approach in many other cases.
2 Rome Statute of the International Criminal Court (adopted 29 July 1998, entered into force 1 July 2002), 2187 UNTS 90 (Rome Statute).
3 Convention on the Prevention and Punishment of the Crime of Genocide (adopted 9 December 1948 and Entered into force 12 January 1951) 78 UNTS 277 (Genocide Convention). Bangladesh put the following Declaration:

> Article IX: For the submission of any dispute in terms of this article to the jurisdiction of the International Court of Justice, the consent of all Parties to the dispute will be required in each case.

4 Prosecutor's Response to the *Amici Curiae* and Alleged Victims Submissions (Office of the Prosecutor), ICC-RoC46(3)-01/18-33 (11 July 2018), §§35-40.
5 This is known as the principle of free choice of means. It is expressed in Latin as *ratione voluntatis.* This principle originated in the *Status of Eastern Carelia*, Advisory Opinion, PCIJ Ser. B, 1923, No. 5, 17. It was reaffirmed in the UN The Declaration on Principles of International Law concerning Friendly Relations and Co-operation among States in accordance with the Charter of the United Nations 1970 (The ICJ held in the *Military and Paramilitary Activities in and against Nicaragua (Nicaragua v. United States of America),* Merits, Judgment, ICJ Reports 1986, 14, §§ 191–193) that the said Declaration reflects customary international law).
6 Hugh Thirlway, *International Court of Justice* (OUP 2006), 35–38.
7 Rome Statute, Article 11. However, a State Party that became a Party to the Rome Statute after 1 July 2002 may lodge an application pursuant to Article 12(3) of the Rome Statute to accept the jurisdiction of the Court from 1 July 2002.
8 ibid, Articles 12(2)(b) and 25(1).
9 ibid, Articles 5 to 8bis and 70.
10 ibid, Article 12(2)(a).
11 ibid, Article 14.
12 ibid, Article 13(b).
13 ibid, Article 15.
14 Under international law, a State may exercise its jurisdiction on the basis of territoriality, nationality of the offenders or active nationality, nationality of the victims or passive nationality, protective principle, and universal jurisdiction. *See* Jan Klabbers, *International Law* (3rd edn, CUP 2020), 100–106.
15 William A Schabas, *An Introduction to International Criminal Court* (6th edn, CUP 2020), 51–58.
16 International Criminal Court, *The States Parties to the Rome Statute*, https://asp.icc-cpi.int/en_menus/asp/states%20parties/pages/the%20states%20parties%20to%20the%20rome%20statute.aspx (last accessed 29 September 2021).
17 This chapter only focuses on the contentious jurisdiction of the ICJ (the other being the advisory jurisdiction).
18 Switzerland, the Netherlands, Uruguay, the United Kingdom, Lithuania, Japan and Botswana, Handbook on Accepting the Jurisdiction of the International Court of Justice: Model Clauses and Templates, A/68/963 (19 August 2014), §23.
19 Yoshifumi Tanaka, *The Peaceful Settlement of International Disputes* (CUP 2018), 141–144.

20 ibid, 144.
21 ibid, 144–147.
22 ibid, 147.
23 Thirlway, *International Court of Justice*, 38-39.
24 The Statute of International Court of Justice, Article 36(6).
25 Cedric Ryngaert, *Jurisdiction in International Law* (2nd edn, OUP 2015), 49. The principle of territoriality is based on the assumption that '[S]tates can exercise authority over all acts that take place on their territory through legislation and prosecute all those who violate the laws in force on that territory'. *See* Klabbers, *International Law*, 101.
26 Michail Vagias, *The Territorial Jurisdiction of the International Criminal Court: Certain Contested Issues* (Bynkershoek Publishers 2011), 29.
27 Ryngaert, *Jurisdiction in International Law*, 49.
28 Cedric Ryngaert, 'Territorial Jurisdiction Over Cross-Frontier Offences: Revisiting a Classic Problem of International Criminal Law' (2009) 9 International Criminal Law Review 187.
29 ibid.
30 Cedric Ryngaert, *Jurisdiction over Antitrust Violations in International Law* (Intersentia 2008), 17.
31 Inter-American Court of Human Rights, Advisory Opinion on Environment and Human Rights Requested by the Republic of Colombia (2017) Oc-23/17.
32 Ryngaert, *Jurisdiction in International Law*, 50.
33 Michail Vagias, *The Territorial Jurisdiction of the International Criminal Court* (CUP 2014), 14.
34 ibid, 15.
35 John Bassett Moore, Report on Extraterritorial Crime and the Cutting Case (US Department of State, Government Printing Office 1887).
36 Harvard Law School, 'Draft Convention on Jurisdiction with Respect to Crime' (1935) 29 American Journal of International Law Supplement 439.
37 Ryngaert, *Jurisdiction in International Law*, 78.
38 Vagias, *The Territorial Jurisdiction of the International Criminal Court,* 10.
39 Harvard Draft Convention on Jurisdiction with Respect to Crime, 484.
40 ibid, 487–488.
41 Crawford commented that this principle is '[g]enerally accepted and often applied'. James Crawford, *Brownlie's Principles of Public International Law* (9th edn, CUP 2019), 442.
42 Vagias, *The Territorial Jurisdiction of the International Criminal Court,* 16.
43 Michael Akehurst, 'Jurisdiction in International Law' (1972–73) 46 British Year Book of International Law 145, 154.
44 Hein Wolswijk, '*Locus Delicti* and Criminal Jurisdiction' (1999) 66 Netherlands International Law Review 361, 366.
45 Vagias, *The Territorial Jurisdiction of the International Criminal Court,* 24.
46 Ryngaert, *Jurisdiction in International Law*, 49.
47 *The Case of the S.S. Lotus (France vs Turkey)*, Judgment, PCIJ Res Serial A, 1927, No. 10.
48 Vagias, *The Territorial Jurisdiction of the International Criminal Court,* 17.
49 Ibid.
50 As of 2018, more than 20 international and regional treaties, which have been ratified by more than 188 States, expressly recognize the principle of objective territoriality. At least 66 States have accepted the international obligation to exercise jurisdiction based on objective territoriality over serious crimes. *See Prosecution's Request for a Ruling on Jurisdiction under Article 19(3) of the Statute* (Office of the Prosecutor), ICC-RoC46(3)-01/18-1 (9 April 2018), §§37–42.

51 *Decision on the 'Prosecution's Request for a Ruling on Jurisdiction under Article 19(3) of the Statute'* (Pre-Trial Chamber I), ICC-RoC46(3)-01/18 (6 September 2018), §§72–73.

52 It did not even sign the Rome Statute of the ICC.

53 The UNFFMM recommended for the UN Security Council referral in its first report dated 18 September 2018 (A/HRC/39/CRP.2, §1691). Up until now, the UN Security Council has not taken any such measures. The People's Republic of China, one of the allies of the Myanmar Government at the UNSC, has been seen voting against the adoption of resolutions against Myanmar in the UN Human Rights Council and UN General Assembly. It is very likely that such proposals for the ICC referral will not see the light of day in the face of a potential veto of China. In one event, China vetoed the adoption of a joint statement after the ICJ Provisional Measures Order at the UN Security on 4 February 2020. *See* Al Jazeera, UN fails to take action on order against Myanmar on Rohingya (4 February 2020), https://www.aljazeera.com/news/2020/2/5/un-fails-to-take-action-on-order-against-myanmar-on-rohingya (last accessed 7 October 2021).

54 It was the first instance of such a type of application in the history of the ICC. *See* Michail Vagias, 'The Prosecutor's Request Concerning the Rohingya Deportation to Bangladesh: Certain Procedural Questions' (2018) 31 Leiden Journal of International Law 981. Subsequently, the Prosecutor also resorted to Article 19(3) application in relation to the Situation in the State of Palestine.

55 In this chapter, the deportation will denote CAH of deportation, not war crime of deportation, unless clearly mentioned.

56 Prosecutor's Request, §4.

57 Article 7(2)(d) of the Rome Statute states that:

> "Deportation or forcible transfer of population" means forced displacement of the persons concerned by expulsion or other coercive acts from the area in which they are lawfully present, without grounds permitted under international law.

58 International Criminal Court, Elements of Crimes (2011) ISBN No. 92-9227-232-2, 6–7. The relevant part is as follows:

> 1. The perpetrator deported or forcibly transferred, without grounds permitted under international law, one or more persons to another State or location, by expulsion or other coercive acts.
>
> …

59 For example: EoC made six sets of elements of crimes for Article 7(1)(g) of the Rome Statute.

60 Prosecutor's Request, §13.

61 The Request took the support of the case laws of the International Tribunal for the Former Yugoslavia and International Tribunal for Rwanda, the academic commentaries on the Rome Statute, the practice of different Chambers of the ICC to consider separate crimes out of the same provision of the Rome Statute, rules of treaty interpretation, and the case laws of the ICC to solidify its assertion. *See* ibid, §§15–26.

62 ibid, §§22–23.

63 ibid, §24.

64 ibid, §25.

65 Decision on Prosecutor's Request, §53.

66 ibid, §§54–55.

67 ibid.
68 ibid. §57. This approach is also known as 'object-and-purpose'-based interpretation.
69 ibid. §§59–60.
70 ibid. §58.
71 ibid. 74–78.
72 In French, it is 'L'État sur le territoire duquel le comportement en cause a eu lieu'.
73 Prosecutor's Request, §28.
74 ibid.
75 ibid. §30.
76 ibid. §§31–32.
77 ibid. §§33–34.
78 ibid. §37–39.
79 ibid. §§40–42.
80 The Prosecutor's Request sought to establish the proposition by using the 'ordinary meaning' based interpretation, contextual interpretation and "object-and-purpose" based interpretation of the Rome Statute. *See* ibid, §§3350.
81 Decision on Prosecutor's Request, §73.
82 ibid. §64.
83 ibid. §65. This position was further solidified with the references of national legislation and international legal instruments, and laws of both Myanmar and Bangladesh. *See* ibid, §§66–68.
84 ibid. §70.
85 *Decision Pursuant to Article 15 of the Rome Statute on the Authorisation of an Investigation into the Situation in the People's Republic of Bangladesh/Republic of the Union of Myanmar* (Pre-Trial Chamber III), ICC-01/19 (14 November 2019).
86 ibid. §§56–58.
87 Douglas Guilfoyle, 'Reforming the International Criminal Court: Is it Time for the Assembly of State Parties to be the adults in the room?,' EJIL:Talk blog (8 May 2019), https://www.ejiltalk.org/reforming-the-international-criminal-court-is-it-time-for-the-assembly-of-state-parties-to-be-the-adults-in-the-room/ (accessed 15 October 2021). The conflicting and inconsistent reasoning regarding the immunity of Omar al-Bashir is well known among international law practitioners. *See* Alexandre Skander Galand, 'A Hidden Reading of the ICC Appeals Chamber's Judgment in the Jordan Referral Re Al-Bashir,' EJIL: Talk blog, (6 June 2019), https://www.ejiltalk.org/a-hidden-reading-of-the-icc-appeals-chambers-judgment-in-the-jordan-referral-re-al-bashir/ (accessed 15 October 2021).
88 Douglas Guifoyle, 'The ICC pre-trial chamber decision on jurisdiction over the situation in Myanmar' (2019) 73 Australian Journal of International Affairs 2. In addition, Kevin Jon Heller made a similar comment in relation to the Palestine situation that may apply *mutatis mutandis* to the Bangladesh/Myanmar situation. He commented that the OTP should appeal to the Decision to Appels Chamber for further judicial ascertainment of the jurisdiction. *See* Kevin Jon Heller, 'The OTP Should Have Appealed the Palestine Decision,' OpinioJuris blog (4 March 2021), http://opiniojuris.org/2021/03/04/the-otp-should-have-appealed-the-palestine-decision-to-the-appeals-chamber/ (accessed 15 October 2021).
89 Decision on Authorisation of Bangladesh/Myanmar Situation, §§56–58. It is interesting to note that the PTC II consisted of a different set of judges than those of the PTC I that handed down the Decision on the Prosecutor's Request.

90 Report of the detailed findings of the Independent International Fact-Finding Mission on Myanmar (17 September 2018), A/HRC/39/CRP.2, §1488.
91 Guilfoyle, The ICC pre-trial chamber decision on jurisdiction over the situation in Myanmar, 3–5.
92 For an opposite scenario, *see* the reactions of a number of States in response to the Prosecutor's Request on the Jurisdiction over Palestine.
93 Guilfoyle, The ICC pre-trial chamber decision on jurisdiction over the situation in Myanmar, 2.
94 This is evident in cases of 'self-referrals'. *See* Schabas, *An Introduction to International Criminal Court,* 155.
95 William A Schabas, *An Introduction to International Criminal Court* (4th edn, CUP 2011), 41.
96 Abdi Latif Dahir, Sudan Inches Closer to Handing Over Ex-Dictator for Genocide Trial. *The New York Times*, 12 August 2021, https://www.nytimes.com/2021/08/12/world/africa/darfur-omar-al-bashir-sudan.html (last visited 15 March 2022).
97 Payam Akhavan, 'The Radically Routine Rohingya Case Territorial Jurisdiction and the Crime of Deportation under the ICC Statute' (2019) 17 Journal of International Criminal Justice 325, 343–344.
98 Ghuna Bdiwi, 'Forced displacement as a crime against humanity: Can the Rohingya criminal case at the ICC bring any justice to the Syrian refugees?' in James C Simeon (ed), *Serious International Crimes, Human Rights, and Forced Migration* (Routledge 2022).
99 Office of the Prosecutor, Report on Preliminary Examination Activities 2020 (14 December 2020), §35, https://www.icc-cpi.int/itemsDocuments/2020-PE/2020-pe-report-eng.pdf (last accessed 17 October 2021).
100 ibid, §69.
101 Dr. Ewelina U Ochab, 'International Criminal Court Will Not Take Further The Case Of The Uyghurs,' Forbes (15 December 2020), https://www.forbes.com/sites/ewelinaochab/2020/12/15/international-criminal-court-will-not-take-further-the-case-of-the-uyghurs/?sh=191cfbf42fe3 (accessed 17 October 2021).
102 Report on Preliminary Examination Activities 2020, §74.
103 It is well established in international law that a treaty does not bind any third State without its consent. *See* Vienna Convention of the Law of the Treaties (Adopted 23 May 1969 and entered into force 27 January 1980) 1155 UNTS 331, Article 34.
104 Akhavan termed the Decision on Prosecutor's Request as 'the routine exercise of territorial jurisdiction over transboundary crimes', though 'radical'. *See* Akhavan, The Radically Routine Rohingya Case Territorial Jurisdiction and the Crime of Deportation under the ICC Statute, 336.
105 Akande argued that the ICC might exercise its jurisdiction over the nationals of Non-Parties if the crime in question has been committed on the territory of a State Party. *See* Dapo Akande, 'The Jurisdiction of the International Criminal Court over Nationals of Non-Parties: Legal Basis and Limits' (2003) 1 Journal of International Criminal Justice 618.
106 *Amicus Curiae Observation on the 'Prosecution's Request for a Ruling on Jurisdiction under Article 19(3)'* (Canadian Partnership for International Justice), ICC-RoC46(3)-01/18 (18 June 2018), §22.
107 Nuri Aydin, 'Myanmar rejects jurisdiction of ICC for Rohingya Muslim Myanmar does not have to comply with ICC decisions on grounds it is not party to Rome Statute, says government,' *Anadolu Agency* (17 November 2019), https://www.aa.com.tr/en/asia-pacific/myanmar-rejects-jurisdiction-of-icc-for-rohingya-muslim/1648020 (accessed 17 October 2021).

108 Kenneth S Gallant, *The Principle of Legality in International and Comparative Criminal Law* (CUP 2009), 11.
109 ibid, 12.
110 Rome Statute, Article 22.
111 International Law Commission, First Report on Crimes against Humanity (4 May–5 June and 6 July–7 August 2015), Doc. A/CN.4/680, §122.
112 Mohamed Shahabuddeen, 'Does the Principle of Legality Stand in the Way of Progressive Development of Law?' (2004) 2 Journal of International Criminal Justice 1007.
113 Christian Dominicé, 'The international responsibility of states for breach of multilateral obligations' (1999) 10 European Journal of International Law 354.
114 ibid, 356-557.
115 Marco Longobardo 'The Standing of Indirectly Injured States in the Litigation of Community Interests before the ICJ: Lessons Learned and Future Implications in Light of *The Gambia v. Myanmar* and Beyond' International Community Law Review (published online ahead of print 2021), 6-7. In his Separate Opinion in the *South West Africa case (Ethiopia v. South Africa; Liberia v. South Africa)*, Preliminary Objections, Judgment (Separate Opinion of Judge Jessup), ICJ Report 1962, 319, 425, Judge Jessup quoted that '[o]ne type of illustration of this principle of international law is to be found in the right of a State to concern itself, on general humanitarian grounds, with atrocities affecting human beings in another country'.
116 Pok Yin Stephenson Chow, 'On *Erga Omnes Partes*' (2020) 52 Georgetown Journal of International Law 469, 480-493.
117 *Barcelona Traction, Light and Power Company, Limited (Belgium v. Spain)*, Judgement, ICJ Reports 1970, 3, §§34–35. The Court held that:

> 34 … In particular, an essential distinction should be drawn between the obligations of a State towards the international community as a whole, and those arising vis-à-vis another State in the field of diplomatic protection. By their very nature the former are the concern of all States. In view of the importance of the rights involved, all States can be held to have a legal interest in their protection; they are obligations *erga omnes*.
>
> 35 … Some of the corresponding rights of protection have entered into the body of general international law.

118 *East Timor (Portugal v. Australia)*, Judgment, ICJ Reports (1995), 90, §29.
119 *Legal Consequences of the Construction of a Wall in the Occupied Palestinian Territory*, Advisory Opinion, ICJ Reports 2004, 136, §155.
120 *Legal Consequences of the Separation of the Chagos Archipelago from Mauritius in 1965*, Advisory Opinion, I.C.J. Reports 2019, 95, §180.
121 Chow, On *Erga Omnes Partes*, 483–493. The provisions of ILC Articles on Responsibility of States for Internationally Wrongful Acts (ARSIWA) have been frequently cited by the ICJ and other international courts and tribunals as having the status of customary international law. For the details of the case laws, *see* A/62/62 (1 February 2007), A/62/62Add.1 (17 April 2007), A/65/76 (30 April 2010), and A/68/72 (20 April 2013).
122 Report of the International Law Commission on the work of its thirty-seventh session (6 May–26 July 1985), A/40/10, 25, 27 (§§25-27 of Commentary of Article 5), Third report on State responsibility, by Mr. James Crawford, Special Rapporteur, A/CN.4/507 and Add. 1–4 (15 March, 15 June, 10 and 18 July and 4 August 2000), 31-32; Report of the International Law Commission on the work of its fifty-third session, 126 (§6 of Commentary of Article 48).

123 James Crawford, *The International Law Commission's Articles on State Responsibility: Introduction, Text and Commentaries* (CUP 2002), 277-278.
124 Report of the International Law Commission on the work of its fifty-third session, 126 (§6 of Commentary of Article 48).
125 ibid, 127 (§8 of Commentary of Article 48).
126 Institut de Droit International, Krakow Session, Resolution of 27 August 2005. Giorgio Gaja was Rapporteur of the Resolution.
127 The language of Article 1 of the Resolution indicates that sub-paragraph (a) denotes obligation *erga omnes* and sub-paragraph (b) denotes obligation *erga omnes partes.*
128 *Questions relating to the Obligation to Prosecute or Extradite (Belgium v. Senegal)*, Judgment, ICJ Reports 2012, 422.
129 *Whaling in the Antarctic (Australia v. Japan: New Zealand intervening)*, Judgment, ICJ Reports 2014, 226, §40.
130 Yoshifumi Tanaka, 'Reflections on *Locus Standi* in Response to a Breach of Obligations *Erga Omnes Partes*: A Comparative Analysis of the *Whaling in the Antarctic* and *South China Sea* Cases' (2018) 17 The Law & Practice of International Courts and Tribunals 527.
131 *Application of the Convention on the Prevention and Punishment of the Crime of Genocide (The Gambia v. Myanmar)*, Provisional Measures, Order of 23 January 2020, I.C.J. Reports 2020, 3.
132 Giorgio Gaja, 'Standing: International Court of Justice' *Max Planck Encyclopedia of International Procedural Law*, Oxford Public International Law (2018), §§5-6.
133 William J Aceves, 'Actio Popularis—The Class Action in International Law' (2003) 2003 University of Chicago Legal Forum 353.
134 *Belgium v. Senegal,* §69.
135 ibid, §70. The Court held that 'there is no need for the Court to pronounce on whether Belgium also has a special interest with respect to Senegal's compliance with the relevant provisions of the Convention'.
136 *The Gambia v. Myanmar* (Provisional Measures), §41. The Court held that '[i]t follows that any State party to the Genocide Convention, and not only a specially affected State, may invoke the responsibility of another State party with a view to ascertaining the alleged failure to comply with its obligations *erga omnes partes*, and to bring that failure to an end'.
137 Evan J Criddle, 'Standing for Human Rights Abroad' (2015) 100 Cornell Law Review 269, 272–275.
138 ibid, 329–332.
139 First Report of the UN Independent International Fact-finding Mission on Myanmar (18 September 2018), A/HRC/39/CRP.2, §1441.
140 Many States have put a reservation on Article IX of the Genocide Convention. The conformity of such reservation was contested in the *Reservations to the Convention of Genocide*, Advisory Opinion, ICJ Reports 1951, p. 15. Article IX states that:

> Disputes between the Contracting Parties relating to the interpretation, application or fulfilment of the present Convention, including those relating to the responsibility of a State for genocide or for any of the other acts enumerated in article III, shall be submitted to the International Court of Justice at the request of any of the parties to the dispute.

141 Interestingly, Myanmar put a reservation on Article VIII, the only country to make such a reservation.
142 The Government of Bangladesh has not explicitly made such speculation. Rather, it cited the political consideration with relation to repatriation of the Rohingya for not following ICJ proceedings.

143 Mucahid Durmaz, 'Abubacarr Tambadou: the man taking on Myanmar's Aung San Suu Kyi,' *TRT World* (11 December 2019), https://www.trtworld.com/africa/abubacarr-tambadou-the-man-taking-on-myanmar-s-aung-san-suu-kyi-32096 (Accessed 27 October 2021).
144 *The Gambia v. Myanmar* (Application Instituting Proceedings and Request for Provisional Measures) (11 November 2019), https://www.icj-cij.org/public/files/case-related/178/178-20191111-APP-01-00-EN.pdf (Accessed 27 October 2021).
145 Quazi Omar Foysal, The Prospects of *The Gambia v. Myanmar* (Provisional Measures) in Protecting the Rohingyas, ILA Reporter (Australia Branch), 4 March 2020 <http://ilareporter.org.au/2020/03/the-prospects-of-the-gambia-v-myanmar-provisional-measures-in-protecting-the-rohingyas-quazi-omar-foysal/> (last accessed 14 March 2022).
146 Press Release No. 2022/5, *Application of the Convention on the Prevention and Punishment of the Crime of Genocide* (The Gambia v. Myanmar), *Conclusion of the public hearings on the preliminary objections raised by Myanmar; The Court to begin its deliberation*, International Court of Justice, 28 February 2022, https://www.icj-cij.org/public/files/case-related/178/178-20220228-PRE-01-00-EN.pdf (Last accessed 14 March 2022).
147 Application Instituting Proceedings, §20.
148 ibid, §§123–124.
149 ibid, §127.
150 *The Gambia v. Myanmar* (Provisional Measures Order), §39.
151 ibid.
152 ibid, §40.
153 ibid.
154 ibid, §41.
155 ibid. It is to be noted that the Court reached the conclusion on a prima *facie* basis. However, Judge Xue expressed her doubt about this conclusion and termed it as 'a sweeping conclusion'. She reasoned that 'it is one thing for each State party to the Convention against Torture to have an interest in compliance with the obligations *erga omnes partes* thereunder, and it is quite another to allow any State party to institute proceedings in the Court against another State party without any qualification on jurisdiction and admissibility'. The same consideration equally applies to the Genocide Convention, or any of the other human rights treaties. *See Application of the Convention on the Prevention and Punishment of the Crime of Genocide* (*The Gambia v. Myanmar*), Order of 23 January 2020 (Separate Opinion of Vice-President Xue), ICJ Reports 2020, 3, 34, §5.
156 *See* Longobardo, The Standing of Indirectly Injured States in the Litigation of Community Interests before the ICJ, 9.
157 *Belgium v. Senegal*, §66.
158 ibid, §70.
159 ibid, §69.
160 *The Gambia v. Myanmar* (Provisional Measures Order), §41.
161 *The Gambia v. Myanmar (Preliminary Objections Hearing),* 1st Round of Oral Observations of Myanmar (21 February 2022), Second Preliminary Objection, https://www.icj-cij.org/public/files/case-related/178/178-20220221-ORA-01-00-BI.pdf (Accessed 14 March 2022).
162 *Land and Maritime Boundary between Cameroon and Nigeria* (*Cameroon v. Nigeria*), Preliminary Objections, Judgment, ICJ Reports 1998, p. 275, §27.
163 *The Gambia v. Myanmar* (Application Instituting Proceedings and Request for Provisional Measures), §122.

164 Dimitrios Kourtis, 'The Rohingya Genocide Case: Who is Entitled to Claim Reparations?,' OpinioJuris (21 November 2019) http://opiniojuris.org/2019/11/21/the-rohingya-genocide-case-who-is-entitled-to-claim-reparations/ (Accessed 30 October 2021).

165 *The Gambia v. Myanmar (Provisional Measures Hearing)*, 2nd Round of Oral Observations of Myanmar (12 December 2021), §§13-14, https://www.icj-cij.org/public/files/case-related/178/178-20191212-ORA-02-00-BI.pdf (Accessed 30 October 2021).

166 In the *Belgium v. Senegal* case, the Belgian extradition request of Hissène Habré created much heat between Belgium and Senegal. Still, Senegal vehemently contested the existence of the dispute. See *Belgium v. Senegal*, §§43–55. Apparently, it would be much more challenging for those States who would assume such a dispute after the actual emergence of the subject matter of the dispute. This proposition can be illustrated by *The Gambia v. Myanmar*, where The Gambia decided to assume the dispute later than the actual emergence of the overall dispute.

167 *The Gambia v. Myanmar* (Provisional Measures Order), §23–24.

168 *The Gambia v. Myanmar (Preliminary Objections Hearing)*, 1st Round of Oral Observations of Myanmar, Fourth Preliminary Objection.

169 A/HRC/39/CRP.2, §24.

170 *The Gambia v. Myanmar (Provisional Measures Order)*, §62.

171 *The Gambia v. Myanmar* (Application Instituting Proceedings and Request for Provisional Measures), §§1015.

172 *The Gambia v. Myanmar (Provisional Measures Order)*, §56.

173 Andrea Gattini, 'Evidentiary Issues in the ICJ's Genocide Judgment' (2007) 5 Journal of International Criminal Justice 889.

174 *The Gambia v. Myanmar* (Provisional Measures Order) (Separate Opinion Of Vice-President Xue), 35–36, §9.

175 Michael A Becker, 'The Plight of the Rohingya: Genocide Allegations and Provisional Measures in *The Gambia v Myanmar* at the International Court of Justice' (2020) 21 Melbourne Journal of International Law 428, 442–443.

176 Priya Urs, 'Obligations *erga omnes* and the question of standing before the International Court of Justice' (2021) 34 Leiden Journal of International Law 505, 523.

177 ibid.

178 ibid.

179 For example, A group of Syrian lawyers submitted an Article 15 Application to the ICC relying on the principle of objective territoriality. On the other hand, the Netherlands is reported to have been preparing a case against Syria under the UNCAT on the basis of the principle of *erga omnes partes* (*See* The Netherlands holds Syria responsible for gross human rights violations, Government of the Netherlands (18 September 2020), https://www.government.nl/latest/news/2020/09/18/the-netherlands-holds-syria-responsible-for-gross-human-rights-violations (Accessed 14 March 2022).

4 Who speaks for the Rohingya?

Ideals and realities of intervention before the World Court

Brian McGarry[1]

The pending case between The Gambia and Myanmar at the International Court of Justice (ICJ, or the World Court) raises several conceptual and practical questions relating to third States, and illustrates the need to consider which form of action may best achieve their strategic aims with regard to ongoing cases. In September 2020, Canada and the Netherlands issued a public statement (the Joint Statement) indicating their intention to intervene in these proceedings.[2] The Joint Statement is ambiguous with regard to certain details which are key to understanding any such intervention's likelihood of success. As of 10 October 2022, neither State had formally filed an intervention in the case. By the same date, the Maldives had yet to file its own intervention following a similar public statement in February 2020.[3] Coinciding with the fifth anniversary of the Rohingya crisis in August 2022, Germany[4] and the United Kingdom[5] each issued statements expressing an intent to intervene in this case.

The present chapter treats the multilateral interest in this case as an opportunity to assess ICJ proceedings from a broader institutional perspective. This is particularly timely in light of a contemporaneous case which also invokes the Genocide Convention, *Ukraine v. Russia*, where many states have filed declarations of intervention.[6] Yet, in so doing, we must reconcile twenty-first-century principles of justice and accountability with twentieth-century limitations on access and participation before international courts and tribunals—and particularly the World Court.

This chapter first briefly recalls the factual and procedural history of the *Genocide* case between The Gambia and Myanmar and introduces the mechanics of third-State intervention in contentious cases before the Court. It next turns to the institution of contentious cases regarding community interests and the hypothesis of third-State intervention in such cases. After assessing the admissibility of third-State intervention in the *Genocide* case, it offers some strategic alternatives and concluding observations.

A brief factual and procedural history of *The Gambia v. Myanmar*

Since Myanmar's independence, the Rohingya have been subjected to cycles of persecution. The UN has characterized the Rohingya as 'the most persecuted

DOI: 10.4324/9781003304883-7

minority in the world'.[7] A 2018 report authored by UN investigators accused Myanmar's military of carrying out mass killings and rapes with 'genocidal intent'.[8] During decades of oppression and human rights violations by Myanmar authorities (especially during military rule), many Rohingya fled to Bangladesh and other parts of the world.[9] Rohingyas, as a stateless people, have thus been referred to as the 'new Palestinians'.[10]

Amidst the discussion of whether atrocities committed against the Rohingya qualify as genocide, two matters were lodged before international courts in November 2019.[11] In one of these, the International Criminal Court (ICC) authorized its Prosecutor to investigate alleged crimes against the Rohingya. Whereas Myanmar is not a signatory to the Rome Statute, the ICC based its jurisdiction in this matter on the membership of Bangladesh, the primary destination for Rohingyas fleeing persecution. This investigation has continued despite Myanmar's refusal to cooperate with the collection of evidence.[12]

The present chapter focuses on the other pending case matter arising from the persecution of the Rohingya: The Gambia's institution of ICJ proceedings against Myanmar under the 1948 Genocide Convention. In its January 2020 decision on The Gambia's request for provisional measures in this case, the ICJ ordered Myanmar to 'take effective measures to prevent the destruction and ensure the preservation of evidence',[13] and required Myanmar to submit a report to the Court every six months.[14]

As suggested in the Court's determination of its jurisdiction at the *prima facie* level in January 2020, the Court drew the same conclusion with binding force in July 2022 when resolving the Preliminary Objections which Myanmar has raised in this case. In its Order of Provisional Measures, the Court had not substantially elaborated upon the *locus standi* of The Gambia—i.e., its standing to institute a case in which it lacks a unique connection to the underlying facts or law.[15] Rather, it had simply confirmed that the obligations to prevent and punish genocide under the 1948 Convention are obligations *erga omnes partes*.[16] In its Judgment on Preliminary Objections, however, the Court formally confirmed The Gambia's standing to seek redress for breaches of obligations *erga omnes partes*.[17]

Importantly, the Court's analysis on this point does not necessarily have any bearing upon the ability of third States to participate in the proceedings. Before recalling the stated aims of Canada, the Netherlands, the Maldives, Germany, and the United Kingdom with regard to this case, it is thus necessary to briefly assess the rationale and mechanisms of intervention under the ICJ Statute, and the key limits and possibilities of intervention identified by the Court in practice.

Third-state intervention in contentious cases before the Court

Article 62 of the ICJ Statute provides that a State may request to intervene in a contentious case if it 'consider[s] that it has an interest of a legal nature which may be affected by the decision in the case.[18] Article 63 appears to confer a more definitive 'right to intervene' for multilateral treaty parties, whenever that treaty's 'construction [...] is in question'. These two provisions were modelled closely on the corresponding Articles of the PCIJ Statute.[19]

By inviting States to inform the interpretation of treaties to which they are parties, Article 63 is rooted in the consent-based origins of international arbitration. It is thus unsurprising to find clear antecedents for Article 63 in an 1875 Resolution of the *Institut de Droit International*,[20] the 1899[21] and 1907[22] conventions establishing the Permanent Court of Arbitration, and the 1907 draft convention[23] and 1910 draft protocol[24] of the International Prize Court. Article 62 of the PCIJ Statute, however, was largely an innovation of the 1920 Hague Committee of Jurists—and one produced under the presumption that the Statute would be an instrument of compulsory jurisdiction.[25] Orphaned from this rationale, Article 62 would become what the earliest commentary on World Court intervention envisioned as '*un monstre presque indéfinissable*' ('an almost indefinable monster').[26]

Some of this fluidity arises from the apparent overlap between Articles 62 and 63. According to its *travaux préparatoires*, the Hague Committee foresaw that an interest in treaty interpretation is also an 'interest of a legal nature'.[27] This overlap has manifested in practice since the first PCIJ case—where Poland's Article 63 intervention in *S.S. Wimbledon* was initially filed under Article 62[28]—and is also evident when interventions are filed under both provisions.[29]

The ICJ has further perplexed intervention by construing Article 62 as itself providing two distinct channels of participation. A State may intervene by meeting the express requirements of Article 62, but if it does so with a jurisdictional link to the parties—encompassing the subject-matter of the case—it can intervene as a full party in its own right.[30] This latter channel has been formally (and unsuccessfully) attempted only by Honduras in *Territorial and Maritime Dispute*.[31] Every State which has actually intervened in a case before the Court has therefore done so in the capacity of a non-party to the case—i.e., as a guest making written and oral submissions on a circumscribed set of issues.

The institution of contentious cases regarding community interests

We may now briefly turn to the concept of community interests, and the institution of cases on this basis, before considering whether this may be adapted as well to third-State participants in such proceedings. Despite being fairly well established in practice and confirmed in academic writings today, the concept of community interests arose in tension with the principle of State sovereignty as a structural foundation of public international law. One of the earliest references in international jurisprudence to the existence of community interests was stated by the ICJ in its Advisory Opinion on *Reservations to the Convention on the Prevention and Punishment of Crime of Genocide*. The Court stated that, under such a convention, 'the contracting parties do not have any interest of their own, they merely have one and all a common interest'.[32]

In the *South West Africa* cases, however, the Court rejected the claims of Ethiopia and Liberia by finding that these Applicants had not established any legal rights or interests in the subject-matter of the case.[33] As such, the Court in these cases did not identify any actionable rights or obligations borne out of common interest. Its 1966 Judgment has been unsurprisingly criticized for its narrow view on obligations owed to the international community as a whole.[34]

The ICJ has shown some reluctance to develop the concept of community interests in subsequent cases, such as *Nuclear Tests*.[35] In that case, Australia (one of the Applicants instituting proceedings) asserted the existence of an *erga omnes* obligation to refrain from atmospheric nuclear testing, which thus establishes a duty of every State towards every other State.[36] In its 1974 dismissal of those cases, however, the Court did not address this issue.

Such instances remind us that the concept of community interests is, to an extent, ill-fitting within the traditional confines of inter-State dispute settlement. Before such courts and tribunals, States commonly invoke the violation of only their uniquely held rights and interests. Because the judicial doctrine of *locus standi* has evolved in this context, it thus encourages counsel for applicant States (when possible) to fit multilateral disputes within the procedural straitjacket of bilateral adjudication.

In the *Barcelona Traction* case, the Court acknowledged in *obiter dicta* that 'in the view of the importance of the rights involved, all States can be held to have a legal interest in their protection, they are obligation *erga omnes*'.[37] The Court illustrated this point by noting that 'such obligations derive, for example, in contemporary international law, from the outlawing of acts of aggression, and genocide, as also from the principles and rules concerning the basic rights of the human person, including protection from slavery and racial discrimination'.[38] This, in turn, finds reflection in the Court's 2020 *Genocide* Order, which acknowledges that 'any state party of the convention may invoke the responsibility of another state party with a view to ascertaining the alleged failure to comply with its obligations *erga omnes partes* and to bring that failure to an end'.[39]

Contemporary scholars have tended to draw clearer links between the concept of community interests and the requirement of *locus standi* to institute judicial proceedings. Tams has found that 'all States can institute proceedings against States principally responsible for violation of obligations *erga omnes*',[40] and Crawford considered that the breach of a fundamental norm requires vindication through international adjudication.[41] In the same vein, Chinkin has recalled that while the bilateral model of international law still prevails, it is increasingly undermined by the expanding horizons of international law and the formation of new relationships between States and other participants. In her view, disputes arising from such developments cannot be satisfactorily resolved by formalistically applying the traditional norms of bilateral adjudication.[42]

Invoking notions of judicial propriety, Rosenne found that such developments 'must give rise to doubt whether a dispute settlement mechanism based on the single assumption that disputes exist only between two parties is adequate or even appropriate for modern needs'.[43] While the 'expansion in the employment of the multilateral treaty [led] to the doctrine of *erga omnes* obligations', he recalled that the bilateralism of ICJ adjudication had always contained a caveat: 'the intellectual exception of a dispute in which the construction of a multilateral treaty is in the issue'.[44]

As this exception is indeed expressly acknowledged in Article 63 of the ICJ Statute, it provides an appropriate juncture for distinguishing these doctrinal bases for an Applicant's standing to sue, on the one hand, from the statutory bases for a third State's capacity to intervene in respect of commonly held interests.

Third-State intervention in contentious cases regarding community interests

In exercising jurisdiction over the present case, the Court's July 2022 Judgment on Preliminary Objections followed a trajectory away from the characterization of *actio popularis* in *South West Africa*. Rather, its acceptance of *locus standi* on the basis of obligations *erga omnes partes* advances a natural evolution of case developments from *Barcelona Traction*, most notably the Court's 2012 Judgment in *Belgium v. Senegal*.[45] It is possible that the Court might characterize the same interest as sufficiently connected to Canada, the Netherlands, the Maldives, Germany, and the United Kingdom to admit intervention under Article 62, despite the absence of any parallel liberalization in the Court's intervention case law. Judge Cançado Trindade indeed encouraged intervention to 'contribute to the progressive development of international law [...] when matters of collective or common interest and collective guarantee are at stake'.[46]

Moreover, in his course at the Hague Academy on the protection of general interests in the international community, Judge Gaja observed that '[w]hatever "interest of a legal nature" is required in Article 62 [...], it cannot be higher than the one that justifies bringing a claim before the Court'.[47] He highlighted in this regard a 2005 resolution of the *Institut de Droit International* produced under his rapporteurship, which advocates that the ICJ 'should give a State to which an obligation *erga omnes* is owed the possibility to participate in proceedings pending' before it.[48]

However, the rubric of 'higher' and 'lower' degrees of interest fits awkwardly with Article 62's framing and practice. The reference to 'legal nature' therein concerns a *kind* of interest—informed by the Court's interpretation of this term—of which any observable degree is sufficient. In contrast, one can find an example of a *degree* of interest in the WTO Dispute Settlement Understanding, which permits intervention by WTO Members which possess a 'substantial' interest in the proceedings.[49]

Indeed, as Judge Gaja acknowledged in his course, intervention on the basis of obligations *erga omnes* amounts to a 'new form of participation' before the Court. The standing to institute new proceedings, and the statutory requirements for incidental proceedings, remain juridically distinct concepts with very different practical consequences.

As of 15 September 2022, the Court has admitted only 20% of Article 62 applications and roughly 29% of Article 63 declarations.[50] The Court's apparent reluctance towards intervention may suggest its concern that the terms of one intervention might 'open the floodgates' of mass participation in contentious cases. In the pending case of *Ukraine v. Russia*—where 41 States issued a Joint Statement precipitating several Article 63 declarations—the Court's decisions on intervention will provide a pivotal opportunity to demonstrate its stance on mass intervention.[51]

To admit *erga omnes partes* intervention under Article 62 by Canada, the Netherlands, the Maldives, Germany, the United Kingdom, or any other party to the Genocide Convention is to accept the challenges of judicial economy in disputes with dozens of participating States. It may also contribute to a potential loss of cases submitted to the Court by *compromis* (due to a perceived erosion of party autonomy in this forum), and a potential increase in respondent non-appearance in cases instituted under multilateral treaties. In this respect, the recent spate of Article 63 interventions declared in *Ukraine v. Russia* shows that States are more at ease with interpretation-based intervention.[52] The copious references in these declarations to each state's 'direct interest' in the case also demonstrate the capacity of Article 63 to assimilate the terms of Article 62.[53]

Admissibility of third-State intervention in *The Gambia v. Myanmar*

In this light, one may consider the suitability of intervention in the current *Genocide* proceedings. The aims of the Joint Statement of Canada and the Netherlands (and the public statements of the Maldives, Germany, and the United Kingdom) directly concern the merits of the case before the Court. The Joint Statement notes the wish of each State to 'assist with the complex legal issues that are expected to arise' and to 'pay special attention to crimes related to sexual and gender-based violence, including rape'.[54] Germany, on the other hand, reasoned its intention to intervene in support of The Gambia as upholding international law and strengthening it in the fight against human rights violations.[55] For its part, the United Kingdom focused on the instrumentalities of ethnic cleansing, including a 'campaign of sexual violence, grave violations against children, torture and village burnings'.[56]

As the simpler pathway for analyzing the prospects of intervention by these States, Article 63 in principle requires only that the Court is tasked with interpreting a convention to which these States are treaty parties. Yet the 'right to intervene' in Article 63 does not prevent the Court from dismissing a declaration of intervention as inadmissible. In *Nicaragua v. United States*, the Court deferred consideration of El Salvador's Article 63 intervention without a hearing and dismissed it upon deciding to apply customary international law (rather than the conventions raised in the application instituting proceedings).[57]

Although jurisdiction in that case derived from the parties' declarations pursuant to the 'Optional .Clause' of the ICJ Statute,[58] jurisdiction in the present case rests solely on the compromissory clause in Article IX of the Genocide

Convention. Therefore, if the Court asserts jurisdiction in the present case, it necessarily engages the 'right to intervene' under Article 63.

As of 15 September 2022, none of the five states which have expressed a desire to intervene in this case have referred in any public statements to a specific form of intervention. Yet, during the oral hearings on preliminary objections in this case, the Agent of The Gambia predicted the Article 63 intervention of both Canada and the Netherlands (with no reference to the Maldives or other States).[59] In this context, the Agent observed that '[j]ustice and accountability for those acts of genocide [alleged to have been committed by Myanmar] is necessary, a solemn obligation shared by The Gambia, every State party to the Genocide Convention, and the international community as a whole'.[60]

The Gambia's characterization of intervention as a universal 'obligation' rather than a voluntary mechanism was clearly hyperbolic. Its characterization of the 'necessary' function of intervention is at odds with the ICJ's finding that it is immaterial whether the participation of an intervener is useful 'or even necessary' to the Court.[61] Yet, by framing the interests of these third States as shared among all parties to the Genocide Convention, the Agent demonstrated precisely why their interventions may be dismissed if instead filed under Article 62.

Should Canada, the Netherlands, the Maldives, Germany, or the United Kingdom instead or additionally request to intervene under Article 62, they must persuade the Court that its decision in the case may affect each State's 'interest of a legal nature'. As noted above, the Court has imbued this vague phrase with some limitations which are relevant to the present case, and which are reflected in the Court's subsidiary procedural rules.

Under Article 81(2)(b) of the ICJ Rules of Court, an application to intervene under Article 62 of the Statute must set out 'the precise object of the intervention'.[62] In the first instance of a successful Article 62 application, *El Salvador/Honduras*, Nicaragua's stated object of intervention was to 'inform the Court of the nature of the legal rights of Nicaragua which are in issue in the dispute'.[63] This uniquely held interest is easy to see in disputes of a spatial character, such as in *Cameroon v. Nigeria*, where Equatorial Guinea successfully proffered a similarly phrased object of intervention.[64] Even in *Germany v. Italy* (the most recent instance of intervention admitted under Article 62), Greece possessed a unique legal interest in the proceedings, stemming from the central role of its judiciary in the case.[65]

This repeated formulation of the 'object of intervention', and the particularization of the 'interest of a legal nature' to the third State's uniquely held rights and obligations, is no accident. In its first Judgment dismissing an Article 62 application, *Libya/Tunisia*, the Court rejected Malta's stated objective to simply 'submit its views to the Court on the issues raised in the pending case'.[66]

The Article 62 intervener thus does not serve to inform the Court of legal areas to which it has no unique connection—a task reserved to the Court, as implied by the principle of *jura novit curia*. Nor does it serve to inform the Court of factual considerations, as the *amicus curiae* is an actor with no role in the

Court's contentious cases.[67] In this manner, the Court distinguishes the *sine qua non* character of an intervener from the informational role of an *amicus curiae.*

If Canada or the Netherlands formulate an Article 62 application according to the laudable aims of their Joint Statement—to 'assist with the complex legal issues that are expected to arise' and to 'pay special attention to crimes related to sexual and gender-based violence, including rape'[68]—it would thus ask the Court to step boldly away from the highly particularized expressions of legal interest in its Article 62 practice.

The Joint Statement implies a potentially distinct legal interest arising from the two States' 'obligation to support' the institution of proceedings under the Genocide Convention, 'which are of concern to all of humanity'.[69] Placed in historical context, however, it would be manifestly absurd to interpret a 1948 convention as obligating its 152 parties to intervene in an ICJ case—and more so in the absence of interventions in two closely watched cases instituted under the same treaty, *Bosnia and Herzegovina v. Serbia and Montenegro*[70] and *Croatia v. Serbia.*[71]

Although the ICJ routinely receives submissions from many States during its advisory proceedings, this kind of mass participation is somewhat alien to the Court's treatment of its judicial function in contentious cases. Because such proceedings concern live disputes between sovereigns, derive from consensual jurisdiction, and bind the parties with *res judicata* force, they are conducted with greater respect to principles such as party autonomy and the free choice of means embodied in Article 33 of the UN Charter.[72] *Ukraine v. Russia* may thus prove to be an inflection point that leads to greater multilateralization in contentious cases before the Court.

In this light, third States closely watching the proceedings between The Gambia and Myanmar must naturally evaluate legal actions on the basis of whether they are likely to not only succeed, but also achieve their interests in the case. For example, the breadth of Article IX of the Genocide Convention recalls that the treaty interpretation function of Article 63 of the Statute may be too narrow to accommodate intervention by States which wish to address clear violations of treaty rules.[73] If Canada, the Netherlands, the Maldives, Germany, or the United Kingdom can frame its interests as strictly concerning the 'construction of a convention', however, it would have little incentive to file for intervention under Article 62. The limited procedural rights given to non-parties under Articles 62 and 63 are essentially the same.

In terms of obligations, the Statute does mandate that 'the construction given by the judgment will be equally binding upon' Article 63 interveners. But as a practical matter, the Court's system of self-referential citation imbues its normative pronouncements with third-party effect, regardless of whether they are de jure binding, and despite the *res inter alios acta* safeguard suggested in Article 59 of the Statute. The very raison d'être of Article 63 presupposes this.

If intervening under Article 62 as a 'full party' to the case, however, Canada, the Netherlands, the Maldives and Germany would in principle have the right to appoint Judges ad hoc, to raise further incidental proceedings, and to participate in framing the scope of issues before the Court. Because the Genocide Convention serves as both a source of applicable law and a source of the Court's jurisdiction, each State possesses the additionally required jurisdictional link for this purpose.

Therefore, if these States meet the statutory requirements of Article 62 and wish to moreover become parties to the case, they will be entitled to do so. Pursuing that long-untested path, however, would substantially slow the justice they are seeking. Indeed, as Prof. Thirlway (the Court's former Principal Legal Secretary) wryly noted, 'the text [of Article 62] is by way of a blank cheque, to be filled in by the Court as and when applications might be made to it'.[74]

Although the expression by Canada and the Netherlands of a 'joint intention to intervene' underscores the absence of legal interests uniquely held by either State, it is worth noting as well that Canada and the Netherlands issued a 'call to all States Parties [...] to support The Gambia in its efforts to address these violations'.[75] The Maldives then confirmed that it 'has held consultations with The Gambia, in order to streamline efforts', and that it 'looks forward to similarly collaborating' with Canada and the Netherlands on their 'common objective'.[76]

If intervening as full parties to the case, this express support for one of the initial litigants would raise questions under Article 31(5) of the Statute ('Should there be several parties in the same interest, they shall, for the purpose of the [appointment of Judges ad hoc] be reckoned as one party only'). In the Court's practice, enforcing this rule has relied upon the mutual generosity of parties, such as the agreement of Denmark and the Netherlands to appoint a 'shared' Judge ad hoc in *North Sea Continental Shelf*.[77] Judge Owada underscored related questions of party equality in *Whaling in the Antarctic*, finding it 'regrettable' that joint media releases published by Australia (as the applicant) and New Zealand (as an Article 63 intervener) 'could be perceived as active collaboration in litigation strategy to use the Court's Statute and the Rules of Court for the purpose of promoting their *common interest*'.[78]

Strategic alternatives and concluding observations

Based on the foregoing analysis, States which are parties to the Genocide Convention will likely be admitted to intervene regarding the merits of the case between The Gambia and Myanmar under Article 63 of the ICJ Statute, but such States will be quite constrained in what they can seek to address through this channel. Although non-party intervention under Article 62 would permit the third State to inform the Court of a significantly broader range of interests, the Court's doctrine restrains it from admitting non-party intervention under Article 62 on the sole basis of collective interests or the fulfilment of obligations *erga omnes*. Yet the untested prospect of intervention as a 'full party' under Article 62 might provide a workaround of sorts, if the Court determines the admissibility of such interventions according to the same standard as the application instituting proceedings.

This assessment does not suggest, however, that intervention is the only (or best) channel for third States to exercise their interests in an ongoing judicial or quasi-judicial proceeding. Rather, as we have seen, the procedural difficulties apparent in the ICJ's contemporary intervention practice raise tactical hurdles which may persuade third States and their counsel to consider whether any alternative approaches would achieve their objectives in a dispute before the Court.

Firstly, Canada, the Netherlands, the Maldives, Germany, and the United Kingdom may each institute new ICJ cases against Myanmar, in keeping with Judge Crawford's observation in *Nuclear Disarmament* that 'a multilateral disagreement can crystallize for adjacent purposes as a series of individual disputes coming within the Statute'.[79] In accordance with Article 47 of its Rules, the Court may join these cases together (or join them to the present case) at its sole discretion. Although the Court has shown a willingness to join cases in the face of procedural difficulties—such as in the *Caribbean Sea and Pacific Ocean* and *Isla Portillos* cases, in which Costa Rica had appointed different Judges ad hoc in either case[80]—the ten *Use of Force* cases may suggest a reluctance to join higher numbers of proceedings, or simply a reluctance to do so when instituted by a common applicant (rather than against a common respondent).[81]

Secondly, the five States' indications of support for The Gambia recall that non-intervening States have remained free to collaborate with litigants 'behind the scenes' since the first ICJ case. In *Corfu Channel*, Yugoslavia (a non-party) made documents available to the Court by way of Albania's submissions.[82] Even without the acknowledgement of the Agent for The Gambia during hearings in the *Genocide* proceedings,[83] it could have been assumed that each of these third States had anticipated collaboration with The Gambia. Indeed, the Court affirmed in *Pulau Ligitan and Pulau Sipadan* that the prospective intervener will require such collaboration in order to obtain the parties' written pleadings while drafting its intervention filing.[84] In contrast to intervening, marshalling resources to directly assist The Gambia with the 'complex legal issues' outlined in the Joint Statement raises few concerns. Indeed, in its January 2020 Order, the Court showed little interest in 'the fact that The Gambia may have sought and obtained the support of other States or international organizations' in bringing the present case.[85]

This chapter has thus acknowledged that States which seek to amplify the voice of the Rohingya have opportunities to more directly serve this cause than through statutory intervention—a mechanism which is prone to failure, and which may substantially delay accountability and justice for victims. In particular, creative alternatives to intervention can avoid the Court's vexed distinction between community interests sufficient to institute a case, on the one hand, and the *lex specialis* 'interest' required to intervene under Article 62 in that case, on the other. Yet States can more robustly achieve these ends by seizing the present opportunity to build a new dispute settlement institution concerning stateless peoples. Recalling this chapter's analysis of intervention before the ICJ, the present author concludes that any such institution should provide for the multilateral settlement of disputes concerning obligations *erga omnes*.

Notes

1 Assistant Professor of Public International Law, Grotius Centre for International Legal Studies, Leiden University. The author wishes to thank the S.J. Visser Fund of Leiden University's Praesidium Libertatis I Foundation for its support of the *Tracing Inherent Powers* research program on judicial procedure, as well as Ms. Beril Sogut, PhD Candidate, University of Bristol, for her assistance during the preparation of this chapter. For further research on the points noted in this chapter, see generally Brian McGarry, *Intervening in International Justice: Third States before Courts and Tribunals* (CUP 2023).

2 'Joint Statement of Canada and The Kingdom of the Netherlands Regarding Intention to Intervene in The Gambia v. Myanmar Case at The International Court of Justice' (Government.nl, 2021), at <https://www.government.nl/documents/diplomatic-statements/2020/09/02/joint-statement-of-canada-and-the-kingdom-of-the-netherlands-regarding-intention-to-intervene-in-the-gambia-v.-myanmar-case-at-the-international-court-of-justice>.

3 'The Republic of Maldives to file declaration of intervention in support of the Rohingya people, at the International Court of Justice' (Foreign.gov.mv, 2020), at <https://www.foreign.gov.mv/index.php/en/mediacentre/news/5483-the-republic-of-maldives-to-file-declaration-of-intervention-in-support-of-the-rohingya-people,-at-the-international-court-of-justice>.

4 'Federal Foreign Office on the fifth anniversary of the attacks against Rohingya communities in Myanmar and the refugee crisis they triggered' (Auswaertiges-amt.de, 2022), at <https://www.auswaertiges-amt.de/en/newsroom/news/-/2548384>.

5 'Fifth anniversary of the Rohingya crisis in Myanmar: UK statement' (Gov.uk, 2022), at <https://www.gov.uk/government/news/uk-statement-on-the-5th-anniversary-of-the-rohingya-crisis>.

6 *Allegations of Genocide under the Convention on the Prevention and Punishment of the Crime of Genocide* (Ukraine v. Russian Federation).

7 Transcript of Secretary General's remarks at press encounter with President of the World Bank, Jim Yong Kim (New York: United Nations Secretary General, 2 July 2018), at <https://www.un.org/sg/en/content/sg/press-encounter/2018-07-02/transcript-secretary-general%E2%80%99s-remarks-press-encounter>.

8 'Myanmar Rohingya: What you need to know about the crisis' (BBC News, 23 January 2020), at <https://www.bbc.com/news/world-asia-41566561>.

9 Jatswan Sidhu, The Rohingya: Myanmar's Unwanted Minority, *European Yearbook of Minority Issues Online*, 18(1), p. 237, at <https://doi.org/10.1163/22116117_01801011>.

10 Craig Considine, 'The Rohingya Are the New Palestinians', Foreign Policy, 26 September 2017, at <https://foreignpolicy.com/2017/09/26/the-rohingya-are-the-new-palestinians/>.

11 Decision Pursuant to Article 15 of the Rome Statute on the Authorization of an Investigation into the Situation in the People's Republic of Bangladesh/Republic of the Union of Myanmar, 14 November 2019, at <https://www.icc-cpi.int/Pages/record.aspx?docNo=ICC-01/19-27>.

12 Priya Pillai, Myanmar Coup d'état – Implications for International Justice (Opinio Juris, 2021), at <http://opiniojuris.org/2021/02/11/myanmar-coup-detat-implications-for-international-justice/>.

13 *Application of the Convention on the Prevention and Punishment of the Crime of Genocide* (The Gambia v. Myanmar), Provisional Measures, Order of 23 January 2020, ICJ Reports 2020, p. 29, para. 81.

14 ibid., p. 29, para. 82.

15 See further Marko Milanovic, 'ICJ Indicates Provisional Measures in the Myanmar Genocide Case' (EJIL:Talk!, 2020), paras. 1, 4 (arguing that, even if The Gambia is found to possess standing in this case, its lack of connection to the underlying facts suggests that it would be unable to provide clear and convincing evidence of genocide).

16 *Genocide*, supra note 13, para. 41.

17 *Application of the Convention on the Prevention and Punishment of the Crime of Genocide* (The Gambia v. Myanmar), Preliminary Objections, 22 July 2022, Judgment, p. 38.

18 Statute of the International Court of Justice (San Francisco, 1945). As stated in Article 92 of the UN Charter, the Statute 'forms an integral part of the present Charter'.

19 Statute of the Permanent Court of International Justice (Geneva, 16 December 1920).

20 Institut de Droit International, 'Projet de règlement pour la procédure arbitrale internationale' (The Hague, 1875).

21 Convention for the Pacific Settlement of International Disputes (The Hague, 1899).

22 Convention for the Pacific Settlement of International Disputes (The Hague, 1907).

23 Convention relative to the Establishment of an International Prize Court (The Hague, 18 October 1907).

24 Additional Protocol to the Convention relative to the Establishment of an International Prize Court (The Hague, 19 September 1910).

25 See generally Institut fur Auslandisches Offentliches Recht und Volkerrecht, Statut et Règlement de la Cour permanente de Justice internationale: Elements d'interpretation (Carl Heymanns Verlag, Berlin 1934); O. Spiermann, 'Who Attempts Too Much Does Nothing Well': The 1920 Advisory Committee of Jurists and the Statute of the Permanent Court of International Justice' (2002). This spirit of innovation is notable as well in the Hague Advisory Committee's consideration of a proposed draft of Article 62 which would have provided the International Labour Organization with the capacity to request to intervene in certain contentious cases. See League of Nations, Permanent Court of International Justice, Documents concerning the action taken by the Council of the League of Nations under Article 14 of the Covenant and the adoption by the Assembly of the Statute of the Permanent Court, p. 80.

26 W.M. Farag, L'intervention devant la Cour Permamente de Justice Internationale (Articles 62 et 63 du Statut de la Cour) (Université de Paris, Faculté de droit et des sciences économiques 1927), p. 59. See reference and translation of the Registry of the Court in *Sovereignty over Pulau Ligitan and Pulau Sipadan* (Indonesia/Malaysia), Application for Permission to Intervene, Judgment, Separate Opinion of Judge Weeramantry, ICJ Reports 2001, p. 630, para 30.

27 See Documents concerning the action taken by the Council of the League of Nations under Article 14 of the Covenant and the adoption by the Assembly of the Statute of the Permanent Court, 45, 50.

28 *S.S. Wimbledon* (United Kingdom, France, Italy v. Germany), Judgment of 28 June 1923 (Question of Intervention by Poland), PCIJ Ser. A, No. 1 (1923), pp. 11, 15.

29 See, e.g., *Request for an Examination of the Situation in Accordance with Paragraph 63 of the Court's Judgment of 20 December 1974 in the* Nuclear Tests (New Zealand v. France) *Case*, Order of 22 November 1995, ICJ Reports 1995, p. 288.

30 *See Land, Island and Maritime Frontier Dispute* (El Salvador/Honduras), Application to Intervene, Order of 28 February 1990, ICJ Reports 1990, p. 3.

31 *Territorial and Maritime Dispute* (Nicaragua v. Colombia), Application for Permission to Intervene (Honduras), Judgment, ICJ Reports 2011, p. 420.
32 *Reservations to the Convention on Genocide*, Advisory Opinion, ICJ Reports 1951, p. 15.
33 *South West Africa* (Ethiopia v. South Africa; Liberia v. South Africa), Second Phase, Judgment, ICJ Reports 1966, p. 6.
34 Giorgio Gaja, 'Claims Concerning Obligations *Erga Omnes* in the Jurisprudence of the International Court of Justice', in *Global Justice, Human Rights and the Modernization of International Law* (Springer 2018), pp. 40.
35 See details in Yoshifumi Tanaka, 'Reflections on *Locus Standi* in Response to a Breach of Obligations *Erga Omnes Partes*: A Comparative Analysis of the Whaling in the Antarctic and South China Sea Cases', The Law and Practice of International Courts and Tribunals, vol. 17(3) (2018), p. 533.
36 Memorial on Jurisdiction and Admissibility Submitted by the Government of Australia, pp. 334–335, para. 448. See also, p. 331, para. 431.
37 *Barcelona Traction* (Belgium v. Spain), New Application, Judgment, ICJ Reports 1970, p. 3, para. 33.
38 ibid., para. 34.
39 *Genocide*, supra note 13, para. 41.
40 Christian Tams, *Enforcing Obligations Erga Omnes in International Law* (CUP 2005), p. 197.
41 James Crawford, *Chance, Order, Change: The Course of International Law* (Brill 2014), 270.
42 Christine Chinkin, *Third Parties in International Law* (OUP 1993), pp. 355–356.
43 Shabtai Rosenne, *The Law and Practice of the International Court, 1920–2005* (Martinus Nijhoff 2006), pp. 1596–97.
44 ibid. ('The conceptual underpinning of the Statute is that normally there are only two parties to a given legal dispute, with the intellectual exception of a dispute in which the construction of a multilateral treaty is in issue. That bilateral approach [...] was certainly appropriate in nineteenth-century arbitration—and indeed in all arbitration. But the unforeseen expansion in the employment of the multilateral treaty on the one hand itself leading to the doctrine of *erga omnes* obligations, and the ever-increasing complexity and multilateralization of international relations in general must give rise to doubt whether a dispute settlement mechanism based on the single assumption that disputes exist only between two parties is adequate or even appropriate for modern needs').
45 *Questions relating to the Obligation to Prosecute or Extradite* (Belgium v. Senegal), Provisional Measures, Order of 28 May 2009, ICJ Reports 2009, paras. 68–70.
46 See *Whaling in the Antarctic* (Australia v. Japan), Declaration of Intervention of New Zealand, Order of 6 February 2013, Separate Opinion of Judge Cançado Trindade, para 76 ('[I]ntervention in legal proceedings, by providing additional elements to the Court for its consideration and reasoning, can contribute to the progressive development of international law itself, especially when matters of collective or common interest and collective guarantee are at stake').
47 Giorgio Gaja, 'The Protection Of General Interests in the International Community General Course on Public International Law', *Collected Courses of the Hague Academy of International Law*, vol. 364 (2011).
48 *Annuaire de l'Institut de droit international*, Vol. 71-II (2006), p. 289.
49 Agreement Establishing the World Trade Organization, Annex 2, (Understanding on rules and procedures governing the settlement of disputes) (Marrakesh, 15 April 1994), Art. 10.

50 For a list of all attempted interventions before the Court, see ICJ, 'Contentious cases organized by incidental proceedings', at <https://www.icj-cij.org/en/cases-by-phase/intervention>.
51 See 'Ukraine's application against Russia before the International Court of Justice: joint statement' (Gov.uk, 2022), at <https://www.gov.uk/government/news/ukraine-joint-statement-on-ukraines-application-against-russia-before-the-international-court-of-justice>.
52 See further in ICJ Press Release, declaration of Romania, the UK, Germany and others, <https://www.icj-cij.org/en/case/182> accessed 15 September 2022.
53 Starting this trend, see Declaration of Intervention of Latvia, 19 July 2022, <https://www.icj-cij.org/public/files/case-related/182/182-20220719-WRI-01-00-EN.pdf>.
54 See *supra* note 2.
55 See *supra* note 4.
56 See *supra* note 5.
57 *Military and Paramilitary Activities in and against Nicaragua* (Nicaragua v. United States of America), Merits, Judgment, ICJ Reports 1986, p. 14, para 292.
58 Article 36(2).
59 *Application of the Convention on the Prevention and Punishment of the Crime of Genocide* (The Gambia v. Myanmar), Public Sitting, Verbatim Record 2022/2, 23 February 2022, ICJ Reports 2022, p. 11, para. 4.
60 ibid., pp. 10-11.
61 *Continental Shelf* (Libyan Arab Jamahiriya/Malta), Application to Intervene, Judgment, ICJ Reports 1984, p. 3, para. 40.
62 ICJ Rules of Court (1978).
63 *Land, Island and Maritime Frontier Dispute* (El Salvador/Honduras), Judgment, ICJ Reports 1992, p. 351.
64 *Land and Maritime Boundary between Cameroon and Nigeria* (Cameroon v. Nigeria; Equatorial Guinea intervening), Application to Intervene, Order of 21 October 1999, ICJ Reports 1999, p. 1029.
65 *Jurisdictional Immunities of the State* (Germany v. Italy), Application for Permission to Intervene, Order of 4 July 2011, ICJ Reports 2011, p. 494.
66 *Continental Shelf* (Tunisia/Libyan Arab Jamahiriya), Application to Intervene, Judgment, ICJ Reports 1981, p. 9.
67 See further *Continental Shelf* (Libyan Arab Jamahiriya/Malta), Application to Intervene, Judgment, ICJ Reports 1984, p. 3, para 40.
68 Joint Statement, *supra* note 2.
69 ibid.
70 *Application of the Convention on the Prevention and Punishment of the Crime of Genocide* (Croatia v. Serbia), Judgment, ICJ Reports 2015, p. 3.
71 *Application of the Convention on the Prevention and Punishment of the Crime of Genocide* (Bosnia and Herzegovina v. Serbia and Montenegro), Judgment, ICJ Reports 2007, p. 43.
72 Charter of the United Nations (San Francisco, 26 June 1945).
73 Article 63 may be more fruitful in regards to 'non-violation' claims, however, as seen in the wave of interventions filed in *Ukraine v. Russia* since July 2022. On the potential challenges of using Article 62 in such cases, see further Brian McGarry, 'Mass Intervention?: The Joint Statement of 41 States on Ukraine v. Russia' EJIL:Talk!, 30 May 2022, <https://www.ejiltalk.org/mass-intervention-the-joint-statement-of-41-states-on-ukraine-v-russia/> (recalling that, in *Ukraine v. Russia*, 'Ukraine requests the Court to find that Ukraine itself has *not* breached the Genocide Convention. Here, the question is not whether states have an Article 62 "interest" in seeking accountability for breaches of obligations

erga omnes, but rather whether they have such an interest in refuting the existence of these breaches').

74 Hugh Thirlway, 'Injured and Non-Injured States before the International Court of Justice', in M. Ragazzi (ed), *International Responsibility Today* (Brill 2005), p. 311.

75 Joint Statement, *supra* note 2.

76 'Maldives welcomes the joint statement by Canada and the Kingdom of the Netherlands announcing their intention to intervene in *The Gambia v. Myanmar* case at the International Court of Justice' (Gov.mv 2020), at <https://www.gov.mv/en/news-and-communications/maldives-welcomes-the-joint-statement-by-canada-and-the-kingdom-of-the-netherlands-announcing-their-intention-to-intervene-in-the-gambia-v-myanmar-case-at-the-international-court-of-justice>.

77 *North Sea Continental Shelf* (Federal Republic of Germany/Denmark; Federal Republic of Germany/the Netherlands), Judgment, ICJ Reports 1969, p. 3.

78 *Whaling in the Antarctic* (Australia v. Japan: New Zealand intervening), Declaration of Judge Owada, ICJ Reports 2013, p. 13, para. 5 [emphasis in original].

79 Obligations concerning *Negotiations relating to Cessation of the Nuclear Arms Race and to Nuclear Disarmament* (Marshall Islands v. United Kingdom), Preliminary Objections, Dissenting Opinion of Judge Crawford, ICJ Reports 2016, p. 1093, para 22 (relying on the Judgment on Preliminary Objections in South West Africa to assert that 'a multilateral disagreement can crystallize for adjacent purposes as a series of individual disputes coming within the Statute'). For Judge Crawford's views on this issue prior to joining the bench, see further J. Crawford, 'The International Court of Justice, Judicial Administration and the Rule of Law', in D. Bowett et al (eds), *The International Court of Justice: Process, Practice and Procedure* (British Institute of International and Comparative Law 1997), pp. 112, 116 ('In some cases, it is entirely appropriate to narrow down the dispute and to see the core issue as a bilateral one, notwithstanding that it may have multilateral ramifications. But in other cases, it may simply belie the character of the dispute').

80 *Maritime Delimitation in the Caribbean Sea and the Pacific Ocean* (Costa Rica v. Nicaragua) and *Land Boundary in the Northern Part of Isla Portillos* (Costa Rica v. Nicaragua), Judgment, ICJ Reports 2018, p. 139.

81 *Legality of Use of Force* (Serbia and Montenegro v. Belgium), Preliminary Objections, Judgment, ICJ Reports 2004, p. 279.

82 *Corfu Channel* (United Kingdom v. Albania), Merits, Judgment of April 9, 1949, ICJ Reports 1949, p. 4, 17.

83 *Application of the Convention on the Prevention and Punishment of the Crime of Genocide* (The Gambia v. Myanmar), Public Sitting, Verbatim Record 2022/2, 23 February 2022, ICJ Reports 2022, p. 11, para. 4.

84 *Sovereignty over Pulau Ligitan and Pulau Sipadan* (Indonesia/Malaysia), Application for Permission to Intervene, Judgment, ICJ Reports 2001, p. 575.

85 See *supra* note 13, para. 25.

5 Racialized denationalization as apartheid

Michelle Foster and Jade Roberts[1]

Introduction

In examining accountability for the Rohingya, much attention has been paid to cross-border movement and the concomitant severe human rights violations associated with forced deportation.[2] In this chapter, we adopt a distinct focus, namely the 'internalization' of the border, characterized by the deprivation of nationality on racialized grounds. As Ayelet Shachar persuasively argues, we can no longer understand borders only by reference to the 'static territorial border'; rather the 'surge of invisible borders'[3] means that the border can and does shift, at times 'penetrat[ing] into the interior'.[4] We consider the shift inwards, specifically in the form of nationality laws as a method of not only controlling migration but *manufacturing foreigners* by transforming citizens into non-citizens through a process of denationalization.[5]

Denationalization has attracted much interest recently from scholars and activists, primarily in the context of 'citizen-stripping' as a security measure. In contrast to that context, which generally applies to individuals, this chapter considers the mass denationalization of whole populations based on race and/or intersectional grounds of race/ethnicity/religion. This phenomenon is not new. As Matthew Gibney highlights, denationalization 'has a dark history, reflecting, in particular, the widespread use of the power by the Nazis in their campaigns of racial exclusion and extermination of the Jews and other minority groups'.[6] Describing widespread denationalization practices during World War II as 'frantic',[7] Gibney observes that 'within thirty years, denationalization had largely disappeared across Western states',[8] in large part because 'the use of mass denationalization by the Soviets in the 1920s and the overtly racist citizenship practices of the Nazis and the Axis countries in the 1930s and 1940s brought denationalization into disrepute.'[9] Yet he notes that, whereas the recent turn to citizenship stripping as a security measure renders 'denationalization's retreat' short lived, he views the revival 'as both widespread and modest'.[10] This is indeed true of the denationalization policies adopted primarily in states of the Global North in response to the phenomenon of so-called 'foreign fighters' and terrorists. Such policies, which in practice have been applied individually to relatively few, have attracted significant attention from scholars[11] and advocates.[12]

DOI: 10.4324/9781003304883-8

Yet the practice of widespread mass denationalization has arguably never witnessed a retreat. Indeed, prominent examples can be traced from the end of WWII and include apartheid South Africa, Bhutan's denationalization of the Lhotshampas, which led to the 'dispossession and banishment of various categories of Lhotshampa citizens';[13] the denationalization of tens of thousands of Ethiopian citizens with Eritrean heritage;[14] the denationalization of citizens of Haitian descent in the Dominican Republic;[15] and, most recently, the millions of Bengali Muslims at risk of statelessness in Assam, India.[16] In this chapter, we focus on the denationalization of the Rohingya and consider whether such denationalization could constitute the crime of apartheid.

In our view, insufficient attention has been paid to denationalization as harm in and of itself.[17] For instance, although the severe persecution and forcible deportation of the Rohingya from Myanmar in 2014 and 2017 has recently been widely condemned by the international community,[18] very little attention was directed in the first instance to the racially discriminatory denationalization of the Rohingya that is a root cause of the predicament.[19] This begs the question—why are states able to pursue such policies? Is there something about citizenship that makes it impervious, or at least resistant, to critique, because the formulation and implementation of nationality laws is considered the ultimate sovereign act? In this way, does nationality law operate as another kind of border, that which keeps out international law? By failing to squarely assess accountability for racialized deprivation of citizenship, we risk allowing the issues to be obfuscated by states' rhetoric, which tends to engage notions of sovereign rights to regulate non-citizens, migrants, or foreigners by reference to ideas of 'influx', 'public order', and security. Analyzing these issues as implicating international criminal law, and in particular the crime of apartheid, may provide a clarity that can expose this flawed reasoning and ensure that attention is paid to what is often the first crucial step in a campaign of crimes against humanity.

In the next part, we reflect on apartheid as a 'forgotten crime', before turning to an assessment of Myanmar's treatment of the Rohingya as apartheid. We then explore the challenges of ensuring accountability for apartheid before discussing the consequences and significance of this analysis.

Apartheid: The forgotten crime

John Dugard and John Reynolds acknowledge that apartheid 'is a loaded term, saturated with history and emotion'.[20] They observe that it 'conjures up images and memories of discrimination, oppression, and brutality; indulgence, privilege, and pretension; racism, resistance, and, ultimately, emancipation. All of [which] come to us … through the history of apartheid in South Africa'.[21] As they note, although prohibited and criminalized by international law in response to the situation in southern Africa, 'the concept of apartheid was never given enormous attention by international lawyers'.[22]

What has apartheid got to do with racialized deprivation of nationality? For a start, the connection between denationalization and international criminal law is hardly novel. It has been argued in the context of German Jews that the deprivation of citizenship was more important 'in sealing their fate than the Nuremberg Laws'.[23] As Cóman Kenny reminds us, the International Military Tribunal at Nuremberg, which tried major political and military leaders, 'held that the discriminatory laws restricting the rights of citizenship amounted to the crime of persecution'.[24]

Turning specifically to apartheid, the International Convention on the Suppression and Punishment of the Crime of Apartheid ('Apartheid Convention')[25]—which, as Christopher Gevers observes at the time had been signed by 'over half the states in the world'[26]—defined 'the crime of apartheid' in Article 2 as including 'similar policies and practices of racial segregation and discrimination as practised in southern Africa' and 'shall apply to the following inhuman acts committed for the purpose of establishing and maintaining domination by one racial group of persons over any other racial group of persons and systematically oppressing them'. This list included:[27]

> (c) Any legislative measures and other measures calculated to prevent a racial group or groups from participation in the political, social, economic, and cultural life of the country and the deliberate creation of conditions preventing the full development of such a group or groups, in particular by denying to members of a racial group or groups basic human rights and freedoms, including the right to work, the right to form recognized trade unions, the right to education, the right to leave and to return to their country, *the right to a nationality.*

There is little discussion in the drafting history of the Apartheid Convention to shed light on the inclusion of denial of the right to nationality; yet it is an unsurprising addition when we consider the centrality of denationalization to the apartheid regime in southern Africa. Writing nearly forty years ago, the esteemed jurist John Dugard wrote of the South African policy of racialized denationalization that the 'new aliens'—as he called the millions of South Africans deprived of their South African nationality—'have lost all claims to participate in the political life of South Africa even if they qualify to reside within the borders of South Africa itself'.[28] He called for an advisory opinion from the International Court of Justice (ICJ) specifically on denationalization as apartheid on the basis that, having created aliens within the borders of South Africa by denationalizing the Black population, the government then claimed that international law justified their treatment as non-citizens. In the words of Dugard: 'the new degradation to which Blacks in South Africa are subjected is perpetrated in the name of international law, behind the fig leaf of nationality'.[29] In our view, this analysis could be applied to many contemporary situations, including the situation of the Rohingya vis-à-vis the government of Myanmar.

These days, the Rome Statute is the source of authority for defining international crimes and, in that statute, apartheid is listed in Article 7(1) as a 'crime against humanity'. The International Law Commission's 1996 Draft Code did not use the term apartheid but included the following in the list of crimes against humanity: '[i]nstitutionalized discrimination on racial, ethnic, or religious grounds, involving the violation of fundamental human rights and freedoms and resulting in seriously disadvantaging a part of the population'.[30] It was not until the United Nations Diplomatic Conference of Plenipotentiaries on the Establishment of an International Criminal Court was convened in 1998 that explicit reference to apartheid was considered.[31] Following interventions from the representatives of several states, the Chairman summarized the discussion by noting that '[i]t had been suggested that the crime of apartheid should be added to the list' of crimes of humanity.[32] On 22 June 1998, representatives from Bangladesh, India, Lesotho, Malawi, Mexico, Namibia, South Africa, Swaziland, Trinidad and Tobago, and the United Republic of Tanzania submitted a proposal concerning the then Article 5, in order to include apartheid.[33] In the Discussion Paper submitted by the Bureau on 6 July 1998 for the Conference, 'the crime of apartheid' appeared in the revised draft, using the definition that was ultimately adopted.[34] The formal proposal submitted by the Bureau on 10 July 1998 also contained these additions,[35] which were added 'without opposition'.[36] There was little discussion of the substance of the definition, but noteworthy is the fact that those states that intervened in favour of its inclusion spoke in very broad terms of its importance; there was no suggestion that its relevance was confined to South Africa.

Yet apartheid has been rather 'forgotten'. The crime against humanity of apartheid has not been charged at the International Criminal Court (ICC).[37] There has been resistance to its application to other contexts, for example to Israel,[38] on the bases that it is a *sui generis* crime (only applying to South Africa); that apartheid in South Africa was overt (while other situations are not as openly discriminatory); and potentially resistance based on the perceived emotiveness of the term apartheid.[39]

None of these reasons are persuasive; on the contrary, the time is ripe for a detailed analysis of the relevance of the crime of apartheid to racialized deprivation of nationality.

Apartheid was ultimately included in the Rome Statute in Article 7(1)(j), with a definition contained in Article 7(2)(h) as follows:

> inhumane acts of a character similar to those referred to in paragraph 1, committed in the context of an institutionalized regime of systematic oppression and domination by one racial group over any other racial group or groups and committed with the intention of maintaining that regime.

Note also the chapeau elements of crimes against humanity in Article 7(1): 'committed as part of widespread or systematic attack against any civilian population, with knowledge of the attack'.

The inhumane acts referred to in paragraph 1 include '[o]ther inhumane acts of a similar character, intentionally causing great suffering, or serious injury to body or to mental or physical health'.[40] There is an element of circularity in this definition, but noteworthy is the reference to 'great suffering' and 'mental or physical health' in Article 7(1)(k), leaving open the possibility that deeply degrading, legislative measures such as those outlined in the Apartheid Convention, including deprivation of nationality, could certainly fall within this definition.[41]

Although to date there has been no mention of the deprivation of nationality as a stand-alone violation in the ongoing investigation by the International Criminal Court, the concept of apartheid has been invoked in relation to the treatment of the Rohingya in other contexts, although often in global terms and not confined to the denationalization element.[42] Yet the Independent International Fact-Finding Mission on Myanmar (IIFFMM) noted that '[t]he extreme levels of violence perpetrated against the Rohingya in northern Rakhine State in 2016 and 2017 … *resulted from* the systemic oppression of the Rohingya' [emphasis added],[43] including the denial of their legal status, identity, and citizenship, and followed the instigation of hatred against the Rohingya on ethnic, racial, or religious grounds.[44]

Certainly, denationalization on racial, ethnic, or religious grounds has been routinely denounced by UN resolutions. The Special Rapporteur on Contemporary Forms of Racism has called attention

> to previous findings within the UN rights system that serve as an important reminder that, historically, citizenship stripping has been a favoured political tool of ethnonationalist governments wishing to isolate, marginalize, or exclude certain racial, ethnic, religious, and national groups.[45]

In support, the Special Rapporteur cited, for example, a resolution calling for Myanmar to review its 1982 Citizenship Law because the law results in human rights deprivations and contributes to 'systematic and institutionalized discrimination against members of ethnic and religious minorities'[46] and a resolution 'denouncing Apartheid South Africa's practices of denationalizing and forcibly removing Black South Africans, and noting that apartheid denied Black South Africans full citizenship rights'.[47]

Notwithstanding these developments, it appears that, to date, deprivation of nationality has not been subjected to a rigorous assessment of the possibility of it amounting to the international crime of apartheid.[48] Yet depriving a subset of the population of nationality on racialized or xenophobic grounds can surely be argued to cause great suffering 'committed in the context of an institutionalized regime of systematic oppression and domination by one racial group over any other racial group or groups and committed with the intention of maintaining that regime'.[49]

While human rights are not in principle dependent on citizenship, in practice the deprivation of citizenship often sets the legal preconditions for wholesale human rights violations. These practices are explicit, intentional, and designed to exclude. What is more, the 'civic death'—or political, social, and economic exclusion that follows—was encapsulated neatly in the US Supreme Court's characterization of denationalization as the 'the total destruction of the individual's status in organized society.'[50]

In the next section, we turn to consider in depth Myanmar's treatment of the Rohingya as constituting the elements of the crime of apartheid before examining accountability for the crime of apartheid.

Assessing Myanmar's treatment of the Rohingya as apartheid

As already mentioned, it has not yet been conclusively established whether deprivation of nationality alone can satisfy the Article 7(2)(h) definition of apartheid in the Rome Statute. However, it is arguable that the deliberate and racially motivated deprivation of nationality from the Rohingya, together with the commission of other human rights violations against this group (violations that were enabled by the act of denationalizing) reveal an 'institutionalized regime of systematic oppression and domination by one racial group' over another, which is the core of the crime of apartheid. As Amnesty International has observed, '[t]o understand the crimes committed against the Rohingya in Rakhine State as crimes of apartheid is to foreground the daily reality of Rohingya in Myanmar: as persons systematically subject to domination and oppression'.[51] The elements of the crime as they relate to Myanmar's treatment of the Rohingya are examined below.

Inhumane acts

As already noted, there is an element of circularity in the Article 7(2)(h) definition of apartheid as 'inhumane acts of a character similar to those referred to in paragraph 1'.[52] What is apparent is the wide scope of the conduct that can constitute the key acts of this crime. It encompasses murder,[53] extermination,[54] enslavement,[55] deportation or forcible population transfer,[56] imprisonment or other severe forms of deprivation of liberty contrary to international law,[57] torture,[58] rape and other forms of sexual violence,[59] and persecution of a group on grounds including race or religion[60] (with persecution defined as 'the intentional and severe deprivation of fundamental rights'[61] on the basis of identity). The key act of apartheid can also be constituted by other acts 'of a similar character intentionally causing great suffering, or serious injury to body or to mental or physical health'.[62] As Article 7(2)(h) is not an exhaustive definition, the acts of apartheid could be those listed in Article 2 of the Apartheid Convention,[63] such as:

> legislative measures and other measures calculated to prevent a racial group or groups from participation in the political, social, economic, and cultural life of the country and the deliberate creation of conditions preventing the full development of such a group or groups, in particular by denying to members of a racial group or groups basic human rights and freedoms, including the … right to a nationality.[64]

It is apparent that many of the acts listed in Article 7(1), as well as other acts of a similar character, have been committed by Myanmar officials against the Rohingya. These acts have been extensively documented by the IIFFMM and in reports of the UN High Commissioner for Human Rights and the Special Rapporteur on the situation of human rights in Myanmar. They include armed attacks against civilians,[65] extra-judicial killings and disappearances,[66] forced displacement,[67] and accounts of torture and deaths in custody.[68] Severe restrictions are enforced on the freedom of movement of the Rohingya, including their confinement within camps,[69] with the effect of denying them access to livelihoods, education, and basic services.[70] These deprivations undoubtedly cause 'great suffering, or serious injury to body or to mental or physical health'.[71]

In 2018, the IIFFMM observed that 'the lack of legal status and identity is the cornerstone of the oppressive system targeting the Rohingya',[72] highlighting the importance of the racialized deprivation of nationality to the regime of apartheid established by Myanmar in respect of the Rohingya.

An institutionalised regime of systematic oppression and domination by one racial group over another

The 'inhumane acts' constituting the key conduct of apartheid are carried out for a purpose: in order to maintain an institutionalized regime of systematic oppression and domination by one racial group over another. Indeed, the institutionalized nature of apartheid distinguishes it from the crime of persecution.[73] According to Guénaël Mettraux, evidence of institutionalization could be established by:

> the adoption of a particular discriminatory legal framework; from the existence of distinct official bodies based on race; from the existence of officially sanctioned restriction of rights affected; from discriminatory administrative, financial, or judicial practices against other racial group(s); or from the stated support for racial discrimination expressed by high-ranking state officials.[74]

The regime must be one of systematic oppression and domination by one racial group over another, which Mettraux suggests refers to 'efforts to keep members of one race in a position of inferiority relative to those persons in control of the regime through violence, restriction, and denial of rights, and other forms of discrimination'.[75]

Guidance on the meaning of 'racial group' can be taken from jurisprudence on this term in relation to the crime of genocide,[76] in which it also features. Race is understood broadly; in line with socio-anthropological understandings, race is a 'social construct, defined and moulded by a group, usually in response to another group'.[77] What matters then is the subjective perception of the perpetrator; '[i]n other words, if a group is perceived and treated as a distinct racial group, it would qualify as a racial group in the meaning of the crime of apartheid, despite the lack of any 'objective' differences between the groups to which the victim and the perpetrator belong'.[78]

As already suggested, the 'cornerstone' of the apartheid regime in Myanmar is the 1982 Citizenship Law. The failure to include the Rohingya in the list of 135 'national races' precluded them from citizenship, thus depriving the Rohingya of a legal status and identity, which not only constituted a serious human rights abuse in and of itself but paved the way for further acts of discrimination and persecution.[79] In the view of the IIFFMM, the reference to national races in the 1982 Citizenship Law makes Myanmar a 'race-based State'.[80] Moreover, it is evident that the discriminatory treatment of the Rohingya is based on a perception of their racial inferiority:

> [t]he hateful rhetoric, well documented in the Mission's 2018 report, which came to the fore at the height of the 2012, 2016 and 2017 violence, demonstrates the hateful, widespread, and mainstream perception by Myanmar's Bamar majority of the 'sub-human' status of the Rohingya.[81]

This perception of the racial inferiority of the Rohingya is reinforced through restrictions on their movement, which have the effect of confining the Rohingya to villages and camps.[82] Indeed, the physical segregation of the Rohingya powerfully captures the idea of 'apartness', the translation of the Afrikaans word 'apartheid'. Although it is not necessary for a situation to resemble the manifestation of apartheid in South Africa to satisfy the Article 7(2)(h) definition of the crime,[83] in many ways the situation in Myanmar does so. The 1982 Citizenship Law is similar in effect to various pieces of apartheid-era legislation in South Africa, including the 1950 Population Registration Act in South Africa, which established four racial groups and required citizens to hold identity cards specifying their racial identity; the Group Areas Act 1950, which established racially segregated neighbourhoods; and the 1970 Bantu Homelands Citizenship Act, which, among other things, stripped Black South Africans of their citizenship.

A widespread or systematic attack directed against a civilian population

To elevate the acts listed in Article 7(1) to a crime against humanity, they must have been committed against a civilian population as part of a widespread or systematic attack. This element is further defined as 'a course of conduct involving the multiple commission of acts referred to in paragraph 1 against any civilian population, pursuant to or in furtherance of a State or organizational policy to commit such attack'.[84] As Pre-Trial Chamber II made clear in the case of *Prosecutor v Bemba*, '[t]he commission of the acts referred to in Article 7(1) of the Statute constitute the "attack" itself and, besides the commission of the acts, no additional requirement for the existence of an "attack" should be proven'.[85] Furthermore, it is clear from the Elements of Crimes that a military attack is not required,[86] and case law demonstrates that mistreatment of a civilian population, and even non-violent attacks, will suffice.[87] The imposition of a system of apartheid on a people has specifically been contemplated as an attack within the meaning of Article 7(2)(a).[88]

The IFFMM has directly addressed this contextual element, concluding that 'a widespread and systematic attack directed against a civilian population existed in both Kachin and Shan States, and in Rakhine State'.[89] The Mission explained that the clearance operations carried out on Rohingya villages in Rakhine State in 2016 and 2017 'were widespread in terms of their geographical reach and the large numbers of targeted persons and victims. They were also organized and implemented in a manner as to rule out the probability of their random occurrence, and thus they were systematic'.[90] The Mission went on to observe though that as 'attack' is understood as 'a course of conduct', it encompasses 'the regime of State-sanctioned discrimination and oppression, that gradually eroded the human dignity of this group of civilians within Myanmar's borders'.[91]

Accountability for apartheid

Even though the crime of apartheid can arguably be made out in Myanmar, holding those responsible to account is not a straightforward exercise. This is because Myanmar is not a party to the Rome Statute establishing the ICC. The issue of accountability is made even more complex following the events of 2021, namely, the *coup d'état* of 1 February 2021, in which the Myanmar military (the Tatmadaw) overthrew the country's democratically elected government, and the formation of the National Unity Government (NUG) in April 2021. Notwithstanding the fact that Myanmar is not a party to the Rome Statute, there are various pathways by which the Court could establish jurisdiction in respect of the crime of apartheid in Myanmar. These pathways, and the prospects for success, are described below.

UN Security Council referral

Regardless of whether a state is a party to the Rome Statute, the UN Security Council, acting under Chapter VII of the UN Charter, can refer a situation involving that state to the ICC.[92] For example, in 2005, the Security Council deemed the conflict in Darfur to amount to a threat to international peace and security and referred the situation to the ICC,[93] notwithstanding that Sudan was not a party to the Rome Statute. However, given that permanent Security Council members, China and the Russian Federation, have a history of blocking collective action against Myanmar,[94] it is likely they would veto such a referral being made in respect of Myanmar.

Article 12(3) declaration

States which are not a party to the Rome Statute can accept the jurisdiction of the Court with respect to a particular crime by lodging a declaration, known as an Article 12(3) declaration, with the Registrar of the Court.[95] On 17 July 2021, the NUG lodged such a declaration. The declaration encompasses crimes committed within Myanmar since 1 July 2002, which is the date the Court began operating.[96] It therefore includes crimes which may have been committed by the military since the coup in February 2021. Indeed, an intention to incorporate these recent crimes is suggested in an NUG media release announcing the declaration, in which the NUG stated their commitment

> to ensuring accountability and ending impunity for all human rights violations. The NUG continues to draw attention to the ongoing atrocity crimes being committed by the military, and it seeks justice for all past crimes. The NUG is steadfastly working towards a future where Myanmar will be known for its international cooperation and adherence to international law.[97]

Myanmar's ambassador to the UN, Kyaw Moe Tun, suggested in a discussion about accountability for the crimes committed following the coup that the Article 12(3) declaration was aimed towards securing accountability for the conduct of the military, observing that '[w]e are not a state party to the ICC, but we need to … explore the ways and means to bring the case to the ICC'.[98] However, even if the intention was to capture the recent crimes of the military, the Article 12(3) declaration opens a pathway for accountability for international crimes committed against the Rohingya, including the crime of apartheid.

The NUG is an underground government,[99] and it comprises members of the National League for Democracy (NLD) as well as representatives of some ethnic minority parties. The Article 12(3) declaration raises the question of whether the NUG is the legitimate representative body of Myanmar and whether it therefore has the authority to act on behalf of and bind the country in international law.[100] This question was addressed in a legal analysis produced by the NGO Fortify Rights, published in August 2021. Fortify Rights argued that the fact that NUG includes the democratically elected representatives of Myanmar means the Unity Government has the authority to represent and act on behalf of the country.[101] The degree of support for the NUG from the people of Myanmar further bolsters its legitimacy.[102] At the same time, Fortify Rights argues that the persistent anti-coup, anti-junta protests throughout the country demonstrate the non-recognition of the military junta.[103]

Control over territory is not of itself sufficient to establish authority to act on behalf of a state[104] (and there is a real question of whether the military does have control of territory in Myanmar). In cases in which a government has been deposed by a military or militia-led coup, with the junta then claiming control over the territory, such as in Sierra Leone following the 1997 coup and Haiti following the 1991 coup, the UN has continued to recognise the authority of officials representing the ousted government.[105] More important than control over territory in determining the legitimacy of a regime is the degree of recognition afforded to it.

For example, international recognition of various Cambodian governments-in-exile in the 1980s legitimized those governments and enabled them to sign multilateral treaties on Cambodia's behalf.[106] The NUG has been recognized as the legitimate government of Myanmar by a number of states and regional bodies,[107] including France,[108] Canada,[109] the Czech Republic,[110] and the European

Parliament.[111] In November 2021, the Credentials Committee of the General Assembly deferred a decision to determine the credentials of the military junta to represent the country in the General Assembly, although the General Assembly's condemnation of the coup and the violence inflicted upon protestors in June 2021[112] does not bode well for the Committee's recognition of the military as the legitimate representative of Myanmar.

State parties to the Rome Statute can challenge the validity of an Article 12(3) declaration.[113] Fortify Rights concluded that a successful challenge to the NUG's accession to the Rome Statue was unlikely, given that the countries most likely to object to the NUG's move, being China or the Russian Federation, are not parties to the Rome Statute and would therefore be prevented from doing so.[114]

To effectively delegate jurisdiction to the ICC, Fortify Rights recommended that the NUG not only submit the Article 12(3) declaration but also accede to the Rome Statute. This is because a State Party to the Rome Statute obtains rights in relation to the governance and functioning of the ICC not available to non-state parties which have delegated jurisdiction through an Article 12(3) declaration. There is a possibility for other states to lodge objections to an accession to a treaty, but Fortify Rights pointed to practice suggesting that the existence of objections was unlikely to prevent the UN Secretary-General from accepting an instrument of accession to a treaty, 'unless the objections are numerous'.[115] Once an instrument of accession is deposited, the Rome Statute will enter into force for that state on the first day of the month following the sixtieth day after the deposit.[116] At the time of writing, the NUG has not deposited an instrument of accession to the Rome Statute. Although even if it does so, acceding would only grant the Court jurisdiction 'with respect to crimes committed after entry into force of this Statute for that State',[117] meaning that this pathway would have little effect in ensuring accountability for crimes against the Rohingya.

Apartheid as a crime under customary international law

In the event that the NUG's Article 12(3) declaration is not accepted by the Court or is the subject of a successful objection, it is worthwhile to examine whether Myanmar is bound by an obligation to not commit apartheid in customary international law. This requires determining whether, firstly, the ICC's jurisdiction includes crimes in customary international law and, secondly, whether apartheid is a crime under customary international law.

The sources of applicable law for the ICC are set out in Article 21 of the Rome Statute. Article 21(1) has a tripartite structure, specifying that the ICC shall apply:

(a) In the first place, this Statute, Elements of Crimes and its Rules of Procedure and Evidence;
(b) In the second place, where appropriate, applicable treaties and the principles and rules of international law, including the established principles of international armed conflict;

(c) Failing that, general principles of law derived by the Court from national laws of legal systems of the world … provided that those principles are not inconsistent with this Statute and with international law and internationally recognized norms and standards.

It is apparent that Article 21 creates a hierarchy in which the second and third listed sources are only referred to if the prior level is not determinative. The Pre-Trial Chamber in the case of *Al-Bashir* outlined two requirements for the application of custom: (i) the existence of a lacuna in the written law (ii) that cannot be filled by the rules of treaty interpretation.[118] In the recent *Palestine* decision, Judge Péter Kovács, in a partly dissenting opinion, argued that the Court should not refrain from referring to other sources as an aid to interpretation when complex issues are at play.[119]

Further provisions of the Rome Statute tend against the idea that the jurisdiction of the Court extends to crimes in customary international law, particularly in application to nationals of, or conduct on, the territory of non-state parties. Article 22(1) codifies the principle of legality, specifying that '[a] person shall not be criminally responsible under this Statute unless the conduct in question constitutes, at the time it takes place, a crime within the jurisdiction of the Court'. According to William A Schabas, '[t]he principal consequence of the reference to "a crime within the jurisdiction of the Court" … is to exclude any possibility of prosecution for offences based solely upon customary law'.[120] Furthermore, Article 22(2) requires a strict construal of crimes, prohibits the extension of crimes by analogy, and requires an interpretation in favour of the accused in the event of ambiguity.

Whether the crime of apartheid has reached the status of customary international law is disputed.[121] John Dugard and John Reynolds, writing in 2013, suggested the prohibition of apartheid (directed at states) is established as a rule of customary international law, but the crime of apartheid (directed at individuals) may not have achieved the status of customary international law, although they noted it was moving towards customary status.[122] More recently, however, Mettraux suggests that the only objection to recognising the crime against humanity of apartheid as a crime of customary international law is whether its definition is adequately settled, given the multiple instruments in which it is defined.[123] Mettraux adds that:

> [t]here is little doubt, however, that, *in principle*, the typical manifestation of apartheid—i.e., inhumane acts and the suppression of rights committed in the context of an institutionalized regime of systematic oppression, discrimination, and domination by a racial group over another with the intention of maintaining that regime—is now prohibited and criminalized as a matter of customary international law.[124]

Overall, and notwithstanding that the factual circumstances reflect a 'typical manifestation of apartheid',[125] it is not likely that custom provides a pathway to accountability in respect of the crime of apartheid in Myanmar. This is principally because, firstly, the two requirements for the application of custom—the existence of a lacuna in the written law that cannot be filled by the rules of treaty interpretation—do not appear to be fulfilled; and secondly, the principle of legality works against a resort to crimes in customary international law, particularly in application to a non-state party.

A jurisdictional link with Bangladesh

Bangladesh is a State party to the ICC, having ratified the Rome Statute in 2010. Since November 2019, the ICC Prosecutor has been investigating crimes against the Rohingya that occurred 'at least in part' in the territory of Bangladesh.[126] The Pre-Trial Chamber was of the view that:

> there exists a reasonable basis to believe widespread and/or systematic acts of violence may have been committed that could qualify as the crimes against humanity of deportation across the Myanmar–Bangladesh border and persecution on grounds of ethnicity and/or religion against the Rohingya population.[127]

The Chamber noted, however, that other crimes not specified could be a part of a future investigation, as long as such crimes occurred 'at least in part' in Bangladesh.[128]

Ronan Lee argues that a jurisdictional link with Bangladesh could be established in respect of the crime of apartheid. Lee's argument is that, because Myanmar requires Rohingya who are seeking to return to the country from Bangladesh to participate in a national citizenship certification exercise and accept a National Verification Card as a condition of their return, this amounts to Myanmar 'export[ing] its apartheid system to Bangladesh'.[129] The National Verification Card identifies its holder as a foreigner and perpetuates their exclusion from the status and rights of citizenship. Accordingly, Lee argues:

> Since Myanmar's discriminatory citizenship system (its laws and the way they are enforced) are necessary to enable the system of apartheid against the Rohingya within Myanmar, making participation in this discriminatory citizenship system a precondition of Rohingya return to Myanmar can be considered a crime committed on the territory of Bangladesh.[130]

It could also be argued that Myanmar's intention, through its discriminatory and persecutory treatment of the Rohingya, was always to facilitate their deportation to Bangladesh, so, in effect, the crime of apartheid, although commencing in Myanmar, was completed in Bangladesh.

Other hurdles to accountability

Other hurdles to accountability appear to be able to be overcome. The Pre-Trial Chamber has already observed that the scale of the alleged crimes and number of victims mean that the gravity threshold for crimes against humanity appears to be met, adding that 'noting the victim's views … there are no substantial reasons to believe that an investigation into the situation would not be in the interests of justice'.[131] It is also worth pointing out that official capacity, including head-of-state status, does not protect the military or its commander-in-chief, General Min Aung Hlaing, from prosecution. Article 27 of the Rome Statute specifies that official capacity does not exempt a person from criminal responsibility under the Statute. The Pre-Trial Chamber I in the *Malawi* decision confirmed that customary international law does not grant heads of states immunity from prosecution by an international court.[132]

Conclusion

In this chapter, we have established that there is a plausible and defensible argument to be made that the typical manifestation of apartheid appears to be present in Myanmar. The cornerstone of the apartheid regime in Myanmar is the racialized deprivation of nationality from the Rohingya and their consequent lack of legal status. While there are multiple pathways to accountability for apartheid, the Article 12(3) declaration is likely to be the most successful method, provided that the NUG is recognized as the legitimate representative authority of the country, which is likely. Arguments about a jurisdictional link in respect of the crime of apartheid with Bangladesh are important and worthy of further exploration.

This analysis of the potential for discriminatory denationalization to be prosecuted as an international crime has significance beyond the immediate context of ensuring accountability for the Rohingya. Despite the ongoing and widescale deprivation of citizenship on racial grounds—in many cases, resulting in statelessness—that continues to occur globally, states continue to resist being held accountable for racial discrimination, especially in matters of nationality. The expressive function of international criminal law highlights the gravity of the harm of denationalization and squarely challenges the practice of the 'manufacture of foreigners' from within as well as states' attempts to retreat behind the invisible border of the *domaine réservé* in respect of nationality laws. It is thus a worthy complement to other mechanisms of accountability for such serious violations of international law.

Notes

1 The authors are grateful to Katya Harrop, Juris Doctor, Melbourne Law School, who provided excellent research assistance, and to participants at the *Undoing Discriminatory Borders* Project Conference, University of Oxford (online) 20 October 2020, especially Tendayi Achiume, Catherine Briddick and Cathryn Costello for thoughtful and incisive feedback. The editors of this collection also provided helpful feedback. Any errors or omissions are our own.

2 The decision of Pre-Trial Chamber III affirmed that the Prosecutor could undertake an investigation with respect to '*any crime* within the jurisdiction of the Court committed at least in part on the territory of Bangladesh, or on the territory of any other State Party or State making a declaration under Article

12(3) of the Statute, if the alleged crime is sufficiently linked to the situation as described in this decision': *Situation in the People's Republic of Bangladesh/ Republic of the Union of Myanmar* (*Decision Pursuant to Article 15 of the Rome Statute on the Authorisation of an Investigation*) ICC-01/19 (ICC Pre-Trial Chamber III, 14 November 2019) 54 [126] (emphasis in original). The Pre-Trial Chamber went on to emphasise [at 126] that:

> the Prosecutor is not restricted to the incidents identified in the Request and the crimes set out in the present decision but may, on the basis of the evidence gathered during her investigation, extend her investigation to other crimes against humanity or other Article 5 crimes, as long as they remain within the parameters of the authorised investigation.

3 Ayelet Shachar, 'Bordering Migration/Migrating Borders' (2019) 37(1) Berkeley Journal of International Law 93, 96.

4 We note that Shachar considers primarily externalization among states of the Global North, yet her analysis is applicable more broadly.

5 Michelle Foster and Jade Roberts, 'Manufacturing Foreigners: The Law and Politics of Transforming Citizens into Migrants' in Catherine Dauvergne (ed), *Research Handbook on the Law and Politics of Migration* (Edward Elgar 2021). Other scholars have used a similar framing, see for example Kristy A Belton, *Statelessness in the Caribbean: The Paradox of Belonging in a Postnational World* (University of Pennsylvania Press 2017) 359. See also Matthew J Gibney, 'Denationalisation and Discrimination' (2020) 46(12) Journal of Ethnic and Migration Studies 2551, 2558 ('foreigner-making'); Neha Jain, 'Manufacturing Statelessness' (2022) 116 (2) American Journal of International Law 237.

6 Gibney (n 5) 2551.

7 ibid 2559.

8 ibid.

9 ibid.

10 ibid 2560.

11 Sangeetha Pillai and George Williams, 'The Utility of Citizenship Stripping Laws in the UK, Canada and Australia' (2017) 41(2) Melbourne University Law Review 845; Audrey Macklin, 'Citizenship Revocation, the Privilege to Have Rights and the Production of the Alien' (2014) 40(1) Queen's Law Journal 1; Elke Cloots, 'The Legal Limits of Citizenship Deprivation as a Counterterror Strategy' (2017) 23(1) European Public Law 57; Laura van Waas 'Foreign Fighters and the Deprivation of Nationality: National Practices and International Law Implications' in Andrea de Guttry, Francesca Capone, and Christophe Paulussen (eds), *Foreign Fighters under International Law and Beyond* (TMC Asser Press 2016).

12 Institute for Statelessness and Inclusion, 'Principles on Deprivation of Nationality as a Security Measure' (February 2020) <https://www.institutesi.org/year-of-action-resources/principles-on-deprivation-of-nationality>.

13 Michael Hutt, *Unbecoming Citizens: Culture, Nationhood, and the Flight of Refugees from Bhutan* (OUP 2005) 159.

14 John R Campbell, (2011) 'The Enduring Problem of Statelessness in the Horn of Africa: How Nation-States and Western Courts (Re)Define Nationality' (2011) 23(4) International Journal of Refugee Law 656.

15 Foster and Roberts (n 5) 219.

16 See articles published in the special issue of the Statelessness and Citizenship Review on Citizenship and Statelessness in India Symposium (2021) 3(1) Statelessness and Citizenship Review <https://statelessnessandcitizenshipreview.com/index.php/journal/issue/view/11>.

17 An exception in the context of international criminal law is Cóman Kenny, 'Legislated Out of Existence: Mass Arbitrary Deprivation of Nationality Resulting in Statelessness as an International Crime' (2020) 20 International Criminal Law Review 1026.

18 See, e.g., United Nations Security Council, 'Statement by the President of the Security Council' (6 November 2017) UN Doc S/PRST/2017/22; Human Rights Council Res 37/32 (23 March 2018) UN Doc A/HRC/RES/37/32; 'Report of the Working Group on the Universal Periodic Review — Myanmar' (23 December 2015) UN Doc A/HRC/31/13 (Second Cycle); United Nations General Assembly Res 70/233, 'Situation of Human Rights in Myanmar' (4 March 2016) UN Doc A/RES/70/233.

19 See, e.g., HRC, 'Report of Working Group on the Universal Periodic Review — Myanmar' (24 March 2011) UN Doc A/HRC/17/9 (First Cycle); See also UNGA Res 66/230, 'Situation of Human Rights in Myanmar' (24 December 2011); UNGA Res 65/241, Situation of Human Rights in Myanmar' (24 December 2010) cited in Michelle Foster and Timnah Baker, 'Racial Discrimination in Nationality Laws: A Blind Spot of international Law?' (2021) 11(1) Columbia Journal of Race and Law 83, 86.

20 John Dugard and John Reynolds, 'Apartheid, International Law, and the Occupied Palestinian Territory' (2013) 24(3) *European Journal of International Law* 867.

21 ibid.

22 ibid 883.

23 Robert E Conot, *Justice in Nuremberg* (Carroll & Grab Publishers 1983). See also the discussion in Kenny (n 17) 1044.

24 Kenny (n 17) 1026.

25 International Convention on the Suppression and Punishment of the Crime of Apartheid (adopted 30 November 1973, entered into force 18 July 1976) 1015 UNTS 243 ('Apartheid Convention').

26 By April 1994, 99 states had signed the Apartheid Convention: Christopher Gevers, 'Africa and International Criminal Law' in Kevin Jon Heller et al. (eds), *The Oxford Handbook of International Criminal Law* (OUP 2020) 154.

27 Apartheid Convention Article 2 (emphasis added).

28 John Dugard, 'The Denationalization of Black South Africans in Pursuance of Apartheid' (1984) 33 International Commission of Jurists Review 49.

29 Ibid. See also John Dugard, 'South Africa's Independent Homelands: An Exercise in Denationalisation' (1980) 10 Denver Journal of International Law & Policy 11.

30 ILC, 'Draft Code of Crimes against the Peace and Security of Mankind' (1996) art 18(f) (emphasis added).

31 William A Schabas, *The International Criminal Court: A Commentary on the Rome Statute* (2nd edn, OUP 2016) 150.

32 'Summary Record of the 3rd Meeting of the Committee of the Whole', UN Diplomatic Conference of Plenipotentiaries on the Establishment of an International Criminal Court (Rome, 15 June – 17 July 1998) (20 November 1998) UN Doc A/CONF.183/C.1/SR.3, 152, 154 (UN Diplomatic Conference).

33 'Bangladesh, India, Lesotho, Malawi, Mexico, Namibia, South Africa, Swaziland, Trinidad and Tobago, the United Republic of Tanzania: Proposal Regarding Article 5', UN Diplomatic Conference (Rome, 15 June – 17 July 1998) (22 June 1998) UN Doc A/CONF.183/C.1/L.12, 239. The Official Records contain this Report and all Reports and Other Documents of the Conference: UN Diplomatic Conference, *The Official Records of the UN Diplomatic Conference on the Establishment of an ICC: Reports and Other Documents* (United Nations

2002) vol 3 <https://legal.un.org/diplomaticconferences/1998_icc/docs/english/vol_3.pdf>.

34 UN Diplomatic Conference, 'Bureau: Discussion Paper Regarding Part 2' (6 July 1998) UN Doc A/CONF.183/C.1/L.53, 204–5. Further, at this stage, within paragraph 2 of Article 5, the definition of apartheid was included in sub-paragraph (d bis) at 213:

> The crime of apartheid means inhumane acts of a character similar to those referred to in paragraph 1 above, committed in the context of an institutionalized regime of systematic oppression and domination by one racial group over any other racial group or groups and committed with the intention of maintaining that regime

35 UN Diplomatic Conference, 'Bureau: Proposal Regarding Part 2' (10 July 1998) UN Doc A/CONF.183/C.1/L.59, 212–13.

36 Schabas (n 31) 151.

37 ibid 206.

38 'Israel's Apartheid against Palestinians: Cruel System of Domination and Crime against Humanity' (Amnesty International, 1 February 2022) <https://www.amnesty.org/en/documents/mde15/5141/2022/en/>.

39 Dugard and Reynolds (n 20).

40 Rome Statute of the International Criminal Court (adopted 17 July 1998, entered into force 1 July 2002) 2187 UNTS 3, art 7(1)(k) (Rome Statute).

41 This has support in the scholarship: Christopher K Hall et al., 'Article 7: Crimes against Humanity' in Otto Triffterer and Kai Ambos (eds), *Rome Statute of the International Criminal Court* (3 edn, Bloomsbury, 2016) 145 (citations omitted) (emphasis added).

42 *Application of the Convention on the Prevention and Punishment of the Crime of Genocide (The Gambia/Myanmar)* (Provisional Measures: Order of 23 January 2020) [2020] ICJ Rep 3, 21 [54] citing UNGA Res 73/264 (22 December 2018). By the same resolution, the General Assembly condemned at 4 [1]:

> all violations and abuses of human rights in Myanmar, as set out in the report of the fact-finding mission, including the widespread, systematic and gross human rights violations and abuses committed in Rakhine State, including the presence of elements of extermination and deportation and the systematic oppression and discrimination that the fact-finding mission concluded may amount to persecution and to the crime of apartheid.

43 HRC, 'Report of the Detailed Findings of the Independent International Fact-Finding Mission on Myanmar' (17 September 2018) UN Doc A/HRC/39/CRP.2, 177 [748]-[749] (emphasis added).

44 ibid 110–77 [458]-[748].

45 UN Special Rapporteur on Contemporary Forms of Racism, Racial Discrimination, Xenophobia and Related Intolerance, *Amicus Brief before the Dutch Immigration and Naturalisation Service* (23 October 2018) [9] <https://www.ohchr.org/sites/default/files/Documents/Issues/Racism/SR/Amicus/DutchImmigration_Amicus.pdf> (Amicus Brief before the Dutch Immigration and Naturalisation Service).

46 UNGA Res 34/22 (3 April 2017) 'UN Doc A/HRC/RES/34/22, 2 para 5.

47 Amicus Brief on the Dutch Immigration and Naturalisation Service (n 43) 4 n 9; UNCHR, 'Situation of Human Rights in South Africa' (3 March 1987) UN Doc E/CN.4/RES/1987/14; HRC, 'Summary Prepared by the Office of the

High Commissioner for Human Rights in Accordance with Paragraph 15(c) of the Annex to Human Rights Council Resolution 5/1’ (25 July 2011) UN Doc A/HRC/WG.6/ 12/SYR/3, 10 paras 60–4.

48 An exception is Cóman Kenny who analyses this question briefly as part of a wider analysis: Kenny (n 17).

49 Rome Statute Article 7(2)(h).

50 *Trop v Dulles* (1958) 356 US 86 [101].

51 ‘“Caged without a Roof”: Apartheid in Myanmar’s Rakhine State’ (*Amnesty International*, 21 November 2017) <https://www.amnesty.org/en/documents/asa16/7484/2017/en/≥ accessed 13 April 2022, 90 (Caged without a Roof).

52 A footnote in the Elements of Crimes explains that ‘character’ means the nature and gravity of the act: International Criminal Court, *Elements of Crimes* (2011) 12 n 29.

53 Rome Statute Article 7(1)(a).

54 ibid Article 7(1)(b).

55 ibid Article 7(1)(c).

56 ibid Article 7(1)(d).

57 ibid Article 7(1)(e).

58 ibid Article 7(1)(f).

59 ibid Article 7(1)(g).

60 ibid Article 7(1)(h).

61 ibid Article 7(2)(g).

62 ibid Article 7(1)(k).

63 Guénaël Mettraux, *International Crimes: Law and Practice* (OUP 2020) vol 2, 741.

64 Apartheid Convention Article II(c).

65 HRC, ‘Report of the Special Rapporteur on the Situation of Human Rights in Myanmar, Thomas H. Andrews’ (29 September 2021) UN Doc A/HRC/46/56, 29 para 26 (Report of the Special Rapporteur on the Situation of Human Rights in Myanmar).

66 ibid.

67 As of February 2021, over 101,000 people were displaced within Rakhine and Chin States: ‘Report of the Special Rapporteur on the situation of Human Rights in Myanmar’ (n 65) 15 para 95.

68 ibid 29 para 26.

69 The confinement of the Rohingya to camps is detailed by Amnesty International in ‘Caged without a Roof’ (n 51) 42–58.

70 ‘Report of the Special Rapporteur on the Situation of Human Rights in Myanmar’ (n 65) 33 para 44. The Special Rapporteur went on to note that, ‘[i]n total, an estimated 600,000 Rohingya live in Rakhine State under highly repressive conditions that severely limit their ability to move or make a living, let alone access health care or education for their children. Conditions for Rohingya in Rakhine State appear designed to be destructive to the survival of the community’: at 36 para 60.

71 Rome Statute Article 7(1)(k).

72 ‘Report of the Detailed Findings of the Independent International Fact-Finding Mission on Myanmar’ (n 65) 118 para 491.

73 Carola Lingaas, ‘The Crime Against Humanity of Apartheid in a Post-Apartheid World’ (2017) 2(1) OLR < https://www.idunn.no/doi/10.5617/oslaw2566> accessed 13 April 2022, 99.

74 Mettraux (n 63) 742.

75 ibid 742.

76 Article 6 of the Rome Statute defines genocide as ‘any of the following acts committed with intent to destroy, in whole or part, a national, ethnic, racial, or

religious group'. The ongoing ICJ proceedings will be of value in producing evidence and findings that could assist in the identification of a racial group for the purpose of identifying a regime of apartheid.

77 Lingaas (n 73) 101.

78 ibid 101.

79 'Report of the Detailed Findings of the Independent International Fact-Finding Mission on Myanmar' (n 65) 118 para 491.

80 'Detailed Findings of the Independent International Fact-Finding Mission on Myanmar' (16 September 2019) UN Doc A/HRC/42/CRP.5, 19, para 63.

81 ibid 170 para 666.

82 ibid 48, para 144.

83 Indeed, it is arguable that the utility of the crime against humanity of apartheid has been constrained by being too closely linked with the apartheid regime in South Africa: see Lingaas (n 73).

84 Rome Statute Article 7(2)(a).

85 *Prosecutor v Bemba* (Decision Pursuant to Article 61(7)(a) and (b) of the Rome Statute on the Charges of the Prosecutor against Jean-Pierre Bemba Gombo)-01/05-01/08-424 (ICC Pre-Trial Chamber II, 15 June 2009) para 75.

86 *Elements of Crimes* (n 50) 5 para 3.

87 ICTY, *Prosecutor v Vasiljević* (Judgment) IT-98-32-T (29 November 2002) paras 29-30; *Prosecutor v Georges Anderson Nderubumwe Rutaganda* (Judgment and Sentence) ICTR-96-3-T (6 December 1999) para 70.

88 *Prosecutor v Jean-Paul Akayesu* (Judgment) ICTR-96-4-T (2 September 1998) para 581.

89 HRC, Independent International Fact-Finding Mission on Myanmar, 'Genocide, Crimes against Humanity, and War Crimes' (Info Note) 2 <https://www.ohchr.org/Documents/HRBodies/HRCouncil/FFM-Myanmar/InfoNoteonCrimesLegalities.docx> accessed 13 April 2022.

90 ibid 2.

91 ibid.

92 Rome Statute Article 13(b).

93 UNSC 1593 (31 March 2005) UN Doc S/RES/1595(2005).

94 'Myanmar Coup: China Blocks UN Condemnation as Protest Grows' *BBC News*, (3 February 2021) <https://www.bbc.com/news/world-asia-55913947> accessed 13 April 2022; Fortify Rights, *Ending Impunity in Myanmar* (19 August 2021) < https://www.fortifyrights.org/mya-inv-2021-08-19/> accessed 13 April 2022, 42.

95 Rome Statute Article 12(3).

96 National Unity Government Myanmar, 'ICC Declaration Accepting Jurisdiction Lodged by Acting President Duwa Lashi La' (*Twitter*, 21 August 2021) <https://twitter.com/NUGMyanmar/status/1428739347717648389> accessed 13 April 2022.

97 ibid.

98 Michelle Nichols, 'Ousted Myanmar Lawmakers Consider International Criminal Court, Says UN Envoy' *Reuters* (19 March 2021) <https://www.reuters.com/article/us-myanmar-politics-un-idUSKBN2BA2PQ> accessed 13 April 2022.

99 The NUG is not strictly a government in exile, as many of its members remain within Myanmar.

100 Whether the NUG adequately represents Rohingya people is debated. The NUG has appointed a Rohingya activist as an advisor in the Ministry of Human Rights: Adam Simpson, 'Two Governments Claim to Run Myanmar. So, Who Gets the Country's Seat at the UN?' *The Conversation* (24 September 2021) <https://theconversation.com/two-governments-claim-to-run-myanmar-so-who-gets

-the-countrys-seat-at-the-un-167885> accessed 13 April 2022. In June 2021, the NUG issued a policy position on the Rohingya which, among other things, promised to amend the country's citizenship laws and abolish the National Verification Card process: 'Policy Position on the Rohingya in Rakhine State' *National Unity Government* (3 June 2021) <https://gov.nugmyanmar.org/2021/06/03/policy-position-on-the-rohingya-in-rakhine-state/> accessed 13 April 2022. Some Rohingya activists and organisations have said the NUG, like the NLD, doesn't represent Rohingya people and they argue that the NUG failed to adequately consult with Rohingya representatives in the drafting of its policy position: 'The NUG's Rohingya Policy: "Campaign statement" or genuine reform?' *Frontier Myanmar* (15 July 2021) <https://www.frontiermyanmar.net/en/the-nugs-rohingya-policy-campaign-statement-or-genuine-reform/> accessed 13 April 2022.

101 *Ending Impunity in Myanmar* (n 94) 31.
102 ibid 9.
103 ibid 31.
104 ibid 32.
105 ibid.
106 ibid.
107 ibid 33.
108 'Myanmar Coup Anniversary: Government in Exile Urges France to Act against Junta' *France24* (1 February 2022) < https://www.france24.com/en/asia-pacific/20220201-myanmar-coup-anniversary-government-in-exile-urges-france-to-act-against-junta> accessed 13 April 2022.
109 ibid.
110 ibid.
111 Sebastian Strangio, 'EU Parliament Voices Support for Myanmar's Opposition Government' *The Diplomat* (11 October 2021) <https://thediplomat.com/2021/10/eu-parliament-voices-support-for-myanmars-opposition-government/>.
112 UNGA Res 75/287 (25 June 2021) UN Doc A/RES/75/287.
113 Rome Statute Article 19.
114 'Myanmar: Engage the International Criminal Court to Hold Military Perpetrators of Mass Atrocity Crimes Accountable' *Fortify Rights* (19 August 2021) <https://www.fortifyrights.org/mya-inv-2021-08-19> accessed 13 April 2022.
115 *Ending Impunity in Myanmar* (n 94) 38.
116 Rome Statute Article 126(2).
117 Rome Statute Article 11(2).
118 *Prosecutor v Al-Bashir* (Decision on the Prosecution's Application for a Warrant of Arrest against Omar Hassan Ahmad Al-Bashir) ICC-02/ 05-01/09-3 (Pre-Trial Chamber I, 4 March 2009) para 44.
119 *Situation in the State of Palestine* (Decision on the 'Prosecution Request Pursuant to Article 19(3) for a Ruling on the Court's Territorial Jurisdiction in Palestine') ICC-01/18-143-Anx1 (5 February 2021) (Partly Dissenting Opinion of Judge Péter Kovács) paras 97–106.
120 Schabas (n 31) 543.
121 Christopher K Hall notes that, on this question, 'different opinions exist': Hall et al. (n 41) 235.
122 Dugard and Reynolds (n 20) 883.
123 Mettraux goes on to suggest that '[a]bsent a clear competing definition, it is likely that the definition of the crime against humanity of apartheid at custom-

ary international law will crystallize around the ICC's definition of this offense': Mettraux (n 63) 738.

124 ibid 363.

125 ibid.

126 'ICC Judges Authorise Opening of an Investigation into the Situation in Bangladesh/Myanmar' *International Criminal Court* (14 November 2019) <https://www.icc-cpi.int/Pages/item.aspx?name=pr1495> accessed 13 April 2022.

127 ibid.

128 ibid.

129 Ronan Lee, 'Myanmar's Citizenship Law as State Crime: A Case for the International Criminal Court' (2019) 8(2) SCJ 241, 259.

130 ibid.

131 'ICC judges Authorise Opening of an Investigation into the Situation in Bangladesh/Myanmar' *International Criminal Court* (14 November 2019) <https://www.icc-cpi.int/Pages/item.aspx?name=pr1495> accessed 13 April 2022.

132 *Situation in Darfur, Sudan* (Corrigendum to the Decision Pursuant to Article 87(7) of the Rome Statute on the Failure by the Republic of Malawi to Comply with the Cooperation Requires Issued by the Court with Respect to the Arrest and Surrender of Omar Hassan Ahmad Al Bashir) ICC-02/05-01/09 (Pre-Trial Chamber I, 13 December 2011) paras 38-43.

6 Identifying 'other Argentinas'

Variables in considering universal jurisdiction Forum States

Jennifer Keene-McCann and Aakash Chandran

Introduction[1]

In November 2019, the Burmese Rohingya Organisation UK (BROUK) initiated proceedings under the principle of universal jurisdiction in Argentina, alleging that genocide and crimes against humanity were committed against the Rohingya community from 2012 to 2018 (the Argentina case).[2] Seeking individual criminal responsibility for crimes *within* Myanmar, the contents of the complaint rectified a gap in avenues for justice for crimes against the Rohingya.

This gap existed because of limited jurisdiction elsewhere. In the International Court of Justice (ICJ), The Gambia's case against Myanmar, also filed in November 2019, alleges that crimes against the Rohingya in Rakhine State violated Myanmar's obligations under the Genocide Convention.[3] Because only States can initiate proceedings against another State at the ICJ, this case can only achieve a form of State responsibility for violations of obligations under treaty law.[4] In January 2020, the ICJ awarded a provisional measures order directing Myanmar: to prevent the commission of genocidal acts; to ensure its military, police, or any other irregular force supported or directed by it or under its control not commit genocidal acts; to preserve all evidence of genocidal acts, and to submit a status report every six months until a final judgement by the Court.[5]

Also in November 2019, the Pre-Trial Chamber (PTC) of the International Criminal Court (ICC) authorized the opening of an investigation by the Office of the Prosecutor (OTP) in the situation of Myanmar/Bangladesh.[6] The PTC's authorization allowed the Prosecutor to investigate not just the crime against humanity of deportation, but *any* crime provided it is within the jurisdiction of the Court and sufficiently linked to the OTP's request covering the 2016–2017 violence. However, the OTP's *proprio motu* request, as sanctioned by the PTC, relates solely to crimes that took place 'in part' in Bangladesh—a party to the Rome Statute[7]—and cannot investigate crimes that took place wholly within Myanmar—a non-State Party.

In this way, the universal jurisdiction complaint in Argentina complements both the ICC and ICJ proceedings by expanding the types and location of crimes that can be considered and by permitting consideration of individual—rather than State—criminal responsibility.[8] It also raises the question: what other 'Argentinas' might exist to bring cases which fill other gaps?

DOI: 10.4324/9781003304883-9

To consider this, it is useful to think about the categories of variables making Argentina a favourable Forum State to bring a universal jurisdiction case regarding crimes against the Rohingya. These involve examining: (1) a Forum State's enabling legal framework; (2) the presence of the accused or victims within a Forum State's territory; (3) a Forum State's resources, including the legal expertise, access to evidence, and basic funding for universal jurisdiction matters; and (4) the political will within a Forum State, including its approach to international legal principles, such as sovereignty and non-interference and its domestic political priorities. The lines between these categories in this chapter are arbitrarily drawn to ease discussion; the term 'variables' is used to indicate that the elements considered are dynamic and intersect with one another. Although no one jurisdiction—or Forum State—will be 'right' for all circumstances, the purpose of this chapter is to explore where else universal jurisdiction—as a tool for seeking justice for the Rohingya—could be used.

This chapter begins by examining the general concept of universal criminal jurisdiction. Then, with reference to Argentina, it examines four categories of variables that may make other Forum States favourable. It applies these variables to three Forum State case studies—India, Australia, and Turkey—to examine how the variables may interact. Nothing in this chapter is intended to constitute legal advice; instead, it provides a foundation on which actors may consider other relevant jurisdictions to support international criminal justice.

Understanding universal criminal jurisdiction

For the purposes of this chapter, 'jurisdiction' most broadly describes a court's capacity and competence to prosecute an individual for a particular crime. It can also be described as the 'link' between a Forum State, its court, and the circumstances of the crime committed. For a hypothetical 'State A', there may be several 'links'.[9] Amongst others, these may include that: the crime at issue was committed on the territory of State A ('territorial jurisdiction'); the alleged perpetrator is a national of State A ('personal' or 'active personality jurisdiction'); the alleged victim is a national of State A ('prescriptive' or 'passive personality jurisdiction'); or the crime affected State A's fundamental interests ('protective jurisdiction').

In contrast, 'universal jurisdiction' refers to the ability of a State A's courts (further, a Forum State) to prosecute non-nationals for crimes against other non-nationals committed outside of State A's territory. In other words, universal jurisdiction requires no 'link'. Instead, the rationale for accepting universal jurisdiction for core international crimes lies in the assertion that certain acts 'are so serious and the magnitude of their impact is so great that their commission shocks the conscience of all humanity'[10] and, as such, demand prosecution from any willing and able State.[11] This conduct includes violations of *jus cogens* norms, including the international crimes of genocide, war crimes, crimes against humanity, and torture.[12]

Bringing a universal jurisdiction matter can provide positive outcomes for both the affected communities and for international accountability in general.

For example, if an accused is found guilty in a fair trial, the accused may serve a custodial sentence if they are in Forum State custody. Depending on Forum State law, its capacity, and the location of the victims, compensation may also be awarded.[13] If no conviction is reached, but a party or the relevant prosecutor is successful in bringing a case, parties can assure that a fair trial has been conducted and the facts were heard, admitted, and litigated. At the same time, if a trial goes ahead, there would ideally be an opportunity for victim participation. Finally, even where a case under universal jurisdiction is brought but does not go ahead, any investigation triggered by the filing of a case can complement findings of other investigation or fact-finding mechanisms. In fact, even an initial investigation may result in an international arrest warrant, hindering the accused from traveling. Therefore, the simple filing of a complaint may represent an opportunity to bring victims' voices, and their lived experiences, to the fore.

However, as with any court proceeding, there are no guarantees of 'success' and proceedings come with considerable uncertainty. Although numbers are growing,[14] universal jurisdiction matters are not common. State consensus is still forming, and many jurisdictions are reluctant to adopt or permit its exercise.[15] The crimes prosecuted through universal jurisdiction are exceedingly complex and often unfamiliar to domestic practitioners. Investigations and trials require the expertise of relevant professional experts, access to victims, the ability to access, store, and often translate evidence, and the funding to sustain lengthy proceedings. Even where financial resources are ample, pursuing a matter under universal jurisdiction can be time sensitive—not because the crimes themselves are temporally limited but because the opportunity to bring a matter may be fleeting.[16] As such, anyone wishing to file a complaint under universal jurisdiction must understand the relevant domestic law, have their resources in place, and be ready to file with little warning.

Each of these challenges requires advance consideration, including being aware of potentially favourable Forum States.

Categories of variables for identifying fora

Thinking broadly about what variables may indicate a 'favourable forum' depends on the purpose or goal of the universal criminal jurisdiction matter. For the purposes of this chapter, the 'goal' considered is simply the initiation of proceedings. This is because there are as many dynamic variables related to the facts in universal jurisdiction matters as there are in considering different Forum States—an attempt to analyze these with the 'goal' of an ultimate conviction is reserved for professional and specific legal advice.

The variables considered below are grouped in broad categories for conceptual ease: the existence of an enabling legal framework; the territorial presence of the accused and relevant victims; the available resources; and the relevant political will. The variables—and the categories themselves—intersect and interact. For example, the valuable role civil society organizations can play in supporting a case can be considered as a 'resource', but ability for civil society organizations to publicly push or pursue a universal jurisdiction matter may only be permitted because of adequate 'political will'. Likewise, the ability to overcome a lack of 'presence' and still initiate a case depends on an adequate 'enabling legal framework'.

There are other factors involved in bringing a universal jurisdiction matter that will not be discussed further. For example, universal jurisdiction is generally considered to be applicable only as a last resort.[17] Where there are other, willing, and competent fora in which another type of jurisdiction may be exercised, those fora are likely to be preferred and a universal jurisdiction matter is unlikely to proceed. Additionally, the strength of a State's justice system and its adherence to international human rights protections and the rule of law will weigh in favour or against a particular Forum State. However, this is a consideration beyond this chapter and should be the subject of further ethical, legal, and strategic examination. Rather, we discuss the following variables in relation to the Argentina case to question broadly what could be procedurally considered in initiating proceedings.

Enabling legal framework

An enabling legal framework is necessary to permit a universal jurisdiction matter to be brought in a potential Forum State's court. For the purposes of this chapter, this framework includes both the incorporation of the relevant international crimes into domestic law and the adoption or adaptation of the relevant criminal procedure to permit proceedings.

An international crime is 'incorporated' into domestic law most often by amending the Forum State's criminal code to include both international and domestic crimes or by establishing a dedicated 'international' crime code. This is important because, although they may relate to similar acts, the complexity and breadth of international crimes require specific articulation: for example, the war crime of murder has different elements than domestic murder or torture as a crime against humanity has different elements than domestic torture. In Argentina, universal jurisdiction can be exercised over crime against humanity (including torture and enforced disappearances), war crimes, and genocide.[18] A complaint under universal jurisdiction can be filed pursuant to Article 118 and Article 75, paragraph 22 of its Constitution and Article 5 of Law 26,200, the legislation that gives effect to Rome Statute obligations.[19] The Argentina judiciary exercise their jurisdiction based on a principle of subsidiary universal jurisdiction, meaning only if no other competent court has investigated or adjudicated on the same matter.[20] Alternatively, Germany created a separate national Code of Crimes Against International Law which enables prosecution for grave breaches of the Geneva Conventions, terrorism, torture, genocide, and trafficking of persons, amongst other offences.[21] There is no requirement of a link between the crime and Germany whatsoever; however, the non-national accused must be found to be voluntarily in Germany.

Once incorporated into domestic law, domestic courts have subject-matter jurisdiction over the crime. However, this subject-matter jurisdiction incorporates the relevant elements of the conduct and does not automatically mean that the court holds jurisdiction to hear matters that took place outside the Forum State's territory, or 'extraterritorially'.[22] In Argentina, the legislation that gives effect to Rome Statute obligations also permits Argentine courts to hear matters related to crimes that took place outside of Argentina by non-nationals if those crimes are listed in treaties to which Argentina is a party.[23]

It is necessary to consult domestic legal practitioners if attempting to initiate a case. However, without access to specific legal advice, State signature and ratification of certain treaties may assist in identifying whether and how a particular Forum State has incorporated international crimes into its courts' subject-matter jurisdiction. Where a potential Forum State is a party to the Rome Statute, it may have incorporated legislation. For example, both Argentina[24] and South Africa[25] make war crimes, crimes against humanity, and genocide crimes domestically prosecutable through legislation domesticating the Rome Statute. This is because the principle of complementarity (Article 1) and State Parties' obligations to 'cooperate fully' (Article 86) with the ICC has been read by parties to incorporate Rome Statute crimes into domestic law.[26]

Where a potential Forum State is not a party to the Rome Statute, signature to other treaties may indicate corresponding domestic legislation. This is because treaties, including the four Geneva Conventions,[27] the Genocide Convention,[28] and the Convention against Torture,[29] also require corresponding domestic obligations to enact relevant domestic legislation to give effect to the State Party's responsibilities. Further, treaty obligations to extradite or prosecute may pressure a Forum State to exercise jurisdiction.[30]

However, such implementing legislation short of incorporation of the Rome Statute may leave justice gaps for some harms. For example, Singapore has ratified the four Geneva Conventions[31] addressing conduct in armed conflict between States (international) but has not ratified Additional Protocol II[32] which addresses conduct in armed conflict other than between States (or non-international). Its implementing legislation—the Geneva Conventions Act 1973—incorporates and criminalizes solely 'grave breaches'[33] of the four Geneva Conventions. Thus, the legislation criminalizes war crimes under *international* armed conflict without criminalizing the same conduct for *non*-international armed conflict. This gap in the legal framework presents a problem for prosecuting crimes against the Rohingya, which have alternatively been classified since 2017 as genocide,[34] crimes against humanity,[35] or war crimes within a non-international armed conflict[36]—but not war crimes within an international armed conflict.

Treaty signature and ratification can also assist if a State has both signed the related treaties and is largely 'monist', meaning that treaties are self-executing and international law obligations automatically become a source of law for domestic practice upon signature. Notably, this is the case in Argentina[37] and arguably Japan,[38] South Korea,[39] and the Philippines.[40] This is as opposed to dualist States, such as Singapore,[41] Malaysia,[42] and Australia,[43] where the government must take some action, such as executive assent or legislative adoption, to have international law take effect in domestic affairs.[44]

Criminal proceedings are generally initiated by a public prosecutor who represents the State. This public prosecutor will generally have relevant guidelines under which their discretion is used to decide to pursue a matter. Separately, in civil law countries, victims' organizations can act as 'civil parties' to petition an investigating judge directly—rather than through the initiation of a prosecutor.[45] Some jurisdictions also permit 'civil parties' to seek damages under civil law at the same time as a criminal matter is determined.[46] Likewise, in many common law countries, private prosecution—or prosecution initiated by a private individual rather than the state prosecutor—may be available. Here, a lawyer may stand in as the listed party representing victims' groups.[47] In Argentina, BROUK made its case for its relevant standing through the Federal Criminal Procedure Code, which permits a private complainant to file a criminal complaint.[48]

However, with international crimes, Forum State criminal procedure may require the consent of a government official (for example, an attorney-general) or the State Prosecutor to file a case that relates to an international crime. In Argentina, this is not required. In contrast, in the UK, no magistrate may issue an arrest warrant in private prosecution cases related to certain offences, such as grave breaches of the Geneva Conventions or torture, without the consent of the Director of Private Prosecutions.[49] Enabling legislation that requires the consent of a government official, including political appointees, may introduce an additional political consideration for parties seeking to bring a universal jurisdiction prosecution, particularly where the prosecution is related to sitting or former State officials.[50]

It is important to differentiate between universal jurisdiction and three other types of jurisdiction that arise when incorporating international crimes in domestic law. Where universal jurisdiction is not available, it may be useful to consider the availability of extraterritorial, active personality, and passive personality jurisdiction.

Where the exercise of universal jurisdiction does not require *any* territorial link to the Forum State, extraterritorial jurisdiction permits a court to hear cases regarding particular crimes committed *outside* the Forum State's territory but requires another link such as the nationality of victims or the accused. Any enabling legal framework that supports the exercise of universal jurisdiction will have the relevant crimes incorporated into its domestic law and ensure that its law applies to conduct outside of its territory—that is, the law applies extraterritorially. Extraterritorial *application* of domestic criminal law is necessary for the exercise of universal jurisdiction for atrocity crimes; extraterritorial *jurisdiction*, while permitting prosecution of international crimes in domestic jurisdictions that have incorporated them, requires links to the Forum State that universal jurisdiction does not.[51]

For example, under Article 43 of the Law of the Republic of Indonesia, Number 26 of Year 2000, Concerning Human Rights Courts (Human Rights Courts Act), specialised ad hoc Human Rights Courts may be recommended by the Indonesian parliament and established by Presidential Decree. Despite not incorporating war crimes into domestic law, Article 7 of the Human Rights Courts Act incorporates both genocide and crimes against humanity within the jurisdiction of the ad hoc courts. However, under Article 5 establishing extraterritorial jurisdiction, the ad hoc courts only have jurisdiction over 'gross violations of human rights perpetrated by an Indonesian citizen'. Thus, any ad hoc Human Rights Court established by the Human Rights Courts Act has extraterritorial jurisdiction over genocide and crimes against humanity committed outside Indonesia—but only if such crimes were committed by Indonesian citizens. This distinction is crucial if the accused in a potential international criminal case brought in Indonesia is *not* themselves Indonesian. Thus, international crimes incorporated into domestic law *must* apply extraterritorially to permit the exercise of universal jurisdiction, but extraterritorial application does not permit universal jurisdiction alone. However, where there is no universal jurisdiction permitted within an enabling legal framework, extraterritorial jurisdiction may still permit the prosecution of international crimes where there is another relevant link to the Forum State.

This is the same for active and passive personality jurisdictions. Active personality jurisdiction describes circumstances where the 'link' to the Forum State is that the accused was a national at the time of the crime or became a national following the crime's commission—this may include dual nationals.[52] Passive personality jurisdiction describes circumstances where the 'link' to the Forum State is that the victim is that State's national. This may occur because the victim was a national at the time of the crime or because the victim became a national following the crime's commission.[53] Active or passive personality jurisdiction may be useful in Forum States that neighbour a State in which crimes are committed or that receive or resettle victims. Where active or passive personality jurisdiction is available, these are likely to be preferred to fora where no traditional link exists.

An enabling legal framework for universal jurisdiction will permit the relevant legislation to apply extraterritorially to harms perpetrated by and experienced by non-nationals. However, even where the enabling legal framework permits pure universal jurisdiction with no traditional link, it may be of assistance to argue that a particular Forum State is the most appropriate venue because of circumstances connected to the Forum State, including the presence of the accused or victims within the State's territory.

Presence

Just as Forum States have incorporated enabling legislation differently, so they also have differing requirements for the presence of the accused or relevant victims within its territory. These requirements are practical. If an accused is within the Forum State's territory, they are more likely to be legally served with their charges, detained, arrested, and physically present at trial.[54] If victims are within the Forum State's territory, this reduces barriers regarding access to evidence (and thus ideally shortens proceedings) and may make it easier for victims to participate in proceedings. Moreover, although not a traditional 'link', the presence of the accused and/or victims may assist in arguing the relevance of bringing a matter under universal jurisdiction in a court that would not otherwise hear international criminal cases.

Regarding the presence of the accused, State opinion and practice is divided regarding whether universal jurisdiction may be exercised if the accused is absent either at the filing of charges or for a trial itself. For example, in France the accused must habitually reside in France for a universal jurisdiction case to be brought against them for Rome Statute crimes.[55] The Netherlands requires voluntary physical presence of the accused in its territory to initiate an investigation and to proceed with trial.[56] The United Kingdom only permits prosecution regarding grave breaches of the Geneva Conventions and torture if the accused is voluntarily in the United Kingdom—however, this includes transit. [57]

'Voluntary' presence excludes extradition. However, the existence of extradition treaties, especially for international crimes, may assist where presence is needed but voluntariness is not.

Further, and in contrast, some States such as Finland[58] and Bangladesh[59] permit both investigation and trial *in absentia*. Such trials may provide symbolic justice to the victims but also carry risks for the rights of the accused. In response, Germany permits *in absentia* proceedings for international crimes, but only as a last resort.[60]

Regarding the presence of victims, the trajectory of universal jurisdiction cases in Europe for international crimes in Syria provides useful insight. Between 2015 and 2019, over 1.7 million Syrians entered Germany.[61] This influx led to a shift in focus of investigation from crimes in African States to those perpetrated in Syria.[62] The Federal Office for Migration and Refugees' standard questionnaire for Syrian asylum seekers asked whether applicants witnessed any potential war crimes and if they had any documentary evidence to support the claim.[63] In so doing, the German asylum unit created a significant docket of alleged perpetrators and international crimes.[64] Thus, the presence of the victim community in the jurisdiction added political weight to the call for accountability and allowed for smoother interactions with the investigative and prosecutorial units.

Applying the presence variables to Argentina, Argentina's enabling legislation is silent and does not prohibit investigation *in absentia*; at the time of writing, none of the accused in the Argentina case are in custody or on Argentinian soil. Argentina's geographic distance, and now its ongoing proceedings, also make it unlikely that any named accused in the case will travel to Argentina voluntarily. Without extradition, the absence of the accused may stymie future proceedings.

Moreover, Argentina's geographic distance means that it does not have a substantial Rohingya population. However, in lieu of access to victims within Argentina's territory, the civil society organization BROUK is involved in facilitating and securing the presence of victims despite their location overseas. Furthermore, the dedicated resources for collecting evidence of the Independent Investigative Mechanism for Myanmar (IIMM) eases some of the challenges posed to Argentina's investigators and the lack of presence of either accused or victims.

In this way, the absence of the relevant accused and victims within Argentinian territory is overcome by both Argentina's enabling legal framework, the involvement of civil society, and the existence of a relevant international investigative mechanism. These same resources could also make other jurisdictions potentially favourable, even where the presence of accused or victims is lacking but the legal framework is permissive.

Available resources

Resources, including legal expertise, access to evidence, and sufficient funding, may each make a Forum State more conducive for bringing a universal jurisdiction matter. This is because investigations and trials regarding international crimes are evidentiarily and legally complex, lengthy, and extremely costly. The geographic scope of a universal jurisdiction matter investigation is often wholly outside the Forum State's territory. Crime scenes and victims may be inaccessible because of ongoing armed conflict or a politically hostile domestic environment in the Territorial State. Distance may also further compound difficulties in securing safety for victims and investigative teams. The large-scale nature of international crimes and the fact they often took place years earlier adds to their complexity. Furthermore, investigating international crimes often involves interaction with hundreds of victims and witnesses to establish 'contextual elements'; for example, for a crime to be classified as a crime against humanity it must be shown that the conduct was widespread or systematic in nature.[65] Questions of command or superior responsibility that arise in international crimes, do not generally arise in domestic criminal matters, creating a further evidentiary burden.

This complexity often results in trials that run for years, if not decades. For example, in Argentina, the ongoing case against Rodolfo Martín Villa and others for the alleged crimes against humanity of torture, extrajudicial killings, and enforced disappearances between 1936 and 1977 was instituted over twelve years ago in 2010.[66] Additionally, lengthy proceedings, securing of documentary and technical evidence, ensuring the presence of victims at trial, and providing legal expertise and translation services all adds to the cost. [67]

Thus, the availability of resources to address these challenges is an important consideration for a case's practicality and viability. Particular mechanisms and entities may ease the resource burden, including: (1) specialised investigative units (SIUs); (2) Mutual Legal Assistance Treaties (MLATs), Joint Investigative Teams (JITs), or other types of regional cooperation; (3) international investigative mechanisms; and (4) the presence and support of relevant civil society organizations (CSOs).

First, SIUs centralize the necessary expertise of analysts, prosecutors, and investigators in international law and criminal law—making a complex process more efficient.[68] SIUs are domestically-constituted units—for example, within a national police force[69] in conjunction with State prosecution services[70]—mandated to conduct cross-border and foreign investigations, support cross-border cooperation by facilitating extradition and monitoring requests, and prepare and prosecute international crimes.[71] Further, these specialized units are often awarded separate budgets,[72] and thus their presence indicates a form of Forum State political will to investigate and prosecute international crimes.

Second, the resource needs for adequate expertise and access to evidence may be eased where JITs, MLATs, or other types of regional cooperation exist. JITs are collaborative efforts put together by two or more States through their respective competent authorities. The establishment of JITs through a legal agreement allows States to pool their investigative, prosecutorial, and judicial resources and share the cost burden.[73] MLATs are bilateral or multilateral treaties signed between States to assist in extraterritorial investigation and prosecution. An MLAT complements the role of a JIT and allows cooperation between States on a horizontal level on matters of criminal law.[74] MLATs may pre-empt political disagreements by clarifying circumstances in which information and resources may be shared between jurisdictions. This can also complement in extradition requests, especially when it concerns a politically fraught crime or situation. Pro-international criminal law architecture, like JITs and MLATs, can be supported by specialized regional cooperation. For example, the European Union's Genocide Network coordinates best practice sharing within the region.[75] Such formalized cooperation reduces the resource burden on potential Forum States.

Third, international investigatory mechanisms, such as the IIMM, reduce the cost, expertise, and access burdens on Forum States. Such international mechanisms are ad hoc, non-judicial, and context specific in nature. Regarding crimes against the Rohingya, the IIMM complements the role of SIUs and reduces the burden on local CSOs by 'collect[ing], consolidate[ing], preserv[ing] and analys[ing]' relevant potential evidence to a criminal law standard in order to specifically 'prepare files … [for] criminal proceedings, in national, regional or international courts or tribunals that have or may in the future have jurisdiction over [the relevant] crimes'.[76] In other words, the IIMM does not conduct legal trials itself but shares the collected information on request by courts. Thus, the IIMM and its precursors support the initiation of universal jurisdiction cases in Forum States that would otherwise be overlooked or impractical because of cost, availability of expertise, or access to evidence.

Fourth, the presence and proactivity of relevant CSOs assists in accessing evidence and agitating for greater resources. Local CSOs specifically have the advantage of being geographically closer to victims and holding greater contextual knowledge than international or foreign entities.[77] Consequently, CSOs may be amongst the first to document atrocities, be best placed to facilitate access to victims, or act as a conduit between the international and domestic actors involved. Depending on their purpose, they may also be the most consistently vocal on the victims' needs.[78] In contexts where there CSOs are active—such as in support of the Rohingya—CSO efforts may help to bridge what would otherwise be gaps in Forum State officials' ability to understand and access information regarding the alleged crimes.

Applying these resource variables to the Argentina case, although lacking a SIU, its judges (and relevantly, the Federal Investigative Judge) are empowered by its civil law system to undertake the international investigation, issue arrest warrants, and request extradition.[79] Prior and ongoing universal jurisdiction cases mean that there is relevant experience within the Argentinian legal profession. Where Argentinian officials are unable to access evidence, the existence of the IIMM may assist. Furthermore, Argentina has legislation that allows for international legal assistance and extradition for the investigation and prosecution of crimes wherever there is no separate existing bilateral treaty between Argentina and the requesting State.[80] Finally, BROUK has played a significant role in documenting atrocities and persuading Argentina to open the current case,[81] including most recently facilitating the testimony of six Rohingya women survivors in court in Buenos Aires.[82]

However, one resource is potentially unique to the case. BROUK is represented in Argentina by Tomas Quintana, former UN Special Rapporteur on the situation of human rights in Myanmar.[83] Prior to his specific role on Myanmar, Quintana practised law for more than two decades in Argentina specializing in human rights and security issues in a regional context—skills highly relevant to this case.[84] The value of Quintana's expertise and specific contextual knowledge cannot be overstated; however, it alone would unlikely be sufficient for the case to proceed.

Political will

Political will is perhaps the most fluid of the categories discussed in this chapter—even where a Forum State may support bringing some cases, it may not necessarily support others. For the purposes of this chapter, 'political will' is defined as government decision-maker willingness to create, support, or pursue a system that permits a Forum State's courts to exercise universal jurisdiction. In the longer term, political will underpins government signature and adherence to the international treaties and the creation of enabling legislation to give courts the power to hear matters under universal jurisdiction. It also underpins funding choices and policy priorities like the establishment of SIUs. In the shorter term and in Forum States where government consent is necessary, political will can dictate whether or not a particular case proceeds. For the purposes of discussion, political will as a variable will be addressed on two levels: (1) in relation to the international legal principles of sovereignty and non-interference; and (2) in relation to domestic political priorities.

As discussed above, universal jurisdiction is predicated on the recognition that certain acts 'are so serious and the magnitude of their impact so great that their commission shocks the conscience of all humanity'.[85] The reasoning follows that, if the conduct offends all humanity, it may be prosecuted anywhere. However, the exercise of universal jurisdiction abuts onto other international *jus cogens* norms: sovereignty and non-interference. Under these principles, the Territorial or Primary State has sovereignty—or retains control of its internal affairs—and a Forum State must refrain from interference in the territorial States' ability to retain that control.

This tension has regularly been voiced by States in the United Nations (UN) General Assembly and its Sixth (Legal) Committee since 2010.[86] States such as Syria, whose nationals are being investigated, charged, or tried under universal jurisdiction, have expressed concern that, 'the existence of serious loopholes and irregular practices in international relations make it impossible to achieve the purposes behind the notion of universal jurisdiction', referring to a concern in broadening its scope and use.[87] In 2019, Myanmar 'highlight[ed to the Sixth Committee] the risk of selectivity and manipulation in the application of the principle of universal jurisdiction', further stating the establishment of the IIMM was 'a blatant attempt to abuse the application of universal jurisdiction which [lacks] consensus amongst nations [... and operates] without the consent of the country concerned'.[88]

Other States, including Argentina, regularly restate the importance of avenues for accountability, but still note concerns about universal jurisdiction's potential use in politically motivated attacks.[89] Even Germany, whose courts now hear roughly the highest number of matters internationally under universal jurisdiction, noted in 2020 that, 'we would prefer for the Security Council to give the ICC more possibilities to try the most serious crimes under international law'.[90]

Positive statements at the Sixth Committee may indicate a potential Forum State's favourability, but even the most supportive statements indicate that the scope of universal jurisdiction is limited and should only be exercised where no other relevant jurisdiction exists.

Furthermore, such statements may be more indicative of political convenience than proactivity. In December 2017, the UN General Assembly adopted a resolution to commission a report by the Secretary-General, collecting 'information and observations on the scope and application of universal jurisdiction'.[91] Only 11 States responded to the Secretary-General's request for information. Of these, the report quotes Argentina, Australia, El Salvador, Mexico, Qatar, and Switzerland as stating that universal jurisdiction was necessary or plays a role in reducing impunity for international crimes.[92] The small response, however, failed to recommend a consensus on the use of universal jurisdiction. Similar points were also made in the International Law Commission's 2018 report to the UN General Assembly proposing a study on the scope of universal jurisdiction.[93] At the time of writing, this study has yet to be published.

Instead, domestic priorities may be a better indicator for political will than international statements. This particularly arises when a government official must provide consent to initiate a matter under universal jurisdiction, to be discussed further below. This applies both where there is a lack of interest in a conflict as well as where there is an active State interest, but in maintaining rather than testing a particular bilateral relationship.

Applying questions of political will to Argentina, Argentina's enabling legal framework and its previous or ongoing trials under universal jurisdiction indicate general, or at least prior, political will towards the use of universal jurisdiction.[94]

'Other Argentinas?'—Application of variables

Thus far, this chapter has examined four categories of variables in relation to the Argentina case to consider what may constitute another favourable Forum State: an enabling legal framework; the presence of the accused or victims; resources, including legal expertise, access to evidence, and ability to cover or reduce costs; and political will. This section applies these variables to three different potential Forum States to examine how they interact. It does not purport to address all variables or circumstances in depth; rather, each example provides a template with which to consider other jurisdictions that may fill gaps in justice for crimes against the Rohingya.

Presence of victims and potential accused? Considering India

India has a high likelihood of the presence of both Rohingya and members of the Myanmar military (relevant as alleged perpetrators). India and Myanmar not only share a 1,700-kilometre-long porous border but also ancestry and deep ethnic ties.[95] This proximity and relationship means that it also hosts a large Rohingya refugee community.[96] Prior to the coup and since 2011, it is estimated that over 40,000 Rohingya crossed to India.[97] India's proximity and relationship also means that it hosts Myanmar military defectors. Since the 2021 coup, it is estimated that over 15,000 to 20,000 people have crossed from Myanmar to the Indian states of Mizoram and Manipur.[98] It has been reported that a handful of sheltering defectors along the Indo-Myanmar border were senior officers within the ranks of the Tatmadaw and could have contributed to the commission of crimes against humanity and war crimes against the Rohingya in the 2016–17 violence.[99] This could enable some access to victim and witness testimony should a universal jurisdiction case regarding crimes against the Rohingya be brought in India.

Regarding its legal framework, India is not a party to the Rome Statute and has no consequent binding legal obligation to incorporate treaty crimes into its municipal laws. Whereas India has ratified the Genocide Convention,[100] it has not passed a law preventing or punishing genocide. Similarly, India is a signatory to the Convention against Torture,[101] but it has neither ratified the Convention nor passed a domestic law criminalizing and punishing torture. In contrast, India has passed a domestic law to give effect to its ratification of the four Geneva Conventions in 1949.[102] The Geneva Conventions Act (in this subsection, the Act), without amending the relevant criminal code, allows for the prosecution of violation of grave breaches[103] and punishes 'any person within or without India [who] commits or attempts to commit or abets or procures the commission by any other person of, a grave breach of any of the Conventions'.[104] The Act indicates a minimum of fourteen years of imprisonment for non-murder cases and awards the death penalty or life imprisonment for wilful killing cases.[105]

The Act criminalizes the commission of grave breaches by any person irrespective of his nationality or citizenship,[106] recognizing universal jurisdiction over the grave breaches.[107] Furthermore, it has extraterritorial application, permitting the treatment of an offence committed outside India 'as if it had been committed at any place within India at which [the accused] may be found'.[108] This phrase 'within India at which [the accused] may be found' indicates that the accused must be present to trigger the criminal justice mechanism. However, this presence requirement could be less cumbersome than in other potential Forum States due to Indian–Myanmar relations and its geographic proximity.

Though the Act facilitates the prosecution of foreign nationals, a court can take cognisance of a complaint only when it is filed by the Government of India through its legal representative with the consent of the Executive.[109] Furthermore, the power to decide on the question of applicability of the Geneva Conventions to the relevant circumstances lies with the Government and not the courts.[110]

Thus, India presents considerable hurdles as a Forum State if solely considering its enabling legal framework. This is because incorporating only grave breaches into domestic law—and therefore establishing subject-matter jurisdiction over only war crimes in international armed conflict—is unlikely to address the harm alleged as crimes against humanity, genocide, and non-international armed conflict war crimes experienced by the Rohingya.

Further, India has indicated little political will to permit universal jurisdiction in its public statements and policies. At the Sixth Committee, India acknowledged that universal jurisdiction may exist under treaty regimes for the crime of genocide, crimes against humanity, and war crimes but emphasized that it is only applicable to State Parties and has *not* become a 'commonly exercisable jurisdiction'.[111] Domestically and with reference to crimes against the Rohingya, the Government of India argued before the Indian Supreme Court in a case concerning the deportation of Rohingya that the influx of 'illegal immigrants' is 'orchestrated for monetary considerations' and constitutes a 'national security' and 'internal security' threat.[112] This argument indicates the Government's conceptualization of Rohingya as 'displaced persons' internationally and 'illegal immigrants' domestically—not victims of mass atrocities and therefore unlikely to warrant Executive consent for potential prosecution.[113]

In addition, it is likely not politically or diplomatically in the interest of India to pursue justice for the Rohingya. India requires the assistance from the Myanmar military to secure its north-eastern border and hand over armed rebels who attack Indian paramilitary forces and seek refuge in Myanmar.[114] Moreover, the growing business of the transfer of arms and armaments to the military junta by the Indian Government, even after the 2021 coup, shows a growing relationship between India and the Myanmar military.[115] Particularly where any accused may be members of the military junta, this may dissuade prosecution in India.

This is not to say that India may never be a favourable Forum State, particularly where grave breaches may be relevant. Even with regard to the Rohingya, India voiced concern about the heightened violence against civilians in Myanmar both before and after the 2021 coup.[116] Furthermore, the growing movement of refugees from Myanmar to India's north-eastern region could increase the financial burden on the Indian Government, with continued armed conflict in

Myanmar heightening India's concerns regarding growing regional instability.[117] It is possible in the future that India's political and security interests may turn and thus make Executive consent in relevant prosecutions, or even further ratification of relevant treaties, more likely.

Until then, the gaps in its enabling legislative framework, when read with the Government's 'anti-Rohingya' rhetoric and increasing anti-Muslim domestic politics,[118] do not instil confidence in India being a favourable site to advance justice through a universal jurisdiction case.

Enabling framework and adequate resources? Considering Australia

Australia is geographically further than India, but still has links to Myanmar and the Rohingya to make it a relevant Forum State. Of the three jurisdictions considered here, Australia has the broadest enabling legal framework. A common law dualist system, Australia is a signatory to the Rome Statute and has incorporated international crimes into its domestic legislation.[119] Furthermore, of the three jurisdictions, Australia consistently ranks highly in rule-of-law indicators, including protection of fair trial rights and independence of the judiciary.[120]

Australia, with Canada and New Zealand, has consistently recognised the importance of universal jurisdiction—indicating some political will and interest—and encouraged UN Member States at the Sixth Committee to 'amend their domestic legislation to apply universal jurisdiction to the most serious international crimes'.[121] In addition, Australia co-sponsored the UN Human Rights Council resolution to establish the Independent International Fact-Finding Mission on Myanmar—despite previously calling for Myanmar itself to investigate atrocities in Rakhine State.[122] Regarding the potential presence of victims, it was reported in 2018 that there were approximately 3,000 Rohingya living in Australia, either on temporary or permanent protection visas.[123]

Australia has incorporated the international crimes of genocide, war crimes, and crimes against humanity in Division 268 of the domestic Criminal Code Act 1995 (Commonwealth Criminal Code or the Code). The crime of torture—separate from torture as a war crime[124] or crime against humanity[125]—is incorporated in Division 274.

Under Section 15.4, the Commonwealth Criminal Code permits jurisdiction over the offences of genocide, war crimes, and crimes against humanity,[126] as well as torture:[127]

> (a) [w]hether or not the conduct constituting the alleged offence occurs in Australia; and
> (b) [w]hether or not a result of the conduct constituting the alleged offence occurs in Australia.

Furthermore, the Code does not prohibit the prosecution of non-Australian nationals.

Criminal procedure, including whether Australian courts can hear matters in the absence of the accused, is dependent on the state or territory legislation in which the case is brought.[128] The Criminal Procedure Act 2009 (Vic) in Australia's second most populous state, Victoria, requires that an accused must attend all hearings in a trial unless excused by the court.[129] 'Attendance' includes by video link,[130] but a refusal of an accused to attend could cause issues for the common law. This is because the 'general rule' within Victorian common law is that proceedings should be in the accused's presence, 'regardless of whether he or she wishes to attend'.[131] This suggests a prosecution would not likely proceed should an accused refuse to attend, especially when not in custody.

Section 268.121(1) of the Commonwealth Criminal Code requires that 'proceedings' for genocide, war crimes, and crimes against humanity 'must not be commenced without the Attorney-General's written consent'. This prevented prosecution of the then-President of Sri Lanka Mahinda Rajapaksa, brought by a Sri Lankan-born Australian citizen in 2011 before Rajapaksa's travel to Australia for a Commonwealth Heads of Government Meeting.[132] An indictment was filed by the citizen in Victorian courts, with a request to the Attorney-General to permit prosecution. The then-Attorney-General Robert McClelland declined prosecution; according to his spokesperson, prosecuting would 'breach Australian and international laws that provide immunity from criminal prosecution for heads of state'.[133]

Like the attempted prosecution of Rajapaksa, in 2018 lawyers brought a matter on behalf of the Rohingya community in Australia against Aung San Suu Kyi, the then-Minister of the Office of the President and Foreign Minister of the Republic of the Union of Myanmar, before her planned attendance in Australia for an ASEAN-Australian Summit.[134] At the time, the then-Attorney General Christian Porter declined to prosecute citing functional immunity.[135]

Despite declining more recent universal jurisdiction cases, Australia has previously indicated its willingness and its ability to try international crimes domestically. Associated with the Allied Powers, Australian military courts held more than 300 trials from 1945 to 1951 under the *War Crimes Act 1945*.[136] Trials under the *War Crimes Act 1945* ceased after 1961, but public interest was renewed in the 1980s. In 1986, the Australian Broadcasting Corporation aired radio and television programmes that raised allegations that Nazi war criminals had been permitted to settle in Australia with impunity since World War II.[137] The issue was raised in the Australian Parliament and the Government established an official inquiry.[138] Following the inquiry, the Government established the 'Special Investigations Unit' (Australian SIU) within the Attorney-General's office—arguably due to public pressure to prevent or address impunity.[139]

Similar to some SIUs today,[140] the Australian SIU's purpose was 'to seek and obtain admissible evidence of the commission of war crimes as defined in the War Crimes Act 1945, as amended [eventually by the War Crimes Amendment Act 1988], for the purpose of charges being laid and prosecutions being undertaken in the ordinary criminal courts of Australia'.[141] However, the War Crimes Amendment Act 1988 only permitted prosecution for war crimes committed 'in Europe in the period beginning 1 September 1939 and ending on 8 May 1945' against Australian citizens and residents, British subjects, or citizens of Allied nations.[142] By the time it was dissolved in 1994,[143] the Australian SIU referred only four cases to the Australian Commonwealth Director of Public Prosecutions,[144] with three going to trial and no convictions.[145] In 27 other cases where the SIU found allegations merited further investigation, the Australian SIU also concluded they were 'unable to obtain sufficient evidence' to refer for prosecution.[146] At the time of writing, no unit to investigate international crimes for domestic prosecution has been reconstituted. In addition, no universal jurisdiction cases have proceeded to prosecution.

Australia's current lack of universal jurisdiction cases could be attributable in part to political will—in addition to citing functional immunity just prior to declining prosecution of Suu Kyi, Government representatives including the Prime Minister were publicly seeking to give Suu Kyi the benefit of the doubt regarding crimes against the Rohingya.[147] In fact, the then-Foreign Minister Julie Bishop stated in October 2017 that she had refrained from criticising Suu Kyi over the violence 'because I can see that Aung San Suu Kyi can't be blamed for what's happening. She has to be part of the solution, otherwise we will be going back decades in terms of Myanmar's growth and prosperity'.[148] Declining prosecution for an accused that, at least then, was seen by the Australian Government to be related to the stability of Myanmar could have been politically and diplomatically strategic.

This raises whether a case with a different accused—especially an accused lacking functional immunity—would have greater success. Given the public and media's role in establishing the Australian SIU, this also raises whether greater success could be had with cases that can argue that prosecution will prevent Australia from becoming a safe haven for perpetrators, particularly following the 2021 Myanmar military coup.

Political will and potential presence? Considering Turkey

Turkey is the most distant geographically from Myanmar of the three jurisdictions considered. However, as Argentina proves, there are potentially relevant Forum States outside of the region as well.

Turkey is relevant potentially for its support of The Gambia's case against Myanmar at the ICJ. The Gambia initiated the 2019 application to the ICJ as a member of the Organisation of Islamic Cooperation (OIC).[149] Created in 1972, the OIC is comprised of 57 member States.[150] Of these, Turkey is a founding member of the OIC.[151] At the time The Gambia petitioned the ICJ, it was reported that Turkey pledged at least $100,000—the same as Malaysia and Nigeria—towards funding the case.[152] Thus, Turkey is one of only five States within the OIC to put forward its own tranche of money indicating its support for accountability. This showed at least a collective willingness to support accountability measures for crimes against the Rohingya.

Like India, Turkey is not a party to the Rome Statute[153] or the Additional Protocols of the Geneva Conventions. However, Turkey is a party to the Geneva

Conventions themselves, as well as the Convention against Torture and the Genocide Convention.[154] This suggests that war crimes in non-international armed conflicts are unlikely to be incorporated into domestic legislation, but that war crimes in international armed conflict,[155] torture as a crime against humanity, and genocide may be available.

Examination of the domestic law confirms this to be the case—to a limited degree. Turkey has criminalized genocide and specific crimes against humanity, including torture, under its domestic Criminal Code (Turkish Criminal Code).[156] Genocide is incorporated under Article 76 and closely reflects the definition of genocide within the Genocide Convention. Crimes against humanity, described in the Turkish Criminal Code as 'offences against humanity', are incorporated into Article 77 and are limited to: 'intentional killing'; 'intentional injury'; 'torture or inhuman treatment or slavery'; 'depriving one [of] his/her liberty'; 'the subjecting of persons to biological experiments'; 'sexual assault [or] sexual abuse of children'; 'impregnation by force'; and 'forced prostitution'. For both genocide[157] and offences against humanity,[158] the Turkish Criminal Code provides no temporal limit within which to bring a case.

Of particular note is the crime of torture. Like many other jurisdictions,[159] an act of torture can be criminalized as a domestic crime, but also as an international crime. The familiarity with torture in domestic criminal law may lessen the learning curve for domestic practitioners who may be unfamiliar with prosecuting international crimes. This may be relevant for crimes against the Rohingya as the Independent International Fact-Finding Mission on Myanmar documented torture of Rohingya by Myanmar officials both before and during the 2017 violence.[160]

Regarding torture, Article 94(1) of the Turkish Criminal Code criminalizes the conduct of 'a public officer who performs any act towards a person that is incompatible with human dignity, and which causes that person to suffer physically or mentally, or affects the person's capacity to perceive or his ability to act of his own will, or insults them'. Notably, unlike the definition in other contexts, the 'torture' under the Turkish Criminal Code does not have to be related to a political purpose but rather only perpetrated by a public official.[161] Related to international crimes, Article 77(1)(c) also lists torture as an 'offence against humanity', of which there is no temporal limit to bringing a case.

Articles 13(1)(a) and 13(1)(b) indicate that Turkish law applies to torture (both singularly and as a crime against humanity), genocide, and other offences against humanity 'committed in a foreign country whether or not committed by a citizen or a non-citizen of Turkey'. This provides extraterritorial application and leaves open prosecution of a non-citizen. Furthermore, Article 13 does not appear to require that a non-national accused be residing in Turkey for prosecution to begin, although it has been stated that it is a 'general rule' that the accused must be on Turkish soil.[162]

There was a brief opportunity in which it was expected that members of the Myanmar junta would physically attend the November 2021 INTERPOL General Assembly[163]—raising the possibility that a representative of the junta implicated in atrocities against the Rohingya could be served with court documents to initiate universal jurisdiction proceedings. Ultimately, the visit did not eventuate, but raised the importance of preparation even for jurisdictions not generally thought to exercise universal jurisdiction and which are geographically distant from Myanmar.

Article 13(2) mandates that the Minister for Justice must initiate criminal justice proceedings in universal jurisdiction matters related to the relevant crimes.[164] Thus, domestic Turkish law permits the prosecution of some international crimes under universal jurisdiction, and it may be possible to begin a matter regarding these crimes without the accused being physically present in Turkey. However, like India and Australia, Turkish domestic law requires a political actor—here, the Minister for Justice—to initiate proceedings.

Turkey has been active in addressing the Sixth Committee regarding the use of universal jurisdiction.[165] In these discussions, it has indicated that it is not opposed to the exercise of universal jurisdiction in Turkish domestic courts but emphasized 'the importance of observing the delicate balance between ensuring the legitimacy and reliability of universal jurisdiction on the one hand, and preventing impunity for specific crimes on the other'.[166]

This, along with the requirement of the Minister of Justice to initiate a case, suggests that any approach pursuing universal jurisdiction may require grounding the request in justification that includes why Turkey is the relevant and appropriate Forum State to hold the accused accountable. This may be where the accused is present or if, although unlikely, Rohingya victims arrive in Turkey.

Barriers to accessing evidence, like in other jurisdictions, is eased somewhat with the work of the IIMM. However, barriers regarding experience in prosecuting international crime remain. Domestic practitioners' experience with prosecution of torture as a domestic crime may help.[167] Here, it may be the case that the international legal obligation to investigate and extradite or prosecute for torture is also a legal obligation under Turkish domestic law. Turkey has ratified the Convention against Torture—meaning its national legislature has accepted that Turkey has duties under the treaty.[168] Under Article 90 of the Turkish Constitution, '[i]nternational agreements duly put into effect have the force of law'.[169] Furthermore, if there is conflict between domestic law and international agreements 'concerning fundamental rights and freedoms and laws … the provisions of international agreements shall prevail'.[170] This suggests that the obligation to investigate and then to extradite or prosecute for torture exists in Turkish domestic law as well as in international law. However, the meaning of the language in Article 90 is contested.[171]

Returning to political will, Turkey's Ambassador to Bangladesh, Mustafa Osman Turan, said in 2021 that 'helping the Rohingya is one of our main foreign policy objectives' and that '[a]ccountability is a primary guarantee for preventing the recurrence of such crimes in the future'.[172] However, Turkey's own domestic human rights record, specifically since its own 2016 coup attempt,[173] may give politicians pause in supporting domestic trials that could encourage other jurisdictions to do the same to Turkish authorities. Thus, Turkey's support of the ICJ case 'in close cooperation with the OIC',[174] may be a way of supporting the Rohingya through a collective international channel without exposing itself to risk.

Conclusion

Although ongoing, the case in Argentina is one example of how the exercise of universal jurisdiction, as a tool, can fill gaps in justice for crimes against the Rohingya. Using Argentina as a springboard for further investigation, this chapter attempts to identify and simplify some of the many variables that make Argentina, and potentially other Forum States, favourable jurisdictions for initiating matters under universal jurisdiction. This chapter has identified four categories of variables that could be relevant in this identification: an enabling legal framework; the presence of the accused or victims; resources, including the legal expertise, access to evidence, and the ability to cover or reduce costs; and political will. Applying them to India, Australia, and Turkey, it has considered how these variables interact and intersect—one way of evaluating other possible Forum States. It has not presumed that any one Forum State will be 'right' for all circumstances. Instead, its purpose has been, using Argentina as a guide, to provide one metric by which other potential Forum States can be identified to seek justice for the Rohingya.

Notes

1 This chapter adapts and builds on an earlier paper by Jennifer Keene-McCann for the Asia Justice Coalition secretariat, 'Universal Criminal Jurisdiction Scoping Paper' (*Asia Justice Coalition,* March 2021) <https://www.asiajusticecoalition.org/_files/ugd/811bc6_4c6c67c3617145b1a98067342a29964b.pdf?index=true> accessed 30 May 2022. The authors are grateful for the stimulating conversations had with expert colleagues in an ongoing convening series held by the Asia Justice Coalition on universal criminal jurisdiction.

2 Burmese Rohingya Organisation UK (BROUK), 'Historic Decision by Argentinian Courts to Take Up Genocide Case against Myanmar' (28 November 2021) <https://www.brouk.org.uk/historic-decision-by-argentinian-courts-to-take-up-genocide-case-against-myanmar/> accessed 24 May 2022.

3 Owen Bowcott, 'Gambia Files Rohingya Genocide Case against Myanmar at UN Court' *The Guardian* (11 November 2019) <https://www.theguardian.com/world/2019/nov/11/gambia-rohingya-genocide-myanmar-un-court> accessed 24 May 2022.

4 Rome Statute of the International Criminal Court (adopted 17 July 1998, entered into force 1 July 2002) 2187 UNTS 90.

5 *Application of the Convention on the Prevention and Punishment of the Crime of Genocide* (*The Gambia* v *Myanmar*) (Order on the Request for the Indication of Provisional Measures) 23 January 2020 <https://www.icj-cij.org/en/case/178/institution-proceedings> accessed 28 May 2022.

6 *Situation in the People's Republic of Bangladesh/Republic of the Union of Myanmar* (Decision Pursuant to Article 15 of the Rome Statute on the Authorisation of an Investigation) 14 November 2019 <https://www.icc-cpi.int/sites/default/files/CourtRecords/CR2019_06955.PDF> accessed on 28 May 2022.

7 ibid.

8 The focus of this chapter is on universal *criminal* jurisdiction rather than civil jurisdiction, but preparation for initiating civil matters will also benefit from many of the same variables considered here.
9 Sienho Lee, 'Universal Jurisdiction: Concept, Logic, and Reality' (2011) Chinese Journal of International Law 503, 504.
10 International Law Commission, 'Annex A: Universal Criminal Jurisdiction' (30 April–1 June and 2 July–10 August 2018) UN Doc A/73/10, [6].
11 See further *Attorney-General of the Government of Israel v Eichmann* (1962) International Law Reports, v 36, 304 (Israel Supreme Court) and *Polyukhovitch v Commonwealth* (1991) 172 CLR 501 [33]-[34] (Australian High Court).
12 Although piracy is sometimes referred to as a crime under universal jurisdiction, see Tamsin Paige, 'Piracy and Universal Jurisdiction' (2013) 12 Macquarie Law Journal 131.
13 For example, *Wetboek van Strafvordering* 1921 (Dutch Criminal Code of Proceedings), art 51(f) as cited in Open Society Justice Initiative and TRIAL International, 'Briefing Paper: Universal Jurisdiction Law and Practice in the Netherlands' (2019) <https://trialinternational.org/wp-content/uploads/2019/05/Universal-Jurisdiction-Law-and-Practice-in-The-Netherlands.pdf> accessed 24 May 2022.
14 Máximo Langer and Mackenzie Eason, 'The Quiet Expansion of Universal Jurisdiction' (2019) 30 The European Journal of International Law 779.
15 For example, UNGA Sixth Committee (76th Session) 'Concluding Debate on Universal Jurisdiction Principle, Sixth Committee Speakers Wrestle with Challenging Balance between State Sovereignty, Fighting Impunity' (22 October 2021) UN Doc GA/L/3642.
16 Some Forum States that permit universal jurisdiction require the accused to be voluntarily present within its territory—even if only in transit. See contrasting practice of Hungary, Finland, Croatia, and Spain (which do not require presence of the accused) versus Turkey and France (requiring presence of the accused) and Romania (requiring voluntary presence) as discussed in: Isidoro Blanco Cordero, 'Universal Jurisdiction: General Report' (2008) 79 Revue Internationale de Droit Pénale 59, 65–66.
17 UNGA Sixth Committee (76th Session) (n 15).
18 See Ley de Implementación del Estatuto de Roma, Ley 26.200 de 2007 (Argentina), art 5.
19 Constitution of the Argentine Nation 1853 (reinst. 1983, rev. 1994); Ley de Implementación del Estatuto de Roma, Ley 26.200 de 2007.
20 Constitution of the Argentine Nation 1853 (reinst. 1983, rev. 1994).
21 The German National Code is unique in its far-reaching jurisdiction. Gesetz sure Einführung des Völkerstrafgesetzbuches, Bundesgesetzblatt Teil I, 2002 Nr 42, 2254, as cited in Luc Reydams. *Universal Jurisdiction: International and Municipal Legal Perspectives* (OUP, 2003) 156–157.
22 Within the Convention against Torture, art 7 does not exclude prosecution *in absentia*, but it also does not explicitly require it. Rather, art 7(1) refers specifically to instances where a suspect is 'in the territory' of the State Party. Convention Against Torture and Other Cruel, Inhuman or Degrading Treatment or Punishment (adopted 10 December 1984, entered into force 26 June 1987) 1465 UNTS 85 (Convention against Torture).
23 Ley de Implementación del Estatuto de Roma, Ley 26.200 de 2007, art 3(d). The same law also requires that an investigation be opened if a person suspected of an international crime be found within Argentina's territory and they are not extradited (art 4).
24 Ley de Implementación del Estatuto de Roma, Ley 26.200 de 2007, arts 8-10.

25 Implementation of the Rome Statute of the International Criminal Court Act 2002 (South Africa), s 2.
26 Britta Lisa Krings, 'The Principles of 'Complementarity' and Universal Jurisdiction in International Criminal Law: Antagonists or Perfect Match?' (2012) 4 Goettingen Journal of International Law 737, 749.
27 Geneva Convention for the Amelioration of the Condition of the Wounded and Sick in Armed Forces in the Field (First Geneva Convention)(adopted 12 August 1949, entered into force 21 October 1950) 75 UNTS 31, art 49; Geneva Convention for the Amelioration of the Condition of Wounded, Sick and Shipwrecked Members of Armed Forces at Sea (Second Geneva Convention) (adopted 12 August 1949, entered into force 21 October 1950) 75 UNTS 85, art 50; Geneva Convention Relative to the Treatment of Prisoners of War (Third Geneva Convention) (adopted 12 August 1949, entered into force 21 October 1950) 75 UNTS 135, art 129; and Geneva Convention Relative to the Protection of Civilian Persons in Time of War (Fourth Geneva Convention) (adopted 12 August 1949, entered into force 21 October 1950) 75 UNTS 287, art 146.
28 Convention on the Prevention and Punishment of the Crime of Genocide (adopted 9 December 1948, entered into force 12 January 1951) 78 UNTS 277, art 5.
29 Convention against Torture and Other Cruel, Inhuman or Degrading Treatment or Punishment (adopted 10 December 1984, entered into force 26 June 1987) 1465 UNTS 85 (Convention against Torture), arts 4–5.
30 See *Arrest Warrant of 11 April 2000 (DRC v Belgium) Judgment* (Merits), [2002] ICJ Rep 75.
31 'UN Treaty Body Database: Ratification Status for Singapore' (*United Nations Human Rights Treaty Bodies*) <https://tbinternet.ohchr.org/_layouts/15/TreatyBodyExternal/Treaty.aspx> accessed 31 May 2022.
32 Protocol Additional to the Geneva Conventions of 12 August 1949, and relating to the Protection of Victims of Non-International Armed Conflicts (Protocol II) (adopted 8 June 1977, entered into force 7 December 1978) 1125 UNTS 609.
33 Geneva Conventions Act 1973 (Singapore), art 3(1).
34 UNHCR, 'Report of the Detailed Findings of the Independent International Fact-Finding Mission on Myanmar' (17 September 2018) UN Doc A HRC 39 CRP.2.
35 ibid.
36 'Two Burmese Soldiers Confess to War Crimes against the Rohingya' *The Economist* (10 September 2020).
37 Constitution of The Argentine Nation 1853 (reinst. 1983, rev. 1994), art 31.
38 Valerio de Oliveira Mazzuoli and Dilton Ribeiro, 'The Japanese Legal System and the *Pro Homine* Principle in Human Rights Treaties' (2015) 15 Anuario Mexicano de Derecho Internacional 239.
39 Wen-Chen Chang, 'The Convergence of Constitutions and International Human Rights: Taiwan and South Korea in Comparison' (2010) 36 North Carolina Journal of International Law 593.
40 Romel Regalado Bagares, 'The Direct Effect of International Law in Philippine Practice' in eds Chesterman, Owada, and Saul, *Oxford Handbook of International Law in Asia and the Pacific* (2019) (Pre-publication Copy) <https://papers.ssrn.com/sol3/papers.cfm?abstract_id=3355212> accessed 24 May 2022.
41 Damien Chng and Jack Tsen-Ta Lee, 'Legal Systems in ASEAN: Singapore' (*ASEAN Law Association* 31 May 2018) <https://www.aseanlawassociation.org

/wp-content/uploads/2019/11/ALA-SG-legal-system-Part-2.pdf> accessed 31 May 2022.

42 Abdul Ghafur Hamid and Khin Maung Sein, 'Judicial Application of International Law in Malaysia: An Analysis' Malaysian Bar (31 March 2006) <https://www.malaysianbar.org.my/article/news/legal-and-general-news/legal-news/judicial-application-of-international-law-in-malaysia-an-analysis#13> accessed 24 May 2022.

43 Michael Kirby, 'Domestic Implementation of International Human Rights Norms' (1999) 5(2) Australian Journal of Human Rights 109.

44 Recognising that most States are a mixture of the two but may take up greater tendencies of monism or dualism, it is unclear whether Indonesia and Thailand can be classified as either. See, respectively, Pranoto Iskandar 'Indonesia and International Law: An Interview with Indonesia's Secretary to the Directorate General of International Treaties and Legal Affairs' (2014) 1 Indonesian Journal of International and Comparative Law 1067 and Kiarttiphorn Umpai 'Judicial Decision and Rethinking the Constitutional Principles Concerning Treaty Making Power and Process in Thailand' (2017) 4(1) Brawijaya Law Journal 1.

45 See, for example, on France, Luc Reydams. *Universal Jurisdiction: International and Municipal Legal Perspectives* (OUP, 2003), 134.

46 See, for example, Código Procesal Penal Federal (T.O. 2019) (Argentina), title IV, chapter V.

47 See *Taylor v Attorney-General* [2019] HCA 30 (Australian High Court).

48 In the amended Federal Criminal Procedure Code (as of 2019), art 82 permits 'any person with civil capacity particularly offended by a crime of public action' to become a plaintiff in a criminal trial, with art 82 *bis* permitting 'associations or foundations, registered in accordance with the law' to become plaintiffs 'in which crimes against humanity or serious human rights violations are investigated'. Código Procesal Penal Federal (T.O. 2019).

49 Magistrates' Courts Act 1980 (UK) s 1(4A); see also s 1(4D)(b), (g).

50 Monique Cormier and Anna Hood, 'Prosecuting International Crimes in Australia: The Case of the Sri Lankan President' (2012) 13 Melbourne Journal of International Law 1.

51 While not the subject of this chapter, Fora that permit extraterritorial jurisdiction for relevant crimes and in which victims or the accused may be nationals—even if they acquire nationality at a later date—can be useful to pursue. This is because extraterritorial jurisdiction is a more 'traditional' mode of jurisdiction—in other words, a type of jurisdiction with which the court may be more familiar. Thus, if seeking to bring a universal jurisdiction matter, it is important first to identify whether there may be a more conducive Forum State because of a link perhaps not readily obvious.

52 See 'German Court Finds Former 'IS' Member Guilty of Genocide' *Deutsche Welle* (30 November 2021) <https://p.dw.com/p/43eYU> accessed 24 May 2022.

53 See 'Justice Prevailed: Salvadoran Ex-Colonel Gets 133 Years for Priest Slayings' *Reuters* (11 September 2020) <https://www.reuters.com/article/us-spain-el-salvador-massacre-idUSKBN2621QP> accessed 24 May 2022.

54 Notably, the accused's ability to know the case against them and their presence at trial assists in ensuring their fair trial rights under international human rights law. International Covenant on Civil and Political Rights (adopted 16 December 1966, entered into force 23 March 1976) 999 UNTS 171, art 14.

55 Code de Procédure Pénale (as modified by Loi n 2019-222 du 23 mars 2019), arts 689-11 & 689-14.

56 Unless the crime has been committed by a Dutch national or committed against a Dutch national. *Wet Internationale Misdrijven* (International Crimes Act) of 19 June 2003, art 2(1)(a) as cited in Open Society Justice Initiative and TRIAL International, 'Briefing Paper: Universal Jurisdiction Law and Practice in the Netherlands' (n 13), 21.

57 However, any arrest warrant for such crimes requires the consent of the Director of Public Prosecutions. *Magistrates' Courts Act 1980* (UK) s 1(4A). For an example of State guidance on bringing a universal jurisdiction matter, see 'Note on the Investigation and Prosecution of Crimes of Universal Jurisdiction' (United Kingdom Government Publications, 2018) <https://assets.publishing.service.gov.uk/government/uploads/system/uploads/attachment_data/file/709126/universal-jurisdiction-note-web.pdf> accessed 31 May 2022.

58 Chapter 1, Section 7 of the Criminal Code of Finland, 39/1889, amendments up to 766/2015 included, translation from Finnish by Ministry of Justice, Finland, as cited in Open Society Justice Initiative and TRIAL International, 'Universal Jurisdiction Law and Practice in Finland' (February 2020) < https://trialinternational.org/wp-content/uploads/2020/03/Universal-Jurisdiction-Law-and-Practice-in-Finland.pdf> accessed 31 May 2022, 12.

59 International Crimes (Tribunals) Act 1973, s 10A. See also *Chief Prosecutor v. Maulana Abul Kalam Azad, alias Bachu* (trial *in absentia*), ICT-BD Case No 05 of 2012 (International Crimes Tribunal in Bangladesh 21 January 2013) paras 49-54.

60 *Strafprozeßordnung* (German Code of Penal Procedure), s153f as cited in commentary by Luc Reydams *Universal Jurisdiction: International and Municipal Legal Perspectives* (OUP, 2003) 144-145.

61 Staff writers and Daniel Ofman, 'Five Years After Migrant Crisis, Integration in Germany is Succeeding, Policy Analyst Says' *The World* (31 August 2020) <https://theworld.org/stories/2020-08-31/five-years-after-migrant-crisis-integration-germany-succeeding-policy-analyst> accessed 31 May 2022.

62 Yuna Han, 'Should German Courts Prosecute Syrian International Crimes? Revisiting the "Dual Foundation" Thesis' (2022) 36 Ethics & International Affairs 37.

63 Ben Knight, 'Refugees in Germany Reporting Dozens of War Crimes' *Deutsche Welle* (11 April 2016) <https://www.dw.com/en/refugees-in-germany-reporting-dozens-of-war-crimes/a-19179291> accessed 31 May 2022.

64 AFP, 'Refugees Spur German Justice to Tackle Syrian War Crimes' (*Justiceinfo.net*, 1 May 2016) <https://www.justiceinfo.net/en/27104-refugees-spur-german-justice-to-tackle-syrian-war-crimes.html> accessed 31 May 2022.

65 'The Long Arm of Justice: Lessons from Specialized War Crimes Units in France, Germany, and the Netherlands' (*Human Rights Watch*, 16 September 2014) < https://www.hrw.org/report/2014/09/16/long-arm-justice/lessons-specialized-war-crimes-units-france-germany-and> accessed 24 May 2022.

66 'Universal Jurisdiction Annual Review 2021' (*TRIAL International* et al) <https://trialinternational.org/latest-post/ujar-2021/> accessed 31 May 2022, 17-18.

67 'A Step-by-Step Approach to the Use of Universal (Criminal) Jurisdiction in Western European States' (*FIDH*, 2009) <https://www.fidh.org/IMG/pdf/ComUniv522a2009.pdf> accessed 31 May 2022, 9-10.

68 'Strategies for the Effective Investigation and Prosecution of Serious International Crimes: The Practice of Specialised War Crimes Units' (*REDRESS, FIDH*, December 2010) <https://trialinternational.org/wp-content/uploads/2016/05/The_Practice_of_Specialised_War_Crimes_Units_Dec_2010.pdf> accessed 31 May 2022, 17-18. This has recently

increased to also include experts on digital evidence and open-source investigations. See generally Karolina Aksamitowska, 'Digital Evidence in Domestic Core International Crimes Prosecutions: Lessons Learned from Germany, Sweden, Finland and The Netherlands' (2021) 19 *Journal of International Criminal Justice* 189.

69 For example, the German SIU or 'War Crimes Unit' is incorporated within the German Federal Police. Benjamin Duerr, 'International Crimes: Spotlight on Germany's War Crimes Unit' (*Justiceinfo.net,* 10 January 2019) <https://www.justiceinfo.net/en/39936-international-crimes-spotlight-on-germany-s-war-crimes-unit.html> accessed 31 May 2022. Sweden has a War Crimes Unit under the Swedish Police. 'War Crime Swedish Police Efforts' (*Polisen*) <https://polisen.se/en/victims-of-crime/war-crime---swedish-police-efforts/> accessed 31 May 2022.

70 For example, Dutch investigation into international crimes is undertaken by its Police International Crimes Team, in partnership with the National Public Prosecutors' Office. 'International Crimes' (*Netherlands Public Prosecution Service*) <https://www.prosecutionservice.nl/topics/international-crimes> accessed 31 May 2022.

71 'Strategies for the Effective Investigation' (n 68), 17–18. Sometimes, a separate court or judge is mandated to hear cases involving international crimes. This may also increase the efficiency and effectiveness of the process.

72 'The Long Arm of Justice' (n 65), 3.

73 On 28 March 2022, a JIT into alleged international crimes committed in Ukraine was set up with the assistance of Eurojust, or the European Union Agency for Criminal Justice Cooperation. 'Eurojust Supports Joint Investigation Team into Alleged Core International Crimes in Ukraine' (*Eurojust*, 28 March 2022) <https://www.eurojust.europa.eu/news/eurojust-supports-joint-investigation-team-alleged-core-international-crimes-ukraine> accessed 31 May 2022.

74 Additionally, some broader treaties include articles specifically addressing mutual legal assistance. See, for example, United Nations Convention against Transnational Organized Crime (adopted 15 November 2000, entered into force 29 September 2003) 2225 UNTS 209, art 14; and United Nations Convention Against Corruption (adopted 31 October 2003, entered into force 14 December 2005) 2349 UNTS 41, art 46.

75 'Genocide Network' (*Eurojust*) <https://www.eurojust.europa.eu/judicial-cooperation/practitioner-networks/genocide-network> accessed 31 May 2022. On 28 March 2022, a JIT into alleged international crimes committed in Ukraine was set up with the assistance of Eurojust, or the European Union Agency for Criminal Justice Cooperation. 'Eurojust Supports Joint Investigation Team into Alleged Core International Crimes in Ukraine' (*Eurojust*, 28 March 2022) <https://www.eurojust.europa.eu/news/eurojust-supports-joint-investigation-team-alleged-core-international-crimes-ukraine> accessed 31 May 2022.

76 UNGA 'Annex: Independent Investigative Mechanism for Myanmar Terms of Reference' (21 January 2019) UN Doc A/73/716, para 1.

77 Jennifer Keene-McCann, 'International Criminal Tribunals and Civil Society: Impediments and Opportunities for Engagement' (*Syria Justice and Accountability Centre,* 2018) <https://syriaaccountability.org/3501/> accessed 31 May 2022, 6-9.

78 ibid. For a fuller discussion on civil society and universal jurisdiction, see Universal Jurisdiction Convening Series, 'Barriers and Opportunities for Civil Society and Universal Jurisdiction Convening Note' (*Asia Justice Coalition* 2021) <https://www.asiajusticecoalition.org/projects/universal-jurisdiction-convening-series

-barriers-and-opportunities%3A-civil-society-and-universal-jurisdiction-convening-note> accessed 31 May 2022.

79 'Universal Jurisdiction Annual Review 2019' (*TRIAL International* et al) <https://trialinternational.org/wp-content/uploads/2019/03/Universal_Jurisdiction_Annual_Review2019.pdf> accessed 31 May 2022, 14–15. Note, an amended 2018 Criminal Code shifts the investigative responsibilities from the judge to the prosecutor with the help of security forces. It is yet to be implemented widely especially for federal crimes. See USDOS, '2020 Country Reports on Human Rights Practices: Argentina' (30 March 2021) <https://www.state.gov/reports/2020-country-reports-on-human-rights-practices/argentina/> accessed 31 May 2022.

80 Law on International Cooperation in Criminal Matters, Ley 24.767 de 1996 (English Translation as available) <https://www.imolin.org/doc/amlid/Argentina/Law_No._24767.pdf> accessed 31 May 2022.

81 BROUK (n 2).

82 'We Need Justice from Argentina [sic] Court' – Women Rohingya Genocide Survivors Get their Day in Court' *(BROUK*, 18 August 2021) <https://www.brouk.org.uk/we-need-justice-from-argentina-court-women-rohingya-genocide-survivors-get-their-day-in-court/> accessed 31 May 2022.

83 Christine Chaumeau, 'Argentina Comes to the Aid of Myanmar Rohingyas' (*Justiceinfo.net,* 10 December 2021) <https://www.justiceinfo.net/en/85392-argentina-comes-aid-myanmar-rohingyas.html> accessed 31 May 2022.

84 UNHCR 'Mr. Tomás Ojea Quintana Special Rapporteur on the Situation of Human Rights in the Democratic People's Republic of Korea, (*UNHCR Special Procedures*) <https://www.ohchr.org/en/special-procedures/sr-dprk/mr-tomas-ojea-quintana> accessed 31 May 2022.

85 International Law Commission (n 10), [6]. See also: *Attorney-General of the Government of Israel v Eichmann* (1962) International Law Reports, v 36, 304 (Israel Supreme Court) (English Translation) and *Polyukhovitch v Commonwealth* (1991) 172 CLR 501 [33]-[34] (Australian High Court).

86 The inclusion of universal jurisdiction as an agenda item was requested by Tanzania, on behalf of the Group of African States, in 2009. UNGA 'Letter Dated 29 June 2009 from the Permanent Representative of the United Republic of Tanzania to the United Nations Addressed to the Secretary-General' (23 July 2009) UN Doc A/63/237/Rev.1.

87 UNGA Sixth Committee (73rd Session) 'Without Clear Definition, Universal Jurisdiction Principle Risks Misuse, Abuse, Sixth Committee Speakers Warn' (10 October 2018) UN Doc GA/L/3571.

88 'Statement by Mr. Nyan Lin Aung, Alternate Representative of the Republic of the Union of Myanmar on Agenda Item 84:"The Scope and Application of the Principle of Universal Jurisdiction"' (October 2019) <https://www.un.org/en/ga/sixth/74/pdfs/statements/universal_jurisdiction/myanmar.pdf> accessed 31 May 2022.

89 UNGA Sixth Committee (73rd Session) (n 87).

90 'Statement by Germany to the Sixth Committee in its 75th Session on Universal Jurisdiction' (2020) <https://www.un.org/en/ga/sixth/75/pdfs/statements/universal_jurisdiction/11mtg_germany.pdf> accessed 31 May 2022..

91 UNGA Res 72/120 (18 December 2017) UN Doc A/RES/72/120.

92 UNGA 'Report of the United Nations Secretary-General: The Scope and Application of the Principle of Universal Jurisdiction' (2018) UN Doc A/73/123 [39]-[47].

93 International Law Commission (n 10).

94 Further and specific to the Rohingya, arms of the Argentinian government have been required to act in relation to universal jurisdiction. The present complaint was initially rejected by the Court of First Instance on account of possible overlap with ongoing ICC proceedings. This was overturned by the Federal Criminal Appeal Court in Buenos Aires in 2020, which requested further clarification regarding the ongoing ICC investigation. The Ministry of Foreign Affairs communicated with the OTP to clarify the jurisdiction of the ICC case, which satisfied the Court of the sufficient distinction between jurisdictions. See Tun Khin, 'Universal Jurisdiction, the International Criminal Court, and the Rohingya Genocide' (*Opinio Juris*, 23 October 2020) <http://opiniojuris.org/2020/10/23/universal-jurisdiction-the-international-criminal-court-and-the-rohingya-genocide/> accessed 31 May 2022; 'Argentinean Judiciary Moves Closer To Opening Case Against Myanmar Over Rohingya Genocide' (*BROUK*, 1 June 2020) <https://www.brouk.org.uk/argentinean-judiciary-moves-closer-to-opening-case-against-myanmar-over-rohingya-genocide/> accessed 31 May 2022.

95 Rupa Chinai, 'Myanmar's Refugees in Mizoram: As India Looks the Other Way, Thousands On The Edge' (*Outlook*, 1 February 2022) <https://www.outlookindia.com/international/myanmar-s-refugees-in-mizoram-as-india-looks-the-other-way-thousands-on-the-edge-news-52001> accessed 27 May 2022.

96 Shreehari Paliath, 'How Stateless Rohingya Struggle to Find Livelihood & Assistance in India' (*IndiaSpend*, 14 March 2022) <https://www.indiaspend.com/welfare/how-stateless-rohingya-struggle-to-find-livelihood-assistance-in-india-807697> accessed 27 May 2022.

97 'India: Rohingya Deported to Myanmar Face Danger' (*Human Rights Watch*, 31 March 2022) <https://www.hrw.org/news/2022/03/31/india-rohingya-deported-myanmar-face-danger> accessed 27 May 2022.

98 Sui Lee-Wee, 'Thousands Flee Myanmar for India Amid Fears of a Growing Refugee Crisis' *The New York Times* (19 October 2021).

99 Saikiran Kannan, 'With Conscientious Objectors from Myanmar Fleeing to Mizoram, India Grapples with Unique Refugee Problem' (*India Today*, 21 March 2021) <https://www.indiatoday.in/india/story/with-conscientious-objectors-from-myanmar-fleeing-to-mizoram-india-grapples-with-unique-refugee-problem-1781759-2021-03-21> accessed 27 May 2022.

100 'Genocide Convention, Status of Treaties' (*United Nations Treaty Collection*) <https://treaties.un.org/pages/ViewDetails.aspx?src=IND&mtdsg_no=IV-9&chapter=4&clang=_en> accessed 27 May 2022.

101 'Convention Against Torture, Status of Treaties' (*United Nations Treaty Collection*) <https://treaties.un.org/pages/ViewDetails.aspx?src=IND&mtdsg_no=IV-1&chapter=4&clang=_en> accessed 27 May 2022

102 Geneva Conventions Act 1960 (Act 6 of 1960).

103 ibid. For the purposes of the Act, 'grave breaches' include commission of any of the acts committed against persons or property protected by the four Geneva Conventions as noted in n 27.

104 Geneva Conventions Act 1960 (Act 6 of 1960), s 3.

105 Geneva Conventions Act 1960 (Act 6 of 1960), s 3(a) and (b).

106 Geneva Conventions Act 1960 (Act 6 of 1960), s 3.

107 This is in contrast to the Indian Penal Code, which only provides extraterritorial jurisdiction if a crime is committed by an Indian national beyond its territories or a crime that has taken place outside India but has an effect on India, given that such a crime is punishable in India under its law. Indian Penal Code 1860 (Act 45 of 1860), s 3, 4.

108 Geneva Conventions Act 1960 (Act 6 of 1960), s 4.

109 Geneva Conventions Act 1960 (Act 6 of 1960), s 17.
110 Geneva Conventions Act 1960 (Act 6 of 1960), s 6.
111 'Statement Mr. Bhartruhari Mahtab, Honourable Member of Parliament on Agenda Item 86, "The Scope and Application of the Principle of Universal Jurisdiction" at the Sixth Committee of the United Nations General Assembly' (*Permanent Mission of India to the UN*, 20 October 2015) <https://pminewyork.gov.in/IndiaatUNGA?id=NDUw> accessed 27 May 2022. The same opposition was seen during negotiations in 1998 where India refused to sign the Rome Statute. See 'Human Rights Watch Disappointed at India's Position on International Court' (*Human Rights Watch*, 1998) <https://www.hrw.org/legacy/press98/june/indi0617.htm> accessed 27 May 2022; 'India Statement on Agenda Item 87 "The Scope and Application of the Principle of Universal Jurisdiction"' (*Permanent Mission of India to the UN*) <https://pminewyork.gov.in/IndiaatUNGA?id=NDA4OA> accessed 27 May 2022.
112 *Mohammad Salimullah v Union of India*, Affidavit filed by Union of India, para 9, Writ Petition (Civil) No. 793 of 2017.
113 Government of India, Ministry of External Affairs, 'Visit of External Affairs Minister to Myanmar' (11 May 2018) <https://mea.gov.in/press-releases.htm?dtl/29889/Visit_of_External_Affairs_Minister_to_Myanmar_May_1011_2018 > accessed 27 May 2022. Notably, the Indian official statements at the UN do not make reference to the Rohingya, nor do they use the term 'refugees'—instead, Rohingyas are described as 'displaced persons from the Rakhine State'. 'Statement by Ambassador T. S. Tirumurti, Permanent Representative' (*Permanent Mission of India to the UN*, 26 February 2021) <https://pminewyork.gov.in/IndiaatUNGA?id=NDE4MA> accessed 27 May 2022.
114 Bertil Lintner, 'Myanmar Military Joining Hands with Indian Rebels' *Asia Times* (6 December 2021) <https://asiatimes.com/2021/12/myanmar-military-joining-hands-with-indian-rebels/> accessed 27 May 2022.
115 UNHRC, 'Conference Room Paper of the Special Rapporteur on the Situation of Human Rights in Myanmar: Enabling Atrocities: UN Member States' Arms Transfers to the Myanmar Military' (22 February 2022) UN Doc A/HRC/49/CRP.1.
116 'Statement By Ambassador K. Nagaraj Naidu, Deputy Permanent Representative on Arria Formula Meeting on Myanmar' (*Permanent Mission of India to the UN*, 9 April 2021) < https://pminewyork.gov.in/IndiaatUNSC?id=NDIxNw> accessed on 31 May 2022; 'Explanation of Vote on the UNGA Adoption of Resolution on Myanmar' (*Permanent Mission of India to the UN*, 18 June 2021) <https://pminewyork.gov.in/IndiaatUNGA?id=NDI3Nw> accessed on 31 May 2022.
117 Vaibhav Kullashri, 'Myanmar Coup: Threat to India's Internal Security and Challenge to India's Foreign Policy' (*Center For Land Warfare Studies*) <https://www.claws.in/myanmar-coup-threat-to-indias-internal-security-and-challenge-to-indias-foreign-policy/> accessed 27 May 2022.
118 Mujib Mahsal, Suhasini Raj, and Hari Kumar, 'As Officials Look Away, Hate Speech in India Nears Dangerous Levels' *New York Times* (8 February 2022).
119 Incorporation into the Criminal Code Act 1995 (Cth) was affected by the International Criminal Court Act 2002 and the International Criminal Court (Consequential Amendments) Act 2002. In specific reference to the ICC, s 268.1(2) of the Criminal Code Act states that the ICC's jurisdiction is to be 'complementary to the jurisdiction of Australia' and s 268.1(3) states that the Act incorporating these crimes and recognizing the ICC's jurisdiction does not affect the 'primacy of Australia's right to exercise its jurisdiction' with respect to the listed crimes.

120 'Worldwide Governance Indicators: Australia' (*World Bank*, 27 September 2021) <https://databank.worldbank.org/source/worldwide-governance-indicators# > accessed on 17 May 2022; 'Rule of Law Index: Australia' (*World Justice Project*, 2021) < https://worldjusticeproject.org/rule-of-law-index/country/2021/Australia/ > accessed on 17 May 2022.
121 Carrie McDougall, 'The Scope and Application of the Principle of Universal Jurisdiction (Agenda Item 85): Sixth Committee: Statement on behalf of Canada, Australia and New Zealand (CANZ)' (*Australian Mission to the United Nations*, 10 October 2017) <https://www.un.org/en/ga/sixth/72/pdfs/statements/universal_jurisdiction/canz.pdf> accessed 31 May 2022; see also Cary Scott-Kemmis, 'The Scope and Application of the Principle of Universal Jurisdiction' (*Australian Mission to the United Nations*, 15 October 2019) < https://www.un.org/en/ga/sixth/74/pdfs/statements/universal_jurisdiction/canz.pdf> accessed on 31 May 2022; and Julia O'Brien, 'The Scope and Application of Universal Jurisdiction' (*Australian Mission to the United Nations*, 15 October 2014) < https://www.un.org/en/ga/sixth/69/pdfs/statements/universal_jurisdiction/canz.pdf > accessed on 31 May 2022.
122 Lindsay Murdoch, 'Turnbull Government Reverses Myanmar Stance to Co-Sponsor UN Resolution on Rohingya Muslims' *The Sydney Morning Herald* (25 March 2017) <https://www.smh.com.au/national/turnbull-government-reverses-myanmar-stance-to-cosponsor-un-resolution-on-rohingya-muslims-20170325-gv69nv.html > accessed 31 May 2022.
123 'Faces of the Rohingya' (*Special Broadcasting Service*) < https://www.sbs.com.au/topics/voices/culture/feature/faces-rohingya > accessed 31 May 2022.
124 Criminal Code Act 1995 (Cth), s 268.25.
125 Criminal Code Act 1995 (Cth), s 268.13.
126 Criminal Code Act 1995 (Cth), s 268.117.
127 Criminal Code Act 1995 (Cth), s 274.2(5).
128 Judiciary Act 1906 (Cth), s 68(1).
129 Criminal Procedure Act 2009 (Vic), s 246.
130 Criminal Procedure Act 2009 (Vic), s 3.
131 *R v Benbrika & Ors* (2008) 18 VR 410; *R v Serrano* (2007) 16 VR 360; and *R v Abrahams* (1895) 21 VLR 343 cited in 'Criminal Proceedings Manual' (*Judicial College Victoria*) <https://www.judicialcollege.vic.edu.au/resources/criminal-proceedings-manual> accessed 28 May 2022.
132 Michael Gordon, 'Sri Lankan President Accused in Australian Court' *The Sydney Morning Herald* (25 October 2011).
133 Cormier and Hood (n 50), 1; see also Aja Styles, 'Sri Lankan PM Will Not Answer War Crimes Claims' *The Sydney Morning Herald* (26 October 2011).
134 Cameron Hill, 'Australia's Response to the Rohingya Human Rights and Migrant Crisis—a Quick Guide' (*Parliament of Australia*, 14 June 2018) <https://www.aph.gov.au/About_Parliament/Parliamentary_Departments/Parliamentary_Library/pubs/rp/rp1718/Quick_Guides/Rohingya> accessed 28 May 2022.
135 Ben Doherty, 'Aung San Suu Kyi Cannot Be Prosecuted in Australia, Christian Porter Says' *The Guardian* (17 March 2018) <https://www.theguardian.com/world/2018/mar/17/aung-san-suu-kyi-cannot-be-prosecuted-in-australia-christian-porter-says> accessed 28 May 2022.
136 Michael Carrel, 'Australia's Prosecution of Japanese War Criminals: Stimuli and Constraints' in David A Blumenthal and Timothy L H McCormack (eds), *The Legacy of Nuremberg: Civilising Influence or Institutionalised Vengeance?* (Martinus Nijhoff Publishers 2008) 239, 243-5 cited in Gideon Boas and Pascale Chifflet, 'Suspected War Criminals in Australia: Law and Policy' 40 Melbourne University Law Review, 9.

137 Attorney-General's Department, *Report of the Investigations of War Criminals in Australia* (Australian Government Publishing Service, 1993), 14.
138 ibid, 14-15.
139 Fergus Hanson, 'Confronting Reality: Responding to War Criminals Living in Australia' (Policy Brief, Lowy Institute, February 2009) 3 cited in Boas (n 136).
140 See 'The Long Arm of Justice' (n 65); Karolina Aksamitowska, *War Crimes Units: Legislative, Organisational and Technical Lessons* (September 2021) <https://www.asser.nl/media/795205/karolina-aksamitowska-war-crimes-units-legislative-organisational-and-technical-lessons-eng.pdf> accessed 24 May 2022.
141 Attorney-General's Department (n 137), 4.
142 War Crimes Amendment Act 1988 (Cth), s 5.
143 Rawan Arraf, 'Australia Needs a Permanent War Crimes Investigation Unit' *The Age* (6 October 2020).
144 Attorney-General's Department (n 137), 5.
145 Gillian Triggs, 'Australia's War Crimes Trials: All Pity Choked' in Tim McCormack and Gerry Simpson (eds), *The Law of War Crimes: National and International Approaches* (Kluwer Law International, 1997) 123, 130–4 cited in Cormier and Hood (n 50), 2.
146 Attorney-General's Department (n 137), 5.
147 Philippa McDonald and Stephen Dziedzic, 'Aung San Suu Kyi Seeks Humanitarian Help for Rohingya from ASEAN Leaders' (ABC News Australia, 19 March 2018) <https://www.abc.net.au/news/2018-03-18/aung-san-suu-kyi-asks-asean-for-help-with-rohingya-crisis/9561058> accessed 31 May 2022.
148 Lindsay Murdoch, 'Australia Softens Rohingya UN Resolution to Accusations of 'Whitewashing'' *The Sydney Morning Herald* (28 September 2017).
149 *Application of the Convention on the Prevention and Punishment of the Crime of Genocide* (*The Gambia* v. *Myanmar*) (Application Instituting Proceedings and Request for Provisional Measures) ICJ 11 November 2019 <https://www.icj-cij.org/en/case/178/institution-proceedings> accessed 28 May 2022.
150 'History' (*Organisation of Islamic Cooperation*) <https://www.oic-oci.org/page/?p_id=52&p_ref=26&lan=en> accessed 28 May 2022.
151 'Member States' (*Organisation of Islamic Cooperation*) <https://www.oic-oci.org/states/?lan=en> accessed 31 May 2022.
152 'OIC Draws $1.2m for Gambia to Run Rohingya Genocide Case' *Dhaka Tribune* (6 December 2020) <https://www.dhakatribune.com/world/2020/12/06/oic-draws-1-2m-for-gambia-to-run-rohingya-genocide-case> accessed 28 May 2022.
153 'Turkey's Relations with the International Criminal Court (ICC)' (*Republic of Turkey Ministry of Foreign Affairs*) <https://www.mfa.gov.tr/turkey_s-relations-with-the-international-criminal-court-_icc_.en.mfa> accessed 28 May 2022.
154 'Genocide Convention: Status of Treaties' (*United Nations Treaty Collection*) <https://treaties.un.org/pages/ViewDetails.aspx?src=IND&mtdsg_no=IV-1&chapter=4&clang=_en> accessed 28 May 2022.
155 In this section, war crimes in international armed conflict will not be further examined because they are not presently relevant to crimes against the Rohingya. War crimes in international armed conflict are incorporated into the Turkish Military Penal Code but would not apply in a case of universal jurisdiction. See: Turkish Military Penal Code, arts 124, 125, 126, 127, as cited in Zeynep Erhan, 'Core International Crimes in Turkish Criminal Law and the Rome Statute: A Comparative Analysis in the Light of International Jurisprudence' (2018) 22 Ankara Hacı Bayram Veli University Faculty of Law Review 111.
156 Criminal Code 2004 (Law No 5237 of September 26 2004).
157 Criminal Code 2004 (Law No 5237 of September 26 2004), art 76(4).

158 Criminal Code 2004 (Law No 5237 of September 26 2004), art 77(4).
159 *Torture in International Law: A Guide to Jurisprudence* (Association for the Prevention of Torture and Center for Justice and International Law 2008).
160 UNHCR, 'Report of the Detailed Findings' (n 34), paras 612, 669-679, 925, 939-941,1070, 1101-1109, 1162-1172.
161 Under art 94(1), the minimum sentence for torture is imprisonment of three years. The Turkish Criminal Code also criminalizes 'aggravated torture' under art 95(1) and 'torment' under art 96(1). Torture is also prohibited under the Turkish Constitution under art 17—the same article also enshrines the right to life.
162 Blanco Cordero (n 16), 21.
163 'National Unity Government calls on Interpol to Review Junta's Invitation to the 89th General Assembly' (*MyanmarNow* 19 November 2021) <https://www.myanmar-now.org/en/news/national-unity-government-calls-on-interpol-to-review-juntas-invitation-to-89th-general> accessed 31 May 2022.
164 Criminal Code 2004 (Law No 5237 of September 26 2004), art 13(2).
165 'Statement by Turkey on Agenda Item 84 "The Scope and Application of the Principle of Universal Jurisdiction" at the Sixth Committee' (*Permanent Mission of Turkey to the UN*, 17 October 2019) <https://www.un.org/en/ga/sixth/74/pdfs/statements/universal_jurisdiction/turkey.pdf > accessed 28 May 2022.
166 'Statement by Turkey on 'The Scope and Application of the Principle of Universal Jurisdiction' (*Permanent Mission of Turkey to the UN*, 23 April 2020) <https://www.un.org/en/ga/sixth/75/universal_jurisdiction/turkey_e.pdf> accessed 28 May 2022.
167 However, a Human Rights Watch submission to the Committee against Torture's 2016 review of Turkey found incidences of domestic torture were increasing while government statistics indicated prosecutions for torture were declining. 'UN Committee against Torture: Review of Turkey' (*Human Rights Watch*, 22 April 2016) <https://www.hrw.org/news/2016/04/22/un-committee-against-torture-review-turkey> accessed 28 May 2022.
168 'UN Treaty Body Database: Ratification Status for Turkey' (*United Nations Human Rights Treaty Bodies*) <https://tbinternet.ohchr.org/_layouts/15/TreatyBodyExternal/Treaty.aspx?CountryID=179&Lang=EN> accessed 28 May 2022.
169 Constitution of the Republic of Turkey 1982.
170 Ikboljon Qoraboyev and Emre Turkut, 'Turkey' in Fulvio Maria Palombino (ed), *Duelling for Supremacy: International Law vs. National Fundamental Principles* (Cambridge University Press 2019).
171 ibid, art 90.
172 Md. Kamruzzaman, 'Helping Rohingya is Turkey's One of Main Foreign Policy Objectives' *Anadolu Agency* (25 August 2020) <https://www.aa.com.tr/en/asia-pacific/-helping-rohingya-is-turkeys-one-of-main-foreign-policy-objectives/1952518> accessed 28 May 2022. Furthermore, with the Turkish representative as General Assembly President, Turkey voted in favour of the June 2021 UNGA Resolution on Myanmar, '[s]trongly condemn[ing] the use of lethal force and violence', by Myanmar security forces following the 2021 coup. See 'UN/ Myanmar General Assembly' (*United Nations UN Audiovisual Library*, 18 June 2021) <https://www.unmultimedia.org/avlibrary/asset/2633/2633966> accessed 28 May 2022.
173 'Torture and Inhuman Treatment in Turkey: 2021 in Review' (*Stockholm Center for Freedom*, 6 January 2022) <https://stockholmcf.org/torture-and-inhuman-treatment-in-turkey-2021-in-review/> accessed 28 May 2022.
174 Kamruzzaman (n 172).

7 A 'patchwork quilt' of fact-finding and international accountability in Myanmar

Priya Pillai

Introduction

Myanmar is currently in the midst of a deep-rooted crisis. The Myanmar military ('Tatmadaw') orchestrated a coup on 1 February 2021, and the situation has deteriorated ever since. Within a few months of the coup, the UN High Commissioner for Human Rights and the Special Rapporteur for Human Rights in Myanmar classified the violations of international law across Myanmar as potential crimes against humanity.[1] However, even before this development, mass atrocity crimes against the Rohingya in Rakhine State resulted in concerted calls for international accountability.[2] With waves of violence against the community ever increasing in ferocity and scale, the 2016 and 2017 'clearance operations' by the Tatmadaw resulted in nearly one million Rohingya fleeing to Bangladesh, with allegations of grave international crimes including war crimes, crimes against humanity and genocide.[3]

Arising from this background, there are multiple legal initiatives for accountability underway—these include the operation of fact-finding institutions (past and present), proceedings before international courts, and a domestic court in Argentina. The Independent International Fact-Finding Mission on Myanmar (IIFFMM), the Independent Investigative Mechanism for Myanmar (IIMM), the International Court of Justice (ICJ), and the International Criminal Court (ICC) are all addressing varied aspects of the violations in Myanmar, and provide different remedies. There are significant differences among all these institutions—that of standards, spheres of action, and underlying basis and methodology, as well as types of violations. They also point to the intersection of fact-finding endeavours, international criminal justice investigations, and human rights investigations. This is a rare instance where multiple fact-finding and international legal initiatives are converging in relation to a country, leading to an inquiry into the implications of such multiple initiatives co-existing, from the perspective of accountability.

Fact-finding is increasingly viewed as a critical component of the push for accountability for international crimes.[4] It has evolved over the years, with often challenging, complex questions and dilemmas in its wake.[5] 'Fact-finding'—construed in the broadest sense—may be undertaken by myriad institutions

DOI: 10.4324/9781003304883-10

including those mandated by the UN, civil society organizations, international courts, and, most recently, by the independent mechanisms for Syria and Myanmar.

This chapter assesses the various fact-finding initiatives in the context of Myanmar, specifically relating to the Rohingya, and how these various initiatives interact in the quest for accountability. At the outset, a few clarifications and caveats in the approach to the topic and underlying assumptions. The first is that 'fact-finding' is construed here to include a wide array of initiatives which all incorporate some or all of the following: ascertaining the facts of violations of international law in a particular context, with or without the attribution of responsibility to a state or an individual, based on legal findings. Admittedly, this may encompass a range of initiatives including peoples' tribunals, truth commissions, international and domestic commissions of inquiry, UN fact-finding missions, and so on. In this chapter, the focus is limited to UN-mandated initiatives and international courts in the context of Myanmar.

The first section provides an overview of fact-finding initiatives—missions and commissions of inquiry—the evolution and context of which to then assess the Myanmar-specific initiatives in the subsequent section. Following this, the international courts and their relationship to fact-finding initiatives are examined. These sections may seem disparate but all tie into how fact-finding initiatives and accountability intersect and interact in this specific context.

UN fact-finding: Transformation from state focus to individual accountability

Fact-finding may be undertaken by non-governmental actors, as well as international commissions of inquiry or as fact-finding missions established by international organizations (such as the United Nations, the Inter-American Commission on Human Rights, as well as the European Union).[6] There has also been much discussion about the role of non-governmental organizations in fact-finding and documentation, as well as the evolution of guidelines.[7] The terms 'commissions' and 'missions' are used interchangeably and are broadly used to

> designate a variety of temporary bodies of a non-judicial nature, established either by an intergovernmental body or by the Secretary-General or the High Commissioner for Human Rights, and tasked with investigating allegations of violations of international human rights, international humanitarian law, or international criminal law and making recommendations for corrective action based on their factual and legal findings.[8]

The ubiquitous term 'fact-finding' covers a range of activities and processes, including inquiries into allegations of violations of human rights, internationally as well as nationally.[9] Although this has been a relatively under-explored area of research compared with international criminal accountability mechanisms, there is a growing body of research and practice upon which to draw.[10]

International commissions of inquiry originated as mechanisms to resolve interstate disputes. These original commissions envisaged in the Hague Conventions were to investigate, verify, and record facts in dispute between states.[11] The Covenant of the League of Nations, Permanent Court of International Justice and subsequently the International Court of Justice also contained provisions for fact-finding in interstate disputes.[12] Over time, the fact-finding commissions have been used to inquire into violations of international humanitarian law and human rights law. Although there is a permanent fact-finding institution for violations of international humanitarian law—the International Humanitarian Fact-Finding Commission—it has been used only once and in limited circumstances.[13] With a greater emphasis on obligations of states *within* their borders, such fact-finding is now used to investigate allegations of violations within states rather than between them.

Multiple international commissions of inquiry or fact-finding missions have been established by the United Nations.[14] Fact-finding within the UN may be undertaken by the Secretary-General, the General Assembly, or the Security Council.[15] Fact-finding was also undertaken by the United Nations Economic and Social Council (ECOSOC) under the Resolution 1503 procedure, though under different conditions from those currently.[16] Furthermore, special procedures mandate holders are also empowered to assess facts.[17] The UN Human Rights Council has also initiated a number of fact-finding missions.[18] Most fact-finding is conducted on an ad hoc basis, in response to particular situations.[19]

The aim of most of the international commissions of inquiry, based on their mandate, relates to ascertaining facts in dispute, and imputing responsibility for violations, if any. The requirement of only fact-finding (without commensurate imputation of responsibility) has been abandoned in the past few years.[20] As a result, commissions of inquiry are under greater scrutiny relating to the legal determination of responsibility and the manner of reaching these conclusions.[21]

Commissions generally have a degree of flexibility regarding their mandate, i.e., the language used and the clarity in definitions, as well as the ability to modify the terms of reference, if required.[22] In regard to the substantive aspects of the mandate, many commissions have been tasked to enquire into allegations of human rights and international humanitarian law violations. The lack of clear separation regarding the categories of international human rights and humanitarian law, each with its own specificities, has an impact on any fact-finding initiative.[23] This is now further compounded with an international criminal law mandate as well as the need to attribute responsibility. In addition, the work of a commission or mission is even more complicated in the case of an ongoing conflict.[24]

In order to undertake its mandate, state co-operation and the ability to conduct on-site investigations is often a problem.[25] In the event of no access, commissions of inquiry solicit information and submissions outside the country as well as via electronic media.[26] However, the lack of access to the affected area and populace may hamper the type and significance of the evidence collected. The safety and security of victims and witnesses, and the threat or reality of reprisals, is a significant concern.[27] Although a commission should conduct its work publicly, due to security concerns, confidential statements as well as closed proceedings are used, which may impact the findings of the commission.[28]

A crucial issue relates to the manner of analysis of facts and evidence collected by the commission—the standard of proof. Typically, the standard of proof is on a 'sliding scale' and various commissions have used different formulations.[29] The criminal law standard of 'beyond a reasonable doubt' is rarely employed, and most commissions use 'reasonable grounds' as the standard of proof.[30] In the few instances where they do find the need to go beyond this minimum threshold, the approach is still unclear.[31]

Whether a higher standard of proof akin to criminal processes should be used for more serious crimes is debatable. The argument made is that an international commission is not a court of law, and therefore criminal law standards are not required. However, in recent years, commission mandates have been explicit in requiring an assessment of violations of international human rights law and international humanitarian law, as well as a finding of potential criminal responsibility.[32] In such situations, a higher standard of proof may be preferable, given the consequences regarding individual criminal responsibility.

The recommendations of fact-finding missions or commissions of inquiry increasingly prioritize prosecution before international or domestic courts.[33] Ultimately, whereas commissions have traditionally been viewed as a mechanism for greater state accountability, there is a pivot now to emphasizing individual criminal responsibility.

From a 'fact-finding mission' to an 'investigative mechanism': A natural continuum?

The background on UN inquiries in the previous section leads to an assessment of the developments related to the Rohingya and application to the Myanmar context at present. A fact-finding body mandated by the UN served as the precursor to one of two substantially similar 'investigative mechanisms' of particular relevance to the question of accountability.[34]

The Independent International Fact-Finding Mission on Myanmar (IIFFMM) —the UN Human Rights Council-mandated body—was established in March 2017 and continued functioning until September 2019.[35] The IIFFMM has had an impact on the legal landscape relating to accountability for Myanmar—not least because it advocated for and was the precursor to the Independent Investigative Mechanism for Myanmar (IIMM).

Para 11 of UN HRC Resolution 34/22 elaborates on the mandate of the mission—to 'establish facts and circumstances' of alleged human rights violations in Myanmar, 'with a view to ensuring full accountability for perpetrators and justice for victims'.[36] The mandate detailed some of the violations, including torture, sexual violence, and killings, but did not restrict the mission to only these. In establishing the IIFFMM, its geographic mandate included all of Myanmar. While it focussed on Rakhine State, it also canvassed violations in Kachin State and Shan State. It was composed of three members appointed by the President of the Human Rights Council, all leading experts in international law and human rights.[37]

To understand the work of the mission, without being privy to its internal workings, its reports are a source of valuable insight.[38] In approach, the IIFFMM used the 'reasonable grounds' standard of proof.[39] It described this as 'sufficient and reliable body of primary information, consistent with other information, [which] would allow an ordinarily prudent person to reasonably conclude that an incident or pattern of conduct occurred'.[40] Arguably, while 'reasonable grounds' has become *de rigueur* for most missions, given the mandate of 'ensuring accountability' and naming those responsible, this may require a higher standard.

The IIFFMM conducted over 800 interviews and collected satellite imagery, as well as other information. It emphasized adherence to the 'principles of independence, impartiality, and objectivity'.[41] The mission was at pains to note that it only relied on 'verified and corroborated' information.[42] It elaborated on its methodology specific to sexual and gender-based crimes, where, if no second source was available, it considered a first-hand account corroborated if it was credible and consistent.[43] In its report detailing its findings, it elaborated upon what it considered first-hand information, how it assessed the reliability and credibility of sources, and the manner of collection of information, in further depth.[44]

The team was not given access to Myanmar by the government—a challenge that many fact-finding bodies contend with and that naturally will have an impact on evidence gathering and verification. However—to be clear—it would be a mistake to equate a lack of physical access with an inability to access evidence and information in its entirety. There are multiple ways of obtaining information and evidence, not least by digital means and through social media.[45]

Despite these challenges, the IIFFMM findings on potential violations indicated patterns of 'gravest crimes'[46] and factors allowing the 'reasonable inference' of genocidal intent.[47] The mission found that responsibility for these international crimes would necessarily include not just individuals but the command hierarchy in the Tatmadaw. To this end, the mission specifically named the commander-in-chief of the army, the deputy commander and four commanders in the report.[48] It also indicated that a more detailed confidential list of names would be held until it could be shared with a body established to ensure accountability in line with international standards.[49] It is not an exaggeration to say that the finding on potential genocidal intent was seismic, and made it hard for the international community to ignore the situation in Rakhine State, paving the way for a more targeted accountability mechanism.

In terms of the focus of this initiative on accountability, the IIFFMM recommended the referral of Myanmar to the International Criminal Court by the United Nations Security Council (UNSC), as well as the creation of an ad hoc international tribunal.[50] It also recommended the exercise of universal jurisdiction by states in order to ensure accountability.[51] Perhaps the most important recommendation was the establishment—by the General Assembly or Human Rights Council—of an independent and impartial mechanism for the collection and preservation of evidence.[52] Thus, in its recommendations as well as its work, the IIFFMM established the need for the IIMM, which was acted upon subsequently.

The Independent Investigative Mechanism for Myanmar was established by the UN Human Rights Council in 2018.[53] The IIMM has been operational since 30 August 2019 and is focused on the crimes against the Rohingya and, more recently, those committed since the military coup on 1 February 2021. The mandate, envisaged in the resolution establishing the IIMM, is:

> to **collect, consolidate, preserve and analyse evidence** of the most serious international crimes and violations of international law committed in Myanmar since 2011, and to prepare files in order to **facilitate and expedite fair and independent criminal proceedings**, in accordance with international law standards, in national, regional, or international courts or tribunals that have or may in the future have jurisdiction over these crimes.[54]
>
> (emphasis mine)

Clearly, the remit of the IIMM is not limited to one area but encompasses the entirety of Myanmar from 2011. It is also a much more specific and targeted mandate—to gather evidence and build files with a view to eventual prosecution, whether in national, regional, or international courts. It goes much beyond the mandate of the IIFFMM and other fact-finding initiatives. Building on this, the terms of reference provide additional insight and detail regarding the approach and functioning of the IIMM.[55]

To ensure continuity, the IIMM was empowered to be the custodian of the information and evidence gathered by the IIFFMM.[56] But even more than this, it was envisaged that the IIFFMM would hand over to the IIMM and would continue to operate until such time as the IIMM was operational.[57] This could be viewed as an evolution towards a greater criminal accountability focus in this transition phase and in the overlap between the institutions. It is also clear that this precise mandate of the IIMM has impacted the IIFFMM's work and approach. For instance, the IIFFMM, in its handover report, stated clearly that it was guided by the IIMM terms of reference and conducted a review of its database for quality control, in particular, related to linkage evidence.[58] Even given the differences in mandates and standards, the very fact of the establishment of the IIMM influenced the approach of the fact-finding mission with a view towards prosecutions.[59]

The terms of reference stipulate the manner in which 'information, documentation and evidence' are to be handled, stored, and used.[60] Clearly, there is a delineation between these various categories to be handled by the IIMM, and all of which are included in the scope. The IIMM is empowered to gather this from other organizations, as well as to conduct interviews and collect physical and digital evidence.[61] The purpose of this information gathering is to 'prepare files focusing on criminal conduct of persons responsible for such crimes', with an emphasis on those 'deemed most responsible'.[62] The evidence is to be analyzed based on 'reliability and probative value'—in other words, whether the evidence could stand up to scrutiny in a criminal trial—based on standards in principal legal systems globally.[63] Safeguards such as informed consent from victims and witnesses to share information or statements and special procedures with regard to those particularly vulnerable are also incorporated in the methods of work.[64]

It seems clear from the mandate and the terms of reference that the transformation from a fact-finding institution *simpliciter* to one that is clearly focused on criminal investigations and eventual prosecutions is complete. Although the IIFFMM and the IIMM are two separate institutions, their roles and functions need to be viewed in conjunction. There are also a few aspects that are common to both bodies—the first is a lack of access to the jurisdiction and an inability to directly obtain information and evidence from the places where these crimes may be occurring. However, reliance on digital and other forms of evidence would lessen this dependence to an extent. The case of the Syrian mechanism is instructive—there have been an increasing number of cases brought in national jurisdictions under the rubric of universal jurisdiction—supported by the IIIM.[65] Clearly, the problems that come with lack of access need to be balanced by a strict adherence to evidentiary standards, particularly given their potential use in national courts.

Aside from the potential for universal jurisdiction cases—discussed in detail in Chapter 6 of this volume—there are also linkages to other legal proceedings. The IIMM is mandated to share information and 'cooperate closely' with the International Criminal Court.[66] The IIMM has also confirmed that it is sharing evidence with the International Court of Justice.[67] It is also the right time to pursue the compelling arguments to establish a permanent standing investigative mechanism.[68]

Two international courts: The ultimate 'fact-finders'?

There are at present two international courts with legal proceedings underway related to accountability for the Rohingya.

In the *Application of the Convention on the Prevention and Punishment of the Crime of Genocide (The Gambia v. Myanmar)*, the International Court of Justice issued its judgement on preliminary objections on 22 July 2022, overruling Myanmar and permitting the case to proceed to the merits phase. The ICJ passed an order indicating provisional measures on 23 January 2020 and instituted a reporting requirement for Myanmar to provide regular reports to the court regarding compliance with the order.[69] At the International Criminal Court, proceedings commenced in 2018, and the prosecutor was given the authorization to investigate in November 2019. This case is premised on Bangladesh being a state party to the Rome Statute, and is somewhat limited in scope.

These two international courts in the Hague, while addressing questions related to justice and accountability for the Rohingya, operate in very different legal realms and contexts. The ICC is concerned with individual criminal responsibility and uses standards that accord to international criminal trials. This includes detailed evidentiary rules and safeguards regarding evidence, with a view to eventual trials and the associated rights.[70] The ICJ is a court, however, that makes legal determinations of state responsibility and does not assess individual culpability.[71] Its approach to evidence is therefore different and not comparable to that of the ICC.

It is relevant to assess the manner and approach to fact-finding and the appreciation of evidence by both these international courts, given their docket of cases pertaining to the Rohingya. The interlinkages between these international courts and fact-finding initiatives, including the work of the IIFFMM as well as the IIMM, need greater elaboration.

International Court of Justice: Weighing evidence of genocide

The statute of the ICJ, as well as the rules of the court, provide for fact-finding, and the court has a record of assessing a variety of evidence.[72] A key aspect of the ICJ's legal framework with regard to fact-finding broadly speaking is 'flexibility'.[73] The ICJ has assessed disputed facts in many scientific issues, such as maritime delimitation and other aspects of the law of the sea, whaling in the Antarctic, and territorial disputes, to name but a few.[74] However, mass atrocity violations, and, in particular, the assessment of specific intent as required by the Genocide Convention may pose a different set of challenges. There is a wide latitude in the appreciation of evidence and facts, and it is important to remember that the ICJ is not a criminal court and does not adhere to the same evidentiary standards. Notwithstanding, the questions that the court is asked to adjudicate involve complex questions of law and fact and have significant repercussions.

The legal framework of the Court is fairly skeletal and much is left to interpretation by the court, found in its case law. Article 48 of the Statute of the ICJ provides that the Court shall 'make all arrangements connected with the taking of evidence'.[75] According to Article 49, the court may call upon agents to provide any document required by the court before the hearings. Article 50 of the Statute is a broad provision whereby the court has the discretion to select 'any individual, body, bureau, commission, or other organization' in order to conduct an enquiry or provide an expert opinion.[76] Oral evidence is guided by certain parameters laid down in Articles 57 and 58 of the Rules of the Court, as well as Article 60.[77] The burden of proof and standard of proof before the ICJ is similar to that of domestic judicial proceedings relating to civil matters.[78]

The manner in which the ICJ has approached factual and evidentiary questions in previous cases relating to the Genocide Convention is instructive. This is also relevant to a new application instituted at the ICJ based on the Genocide Convention by Ukraine against Russia.[79] In particular, the reliance upon fact-finding mission reports or other legal proceedings in assessing complex facts needs to be explored.

In *The Gambia v. Myanmar*, heavy reliance has been placed on IIFFMM reports by the applicant state.[80] These reports have been referenced in the order of provisional measures. Due to the preliminary stages of the proceedings, the court did not delve into detail regarding the substance of the IIFFMM reports. It did, however, rely on the IIFFMM reports in its assessment of the denial of plausible rights under the Genocide Convention, as required for the issuance of provisional measures.[81] The court also referenced the reports to indicate existence of a dispute according to Article 9 of the Genocide Convention, due to Myanmar's objections to these reports at the UN General Assembly.[82] Thus, the fact-finding body of the UN has served two purposes in these initial stages of the proceedings so far. But at a later stage, what weight might be given to these findings?

In *Bosnia and Herzegovina v. Serbia and Montenegro*, in its judgment on merits, the ICJ relied on a report by the UN Secretary-General (entitled 'The Fall of Srebrenica')[83], prefacing this reliance on the basis of

> among other things, on (1) the source of the item of evidence (for instance, partisan or neutral), (2) the process by which it had been generated (for instance, an anonymous press report or the product of a careful court or court-like process), and (3) the quality or character of the item (such as statements against interest, and agreed or uncontested facts).[84]

In its assessment of the report 'The Fall of Srebrenica', the court elaborated on what gave it 'considerable authority'—the fact that it was based on classified UN files, interviews with key personnel involved in decision making, as well as areas which were accessed by the International Criminal Tribunal for the Former Yugoslavia (ICTY), which provided corroboration of victim testimony with forensic evidence.[85] This report was therefore given substantial weight, *in part* due to the functioning of *another court*—the ICTY—and not on a stand-alone basis. It is worth asking whether the report without the ICTY access to the region would have been given the same weight by the court.

In its determination of whether genocide occurred or not, the ICJ relied extensively on the judgments of the ICTY, as trials of those accused of genocide in Srebrenica had taken place already.[86] But the reason for this reliance is important—was it sufficient that the ICTY was an international ad hoc tribunal and that in itself would lend its judgments significant weight? In fact, the ICJ determined that fact-finding by the ICTY would fall within the previous formulation by the court in *Armed Activities on the Territory of the Congo (Democratic Republic of the Congo) v. Uganda*, i.e., of 'evidence obtained by examination of persons directly involved', tested by cross-examination, and credible.[87] However, not all proceedings before the ICTY were the same—of the various stages of cases at the ICTY, only the final judgment consisted of definitive findings and would be given weight.[88] The previous stages, such as framing of charges and motion for acquittal after the prosecution case, would not meet the standard of proof required.[89]

In assessing Article II of the Genocide Convention, the ICJ analyzed the factual context and the elements relying on the jurisprudence of the ICTY, in particular, the *Krstić* and *Blagojević* cases.[90] The ICJ did not find that genocide had been committed in other locations in Bosnia but did find *dolus specialis* regarding the crimes committed in Srebrenica, finding that it constituted genocide.

The ICJ detailed its methodology regarding the assessment of factual issues and evidence pertaining to the commission of genocide.[91] Whereas the court placed most weight on the judgments of the ICTY, it also relied on documentation arising from the processes at the tribunal (such as indictments, interlocutory decisions, etc.).[92] The court emphasized that fact-finding in a case relating to the genocide convention 'requires proof at a high level of certainty appropriate to the seriousness of the allegation'.[93]

Overall, there is considerable flexibility available to the court and few restrictions that would hamper the court's appreciation of the evidence. This may provide an opportunity to adduce evidence hitherto unfamiliar to this court, such as that related to social media and digital evidence.[94] The Gambia has also initiated legal proceedings against Facebook before federal courts in the United States, with the aim of submitting the evidence obtained from Facebook before the ICJ. A federal judge in the District of Columbia has partially granted The Gambia's request for de-platformed content as well as internal investigation documents from Facebook.[95]

The approach of the court towards disputed facts and evidence will be guided by the subject matter at hand, and, given the high stakes relating to the genocide convention, it is assumed that, based on the track record of the court, the evidentiary threshold will be quite high. There are also other avenues that the court may rely upon, depending on the sequence of proceedings, such as potential cases before the ICC and national courts, in addition to the fact-finding mechanisms.

International Criminal Court: Different stages, varied approach?

When assessing proceedings before an international court that addresses individual criminal responsibility—in this case, the ICC—the assumption is that there is a robust fact-finding process that is inherent to the functions of the court. There are clear rules of procedure and evidence, and clarity in the function and scope of the prosecutor. However, unlike domestic courts, the ICC comes with inbuilt constraints—limited enforcement powers and, in cases such as this, difficulties in accessing one of the jurisdictions in question (given that Myanmar is not a state party and jurisdiction over the crimes is by virtue of the link to Bangladesh).

It is in the assessment of international criminal law that the turn towards a greater focus on accountability and individual responsibility by commissions or fact-finding missions has become a source of controversy. This is for two reasons. The first relates to the (in)ability of fact-finding missions to obtain information and assess evidence in line with the standards required for criminal proceedings, particularly in the instances where they are asked to name perpetrators. The second relates to the reliance on such reports by other institutions, and, in particular, by an international court, such as the ICC. There is also the question of simultaneous functioning of institutions with varying mandates and the interlinkages and possible conflicts that may arise based on their work.

First, we will address the issue of overlaps between these entities and the potential repercussions. The investigation at the ICC was authorized in 2019, after the IIFFMM had concluded its work. The Prosecutor had occasion to rely on the work of the IIFFMM in the preliminary examination stage—where the standards required are lower. The question here, therefore, is not of compatibility or conflict between the work of the IIFFMM and the ICC, but rather about reliance by the Court on the reports and records of the mission. However, in the case of the IIMM, there is scope for overlap between its work and that of the ICC. This is tempered, though, by the proximity of the mandate and the aims of both, i.e., focused on individual criminal accountability (unlike the mandate of the IIFFMM). Inevitably, there will be synergies between these institutions, which have been acknowledged. The IIMM has indicated clearly that it is cooperating and providing evidence to the ICC.[96] However, it is worth noting that, like many fact-finding missions, the IIMM also does not have direct access to the territory of Myanmar, which is also problematic given its mandate and focus.

Turning now to the reliance by the ICC on the reports of fact-finding missions or commissions more generally, there are a few reasons for this. The first is invariably a lack of access to the jurisdiction due to the refusal of the state to co-operate, which in turn means reliance on civil society organizations or UN-mandated entities that are present and have access.[97] Other reasons include a lack of resources as well as the inability to harness the legal tools that are available to national prosecutors, such as the ability to compel witnesses.[98] Another factor is the stage of the proceedings at the ICC, with the early stages more amenable to reliance on such reports.

The Office of the Prosecutor (OTP) Policy Paper on Preliminary Examinations makes clear that, at this stage of the proceedings, the OTP examines open-source material, indicating the methodology used in such instances.[99] This policy paper is of particular relevance, as it details the manner and approach to collect information, documentation, and evidence. While information may be sought from a variety of sources including 'States, organs of the United Nations, intergovernmental or non-governmental organizations, or other reliable sources,' the information is 'subject to critical analysis and evaluation'.[100] Given the need for objectivity, the Policy Paper stresses the importance of source reliability and credibility of information.[101] Elaborating on this, the need for coherence, as well as diverse and independent sources of information to control for bias, is emphasized.[102] As to the standard of proof at this stage, 'reasonable basis' as indicated in Article 15(3)[103] and interpreted by the court to mean 'a sensible or reasonable justification for a belief that a crime falling within the jurisdiction of the Court "has been or is being committed"' is adopted.[104] The need for reliance on reports and field missions is clear—due to the lack of investigative powers at this stage.[105] In applications to authorize an investigation by the Prosecutor, there is a clear reference to such materials.[106]

Coming specifically to the Situation in Bangladesh/Myanmar, the ICC is currently investigating based on Article 15 of the Rome Statute.[107] The threshold preliminary examination stage is over, with an investigation underway. However, the Prosecutor has been criticized for reliance on fact-finding reports in the preliminary examination stage.[108] This includes lack of detailed methodology, anonymity of sources, and the lack of legal authority of these bodies to make legal findings.[109] This needs further assessment, including the manner in which reports are relied upon—whether as part of the background and context, or for specific charges and crimes alleged.

In the 4 July 2019 request to authorize an investigation by the Prosecutor, per Article 15, the request clarified that the sources relied upon were considered 'sufficiently reliable and credible,' and that the office relied extensively on the detailed findings of the September 2018 report of the IIFFMM, given that it followed best practices for fact-finding missions and commissions.[110] Although the prosecutor noted the 'relatively low threshold' under Article 15, even if it is not meant to be comprehensive or conclusive, the available information must be evaluated as a whole to assess whether a positive conclusion to proceed with an investigation is warranted.[111] When the pre-trial chamber assessed the request to authorize the investigation, it placed reliance upon victims' representations for evidence.[112] In perusing the decision of the chamber, it referred to the IIFFMM report relating to the background of the case—the ethnic composition of Rakhine State,[113] deprivation of citizenship,[114] and the waves of violence in 2016 and 2017.[115] It also relied upon the report when assessing the systematic or widespread attacks against a civilian population, referencing it as 'supporting material'—with regard to attacks by the Arakan Rohingya Salvation Army (ARSA),[116] the clearance operations and destruction of homes,[117] sexual violence,[118] and the leading of the clearance operations by the Tatmadaw.[119] Clearly, while the ICC pre-trial chamber relied on the IIFFMM report, it also relied on other reports, as well as supporting material.[120]

Although there may be legitimate concerns, it is good to remember that this stage is a preliminary assessment, and it is not possible to rely on evidence directly adduced by the Prosecutor, given the lack of power to do so. The concern should be less about the preliminary examination stage but rather more focused on how information and evidence stands up to scrutiny later in proceedings, when it will be tested. This also ties into what is becoming more obvious—the dangers of over-documentation and documentation not undertaken correctly—and the impact particularly in the later stages of the criminal process.[121] At the preliminary examination stage, there should be less apprehension of reliance on reports of a UN-mandated commission, given its mandate, authority, veracity, and use of appropriate methods, given the threshold requirements as well as what the reports are being relied upon for.

The ICC investigation in relation to Bangladesh/Myanmar is underway currently and there is naturally little information regarding its progress available in the public domain. However, based on the first trip by the current Prosecutor to Bangladesh in February 2022, where he urged victims of sexual and gender-based violence to come forward to assist the investigation, it is no surprise that direct testimony and other evidence will be the focus.[122] It remains to be seen the extent to which these proceedings will overlap or complement those at the IIMM, as well as potentially those before domestic courts as a result of universal jurisdiction.

Conclusion

There is truly a 'patchwork quilt' of accountability initiatives underway for the situation in Myanmar. The existence of these varied institutions with differing mandates is unprecedented, and is a test case of sorts, in how these initiatives interact, complement, or detract from each other's work.

Each of the institutions canvassed in this chapter is tasked with fact-finding, with the aim of legal accountability. The quest for accountability inevitably rests on effective fact-finding and documentation, whether this is with the aim of identifying state responsibility or individual criminal responsibility. The departure from solely 'human rights fact-finding' to a broader mandate encompassing criminal responsibility seems a *fait accompli*. So, now the task is to ensure the most effective fact-finding that can stand up to legal scrutiny, but also keeping in mind the wider aims and mandates of the institution, which may not be limited solely to attribution of criminal responsibility but also the broader context of the violations. This is a difficult balancing act, and one that needs to be carved out with clarity of purpose. In addition, the complex interlinkages between these multiple institutions—international courts, fact-finding bodies, investigative institutions—need to be understood better and examined in greater depth. The situation of Myanmar is unique in that all these institutions are in existence and working on different pieces of the puzzle at the same time—which poses challenges to each institution but also potential opportunities in the ability to rely on and complement one another. However, this is as yet a work-in-progress, and the results will not be known for some time.

Notes

1 Office of the High Commissioner for Human Rights, Statement by Michelle Bachelet, UN High Commissioner for Human Rights, 6 July 2021, <https://www.ohchr.org/EN/HRBodies/HRC/Pages/NewsDetail.aspx?NewsID=27274&LangID=E> accessed 1 June 2022; Office of the High Commissioner for Human Rights, Statement by Thomas H. Andrews UN Special Rapporteur on the Situation of Human Rights in Myanmar, 11 March 2021 <https://www.ohchr.org/EN/NewsEvents/Pages/DisplayNews.aspx?NewsID=26884&LangID=E> accessed 1 June 2022.

2 Report of the Special Rapporteur on the situation of human rights in Myanmar, A/HRC/37/70, 9 March 2018.

3 Report of the Independent International Fact-Finding Mission on Myanmar, A/HRC/39/64, 12 September 2018 ('IIFFMM September 2018 Report'); Amnesty International, 'My World Is Finished', 18 October 2017, <https://www.amnesty.org/en/documents/asa16/7288/2017/en/> accessed 1 June 2022.

4 Frederica D'Alessandra, 'The Accountability Turn in Third Wave Human Rights Fact-Finding' (2017) 33(84) Utrecht Journal of International and European Law 59; Chatham House International Law Discussion Group Meeting Summary, 'UN Fact-finding and International Criminal Investigations', 22 January 2014 <https://www.chathamhouse.org/sites/default/files/public/Meetings/Meeting%20Transcripts/220114UNFact.pdf Chatham House 2014> accessed 2 June 2022.

5 Richard J. Goldstone, 'Quality Control in International Fact-Finding Outside Criminal Justice for Core International Crimes', in Morten Bergsmo and Carsten Stahn (eds), *Quality Control in Fact-Finding* (Torkel Opsahl Academic EPublisher, 2nd edn, Brussels, 2020)

6 Within these organizations, there may be separate bodies that mandate the functioning of such commissions such as the UN General Assembly, Security Council, the Human Rights Council, as well as special procedures and thematic rapporteurs. For a discussion of fact-finding within the context of the European Union, see Andrew Drzemczewski, 'Fact-finding as Part of Effective Implementation: the Strasbourg Experience', p. 115–136, in Anne F. Bayefsky (ed.), The UN Human Rights Treaty System in the 21st Century (Martinus Nijhoff, 2000); For a discussion of fact-finding in the context of Latin America, see Douglas Cassel, 'Fact-Finding in the Inter-American System', p. 105–114, in Anne F. Bayefsky (ed.), The UN Human Rights Treaty System in the 21st Century (Martinus Nijhoff, 2000).

7 Guidelines developed in relation to non- governmental investigations and fact-finding are relevant to commissions of inquiry. See 'Belgrade Minimal Rules of Procedure for International Human Rights Fact-Finding Missions', para. 1, adopted at the 59th Conference of the International Law Association (Belgrade 18–23 August 1980), 75 Am. J. Int'l L. 163 (1981); 'The Guidelines on International Human Rights Fact-Finding Visits and Reports', The Lund—London Guidelines (1 June 2009), <https://www.refworld.org/pdfid/4a39f2fa2.pdf> accessed 1 June 2022. While these are not binding, or applicable in their entirety, they are indicative of the concerns that arise in regard to fact-finding, irrespective of the type of organization conducting it. See also, Asia Justice Coalition, 'Toolkit on Justice Avenues for International Crimes', https://www.asiajusticecoalition.org/_files/ugd/811bc6_be7bf72cb86140a9a5a4f3d54048d2bd.pdf?index=true> accessed 1 June 2022.

8 Office of the High Commissioner for Human Rights, 'Commissions of Inquiry and Fact-Finding Missions on International Human Rights Law and Humanitarian Law—Guidance and Practice' (OHCHR, 2015), p. 7.

9 Joan Fitzpatrick, 'Human Rights Fact-Finding', p. 65–95, in Anne F. Bayefsky (ed.), *The UN Human Rights Treaty System in the 21st Century* (Martinus Nijhoff, 2000).

10 Philip Alston, 'Introduction: Commissions of Inquiry as Human Rights Fact-Finding Tools', Proceedings of the Annual Meeting *(American Society of International Law)* 105 (2011) 81, 84.

11 See Articles 9–14, Convention for the Pacific Settlement of International Disputes (Hague I) (29 July 1899), entered into force 4 September 1900.

12 Article 12 provided for either arbitration or an inquiry by the Council, and Article 15 provided detail in regard to the process to be undertaken in case of a commission of inquiry. See League of Nations, *Covenant of the League of Nations*, 28 April 1919, <https://www.refworld.org/docid/3dd8b9854.html> accessed 2 June 2022. See also, Article 50, Statute of the PCIJ and the ICJ.

13 In 2019, at the request of the OSCE, the Independent Forensic Investigation (IFI) team was set up by the IHFFC to investigate the death of a paramedic in Eastern Ukraine on 23 April 2017, part of the OSCE Special Monitoring Mission to Ukraine (SMM). The mandate was to 'establish the facts of the incident by conducting a post-blast scene forensic investigation and technical assessment against the background of international humanitarian law'. The mandate was explicit—that it was not to establish criminal responsibility or accountability for the incident. The team did find that IHL was violated due to the indiscriminate laying of mines, but that the SMM was not targeted specifically. This was an

unusual investigation in another respect—that it was initiated by an international organization, and not a state. For more, see <https://www.ihffc.org/index.asp?mode=shownews&ID=831> accessed 2 June 2022.

The International Humanitarian Fact-Finding Commission is set up pursuant to Article 90, Additional Protocol I of the Geneva Conventions. For details regarding the commission, see <http://www.ihffc.org/index.asp?Language=EN&page=home> accessed 2 June 2022.

14 For a detailed list, see United Nations Research Guide, 'International Commissions of Inquiry, fact-finding missions: Chronological List' <https://libraryresources.unog.ch/factfinding/chronolist> accessed 1 June 2022.

15 See *Declaration on Fact-finding by the United Nations in the Field of the Maintenance of International Peace and Security*, General Assembly, A/RES/46/59 (67th Plenary Meeting, 9 December 1991), para. 7, <https://legal.un.org/avl/pdf/ha/ga_46-59/ga_46-59_ph_e.pdf> accessed 2 June 2022 ('U.N. Fact-Finding Declaration').

16 See Economic and Social Council Resolution 1503 (XLVIII), 48 U.N. ESCOR (No. 1A) at 8, U.N. Doc. E/4832/Add.1 (1970), <http://www1.umn.edu/humanrts/procedures/1503.html> accessed 2 June 2022). As per this resolution, upon a referral by the Sub-Commission on Prevention of Discrimination and Protection of Minorities to the Commission on Human Rights, it could set up an *ad hoc* commission to further inquire and investigate. However, this was to be with consent of the state and 'constant cooperation' (para. 6(b)), and the procedures as well as reports of the ad hoc commission were to be confidential (para. 7 (b) & (c)).

17 See *Code of Conduct for Special Procedures Mandate-holders of the Human Rights Council*, Human Rights Council Res. 5/2 (June 18, 2007), <http://www.ohchr.org/Documents/HRBodies/SP/CodeofConduct_EN.pdf> accessed 2 June 2022.

18 Relating to the role of the General Assembly in regard to the maintenance of peace and security, and its deployment of fact-finding, see U.N. Fact-finding Declaration, paras. 10 & 11. While there is no explicit mandate in regard to fact-finding by the Human Rights Council, given that it has been set up as a subsidiary body to the General Assembly, it is also imputed with the same responsibilities and has implied powers in regard to the maintenance of peace and security. For more on this argument, see Christine Chinkin, 'UN Human Rights Council Fact-Finding Missions: Lessons from Gaza', 475, 480–481, in Mahnoush H Arsanjani, Jacob Katz Cogan, Robert D Sloane and Siegfried Wiessner (eds.), *Looking to the Future—Essays on International Law in Honor of W. Michael Reisman* (Martinus Nijhoff, 2011).

19 Philip Alston, 'Introduction: Commissions of Inquiry as Human Rights Fact-Finding Tools', Proceedings of the Annual Meeting *(American Society of International Law)* 105 (2011) 81, 84.

20 Earlier, imputation of responsibility was not contemplated. See UN Fact-Finding Declaration, para. 17, which states, 'The report should be limited to a presentation of findings of a factual nature.' However, recent commissions—whether established by the Human Rights Council or the UN Secretary-General now include the language of responsibility. See Libya Independent Fact-Finding Mission, A/HRC/RES/43/39, 6 July 2020, para. 42(a); Independent International Fact-Finding Mission on the Bolivarian Republic of Venezuela, A/HRC/RES/42/25, 8 October 2019, para. 24; International Commission of Inquiry for Mali, S/2018/57, 23 January 2018, para.1(a)-(c).

21 For example, questions related to the Israeli–Palestinian conflict, which is particularly polarized and has resulted in allegations of bias, as well as erroneous

conclusions. See Christine Chinkin, 'UN Human Rights Council Fact-Finding Missions: Lessons from Gaza', 475, 482, in Mahnoush H Arsanjani, Jacob Katz Cogan, Robert D Sloane and Siegfried Wiessner (eds.), *Looking to the Future—Essays on International Law in Honor of W. Michael Reisman* (Martinus Nijhoff, 2011). In regard to the criticisms of the Goldstone commission (in regard to Gaza, undertaken in 2009) and the response of the Rwandan government in regard to the inquiry undertaken regarding the Democratic Republic of Congo and criticism by the government regarding purported flaws in methodology (such as use of anonymous sources, hearsay evidence etc.), see Philip Alston, 'Introduction: Commissions of Inquiry as Human Rights Fact-Finding Tools', Proceedings of the Annual Meeting (American Society of International Law) 105 (2011) 81, 84.

22 See UN Office of the High Commissioner for Human Rights (OHCHR), *Istanbul Protocol Manual on the Effective Investigation and Documentation of Torture and Other Cruel, Inhuman or Degrading Treatment or Punishment*, 2004, HR/P/PT/8/Rev.1, para. 107, p. 22–23, <http://www.ohchr.org/Documents/Publications/training8Rev1en.pdf> accessed 2 June 2022 ('Istanbul Protocol'). The Istanbul Protocol also includes the requirement to inform the public as well as interested parties, in case of any amendment of the mandate.

23 Christine Chinkin, 'UN Human Rights Council Fact-Finding Missions: Lessons from Gaza', 475, 486, in Mahnoush H Arsanjani, Jacob Katz Cogan, Robert D Sloane and Siegfried Wiessner (eds.), *Looking to the Future—Essays on International Law in Honor of W. Michael Reisman* (Martinus Nijhoff, 2011).

24 See Technical assistance to the Government of the Democratic Republic of the Congo and urgent examination of the situation in the east of the country, constituted following HRC Res S-8/1 (1 December 2008).

25 Relating to the rejection by the Democratic People's Republic of Korea of the commission of inquiry and its refusal to co-operate with the commission, see UN General Assembly (Human Rights Council), *Report of the commission of inquiry on human rights in the Democratic People's Republic of Korea*, A/HRC/25/63 (7 February 2014), para. 9–11 (p. 4), <www.ohchr.org/Documents/HRBodies/HRCouncil/CoIDPRK/Report/A.HRC.25.63.doc> accessed 2 June 2022 ('DPRK Commission of Inquiry Report'); Relating to the lack of access to Syria, see UN General Assembly (Human Rights Council), *Report of the independent international commission of inquiry on the Syrian Arab Republic*, A/HRC/25/65 (12 February 2014), para. 2, p. 4. ('SAR Commission of Inquiry Report'). However, the UN inquiry into Lebanon had powers under Chapter VII of the U.N. Charter, thereby obligating states to co-operate See United Nations International Independent Investigation Commission, UN Security Council, *Security Council Resolution 1595 (2005) on Lebanon*, 7 April 2005, S/RES/1595 (2005).

26 For instance, the commission of inquiry for the Democratic People's Republic of Korea conducted public hearings in Seoul, Tokyo, London, and Washington D.C. See DPRK Commission of Inquiry Report, para. 12–16, p. 4–5.

27 The commission of inquiry for the Democratic People's Republic of Korea (DPRK) made a special note of the fear of reprisals, for victims (who feared clandestine monitoring), and especially their family members who were still within the DPRK (even with regard to confidential testimony). This was seen as the most significant challenge, after the lack of access to the country, giving an idea of the significance of this factor in the work of commissions of inquiry. See DPRK Commission of Inquiry Report, para. 19, p. 5.

28 In regard to confidentiality of information and the protection of witnesses, see Istanbul protocol 1991, para. 112 & 113, p. 23; see also, DPRK Commission of Inquiry Report, para. 14, p. 5 (recording the fact that 240 confidential interviews were conducted, in addition to the public hearings).
29 For standard of proof to be used by international commissions of inquiry, see Office of the High Commissioner for Human Rights, 'Commissions of Inquiry and Fact-Finding Missions on International Human Rights Law and Humanitarian Law—Guidance and Practice' (OHCHR, 2015), p. 62–63; Geneva Academy of international humanitarian law and human rights and UNO, 'The UN Human Rights Council: Commissions of Inquiry Conference Brief' (2011), p. 3, on file with author.
30 The same formulation was used by the commission of inquiry for Syria. See SAR Commission of Inquiry Report, para. 6, p. 4. The commission of inquiry for the Democratic People's Republic of Korea included the following elaboration in regard to this standard of proof: 'The commission bases its findings on a "reasonable grounds" standard of proof. It concluded that there are reasonable grounds establishing that an incident or pattern of conduct had occurred whenever it was satisfied that it had obtained a reliable body of information, consistent with other material, based on which a reasonable and ordinarily prudent person would have reason to believe that such an incident or pattern of conduct had occurred'. See DPRK Commission of Inquiry Report, para. 22, p. 6. For similar formulations, see International Commission of Inquiry on Mali Report, S/2020/1332 (29 January 2021), para. 9; Independent International Fact-Finding Mission on the Bolivarian Republic of Venezuela, A/HRC/RES/42/25, 8 October 2019, para. 24; International Commission of Inquiry for Mali, S/2018/57, 23 January 2018, para.1(a)-(c).
31 The Independent Fact-Finding Mission on Libya stated: 'While the "reasonable grounds to believe" standard established a minimum evidentiary threshold, there were circumstances where a higher level of certainty was warranted, in particular when a finding entailed a legal qualification that carried with it a higher degree of stigma due to its gravity, such as crimes against humanity and torture. In relation to such findings, the Mission exceeded the minimum evidentiary threshold'. See 'Report of the Independent Fact-Finding Mission on Libya', A/HRC/48/83 29 November 2021, para. 20.
32 See UN Security Council, Security Council resolution S/Res/2127 (5 December 2013) (adopted by the Security Council at the 7072nd meeting, authorizing the Secretary General to establish an international commission of inquiry for the Central African Republic), para. 24, p. 6, <http://www.un.org/press/en/2013/sc11200.doc.htm> accessed 2 June 2022. See also, Libya Independent Fact-Finding Mission, A/HRC/RES/43/39, 6 July 2020, para. 42(a); Independent International Fact-Finding Mission on the Bolivarian Republic of Venezuela, A/HRC/RES/42/25, 8 October 2019, para. 24; International Commission of Inquiry for Mali, S/2018/57, 23 January 2018, para.1(a)-(c).
33 For instance, the recommendation by the DPRK commission of inquiry urging the Security Council to refer the matter to the ICC. DPRK Commission of Inquiry Report, para. 94 (a), p. 20.
34 'International, Impartial and Independent Mechanism to Assist in the Investigation and Prosecution of Those Responsible for the Most Serious Crimes under International Law Committed in the Syrian Arab Republic since March 2011' UN Doc. A/71/L.48, 21 December 2016. More details regarding this mechanism, <https://iiim.un.org> accessed 2 June 2022.
35 A/HRC/RES/34/22 (24 March 2017)

36 '11. Decides to dispatch urgently an independent international fact-finding mission, to be appointed by the President of the Human Rights Council, to establish the facts and circumstances of the alleged recent human rights violations by military and security forces, and abuses, in Myanmar, in particular in Rakhine State, including but not limited to arbitrary detention, torture and inhuman treatment, rape and other forms of sexual violence, extrajudicial, summary, or arbitrary killings, enforced disappearances, forced displacement, and unlawful destruction of property, with a view to ensuring full accountability for perpetrators and justice for victims, and requests the fact-finding mission to present to the Council an oral update at its thirty-sixth session and a full report at its thirty-seventh session'; A/HRC/RES/34/22 (24 March 2017)

37 Mr. Marzuki Darusman (Indonesia), Chair, Ms. Radhika Coomaraswamy (Sri Lanka), Mr. Christopher Dominic Sidoti (Australia). Two of the members of the mission have continued their advocacy in relation to Myanmar as part of the 'Special Advisory Council for Myanmar', along with a former UN Special Rapporteur for human rights in Myanmar, Ms. Yanghee Lee.

38 'Report of the Independent International Fact-Finding Mission on Myanmar', A/HRC/39/64, 12 September 2018 ('IIFFMM September 2018 Report'), read with 'Report of the detailed findings of the Independent International Fact-Finding Mission on Myanmar', A/HRC/39/CRP.2, 17 September 2018; 'Sexual and Gender Based Violence in Myanmar and the Gendered Impact of its Ethnic Conflicts', A/HRC/42/CRP.4, 22 August 2019; 'The Economic Interests of the Myanmar military', A/HRC/42/CRP.3, 12 September 2019

39 Para. 6, 'Report of the Independent International Fact-Finding Mission on Myanmar', A/HRC/39/64, 12 September 2018 ('IIFFMM September 2018 Report'), read with para.10, 'Report of the detailed findings of the Independent International Fact-Finding Mission on Myanmar', A/HRC/39/CRP.2, 17 September 2018.

40 Para. 6, IIFFMM September 2018 Report

41 Para. 11, IIFFMM September 2018 Report

42 Para. 7, IIFFMM September 2018 Report

43 'Sexual and Gender Based Violence in Myanmar and the Gendered Impact of its Ethnic Conflicts', A/HRC/42/CRP.4, 22 August 2019, Para. 20: 'In cases of sexual and gender-based violence, where a second independent source of information was often unavailable, the Mission considered the case or incident corroborated when it obtained one first-hand account which it assessed as credible and as consistent with what was known about the incident or the established patterns of similar incidents in the area, and in line with the interviewer's own observations'.

44 'Report of the detailed findings of the Independent International Fact-Finding Mission on Myanmar', A/HRC/39/CRP.2, 17 September 2018, Para. 11–24.

45 See Sam Dubberly, Alexa Koenig and Daragh Murray (eds.), *Digital Witness* (Oxford University Press 2020)

46 Para 100, IIFFMM September 2018 Report.

47 Para 85-87, IIFFMM September 2018 Report.

48 Para 92, IIFFMM September 2018 Report.

49 Para 92, IIFFMM September 2018 Report.

50 Para 105, IIFFMM September 2018 Report.

51 Para 116, IIFFMM September 2018 Report.

52 Para 106, IIFFMM September 2018 Report.

53 A/HRC/RES/39/2, 27 September 2018.

54 Para. 22, A/HRC/RES/39/2, 27 September 2018.

55 Terms of Reference, A/73/716, 21 January 2019. ('IIMM ToR')

56 IIMM ToR, para. 8 (a).
57 Para. 30, A/HRC/RES/39/2, 27 September 2018 extended the mandate of the IIFFMM in order 'to ensure that the large and continually increasing amount of evidence of human rights violations and abuses it has collected is fully documented, verified, consolidated, and preserved in order for the material to be effectively shared, accessed, and used by the mechanism …'. See also, Paras. 45 & 46, IIMM ToR.
58 Paras. 14–17, 'Report of the Independent International Fact-Finding Mission on Myanmar', A/HRC/42/50, 8 August 2019.
59 'The mission's approach was to ensure that, to the fullest extent possible, its materials were shared with the Mechanism and that the organization and presentation of the material was accessible and useful, particularly for potential future criminal prosecution'. Para. 14, 'Report of the Independent International Fact-Finding Mission on Myanmar', A/HRC/42/50, 8 August 2019.
60 These three terms are used throughout the IIMM ToR.
61 IIMM ToR, para. 8 (b)–(d).
62 IIMM ToR, para. 15.
63 IIMM ToR, Para. 9.
64 IIMM ToR, Para. 29–31
65 'Report of the International, Impartial and Independent Mechanism to Assist in the Investigation and Prosecution of Persons Responsible for the Most Serious Crimes under International Law Committed in the Syrian Arab Republic since March 2011', A/76/690, 11 February 2022, para. 4.
66 UNHRC Resolution 39/2 of Para. 24, 25 September 2018.
67 Statement to the Human Rights Council by Mr. Nicholas Koumjian, Head of the Independent Investigative Mechanism for Myanmar, on the 48th Regular Session of the Human Rights Council, 13 September 2021, <https://iimm.un.org/statement-to-the-human-rights-council-by-mr-nicholas-koumjian-head-of-the-independent-investigative-mechanism-for-myanmar-on-the-48th-regular-session-of-the-human-rights-council/> accessed 2 June 2022.
68 Frederica D'Alessandra, Ambassador Stephen J. Rapp, Kirsty Sutherland, and Sareta Ashraph, 'Anchoring Accountability for Mass Atrocities—The Permanent Support Needed to Fulfil UN Investigative Mandates', Oxford Institute for Ethics, Law and Armed Conflict (May 2022). See also, Kingsley Abbott and Saman Zia-Zarifi, 'Is It Time to Create a Standing Independent Investigative Mechanism (SIIM)? Part I' (*Opinio Juris*, 10 April 2019) <http://opiniojuris.org/2019/04/10/is-it-time-to-create-a-standing-independent-investigative-mechanism-siim/> accessed 2 June 2022; Kingsley Abbott and Saman Zia-Zarifi, 'Is It Time to Create a Standing Independent Investigative Mechanism (SIIM)? Part II' (*Opinio Juris*, 11 April 2019)
<http://opiniojuris.org/2019/04/11/is-it-time-to-create-a-standing-independent-investigative-mechanism-siim-part-ii/> accessed 2 June 2022.
69 *Application of the Convention on the Prevention and Punishment of the Crime of Genocide (The Gambia v. Myanmar)*, Provisional Measures, Order of 23 January 2020, I.C.J. Reports 2020, p. 3.
70 International Criminal Court, Rules of Procedure and Evidence, ICC-ASP/1/3 and Corr. 1 (2013).
71 Charter of the United Nations and Statute of the International Court of Justice, June 26, 1945
59 Stat. 1031.
72 Charter of the United Nations and Statute of the International Court of Justice, June 26, 1945

59 Stat. 1031; Rules of Court (1978), adopted 14 APRIL 1978, entered into force 1 JULY 1978, < https://www.icj-cij.org/en/rules> accessed 2 June 2022.

73 Speech by HE Judge Peter Tomka, President of the International Court of Justice, to the Sixth Committee of the General Assembly, 31 October 2014 < https://www.icj-cij.org/public/files/press-releases/8/18398.pdf> accessed 2 June 2022.

74 James Gerard Devaney, 'The Law and Practice of Fact-Finding before the International Court of Justice,' *Thesis submitted for the Doctor of Laws degree at the European University Institute (2014)*, < https://cadmus.eui.eu/bitstream/handle/1814/33884/2014_Devaney.pdf> accessed 1 June 2022.

75 Article 48, Statute of ICJ, states: 'The Court shall make orders for the conduct of the case, shall decide the form and time in which each party must conclude its arguments, and make all arrangements connected with the taking of evidence'.

76 Article 50, Statute of the ICJ: 'The Court may, at any time, entrust any individual, body, bureau, commission, or other organization that it may select, with the task of carrying out an enquiry or giving an expert opinion'.

77 Article 57 indicates the information that the parties are to provide the court, including details of the witnesses and experts, as well as the points that they will address. Article 58 allows the court to determine whether arguments precede or follow the presentation of evidence, notwithstanding the parties have a 'right to comment on the evidence given'.

78 Peter Tomka and Vincent-Joël Proulx, 'The Evidentiary Practice of the World Court', NUS Law Working Paper Series, 2015/010 (December 2015), p. 16, <https://law.nus.edu.sg/wp-content/uploads/2020/04/010_2015-_Vincent-Joel-Proulx_Tomka.pdf> accessed 2 June 2022.

79 *Application of the Convention on the Prevention and Punishment of the Crime of Genocide (Ukraine v. Russian Federation)*, Provisional Measures, Order of 16 March 2022 <https://www.icj-cij.org/public/files/case-related/182/182-20220316-ORD-01-00-EN.pdf> accessed 2 June 2022.

80 Paras. 10–14, 'Application instituting proceedings and Request for the indication of Provisional Measures', *Application of the Convention on the Prevention and Punishment of the Crime of Genocide (The Gambia v. Myanmar)*, 11 November 2019, <https://www.icj-cij.org/public/files/case-related/178/178-20191111-APP-01-00-EN.pdf> accessed 1 June 2022.

81 *Application of the Convention on the Prevention and Punishment of the Crime of Genocide (The Gambia v. Myanmar)*, Provisional Measures, Order of 23 January 2020, I.C.J. Reports 2020, p. 3, p. 22–23, para. 55–56.

82 *Application of the Convention on the Prevention and Punishment of the Crime of Genocide (The Gambia v. Myanmar)*, Provisional Measures, Order of 23 January 2020, ICJ Reports 2020, p. 3, p. 13–15, para. 27–31.

83 'The Fall of Srebrenica', UN Doc. A/54/549, 15 November 1999.

84 *Application of the Convention on the Prevention and Punishment of the Crime of Genocide (Bosnia and Herzegovina v. Serbia and Montenegro)*, Judgement, ICJ Reports 2007, p. 43, para. 227.

85 *Application of the Convention on the Prevention and Punishment of the Crime of Genocide (Bosnia and Herzegovina v. Serbia and Montenegro)*, Judgement, ICJ Reports 2007, p. 43, para. 228–230.

86 *Prosecutor v. Krstić*, IT-98-33-T, Trial Chamber Judgement, 2 August 2001; *Prosecutor v. Krstić*, IT-98-33-A, Judgment, 19 April 2004; *Prosecutor v. Stakić*, IT-97-24-T, Judgement, 31 July 2003.

87 *Application of the Convention on the Prevention and Punishment of the Crime of Genocide (Bosnia and Herzegovina v. Serbia and Montenegro)*, Judgement,

ICJ Reports 2007, p. 43, p.95, para. 214, referring to (*Armed Activities on the Territory of the Congo (Democratic Republic of the Congo v. Uganda), Judgement, ICJ Reports 2005*, p. 35, para. 61.

88 'In view of the above, the Court concludes that it should in principle accept as highly persuasive relevant findings of fact made by the Tribunal at trial, unless of course they have been upset on appeal. For the same reasons, any evaluation by the Tribunal based on the facts as so found for instance about the existence of the required intent, is also entitled to due weight'. *Application of the Convention on the Prevention and Punishment of the Crime of Genocide (Bosnia and Herzegovina v. Serbia and Montenegro), Judgement, ICJ Reports 2007*, p. 133, para. 223.

89 *Application of the Convention on the Prevention and Punishment of the Crime of Genocide (Bosnia and Herzegovina v. Serbia and Montenegro)*, Judgement, ICJ Reports 2007, p. 134, para. 219.

90 *Prosecutor v. Krstić*, IT-98-33-T, Trial Chamber Judgement, 2 August 2001; *Prosecutor v. Blagojević*, IT-02-60-T, Trial Chamber Judgment, 17 January 2005. The finding of complicity in genocide by the trial chamber in *Prosecutor v. Blagojević* was subsequently reversed on appeal, in May 2007, a mere three months after the ICJ judgement in February 2007. See *Prosecutor v. Blagojević*, IT-02-60-A, Appeals Chamber Judgement, 9 May 2007.

91 *Application of the Convention on the Prevention and Punishment of the Crime of Genocide (Bosnia and Herzegovina v Serbia and Montenegro)*, Judgement, ICJ Reports 2007, p. 43, p. 127–130, Para. 202–210.

92 *Application of the Convention on the Prevention and Punishment of the Crime of Genocide (Bosnia and Herzegovina v Serbia and Montenegro)*, Judgement, ICJ Reports 2007, p. 43, p. 133–134, Para. 220–223.

93 *Application of the Convention on the Prevention and Punishment of the Crime of Genocide (Bosnia and Herzegovina v Serbia and Montenegro)*, Judgement, ICJ Reports 2007, p. 43, p. 130, para. 210.

94 *Application of the Convention on the Prevention and Punishment of the Crime of Genocide (Bosnia and Herzegovina v Serbia and Montenegro)*, Judgement, ICJ Reports 200

95 >7, p. 43, p. 130, para. 210.
Republic of The Gambia v. Facebook Inc., Order, U.S District Court for the District of Columbia, 22 September 2021, <https://globalfreedomofexpression.columbia.edu/wp-content/uploads/2021/10/In-re-Gambia-v-Facebook.pdf>, accessed 1 June 2022.

96 Statement to the Human Rights Council by Mr Nicholas Koumjian, Head of the Independent Investigative Mechanism for Myanmar, on the 48th Regular Session of the Human Rights Council, 13 September 2021, <https://iimm.un.org/statement-to-the-human-rights-council-by-mr-nicholas-koumjian-head-of-the-independent-investigative-mechanism-for-myanmar-on-the-48th-regular-session-of-the-human-rights-council/> accessed 1 June 2022.

97 Chatham House International Law Discussion Group Meeting Summary, 'UN Fact-finding and International Criminal Investigations', 22 January 2014, p. 3 <https://www.chathamhouse.org/sites/default/files/public/Meetings/Meeting%20Transcripts/220114UNFact.pdf Chatham House 2014> Accessed 2 June 2022.

98 Chatham House International Law Discussion Group Meeting Summary, 'UN Fact-finding and International Criminal Investigations', 22 January 2014, p. 4 <https://www.chathamhouse.org/sites/default/files/public/Meetings/Meeting%20Transcripts/220114UNFact.pdf Chatham House 2014> Accessed 2 June 2022.

99 Office of the Prosecutor, ICC, Policy Paper on Preliminary Examinations (November 2013), para. 31 <https://www.icc-cpi.int/news/policy-paper-preliminary-examinations> accessed 2 June 2022 ('PE Policy Paper')
100 Para 27, PE Policy Paper, referencing Articles 14(2) & 15(2).
101 PE Policy Paper, para 31: 'As information evaluated at the preliminary examination stage is largely obtained from external sources, rather than through the Office's own evidence-gathering powers (which are only available at the investigation stage), the Office pays particular attention to the assessment of the reliability of the source and the credibility of the information'.
102 PE Policy Paper, para 32: 'The Office uses standard formats for analytical reports, standard methods of source evaluation, and consistent rules of measurement and attribution in its crime analysis. It checks internal and external coherence and considers information from diverse and independent sources as a means of bias control'.
103 Article 15(3), Rome Statute: 'If the Prosecutor concludes that there is a reasonable basis to proceed with an investigation, he or she shall submit to the Pre-Trial Chamber a request for authorization of an investigation, together with any supporting material collected. Victims may make representations to the Pre-Trial Chamber, in accordance with the Rules of Procedure and Evidence'.
104 Para 34, PE Policy Paper.
105 Para. 85, PE Policy Paper.
106 See *Situation in the Republic of Kenya*, Request for Authorization of an Investigation Pursuant to Article 15, ICC-01/09-3, 26 November 2009; *Situation in the Republic of Cote D'Ivoire*, Request for Authorization of an Investigation Pursuant to Article 15, ICC-02/11-3, 23 June 2011; *Situation in Georgia*, Request for Authorization of an Investigation Pursuant to Article 15, ICC-01/15-4, 13 October 2015.
107 Article 15 of the Rome Statute relates to the power of the Prosecutor to 'initiate investigations *proprio motu* on the basis of information on crimes within the jurisdiction of the court' and goes on to specify the requirements that must be met in order to proceed.
108 Dov Jacobs, 'Limitations of Using Fact-Finding Reports in Criminal Proceedings: The Case of Myanmar', Policy Brief Series No. 118 (2020), Torkel Opsahl Academic E-Publisher (2019).
109 Dov Jacobs, 'Limitations of Using Fact-Finding Reports in Criminal Proceedings: The Case of Myanmar', Policy Brief Series No. 118 (2020), Torkel Opsahl Academic E-Publisher (2019), p. 2 & 4.
110 Situation in the People's Republic of Bangladesh/Republic of the Union of Myanmar, 'Request for authorization of an investigation pursuant to Article 15,' 4 July 2019, ICC-01/19-7, para. 29.
111 Situation in the People's Republic of Bangladesh/Republic of the Union of Myanmar, 'Request for authorization of an investigation pursuant to Article 15', 4 July 2019, ICC-01/19-7, para. 30, 33–34.
112 Situation in the People's Republic of Bangladesh/Republic of the Union of Myanmar, 'Decision Pursuant to Article 15 of the Rome Statute on the Authorization of an Investigation,' 14 November 2019, ICC-01/19-27, para. 35–39. ('Decision to Authorize Investigation')
113 Decision to Authorize Investigation, Para. 66.
114 Decision to Authorize Investigation, Para. 67.
115 Decision to Authorize Investigation, Para. 68.
116 Decision to Authorize Investigation, Para. 74 & 77.
117 Decision to Authorize Investigation, Para. 84.
118 Decision to Authorize Investigation, Para. 84.

119 Decision to Authorize Investigation, Para. 91
120 Situation in the People's Republic of Bangladesh/Republic of the Union of Myanmar, 'Decision Pursuant to Article 15 of the Rome Statute on the Authorization of an Investigation,' 14 November 2019, ICC-01/19-27.
121 Frederica D'Alessandra, Sander Couch, Ilina Georgieva, Marieke De Hoon, Brianne McGonigle Leyh, Jolien Quispel (eds.), 'Handbook on Civil Society Documentation of Serious Human Rights Violations—Principles and Best Practices' (PILPG 2016) https://static1.squarespace.com/static/5900b58e1b631bffa367167e/t/59dfab4480bd5ef9add73271/1507830600233/Handbook-on-Civil-Society-Documentation-of-Serious-Human-Rights-Violations_c.pdf> accessed 2 June 2022.
122 https://www.icc-cpi.int/news/icc-prosecutor-karim-khan-qc-concludes-first-visit-bangladesh-underlines-commitment-advance February 2022

Theme 3

Towards sustainable solutions

Multi-faceted engagements for concrete action

8 Are you real, seriously?

Ethical dilemmas of an online role play in the Rohingya crisis

Helen Hintjens, Md Mizanur Rahman, and Ron Linser

Introduction

For some time, online role-play simulations have been recognized as an effective method for learning about practice, including in situations of crisis.[1] In the winter of 2019, at the International Institute of Social Studies (The Hague), we ran an assessed, online role-play simulation with around 37 MA participants. This chapter considers some ethical dilemmas raised by this online exercise which took place shortly before COVID-19 restrictions put an end to in-person classrooms in the Netherlands. Requiring MA students to take part in online teaching would soon become the norm across all degree programmes, as in-person teaching was suspended. Back in autumn 2019, we did not anticipate how online teaching would become the rule, almost everywhere. One feature of online role-play simulations noted by Linser and Hintjens is that they involve: 'exploring a sort of interactive and collaborative thought experiment about some reality being modelled. The roles that populated these [role plays]...were in most cases drawn from the reality being modelled, i.e., they were particular individuals rather than generic ones'.[2] For the past 20 years, two of us, as teachers and designers, have been designing and delivering online role-play simulations 'in the hope that the Reality being modelled by the role-play medium filters through the porous layers of identity to become a transparent model for the students'.[3] The aim of such simulations, according to Gredler, is to 'bridge the gap between the classroom and the real world by providing experiences with complex, evolving problems', making such exercises 'social microcosms' of the real world; in this case the world of the Rohingya crisis.[4] When an online role play of this kind works well, participants: 'take [on] a bona fide role, address the issues, threats or problems arising in the simulation, and experience the effects of [their] decisions'.[5]

In the past, we have run simulations on Venezuela and post-genocide Rwanda, and Linser has run simulations on the Holocaust but, given that the genocide in Myanmar took place just two years before the role play, the case of the Rohingya simulation was particularly intense, disturbing, trauma-laden, and seemed to lack hop, for those who experienced the simulation role play. One participant in this role-play simulation questioned the whole premise. Co-playing the role of Razia Sultana, a Rohingya lawyer and human rights activist, she reflected at the

DOI: 10.4324/9781003304883-12

end of the exercise, just as the ICJ (International Court of Justice) Gambia case against Myanmar was getting started five minutes from the ISS (the International Institute of Social Studies), in the Peace Palace:

> The most problematic thing for me came up in the latest days of this role play, since I realized that the main purpose was to represent characters and roles that were actually passing through an actual humanitarian crisis and that a few days ago have been asking for justice in the international court [ICJ] located in The Hague. If I have to select a positive thing, it could be the fact that I became more aware of what is happening with the Rohingya community in Myanmar and Bangladesh, however I found it really problematic that we had been representing an ongoing problem. As student of Social Justice, I think I wish to be more involved into other type of activities related with the support of the vulnerable and oppressed members of that community, rather than representing roles in a simulation. Because as respectful and methodologically underpinned as it may be, we are again objectifying a marginalized population with no real outputs that could be beneficial for them … In sum, I had some troubles at the end in finding out what all the role-play simulation was about; however, we tried to give our best in this simulation, with the awareness that we were representing a real person struggling day by day to gain respect for the rights of her compatriots.[6]

This comment raises serious questions as to what the purpose of such a pedagogic exercise is *for the Rohingya*, and whether it is ethical in the classroom. In the rest of this chapter, we will try to address that participant's very legitimate questions about the ethics of playing the role of a real person, in this case a Rohingya woman activist and lawyer, as if it were possible to game around so serious a real situation. As she suggests, any simulation of this kind, if not taken seriously and played responsibly, does run the risk of 'objectifying a marginalized population with no real outputs that could be beneficial for them'. It also raises the question of whether the educational purpose would have been better served had we invented an unreal traumatic situation to enable participants to deal with difficult human rights, gender, and conflict and peace issues, the areas covered by the full title of our MA programme (Human Rights, Gender and Conflict: Social Justice Perspectives).

This chapter considers how simulating the Rohingya crisis online, through role play, involving real individuals, led participants to construct their own experience-based knowledge of the Rohingya crisis. We suggest this kind of learning can go beyond the usual knowledge of formal academic writing and reports, associated with classroom-based learning. Tacit aspects of the Rohingya crisis, and ethical dilemmas, became more apparent to participants, as we will show. Immersing themselves in a given context, most participants were led to acknowledge the atrocities committed against Rohingya, from a range of perspectives. We consider what ethical dilemmas this raised for participants, and for us as staff responsible for the Rohingya role play. Did some roles achieve greater insights into the Rohingya crisis than others? Did some participants go further than others, imagining and proposing possible ways out of the existing crisis? The ethical dilemmas involved in running a role-play simulation on such a fraught and sensitive issue are considered. We ask if this experience can generate anything of value to the Rohingya themselves and those who advocate for their rights. We ask: can simulating a situation of genocide, characterized by extreme violence, trauma, and suffering, be justified on pedagogic grounds? Can it be justified on practical grounds, for Rohingya themselves? We identify a number of ethical dilemmas and limitations of such an exercise. We also consider some key insights arising from participants' self-reflection and feedback on the experience.

We start by considering how online role-play simulations around themes of suffering and loss can be conceived. Then, we move on to critically reflect on how the situation of Rohingya in flight was framed in this particular exercise, through the lenses of history, citizenship, ethnic and religious identity, and victim status. How were atrocities, gender violence, and loss of citizenship represented by participants in their communications? We draw throughout on the record of online interactions among 34 participants, including simulated media publications. In the third section, we analyze how participants reflected on their roles, linking their framings to existing UN and NGO reports and academic literature. How the realities of suffering and trauma are integrated into their analysis of the role-play experience is of particular interest. Finally, we seek whether any participants developed deeper insights into how real-world solutions could be imagined amidst the apparently irresolvable dilemmas facing the Rohingya, focusing mainly on those who are stateless in Bangladesh. What kinds of solution-oriented insights arose in self-reflection reports of participants? How did they manage to integrate experience-based knowledge with more academic and explicit reporting on the Rohingya situation? We reflect on how participants negotiated the idea of play, contrasting it with the deadly seriousness, and apparent hopelessness, of the context facing Rohingyas collectively. Towards the end of the chapter, we reflect on some overall lessons from this pedagogic exercise, asking whether its implications can move us beyond the virtual global classroom into real life?

Setting and resources

Displaced Rohingya today find themselves in an impossible situation, especially in Bangladesh and Myanmar. Their legal status remains unresolved, and for the most part they are stateless. Rohingya lives are in limbo as far as their refugee status and legal protection are concerned. Interestingly, although the Rohingya situation is distinctive in many ways, the fact is, it is far from unique in Myanmar. UN Human Rights Special Rapporteur, Tomas Ojean Quintana reported in 2018, to the UN Human Rights Council about another group of displaced Myanmar citizens:

> Karen refugees told me that the humanitarian assistance they depend on is declining, while Shan refugees informed me that their aid has been cut by

> foreign donors entirely. This is occurring in a context where people are being encouraged to return home despite feeling that it is premature or unsafe to do so. They are left to choose between empty stomachs on the Thai side of the border and a return to a precarious peace on the Myanmar side and the risk of being made refugees all over again.[7]

Replacing the words Karen with Rohingya and Thailand with Bangladesh, this statement perfectly reflects the current plight of Rohingya who have fled across the border, most of them from August to September 2017. The dominant response of powerful state players has been indifference to the suffering of the Rohingya, whose lives, it sometimes appears, do not matter much to anyone but the Rohingya themselves and the human rights community. With on-going geo-strategic power plays in South Asia today, many Rohingya find themselves in a fearful and hopeless situation, abandoned to their 'fate', in Bangladesh, as in Myanmar and elsewhere in the diaspora. Speaking of the mass flight of stateless Rohingya into Bangladesh in 2017, Wade suggests this was: 'the culmination of a decades-long strategy, driven by a racist ideology, to wipe Rohingya off the national map'.[8]

By combining the roles of Rohingya, Bangladeshis, international agencies, academics, and journalists, the simulation sought to have these lenses convey a range of perspectives, only some of which fully recognize Rohingya as victims of atrocities. Ultimately, to rethink the shape of future justice for the Rohingya, insight is needed into how these different lenses, or perspectives, and interests can be reconciled productively. This chapter reflects on broad ethical and pedagogic lessons from simulating roles around the Rohingya crisis, through an online simulation. It critically reflects on the ethics of conducting a pedagogic exercise that centres on the suffering and trauma of a group of marginalized people. The question is how participants were able to tread the thin line between empathy and objectification, and to avoid vicarious trauma for simulation participants. On the way through this maze, we seek insights into post-traumatic recovery and the resilience of Rohingya, both as a stateless people and an unwanted minority. The starting point, and fundamental assumption, is the full entitlement, as a people and as individuals, to various forms of collective and personal self-determination and justice.

Drawing on both existing scholarship on the Rohingya situation and on role-play simulations online, we analyze participants' self-evaluations, reflecting on their insights into connection and dilemmas of portraying a range of actors involved somehow in Rohingya's daily lives, especially in Bangladesh. Drawing on these self-evaluations, we reflect on the thin line between vicarious trauma, the denial of extreme suffering, and the insights of some participants around the ways and means towards post-traumatic growth for Rohingya people. Given their status as both stateless and unwanted, can a role-play simulation exercise be justified on any other than pedagogic grounds? Can any aspects of such an exercise somehow contribute to resolving practical dilemmas faced by the Rohingya? Issues of historical representation, citizenship, ethnic and religious identity markers, and representations of organized violence, army atrocities, and gender violence are considered as part of the wider picture. The online interactions and self-reflections of the 37 Masters participants provide significant insights. By identifying with Rohingya experiences, and with agencies that work with the Rohingya, some participants were able to draw lessons from this exercise, lessons that extended beyond the classroom.

Prior to the start of the course, by a fortunate coincidence, an event took place in person at the ISS, to which many notable figures around the Rohingya question were invited, several of whom we included in the role-play exercise. The summary and full report of the International Conclave on Justice and Accountability for Rohingya, which took place in The Hague on 18 October 2019, was jointly organized by BRAC University of Bangladesh, Centre for Peace and Justice, the Asia Justice Coalition, and ISS. The Conclave brought together key players to provide in-person observations, recorded and transcribed into a unique record of various viewpoints and priorities at this point in time. The Final Report is another key source for this chapter, showing which issues were of primary concern to international actors and to Rohingya representatives themselves. Since the Conclave took place just two weeks before the simulation started, the report is a relevant snapshot of positions. The event also made it possible for two of us to personally meet with some individuals whose real-life 'selves' our MA participants would soon be 'playing' online. This quite exceptional coincidence definitely enhanced the sensation of 'realism' of the simulation. So too did the start of the ICJ hearing against the Myanmar government, led by the Gambian Minister of Justice, who also spoke at the Conclave. The ICJ being located just a short walk from ISS meant the course participants were very much aware, at the time of their self-reflective evaluations, that the legal case against the Myanmar government, with Aung San Suu Syi present, was proceeding just 'down the road'. Asked to reflect on the experience of identifying as someone else, participants' reflections are a key source of insights for this chapter, alongside other UN material and the Final Report of the Conclave.

Online through the looking-glass

'When we step through the screen into virtual communities, we reconstruct our identities on the other side of the looking glass. This reconstruction is our cultural work in progress'.[9] On the first day of the simulation, we posted the scenario, which signalled to participants that they should start to read one another's profiles and familiarize themselves with the cast of characters. These profiles were prepared in the preceding days, either individually or as a team of two. Thus, at the start of the simulation, there are just their own general knowledge, a lecture input on background, and some readings provided. The specifics of the simulated environment are unknown to almost all participants. Once the profiles are submitted, the scenario (see below) was posted and they could then start communicating with one another, without any mediation from the teacher, who performs the role of a moderator and should remain, as much as possible, in the background, and preferably anonymized (e.g., as 'conference organizer', mod or 'ghost in the machine'). Participants were reminded at the start to only communicate in character, and sometimes told they needed to step up their online interactions, as well as using the full range of virtual spaces available for communicating (posting sim-mails, using chat rooms, writing to media, posting media, and so on). In three weeks, in the Rohingya simulation exercise, which has only been run once, over 1200 messages were sent by sim-mail and 30 articles were posted by four participants playing journalists in two media outlets (*The Guardian* and *Rohingya Human Rights Network*).

One study on this question of how we learn online suggests that: 'While this mode of learning offers convenience and flexibility, it has also increased the difficulty of instructors and students engaging on an emotional level'.[10] Yet role-play simulations portraying real characters are designed to enhance emotional attachment and identification; this is built into the design. As one participant in an earlier simulation at the same institution noted: 'such simulations can be called new experiments for social change by using real life content and advanced technology practice. I found it beyond … the traditional teaching and learning procedures' (2014, participant, role-play on Rwanda, ISS, the Netherlands).

The Scenario:

> The Rohingya now in Bangladesh, faced systematic discrimination in Myanmar over several decades, including denial of citizenship. They are now stateless refugees (sic) living in a congested, fragile area of Cox's Bazar, right next to the Myanmar border, and an area very prone to natural disasters and flooding. In December 2018, the US Congress declared that the crimes committed by Myanmar's security forces against Rohingya Muslims constituted a genocide. The Rohingya fled following horrifying atrocities committed against them, widely reported on by the UN, NGOs and academics. An independent United Nations fact-finding mission completed its work in September 2019, collecting evidence of serious crimes against humanity, and violations of international law. Bangladesh and parts of the international community claim Rohingya should return to Myanmar voluntarily and seek to ensure the right conditions are in place. However today, the right conditions are not yet in place. Will the principle of voluntary return be respected by UNHCR, IOM, the Bangladesh government, and international agencies? Might Rohingya sooner or later be forced to return? What can be done to avoid that?[11]

This is how the online role play was framed from the start, by very broad questions following a sweeping and very general scenario. On reflection, we could have introduced more hints that the Rohingya—especially through their diaspora—might be able to do some advocacy for themselves (self-advocacy) rather than focusing on international and state actors alone. Our biases show in the way the scenario is framed, and the comment from the participant who played Razia Sultana A is quite correct: Rohingya are indeed framed as passive victims, subject to the power plays of other actors and agencies. Yet, realistically, people subjected to such atrocities are almost uniformly living with trauma. However plucky they are as survivors, accepting their allotted role as an unwanted minority is not something they can easily fight, given their statelessness and the lack of protection of their community. The seriousness of the simulation comes across well in some of the reflective comments. A woman who played Tun Khin, a Rohingya exiled activist living in the UK, expressed her mixed feelings about how simulation experience related to reality:

> On a more sombre note, the simulation also highlighted the various constraints when seeking to further justice through different national and international channels: NGOs' inflexible agendas, state officials' diplomatic manoeuvres, IOs' [international organisations] technocracy and dependence on states' political will, etc. Power relations between different actors also became evident. Actors that I felt were missing from the simulation were grassroots community representatives without public profile—which is probably reflective of the reality of international politics, where the actions of these actors go largely unnoticed. As a privileged white German, I had difficulties trying to 'represent' my character.
>
> (a Rohingya genocide survivor)[12]

The comment is very interesting, as she failed to make a connection in this reflection between the history of trauma and genocide associated with German nationalism and the position of Rohingya in relation to Myanmar Buddhist nationalism. Playing the unfortunate and formerly lauded leader of democracy, Aung San Suu Kyi, one participant was shocked to discover that she was neither blameless nor entirely responsible for the crisis affecting the Rohingya. The participant reflects:

> I have realised one important thing which is never to judge anything by its cover, not even media. Because often times, whatever you see in real is just an iceberg and not the complete reality which one finds in the bottom. From the perception of Aung Suu Kyi, I have gained several insights both before and after the face-to-face conference and those are: being the leader of a nation, it's extremely difficult and a challenging task to deal with both sides of the coin.[13]

Moral ambivalence and emotional engagement

One of the interesting features of our particular role-play simulation on the Rohingya was that it did not prescribe to participants how they should treat ethical dilemmas, nor did it lay down a code of conduct. The only prescriptions were that they must participate quantitatively, that they stay in character, and that they should not knock other players out of the role play. Participants were thus involved in a scenario where the:

> Player of a game is actively participating in co-creating a story and making decisions within the game … This exploration is critical when, rather than telling the player what to believe, it offers players a number of ways to interpret the situation, and a number of potential reactions to it. The exploration is descriptive when it sets up a rich social environment within necessarily taking them on as a player, possibly changing their norms by playing a different way. The norms are not therefore seen as universal, but as tied to culture or community.[14]

Online role-play simulations are particularly good at affording to the player a critical and descriptive exploration of ethical issues. This can be supported by effective game design, involving:

> the balanced use of consequence, mirroring, social context, and freedom (Ultimately, the purpose of a role-play simulation is to encourage participants' (re)making of meanings, by encouraging what Pierre Bourdieu terms 'second-order reflexivity' around the themes of the role play.[15]

To elaborate on this point:

> critical reflexion on the limits of theoretical understanding is … to give it [i.e., theoretical knowledge] a solid basis by freeing it from the distortions arising from the epistemological and social conditions of its production.[16]

Diverse opinions about the significance and degree of realism of the online role-play exercise, are apparent in participants' responses.

Dealing with difficult and triggering subject matter in class is always a dilemma. Participants may become disturbed. They may have to leave the class after a discussion about trauma or cases of atrocities and suffering. Sometimes, informal or even professional counselling may be required, so 'triggered' can they be by painful material, especially if conveyed without sensitivity, but even if much thought has gone into making the material palatable and 'playful'. This is an issue that can only be avoided if teachers working on subjects connected with violence, injustice, and cruelty decide to exclude all triggering references altogether. This will rule out the use of much film, imagery, and the editing and even censoring of texts that might be able to trigger a strong negative emotional response in some participating students. In many different and applied disciplines, when dealing with disturbing or unpalatable situations, such as a serious human rights abuse, or effects and justifications for violence and persecution, is it our job as educators to protect participants from potentially disturbing subjects? Is it enough to give a 'trigger warning', as we did for certain UN reports, and continue undeterred to expect participants to deal with this difficult material? Can teachers themselves become indifferent to the emotional impact such contexts and studies (such as Holocaust or genocide studies) can have on learners? If we can encourage those taking place in role-play simulation exercises of this kind, to be inspired, to imagine solutions to the real-world problems of the Rohingya, does this justify the game, linking it to reality? Or is this also a form of rationalization, to justify to ourselves the entire pedagogic exercise, and its necessary connections with serious and often depressing realities? When dealing with as sensitive an issue as the Rohingya crisis, and through student-centred participatory online learning, with a simulated context that relates to a real situation, what interactions can be expected with that real context? Are there some serious lessons learned? During COVID-19 in particular, these have been vital questions to ask about the 'new normal' of online university classes.

Identification takes place, not via instructor validation, but with information that then is used by the person playing the role in building their own profile for other roles to read. Identification can be very powerful and demanding, and that in itself may even account for the urgency with which the woman co-playing Razia Sultana A sought real-life solutions in this online exercise. In one sense, her demand for impact betrays a deeper identification with the role, who precisely is immersed in a serious offline struggle for real-life solutions for Rohingya people as a community of forced exiles in Bangladesh and worldwide. Another feature of online learning through role play is the space for anonymity and a certain freedom for otherwise more inhibited learners in the classroom. One participant in an earlier Rwanda simulation had this to say:

> I usually don't speak a lot in class. But through the simulation exercise I could openly and critically communicate with others and write freely to advance my agenda. It was fun. The simulation was based on real life situation. The scenario was real, the characters were real who actually exist in real life, the issues we dealt with were real, so it was a practical exercise that put together [what] we have learned so far. Through all that, I could see the diversity of opinions, the different stakeholders, and the power relations of the actors involved, and complexity and possibility of realizing rights. It somehow felt like my first work experience.[17]

Both within the physical classroom, and in online teaching and learning spaces, '[w]hether we like it or not, researchers [and student participants] remain human beings, complete with all the usual assembly of feelings, failings, and moods'.[18] In our experience, the emotions expressed by participants varied greatly. From the self-reflections, a few phrases can convey this, as shown in Table 8.1.

What we observe in these, besides feelings of discomfort and engagement, is 'the recursive resonance between the identity of the role and identity of the student created by playing a role'.[19] Emotions, feelings, and mixed sentiments play an important role in the online learning process, including those that can be described as 'negative', such as outrage and regret. Initial sentiments of

Table 8.1 Emotional content of responses to playing a role (Rohingya Simulation)

Role played	
Co-played Razia Sultana B	The role play simulation at first did not prepare me for the roller-coaster of emotions I was in for. It took me back to the armed conflict I experienced as a child in my home country, Nigeria, in 1992 in Kano State, where I was born[a]
Saiful Huq Omi	Overall, I have mixed feelings about the online simulation. On the one hand, I got really excited and inspired by the real poetry-photo-collaboration with another character (Mayyu Ali) that we also brought to the face-to-face conference as well as my space for giving a speech as Saiful Huq Omi. On the other hand, the fact that all was simulated was something that confused and deterred me[b]
Tun Khin	Perhaps most regrettably, I feel that there is no 'real' outcome in terms of tangible support for the cause. We might be able to build on our gained insights in the future[c]
Aung San Suu Kyi	I was bombarded with five to six messages a day with the title "Stand up for your nation! Act now!" etc. And yes, for a moment I was taken aback by the long accusations in the form of emails against me. The toughest moments were when I dug up on her history in order to provide a valid and strong response to the sim-mails. Not just for the sim exercise but individually as a person my notion towards this person has completely changed for the greater good[d]
Hasina Sheikh	Sincerely am still filled up with joy and happiness for being part of the Rohingya crisis conference … I felt honoured to be assigned such a good role to play that introduced me to the world of politics and exposed my mind on how to solve such disasters in case they happen along my way[e]
Prayut Chan-o-cha	I found it interesting because the theme is so current so that we unconsciously analyze present issue in a theatrical way. I got Prayut Chan-o-cha as my character to play and it's kind of weird because I got to play a military man even though I'm a pacifist. It was quite challenging, because you have to do different way of thinking despite your personal mental state[f]

[a] Razia Sultana (B), Co-player, MA participant, excerpt from Self-reflection, December 2019.
[b] Saiful Huq Omi, Sole Player, MA participant, excerpt from Self-reflection, December 201.
[c] Tun Khin, except from 'Self-reflection' ff. 12.
[d] Aung San Suu Kyi, excerpt from Self-reflection, see ff. 13.
[e] Hasina Sheikh, Sole Player, MA Participant, excerpt from Self-reflection, December 2019.
[f] Prayut Chan-o-cha, Sole Player, MA Participant, excerpt from Self-reflection, December 2019.

excitement at anticipating fun learning alternate with confusion and frustration at not knowing what to do. The dominant trope appears to be mixed feelings and internal tensions. For role-play participants whose immersion in their online role-play character can remove them somewhat from their own comfort zones, the whole experience can engender dissonance, their role conflicting with their own habitual responses. Several feel, in a sense, trapped inside the role and only come to identify with it towards the end of the exercise. The participant with the role of Aung San Suu Kyi reflected on this:

> When questions were being posed at the conference, there was a continuous struggle between the "real me" and "the character" to exchange positions and speak out for "what is justifiable and right", not just because I am playing the role of the *de facto* leader of Myanmar but because this is not who I am in real life.[20]

Several participants reflect on how 'conflicted' they feel in their experience of playing another person. Yet, interestingly, Razia Sultana A's challenging reflection, which kick-started this chapter, conveyed less a sense of ambiguity of unconscious identification with Razia Sultana, a feminist activist like herself. She was as preoccupied as Razia Sultana would presumably be herself, with achieving feminist goals in the real world, and placed herself in the position of her role without the apparent inner turmoil mentioned by some other participants between the self and the role.

> At the beginning, I had some hesitations about the main objectives of my character because, even though I admire her work, I also think that her discourses were mostly related with humanitarian interventions for women refugees but there was a lack of solutions to put an end to the crisis and my partner and I decided to focus on what was important for Razia in real life, which was the Rohingya women … As part of our strategy, at some moment, we decided to start making emails to get allies for the conference and we even meet a group of people in real life, I must say that we did the best output from that meeting was that we heard each other and get to know more closely by explaining each other's struggles, and also by sharing our issues for the future agenda.[21]

Here what emerges is the importance of unmediated peer-to-peer learning during the course of the simulation role play, both online and face-to-face. For painful but important issues, like psychiatric and psychological problems, childhood illness, sexual abuse, gross human rights violations like torture, or even the collapse of ecosystems, there are risks for both the teacher and classroom participants to engage emotionally. What is sometimes termed vicarious trauma can result, for example, from teaching students about the Holocaust, racism, climate change, poverty, or colonial history and slavery. Referring to this possibility in the conventional classroom setting, one author comments that, in general, even in fields like genocide studies: 'instructors … speak little of how their pedagogy should address students' emotions, and even less of their own emotional states'.[22] The aim of our pedagogy was to encourage students to make: 'the sojourn from not-knowing to knowing about these literatures' so that they could bridge the gap between experiential knowing and understanding academic texts.[23]

Being someone else

Online role-play simulation is really a form of being in the skin of another person, online and off. Long ago, in his book *The Road to Wigan Pier*, George Orwell referred to his ambiguous class position when he decided to live in a working-class mining community. In a sense, he was simulating membership of this world, and he himself was engaged in a form of face-to-face role play. And, as Orwell reflected:

> In a way it is even humiliating to watch coal-miners working. It raises in you a momentary doubt about your own status as an 'intellectual' and a superior person generally. For it is brought home to you, at least while you are watching, that it is only because miners sweat their guts out that superior persons can remain superior … all of us [in the middle classes] really owe the comparative decency of our lives to poor drudges underground, blackened to the eyes, with their throats full of coal dust, driving their shovels forward with arms and belly muscles of steel.[24]

Although the relationship of dependency through exploitation may be more distant, there is little doubt that the Rohingya have been displaced from their land in Myanmar and had their citizenship removed, in order to benefit political and socio-economic elites in the country and international strategies of 'Belt and Road', agreed between China and Myanmar in January 2020, at the very start of the pandemic.[25] Their oppression is less about gross physical exploitation, as for miners in northern England in the twentieth century, and more about expulsion from their land and dispossession of their citizenship.

The power relations implicit in academic texts and intellectual concepts are made tangible by juxtaposing classroom teaching with the specific life experiences and contexts of specific individuals in the role play. Through the online and face-to-face elements of the simulation, participants reconsider some previous assumptions and perhaps also look back to see things differently which they thought they knew. This is what is sometimes termed second-order reflexivity, which means that: 'social actors become aware of prior behaviour and revise their actions and their self-awareness accordingly'.[26]

Fortunately, emotions are taken more seriously in higher education and scholarship than they once were, and this matters where, as in Development Studies and Peace Studies, 'emotions should not be regarded as psychological states, but as social and cultural practices' and as expressing forms of emotional intelligence.[27] Personalized identification in pedagogic situations can initiate processes of intellectual discovery that are more effective and meaningful to learners precisely because their emotions are more fully engaged.[28] What they develop in the exercise of role play is what Lederach calls 'moral imagination' which can be defined as 'the capacity to imagine something rooted in the challenge of the real world yet capable of giving birth to that which does not exist yet'.[29]

The politics of emotions in response to dealing with traumatic material has been discussed in the work of Jo Hamilton on climate change.[30] She suggests three possible emotional responses to suffering, atrocities, and the resulting emotions of pain and anger: denial, which involves avoidance or refusal to acknowledge facts and feelings; 'maladaptive coping strategies', which involve partial denial or partial acceptance of some facts, but negation of others which may cause emotional discomfort. A third possible response involves what she terms 'adaptive coping strategies', which enable individuals to acknowledge and integrate 'negative' and painful emotions, and on this basis move on to propose some coherent responses, including advocating for alternative scenarios.[31] All three types of responses can be expected from participants' retrospective reflections on the role-play simulation exercise.

It is in the third type of response, where the hope arises of participants coming up with some creative suggestions for how suffering might be reduced in practice. Drawing on her research on grief, despair and anger felt in relation to climate change realities, she suggests that: 'the emotional or affective aspect of engagement, alongside connections to others which can enhance collective agency, is not just a "nice to have", but a core component of active engagement for some'.[32] In answer to the ethical question posed by Razia Sultan A, this implies that there will be no single path through which individuals are able to work through unpleasant emotions in order to engage more determinedly with the practicalities of resolving painful issues. This may be true for some; emotional engagement can produce an opening towards action. For others, emotional engagement can undermine their belief in their own capacity to change realities through acting rationally in the world.

Some lessons: generating empathy, failing to collaborate

Not surprisingly, during the course of the emotional roller-coaster of this online role-play simulation, participants playing different characters doubted the real-life relevance of their experience in terms of finding practical solutions to the Rohingya crisis. Some experienced a conflict between their personal stance on the Rohingya issue and the position of the character they were assigned. However, some positive learning can also be traced in the interactions and reflections of participants, of some practical relevance to the delicate and complex social justice struggles required to address the Rohingya crisis in 'real life'.

Drawing on participants' interactions through sim-mail and self-reflections, two kinds of lessons emerged. The first was that most participants, by relating emotionally to the suffering of Rohingya people, also expressed their motivation to devote themselves to working for more positive change in their future life journey, for Rohingya people, and for other, similarly vulnerable minority communities. The considerable empathy generated among participants during this role-play simulation can be tied to their reinforced commitment to action, in some cases. It was particularly the more painful emotional responses that seemed to galvanize certain individuals, giving them a positive will to act for social justice in future.

Secondly, we noticed a lesson in the lack of any real collaboration among different sets of stakeholders, such as government representatives, representatives of UN agencies, local civil society organizations from Bangladesh, the media, and Rohingya activists and organizations. This lack of cross-boundary cooperation was very much evident throughout the simulation process, and most participants expressed their frustration at how difficult it was to initiate collaborative relationships across these divisions. To find concrete solutions to the Rohingya crisis, the majority of participants ended up seeing effective collaboration and communication among different kinds of stakeholders as the vital ingredient. However, they also recognized that this was more or less impossible, not only in the simulation but also in the 'real world', where any such collaboration was mostly lacking. One important observation was that in order to advocate for serious social change, new relationships need to be forged across the dividing lines of key actors' 'framings' of the crisis and its root causes. In relation to the hope of contributing to peaceful and dignified solutions for Rohingya in the future, these two lessons can briefly be discussed in turn.

Lesson 1: Generating empathy: advocating for social justice for Rohingyas

This kind of role-play simulation revolves around each player becoming involved with—and identifying to some degree—with their real-world character. Clapper, for example, suggests that through role-playing most people will feel some level of emotional identification with the role.[33] This involvement can trigger conflicting emotions among players as they grapple to understand their characters and critically elaborate on their role, as we have already seen. Role-playing is putting one's feet in the shoes of the characters being played. This enables players to engage with their characters *as if* they were in real life. Drawing from their interactions and reflections we noticed how playing their characters triggered feelings ranging from disbelief and distrust, to sadness and anger, to joy and the hope for a better future for their characters. All those emotions, discussed earlier, seem to arise from genuine feelings of empathy with Rohingya people. This inspired some participants to reflect on how they themselves could challenge injustices of vulnerable communities in their own societies. For example, one participant playing Khin Mai Aung, an activist who writes about atrocities Rohingya people face in Myanmar, stated in her self-reflection:

> I found myself rooting for my character, but that may be because I agree with so many of her standpoint … I really started to feel a kind of kinship with her when she described how similar the religious and ethnic extremism in Myanmar is to that of the United States. As a Buddhist of Burma and Rakhine descent, Khin Mai speaks from a place of privilege in Myanmar. Being white from the United States, I also see the extremism in my country, but I often don't know exactly how to go about fighting it without taking away space from other voices. I think I can learn from Khin Mai about how to raise awareness among privileged groups while making space in the conversation for silenced or marginalized voices.
>
> (Self-reflection, Khin Mai Aung, sole player)

One participant played Rohingya leader and activist, Mohibullah, who, in real life, was killed recently in one of the Rohingya camps in Bangladesh.[34] This participant ended up deeply empathizing with the Rohingya as victims of ethnic cleansing and persecution, and as stateless because they are not recognized as citizens by Myanmar. Being forced to flee to countries such as Bangladesh, Thailand, and further afield, this participant expressed her intense emotional disturbance and sorrow at the situation, as follows:

> The online simulation on the topic 'Rohingyas at Risk' to me was a very interactive and participatory method of learning. I understood more about lives of refugees in a host country, especially in camps, and the challenges and sufferings they face. What struck me as strange was how sometimes I got so engaged and attached to my role ... The insight I gained into realizing rights were that, I learnt the importance of rights in decision making and protection of marginalized groups, looking at how the Rohingyas whose rights were not recognized are suffering in the camps. I also realize how people in power use their positions to violate people's rights for their own interest, as done by the Myanmar army and government. I understood how women and children in camps are deprived of right to proper education, decent lives, proper shelter and medical care, and the impact on their future and wellbeing.[35]

Thus, role-play simulation can be decisive in transmitting empathy among the players, which in turn would help the cause of marginalized groups of people, in this case, Rohingyas. Empathy can start cumulative responses for future actions, and each response from an empathetic attribution is likely to start other empathetic processes and responses.[36] Most importantly, as a set of practices, empathy produces a feeling of 'shared emotions' and relates participants to 'social identities very different from their own'.[37] This kind of identification is very much needed in the case of the Rohingyas, who need others to work in their future alongside their own community organizations.

Lesson 2: Just like real life: No effective collaboration

During the role-play simulations we observed that participants playing different characters, including political leaders, staff of NGOs, and UN agencies, Rohingya activists, and academic researchers, did not get always get along with each other as might be hoped. Their lack of collaboration reflected this pervasive reality among real stakeholders in the context of the Rohingya crisis. Interestingly, players who shared similar interests or positions did collaborate and formed alliances fairly easily but ignored other groups of characters they could have communicated with, as they pursued their own group's shared goals. They in turn were ignored by others, who achieved similarly predictable alliances among other, similar characters. One example was the participant who played Khin Mai Aung, who we heard from earlier. As she reflected, she found it hard to communicate with other interest groups:

> One of the most interesting things I found from the role-play simulation was in how we built alliances and coordinated before the conference. Early on, Tun Khin, Razia Sultana, Yasmin Ullah, and I formed a group for collaboration because we had similar common goals. However, it wasn't until we did more research into our characters that we actually realized they all worked together as coordinators of the Free Rohingya Coalition, AND that they had all been on a panel together at a conference speaking on the Rohingyas in New York! Watching the video was really helpful in seeing how they each bring different interests and skills to the table, yet support a common goal. It was funny to me that we had naturally gravitated toward each other without knowing that these characters worked together often in real life, too. Something else that was interesting was that some of the characters that I thought I could work with formed other groups or were not as active in the Sim-Mail or attending face-to-face meetings, so we didn't end up collaborating on anything.[38]

Similarly, another participant who jointly played Hannah Ellis-Petersen, a *Guardian* newspaper journalist, expressed frustration at some of the other characters' lack of interest in communicating their 'news' to the media. This was especially the case with the Bangladesh government, she said. As she wrote,

> Some information was hard to get and some delegates never got me proper information [and we] failed to get to every office. I was at times blocked by the government of Bangladesh to the camp to get information.
>
> (Self-reflection, Hannah Ellis-Petersen, sole player)

Quite interestingly, this reflection echoes real-life situations, since government stakeholders often clash with those who wish to freely report the news inside the Rohingya camps. The lack of any real collaboration here can potentially prevent more meaningful solutions being thought of and proposed that could start to address the Rohingya crisis, offering prospects of longer-term solutions. Indeed, the general lack of collaboration worsens the crisis, both in the simulation and in real life.

To ensure human rights, dignity, and social justice for Rohingyas, collaboration and communication across different stakeholders emerge as the key, with the need for dialogue around the rights of this community.[39] The urgency of achieving effective collaboration among different stakeholders—including Rohingyas themselves—was expressed during the simulation by one participant who played real-life character Richard Ragan (head of the UN World Food Program for Bangladesh in 2019). This participant wrote:

> The things I noted that could be taken forward from the role play is the fact that in solving problems, making a change or carrying out interventions, the

> principle of collaboration cannot be over-emphasized. All actors must work together, interpolate their activities and come up with a plan or strategy that captures the individual inputs of the actors. With this approach, a better outcome is achieved and the chances of duplication of effort eliminated. It is also worthy of note to state that in providing humanitarian assistance, development project, and or interventions, it is imperative to take into cognizance the culture and preference of the people—the target group of any intervention should be part of the process in order to ensure a valuable outcome and participation.[40]

Considering how badly things are going in the real world, perhaps it is not surprising that no clear solutions were thrown up in the simulation, and that effective collaboration and communication was highlighted as something vital, yet which does not exist, either in 'real life' or in the simulation exercise. The role-play simulation underlines how crucial dialogue is if the world really wants to find solutions for the Rohingya crisis. For the participants, the best they could do was to express the hope that this would be possible in the future.

Is this real life?

Initial sentiments of excitement at anticipating fun learning alternate with confusion and frustration at not knowing what to do. A sense of unreality not surprisingly made itself felt as reflected in some of the self-reflections:

> As I try to put on the shoes of my character, there was this constant wonder of how Iffat feels as she connects with the people on the ground and sees all these injustices right before her eyes, as I sit comfortably in front of my laptop screen.[41]

This sense helped learners tap into personal experiences of living through post-war and authoritarian settings, incorporating their own worldviews, native vocabularies, indigenous histories, and cultural resources into their essays. For us, as educators, the entire exercise was a welcome reminder of how often we take broad concepts like Human Rights, Peace, or Social Justice for granted, especially when the global Development Studies classroom is in a European setting.

Echoing the difficulties that Rohingya have in a clear presentation of their collective self-identity to other, non-Rohingya people and identities, the MA participants playing Rohingya roles in the simulation (five out of the total) often struggled with identification. This is consistent with other simulation role-play exercises, where the most disadvantaged often struggle to form alliances and to represent themselves in communication and the simulated media. Such marginal status reflects real-world power dynamics that serve to exclude the under-privileged from serious consideration. One participant in the Rohingya simulation explained how hard it was for him to identify with his allotted role, Saiful Huq Omi, a talented Rohingya photographer, whose subject matter is often extremely painful, usually in black and white, and somewhat resonant with the style of Salgado. This participant had a breakthrough, however, late in the process of playing this role. As he describes:

> The arrival of my character's book at the library was therefore a crucial moment for me—by mistake I found it too late into the simulation. Nonetheless, it was a direct communication with my role and an inspiration to be more active—to think outside the limitations. However, I still prefer having discussions in a circle or else rather than via e-mail. The way the simulation was played out—mostly via bilateral sim-mails—made me less interested into the role-play and eventually my learning was not much stimulated. The face-to-face conference thus was a welcoming change: the transition from virtual to real. However, as already reviewed there was not enough time for real discussions and also such conferences are for me a waste of time. I know they are important but over the course of my life I didn't see real outcomes from them. It's just another forum where the already established opinions are exchanged without real listening or activities justified while being inactive. Also, there were too many topics that would have been interesting to go into depth. That having said, the way the Rohingyas at Risk Conference played out was close to reality—at least to the reality I got to know having worked in international relations. *That is why I disliked it.*[42]

What is interesting here in the last sentence is an apparent desire for the simulation not to reflect the world of everyday face-to-face realities, but to be an enhanced or more hopeful version of this online, as well as face-to-face. We see here a participant dissatisfied overall with the pedagogic experience, the online simulation platform, which did not allow for easy sharing of visual material, but also with the realism of the exercise and its final conference. One study notes how: 'Reference to contemporary politics reminds us that the written word is less powerful today than the image. Now the camera becomes the medium and guarantee of truth'.[43] And yet, this individual felt his playing the part of a photographer was stymied both by technical issues and a sense of déjà vu; disappointment that things did not turn out 'better than in real life'. During the conference, he did, however, collaborate with the Rohingya poet Mayyu Ali, and they produced a poster for the event, held in person in the Attic of the ISS building. They contributed creatively, and in role, not so much online, but during the face-to-face conference that concluded the simulation.

His objection to the conference at the end of the simulation, where participants presented position-papers, was precisely because of it reminding him of conferences he had attended in the past, which in his experience were 'a waste of time' without 'real outcomes'. This was because the failure of 'real listening' meant 'established opinions' were reiterated 'while being inactive' (i.e., without an alteration in individuals' positions in practice). It is interesting that this participant did not see a shift in his own position, since during the simulation, he played the unfamiliar role of a photographer. He was unable to connect with that emotionally until he got hold, physically, of a book of the photographer's images. What seems of note here is that the hardcopy book made such a difference to his feeling of identification, since most of Saiful Huq Omi's photographs of Rohingya in flight can be viewed online through a simple image search. As another participant, who played the character of Rohingya poet Mayyu Ali, noted:

> I lucked out, because, as a poet and youth empowerment activist, my character reflected my own creative spirit and passion. It was, therefore, an honor and pleasure to try and do right by him. I am not sure I solved any difficulties (within the simulation or in the real world) beyond hitching a fictitious ride to the conference with another attendee. I will say that the collaborations with my classmates (and their role-play counterparts) were meaningful and encouraging. If we can find ways to connect in such a short time, surely the real-world players with years of engagement should be able to do the same.[44]

An interesting feature of the Rohingya online role play simulations was reiteration by several participants of the relative importance of face-to-face, tangible, and in-person elements compared to online interactions alone. Yet these are the same elements that the participant who played Saiful Huq Omi saw as ritualistic and ineffective, the worse it seems for resembling actual conferences, where listening itself may be simulated offline! Performance of roles certainly does not end in the virtual world of simulations, since the presentation of self, individually and organizationally, in real-life conferences is also part of a sort of on-going performance.[45]

Concluding thoughts

From the start in this chapter, we asked whether it is possible to design a role-play simulation so that meaningful collaboration among different participants helps point the way towards paths to justice and human rights in real life. Whether role-play simulations can be expected to generate solutions, when in reality no such solutions appear to be discussed, is a different question, one raised by this second lesson. However, following the recent coup in Myanmar, the situation has shifted markedly. The government in exile was finally pressed into acknowledging the identity of Rohingya *as* Rohingya and not as 'Rakhine Muslims'.

Role-play simulations that use real-world individuals as roles played by participants, by necessity require the latter to delve into the real-life biographies of those individuals in the context of the simulation scenario that provides background for their actions. In the case of a series of online role-play simulations run on post-genocide Rwanda, the emotional responses were less notable than in the Rohingya simulation. This may have been because genocide had receded into the past. In the post-genocide Rwandan simulated context, divergent framings were expressed through the incompatible worldviews of government, media, and civil society but were not, as in the Rohingya simulation, derived from raw, recent memories of the main characters involved. It might have been possible to diminish the traumatic potential, through using fictional characters. Yet this would have required either participants or teaching staff to invent individual biographies, a much less satisfactory form of relating external realities to strategies in the classroom and online. In the Rohingya simulation, the emotional life of real, individual people became very significant and personal for the players. In the Rwandan online simulations, real characters were also the basis for roles, but the genocide itself had become a matter of representational dispute, being processed already through secondary discourses, and not, as in the Rohingya case, still a raw, open wound. Perhaps the use of fictional characters could work in particularly traumatic situations, say as now in the Ukraine, with identifiable characters being more suitable for situations where conflict is on-going like the Rohingya case. This suggests quite porous boundaries between players' identities and those of the role they play.[46] The cognitive dissonance that accompanies engagement in this kind of exercise means that emotional dilemmas will arise for players, and these dilemmas were more likely to arise in the Rohingya simulation, given its proximity to the events of genocide and mass flight.

For those who teach and design online role-play simulations, the onus is on us to ensure a 'duty of care' towards participants. This is especially the case when the emotional dynamics are as sensitive as in the Rohingya case discussed in this chapter. Emotional dynamics are unavoidable and even desirable in most role-play simulations. Yet to be educationally acceptable, careful and effective debriefing of players at the conclusion of the exercise is vital, so they are able to emerge from the experience appreciating the way it has impacted them. During the entire simulation, a vital part of the moderator's role is to notice those struggling to identify and those over-identifying with their roles. For all role-play simulations, the debrief permits a healthy distance to be restored from the role and focuses attention on lessons learned, and take-aways from the exercise overall. More attention and research are needed so that role-play simulations on real-world issues that raise intense ethical questions and emotional turbulence for participants can nonetheless produce learning about praxis, bringing classroom-based learning around texts, together with insights into practice through experiential learning. In the end, many of the deficiencies of the real world were mirrored in how the simulation unfolded, suggesting that art does mirror life rather than the reverse.

Notes

1 See, e.g., Juho Hamari and others, 'Challenging Game Help Students Learn: An Empirical Study on Engagement, Flow and Emmerson in Game-based Learning' (2016) 54 *Computers in Human Behavior* 170; Klaudia Bovermann, Joshua Weidlich and Theo Bastiaens, 'Online Learning Readiness and Attitudes Towards Gaming in Gamified Online Learning—A Mixed Methods Case Study' (2018) 15(27) *International Journal of Educational Technology in Higher Education* 1 <https://educationaltechnologyjournal.springeropen.com/articles/10.1186/s41239-018-0107-0> accessed 15 September 2021; Mark Peterson, 'Massively Multi-Player Role-playing Games as Arenas for Second Language Learning' (2010) 23(5) *Computer Assisted Language Learning* 429 <http://dx.doi.org/10.1080/09588221.2010.520673> accessed 10 September 2021.

2 Roni Linser and Helen Hintjens, 'Reflections on Promoting Engagement and Learning in Higher Education Multiplayer Online Role Play Simulation Games (MORPSGs)' in Saul Carliner (eds), *Proceedings of E-Learn: World Conference on E-Learning in Corporate, Government, Healthcare, and Higher Education*, New Orleans, Louisiana (United States: Association for the Advancement of Computing in Education 2019) 15 <https://www.learntechlib.org/j/ELEARN/v/2019/n/1/> accessed 10 September 2021.
3 ibid.
4 Margaret E. Gredler, 'Games and Simulations and their Relationships to Learning' in David Jonassen and Marcy Driscoll (eds), *Handbook of Research on Educational Communications and Technology*, (Taylor-Francis: London-New York 2013) 571, 572.
5 ibid 573.
6 Razia Sultana (A), Co-player, MA participant (Excerpt from Self-reflection, December 2019).
7 Tomas Ojean Quintana, 'Mission statement by Special Rapporteur on the situation of human rights in Myanmar' (OHCHR 2018) <https://www.ohchr.org/EN/NewsEvents/Pages/DisplayNews.aspx?NewsID=22619&LangID=E>
8 Frances Wade, *Myanmar's Enemy Within: Buddhist Violence and the Making of a Muslim 'Other'* (Zed Books 2018).
9 Sherry Turkle, *Life on the screen: Identity in the age of the internet* (Simon & Shuster 1995) 177.
10 Danielle Sonnenberg, 'The Emotional Challenges of Teaching Online' (DPhil Thesis, Fielding Graduate University 2021).
11 Helen Hintjens, Course leader (Course Curriculum, July 2019) (copy on hand with author).
12 Tun Khin, Sole player, MA participant (Excerpt from Self-reflection, December 2019).
13 Aung San Suu Kyi, A sole player, MA Participant (Excerpt from Self-reflection, December 2019).
14 David Simkins, 'Playing with Ethics: Experiencing New Ways of Being in RPGs' in Karen Schrier and David Gibson (eds), *Ethics and Game Design: Teaching Values through Play* (University of Vermont 2010) 69.
15 Pierre Bourdieu, *The Logic of Practice* (Polity Press 1990); Kevin Kester & Hilary Cremin, 'Peace education and peace education research: Toward a concept of post-structural violence and second-order reflexivity' (2017) 49(14) *Educational Philosophy and Theory* 1415.
16 Bourdieu, 'The Logic of Practice' (n 15) 27.
17 As cited in Roni Linser and Helen Hintjens, 'Reflections on Promoting Engagement and Learning in Higher Education Multiplayer Online Role Play Simulation Games (MORPSGs)' (n 2) 16.
18 Lis Stanley and Sue Wise, *Breaking Out Again: Feminist Ontology and Epistemology* (Routledge 2002) 156.
19 Ron Linser, 'Multi-player Online Role-play Simulation Games for Learning in Higher Education: Student Motivation and Engagement' (Master's Thesis, Open University of Israel 2019).
20 Ibid (n 13).
21 Razia Sultana (A) 'Self-reflection' (n 6).
22 Katherine Bischoping, '*Timor mortis conturbat me*: genocide pedagogy and vicarious trauma' (2004) 6(4) *Journal of Genocide Research* 545, 545.
23 ibid 548; See also, Caroline Yoder, *The Little Book of Trauma Healing* (Good Books: Pennsylvania 2005).

24 George Orwell, *The Road to Wigan Pier* (Victor Gollancz 1937).
25 John Reed, 'China and Myanmar sign off on Belt and Road projects' *Financial Times* (London, 18 January 2020); See also, Editorial, 'China and Myanmar sign off on Belt and Road projects' *China Economic Review* (China, 20 January 2020) <https://chinaeconomicreview.com/china-and-myanmar-sign-off-on-belt-and-road-projects/> accessed 20 January 2020.
26 Jan Zienkowski, 'Reflexivity in the transdisciplinary field of critical discourse. Studies' (2017) 3 *Palgrave Communications* 1, 6. Available <https://doi.org/10.1057/palcomms.2017.7 > accessed 20 June 2021.
27 Sara Ahmed, *The Cultural Politics of Emotions* (2nd edn, Edinburgh University Press-Routledge: Edinburgh-London-New York 2017) 9.
28 Jens Brockmeier, 'Remembering and Forgetting: Narrative as Cultural Memory' (2012) 8(1) *Culture & Psychology* 15, 28.
29 John Paul Lederach, *The Moral Imagination: The Art and Soul of Building Peace* (Oxford-New York: Oxford University Press 2005) 29.
30 Jo Hamilton, 'Emotional Methodologies for Climate Change Engagement: towards an understanding of emotion in Civil Society Organisation (CSO)-public engagements in the UK (DPhil thesis, University of Reading 2020).
31 ibid 54.
32 ibid 214.
33 Timothy C. Clapper, 'Role-Play and Simulation: Returning to Teaching for Understanding' (2010) 75(8) *Education Digest: Essential Readings Condensed for Quick Review* 39, 41.
34 Editorial, 'Prominent Rohingya Leader Shot Dead in Bangladesh Refugee Camp' *Al-Zazeera online* (29 September 2021) <https://www.aljazeera.com/news/2021/9/29/top-rohingya-leader-in-bangladesh-shot-dead> accessed 10 October 2021.
35 Mohib ullah, Sole Player, MA Participant (Except from elf-reflection, December 2019).
36 Ralph Adolphs, 'The Social Brain: Neural Basis of Social Knowledge' (2009) 60 *Annual Review of Psychology* 693, 716. <https://www.ncbi.nlm.nih.gov/pmc/articles/PMC2588649/> accessed 15 October 2021.
37 Thomas Szanto and Joel Krueger, 'Introduction: Empathy, Shared Emotions and Social Identity' (2019) 38(11) *Topoi* 153, 162.
38 Khin Mai Aung, Sole Player, MA Participant (Excerpt from Self-reflection, December 2019).
39 Syed Badrul Ahsan, 'The Rohingya Crisis: Why the World Must Act Decisively' (2018) 49(4) Asian Affairs 571.
40 Richard Ragan (A), Double Role, MA Participant (Excerpt from Self-reflection, December 2019).
41 Iffat Tahmid Fatema, Double Role, MA Participant (Excerpt from Self-reflection, December 2019).
42 Ibid (n 20).
43 Paul Atkinson and David Silverman, 'Kundera's Immortality: The interview society and the invention of the self' (1997) 3(3) *Qualitative Inquiry* 304, 308.
44 Mayyu Ali, Sole Player, MA Participant (Excerpt from Self-reflection, December 2019).
45 Erving Goffman, *The presentation of self in everyday life* (Doubleday: New York 1959).
46 Roni Linser, 'Reflexivity of Roles and Rules in Role Based E-learning' in C. Ho and M. Lin (eds), *Proceedings of E-Learn 2011--World Conference on E-Learning in Corporate, Government, Healthcare, and Higher Education* Honolulu, Hawaii (USA: Association for the Advancement of Computing in Education 2011) 2409.

9 NGO roles in achieving Transitional Justice for crimes against the Rohingya

Tonny Raymond Kirabira and Emma Palmer

Introduction

This chapter explores the role of Non-Governmental Organizations (NGOs) in relation to Transitional Justice (TJ) mechanisms for the Rohingya. Transitional Justice (TJ) encompasses measures to redress gross violations of human rights following periods of authoritarian rule or armed conflict.[1] Such measures include truth commissions, structural reforms, reconciliation, amnesty, and criminal accountability. International criminal justice involves the investigation and prosecution of individuals for international crimes with reference to international institutions or laws.[2] TJ processes may create pathways for conflict transformation, by fostering reconciliation and societal reconstruction.[3] It is thus important that the existing TJ processes link with wider, long-term transformation and conflict management.

The ongoing measures for justice and accountability for crimes against the Rohingya can be used as a starting point to examine how NGOs contribute towards TJ. The Rohingya context is particularly instructive since it combines accountability mechanisms directed at both individuals and the state at the International Criminal Court (ICC) and International Court of Justice (ICJ). There have also been calls for other mechanisms and the Myanmar government to provide accountability for gross human rights violations or alleged international crimes committed against the Rohingya.[4]

In theory, the accountability mechanisms in The Hague remind us that international crimes and crimes against humanity transcend sovereign jurisdiction in this international legal order.[5] The inadequacy or absence of domestic accountability mechanisms in complex contexts like that of the Rohingya calls for the implementation of globalized forms of TJ. This chapter seeks to amplify the vital role of non-state actors in TJ, focusing on the role of NGOs, in relation to the ICC and ICJ Myanmar proceedings.

Recent years have seen a rise in the profile and work of NGOs with international criminal law institutions; for example, the ICC has exhibited some dependence upon NGO intermediaries to connect with affected communities.[6] NGO intermediaries also have the potential to amplify counter-hegemonic voices in international criminal law.[7] However, there are some scholarly concerns about

DOI: 10.4324/9781003304883-13

the extensive involvement of NGOs in international criminal justice, due to their perceived lack of legitimacy, representativeness, or accountability.[8] To Haddad, NGOs are the 'Hidden Hands of Justice' that serve to legitimize international institutions like the ICC.[9] In any case, it is increasingly recognised that NGOs play an important role in relation to TJ, including international criminal justice, and are key stakeholders in these contested processes.[10]

In addition, the present-day world is characterized by increased interconnectedness between domestic and international NGOs (INGOs),[11] and scholarship has long recognized the important role of 'transnational advocacy networks' in promoting human rights and justice norms.[12] 'Local' NGOs are thought to be in a position to 'translate' or 'vernacularize' 'global' international norms to align with 'local' needs or issues.[13] For instance, in Myanmar, the pursuit of international criminal justice as a primary measure for accountability might not necessarily resonate with measures for long-term development and stability without adaptation.[14] However, there is a contested relationship between 'local' and 'global' in TJ.[15] Although there is scope for greater analysis of how NGOs working in the Asia-Pacific and INGOs engage with the ICC and ICJ, in Myanmar many NGOs have historically been formally 'based' outside of the country (often in Thailand)[16] for security and other reasons, while funding and secondments can complicate the identification of organizations as 'local' or otherwise.[17] This chapter recognizes that there are both distinctions and overlaps between NGOs and INGOs, and so explores the engagement and interaction between NGOs of various types, often working in transnational advocacy networks and coalitions, with the ICC and ICJ.

Whereas some NGOs focused on Myanmar issues have been working towards TJ measures of reconciliation, others have documented and investigated atrocities, with the goal of criminal prosecution.[18] The United Nations Independent Investigative Mechanism for Myanmar (IIMM) is considered to act as a legal bridge between NGOs and the state's obligation to investigate gross atrocities.[19] The IIMM has a broad mandate to:

> collect, consolidate, preserve, and analyze evidence of the most serious international crimes and violations of international law committed in Myanmar since 2011, and to prepare files in order to facilitate and expedite fair and independent criminal proceedings, in accordance with international law standards, in national, regional, or international courts or tribunals that have or may in the future have jurisdiction over these crimes, in accordance with international law.[20]

It provides another avenue for NGOs to document and communicate experiences of violence that could support ICC, ICJ, and other prosecutions. International networks have also worked to drive justice and accountability mechanisms in other jurisdictions. In November 2019, the Burmese Rohingya Organisation UK (BROUK) initiated the first universal jurisdiction case for the Rohingya, with a petition in Argentina against the Myanmar government.[21] Cognisant of the ongoing ICC investigation, BROUK maintained that they only sought to complement the existing mechanisms 'in order to offer the best possible prospect of justice for the Rohingya'.[22] Litigating universal jurisdiction proved successful in the case against former Chad dictator Hissène Habré before the Extraordinary African Chambers in Senegal.[23] This creates another pathway for NGOs to engage with a broader range of actors within TJ. As the Public International Law & Policy Group (PILPG) asserts in relation to the IIMM, 'If the international community cannot yet provide justice for victims, it must at least support a mechanism that can act now to secure the evidence necessary for any accountability proceedings in the future'.[24] Ultimately, the role of transnational networks may be vital in achieving accountability and justice via a range of potential institutional mechanisms. However, this chapter focuses on the narrower issue of how NGOs interact with the ICC and ICJ mechanisms for the Rohingya.

NGO work can be assessed using the theory of legitimacy,[25] while Lohne explores the role of NGOs in international criminal justice using sociology of punishment as a theoretical orientation.[26] This chapter is interested in the role of NGOs in the reconstruction of ideas about accountability and international justice and so instead adopts the framework of localization. Like Lohne's approach, localization offers a spatial analysis of NGO work across 'global' and 'local' sites of accountability.[27] However, localization considers how apparently global ideas about authority and legitimacy are not just accepted by 'locals', but can be constructed and reconstructed in light of different contexts.[28] Similarly, Zaum stresses the vital role played by NGOs in the diffusion of norms, arguing that they are 'benchmarks against which different audiences assess the legitimacy of international organizations and their practices'.[29]

The key question, then, is how do NGOs localize ideas about accountability mechanisms for the Rohingya, while also 'localizing' the practices of TJ institutions? By examining their practices and discourses, the chapter will examine how NGOs have responded to and adapted existing justice and accountability norms. The chapter will show the influence of NGOs in the dissemination of The Hague-based norms of justice, and how they tailor their messages towards the local audiences and victims/survivors ('victims')[30] and international institutions. We argue that NGOs contribute to the localization of TJ in two ways. First, through engagement with transnational networks and coalitions, NGOs localize the work of global justice mechanisms, adapting their actions and statements for the communities they work with. Second, NGOs offer support to victims and justice advocates. As this chapter reveals, victim-oriented discourse serves to connect global justice mechanisms with the victims and affected communities. These practices, in turn, contribute to international norms concerning TJ, including by engaging with ICC and ICJ proceedings. In this way, NGOs play an important role in attempting to reshape and reconstruct approaches toward TJ.

This chapter is based on a critical review of literature on TJ, NGO reports, court documents, media reports, and United Nations reports on the Rohingya human rights situation. The primary goal was to understand how NGO interventions feed into the work of the existing accountability mechanisms and into

NGOs' advocacy. It also aimed to identify the common themes that pervade this work. In doing so, it explores the socio-legal contexts that have shaped the ICC and ICJ interventions for the Rohingya. For example, what sort of factors or arguments feature in the local discourses and policies within this context? The analysis explores the links between these factors and the NGOs in shaping the TJ decisions and accountability mechanisms.

The chapter consists of four main sections. The second section analyzes NGO work in the broader context of TJ. It identifies ways in which NGOs contribute to the localization of international TJ norms and also highlights critical concerns about NGO work within the Global South. Next, the third section turns to the Rohingya context, exploring the links between the existing accountability mechanisms and NGO activities, focusing on the ICC and ICJ. Finally, the fourth section concludes with potential avenues for the ICC and ICJ to adjust their engagement with NGOs seeking justice and accountability so as to better resonate with the realities of the Rohingya.

NGOs and Transitional Justice: Protagonists for accountability

This section explores the work of NGOs in TJ, with an emphasis on justice and accountability mechanisms. The term NGOs is considered here to be synonymous with civil society organizations (CSOs), operating separately from the state and political parties, within wider 'civil society'.[31] As defined in the introduction, TJ relates to measures to redress gross violations of human rights following periods of authoritarian rule or armed conflict.[32] Accountability is a fundamental goal of TJ,[33] encompassing state's obligations to investigate, prosecute, punish perpetrators and make reparations to victims of gross human rights violations,[34] which we consider include ICJ determinations. TJ is a broad term that may also encompass community reconciliation and memorial initiatives, security sector reform, lustration, or truth commissions, for example, whereas we understand international criminal accountability or justice as focusing upon prosecutions, for instance at the ICC.[35]

In recent years, there has been increasing scholarship on the role of NGOs within the field of TJ. Paul Gready and Simon Robins illustrate five ways in which NGOs interact with TJ mechanisms: persuasion, support, mobilization, substitution, and space for modelling alternatives.[36] On the other hand, Aaron Boesenecker and Leslie Vinjamuri conceptualize NGOs in line with their normative diffusion roles: norm makers like faith-based organizations, norm adopters akin to negotiators, and norm facilitators akin to agents of international accountability norms.[37] Van der Merwe and Brankovic locate the work of NGOs in five dimensions: implementers, opponents, reframers, and alternatives and mediators.[38] These frameworks offer different typologies or categorizations to explore how both local and international NGOs adopt, adapt, or implement accountability mechanisms like the ICC and ICJ. Rather than determining which labels might apply to specific NGOs, in the present context, we could ask more generally: how do NGOs localize the international justice norms of these mechanisms in complex situations within the Global South?

The localization approach suggests that it is important to consider how NGOs implement or shape TJ at the 'local' levels, adapting and even reconstructing the norms surrounding TJ in light of local contexts. Scholarship has identified a 'turn' toward the 'local' in TJ, which has since been contested (see below).[39] Some TJ scholars emphasize the need for locally or Global South-driven approaches that are informed by the needs of people within affected communities.[40] To this end, NGOs organise local dialogues and workshops where stakeholders hold discussions outlining what TJ should look like.[41] In the Democratic Republic of the Congo (DRC), local people's discussions during NGO workshops proposed decentralized approaches through the use of local committees in order to mitigate context-sensitive dynamics of TJ.[42] As observed by Arnould, a 'grounded decentralization' allows the adoption of TJ based on victims' own conceptions of 'justice', instead of normative positions.[43] Crucially, local NGOS are vital in the decentralization of TJ approaches. In other words, TJ processes form part of the wider goals of conflict transformation and societal reconstruction, if embedded within local direction and expertise via the work of local NGOs.

Transnational NGO networks and coalitions play a pivotal role in the localization of truth and justice mechanisms, through their engagement with the public, media, donors, and states.[44] Noha Aboueldahab uses the Egyptian case to emphasize the importance of NGOs in shaping TJ, in addition to other priorities like social justice and judicial activism, as a solution to what she terms 'renewed authoritarianism'.[45] This suggests that NGOs play an important force in the structural reforms that may be encouraged by a broader understanding of TJ.

With respect to international criminal accountability, NGOs have been influential in the work of the ICC and other specialized criminal tribunals. The adoption of the Rome Statute in 1998 benefitted from the work of a coalition of 138 NGOs.[46] In terms of participation, NGOs form the largest percentage of civil society *amicus curiae* applications at the ICC and most international criminal tribunals and also represent victims' interests.[47] In relation to enforcement, a transnational coalition of 300 NGOs was pivotal in the arrest and prosecution of Charles Taylor at the Special Court for Sierra Leone (SCTL).[48] Reed Brody, a leading lawyer with Human Rights Watch, attributes the prosecution of the former President of Chad, Hissène Habré, to the 'persistence, imagination, and (legal) creativity, cooperation between local and global victim groups, and other NGOs, outreach to the public, non-stop lobbying and the search for (political) allies—as well as a big budget'.[49] Hence, we could consider transnational NGO networks as protagonists for justice and promoting victims' rights. Similarly, Stahn views NGOs as 'advocates and voices of judicial action'.[50]

Organizations like Human Rights Watch (HRW), Amnesty International, and the Coalition for the International Criminal Court (CICC) have been the most prominent INGO advocates for international criminal accountability for mass atrocities.[51] These organizations, including CICC's NGO members, fill gaps where the states lack capacity—drafting TJ legislation, documenting violence, and working directly with victims.[52] For instance, NGOs were influential in the interpretation of the Special Court Agreement (Ratification) Act 2002 of the SCSL, in regard to the contested legal relationship between the Tribunal and the Truth and Reconciliation Commission.[53] Similarly, civil society groups worked with politicians to draft and promote various adapted versions of international criminal law legislation in the Philippines.[54]

It can be argued that by articulating TJ norms and working toward their institutionalization, NGOs have the potential to localize norms associated with international accountability mechanisms. Similarly, community-based NGOs have the potential to question top-down approaches that do not resonate with the local realities.[55] Away from criminal accountability, NGOs also play critical roles in the work of truth commissions and reconciliation mechanisms, while engaging the public through seminars and victim-oriented work.[56] Victims' groups, in particular, are considered pivotal in the mobilization of affected communities seeking different forms of justice.[57]

However, this 'local turn' in TJ has also been critiqued as potentially romanticized.[58] For instance, one key question relates to the process of local participation and ownership, including the representation of women, children, and minority groups within local consultation processes.[59] Whereas there are calls for the incorporation of local approaches like Islamic principles in Muslim-majority countries,[60] there are also concerns about how these processes can be affected by local power struggles, as observed in Tunisia,[61] and '*islah*' processes in Indonesia.[62] In Nepal, for example, there was contestation about the role of human rights NGOs in TJ, since their approaches did not always resonate with the affected communities.[63] Corri Zoli et al. pose important questions, including: 'Are these [TJ] tools, both practical and analytical, confined to specific cultures and histories, advanced best by states and international and nongovernmental organizations, or merely a product of good timing and luck?'[64] What such questions suggest for situations like violence against the Rohingya is that NGOs and other TJ advocates should maintain an attachment to local communities and their norms of justice.

NGOs are also faced with challenges in relation to how they execute their mandates. International NGOs, for example, tend to carry out advocacy work while also being involved in the implementation of particular TJ project activities, like ICC outreach.[65] At the local levels, these kinds of strategies have the potential to obscure the work of smaller NGOs that do not have the necessary finances to implement their work. Sara Kendall is critical of the extensive involvement of non-state actors like donors in TJ, following the way in which criminal accountability was implemented in Sierra Leone.[66] In an arena of divergent and sometimes contested forms of justice, NGOs may not always reflect the views of the local constituencies of TJ (victims) but emphasize donor goals.[67] This mixed practice suggests a need to explore how NGOs engage with existing TJ mechanisms in contexts like Myanmar. As proponents of international justice and accountability call for the reconciling of global accountability norms with local agency,[68] it is important to assess the activities of NGO actors.

Against the background of these discussions, the next section will consider how NGOs engage with and impact the existing international accountability mechanisms for the Rohingya, focusing on the ICC and ICJ. This provides an example of how NGOs negotiate the boundaries between The Hague and local contexts in relation to a stateless population that has been subjected to marginalization and violence.

NGOs and accountability for the Rohingya

This section analyses how NGOs engage with two existing accountability mechanisms for the Rohingya, the ICC, and the ICJ. This analysis focuses on two spheres of NGO activity to show how organizations localize the norms promoted by these accountability mechanisms. First, it will examine the NGO discourses on TJ to show how they link with accountability and justice for the victims. Second, it will unpack the work of transnational NGO networks prior to and during proceedings to show the discursive strategies that they undertake on accountability.

To shed light on how NGOs impact on the existing accountability mechanisms for the Rohingya, it is important to explore NGO understandings of TJ, ideas about justice, and how and why they work on issues of TJ. With this context, we can then analyze the common frames that pervade their work in relation to the Rohingya. In general, the idea of TJ for Myanmar is itself the subject of debate, considering the ethnic diversity across the country. Many NGOs within Myanmar have tended to avoid publicly speaking about TJ.[69] The limited public discourse on TJ, specifically accountability, is considered to be a strategic decision by the local NGOs to avoid retaliation from the military.[70] However, some NGOs have argued for justice or accountability. Some examples concerning the Rohingya are mentioned below, but more broadly, in 2015, ND-Burma, a Myanmar-based network of NGOs (that does not include a Rohingya organisation), argued that:

> The Government of Burma must acknowledge ... accounts of extrajudicial killings, torture, and mass displacement caused by land confiscation, and *take responsibility* for these crimes. Acknowledging and utilizing these experiences as a basis from which to develop *transitional justice* programs is a key step towards achieving true national reconciliation in Burma.[71]

ND-Burma has also produced research from interviews with victims suggesting that the 'most common desire for justice was an institutional change to guard against human rights violations happening again', that is, guarantees of non-recurrence, although many 'victims asked for justice, but voiced low levels of confidence in the domestic legal system' to deliver it.[72] Indeed, empirical research illustrates a strong disconnect between official avenues for justice and the reality of accessing justice in Myanmar.[73] It is important to recognize the impact of ethnic pluralism on the local people's perceptions of justice. Many communities have experienced extensive violence perpetrated by the Myanmar military, prompting ND-Burma to argue in 2017 that '[a]buses reportedly being carried out in

Rakhine are the same as have been documented across the country—especially in ethnic nationality areas—since 2004'.[74] With these challenges in mind, the next subsection is focused on NGO engagement with the ICC in relation to violence against the Rohingya.

NGOs and the ICC intervention: Mediators for victims

There are a range of ways that NGOs can engage with the ICC beyond advocating for Rome Statute ratification. These include efforts to secure ICC attention or jurisdiction in relation to situations of violence by documenting and reporting upon crimes, advocating for UN Security Council referrals, submitting communications to the ICC Prosecutor, or lobbying states parties of the ICC to support justice initiatives, for instance during annual ICC Assembly of States Parties (ASP) meetings. The ICC, particularly its Registry, also has formal avenues for engagement, including NGO consultations, outreach (ranging from fact sheets and 'Q&A' documents to in-country offices during active investigations), and working with NGO intermediaries who might advocate for or represent witnesses or gather evidence. During proceedings, NGOs can support, critique, and publicize ICC proceedings, work with and around outreach services (including arranging visits to courts or victims, for instance), submit *amicus curiae* briefs, and assist with reparations project development and implementation.[75] NGOs have undertaken all of these roles in relation to the Rohingya.

Reporting, communications, and advocacy

NGOs have documented violence across Myanmar for decades, including sexual and gender-based violence committed by military perpetrators,[76] for 'many years' arguing that violations amounted to international crimes within the meaning of the Rome Statute of the ICC.[77] Efforts to persuade the UN Security Council to refer the situation in Myanmar to the ICC have continued. For instance, in 2018, a joint press release signed by the Rohingya Women Welfare Society argued that the 'UN Security Council (UNSC) must exercise its authority and urgently act to refer the situation in Myanmar to the International Criminal Court'.[78] Successive UN Special Rapporteurs[79] and organizations have documented violence in a series of well-publicized reports[80] and submitted communications to the ICC.[81] In addition to these communications, NGOs held direct consultations with the ICC Prosecutors to represent the victims' justice interests.[82] They also organized and hosted 'side events' held alongside the annual ASP.[83]

Fortify Rights, an international NGO, also has a history of advocating for criminal accountability for crimes against the Rohingya and other ethnic minorities in Myanmar.[84] The organization emphasizes the relevance of international intervention and the ICC mechanism as a way of providing justice for victims of genocide and crimes against humanity.[85] It has published reports and organized webinar events, including, for instance, explaining how the National Unity

Government might accede to the Rome Statute and delegate wider jurisdiction to the ICC. [86]

To give a more detailed example, in March and April 2018, the PILPG, a *pro bono* law firm, documented atrocities in Myanmar from interviews with Rohingya refugees in 34 refugee camps in Eastern Bangladesh.[87] The findings revealed a coordinated state campaign against the Rohingya across the northern Rakhine State.[88] Following the conclusion of the investigations, PILPG published a detailed legal analysis of the factual findings:

> intended primarily for policymakers to provide guidance on the international legal ramifications of the investigation mission's factual findings and to facilitate the formulation of effective measures to respond to the documented atrocities.[89]

A notable aspect of the PILPG Factual Findings and Legal Analysis Report is the conclusion that there are reasonable grounds to believe that crimes against humanity, genocide, and war crimes were committed against the Rohingya.[90] Although the Report did not recommend any particular accountability mechanism for pursuing justice and accountability, the authors emphasized:

> [T]he international community's duty to ensure accountability to be primarily one of result. The ultimate purpose of this duty is to provide justice to victims, deter potential perpetrators, and prevent future mass atrocities.[91]

This appeared to allow scope for localization, by focusing on the end goal rather than prescribing a particular TJ mechanism. The factual findings and legal analysis of the PILPG Report were discussed at a conference held at the Vrije Universiteit Amsterdam on 21 February 2019.[92] Maung Tun Khin, a Rohingya rights advocate and President of Burmese Rohingya Organization UK, gave a keynote speech, emphasizing:

> how they [Rohingya victims] want to gain their rights back, seek justice for the atrocious crimes committed against them, and see the perpetrators held accountable and tried at the International Criminal Court.[93]

Dr. Marieke de Hoon, the director of PILPG's Netherlands Office, emphasized the need for criminal accountability, together with other forms of TJ, like truth-telling, reparations, and structural reforms.[94] However, she was sceptical of their practicability, due to the polarized political situation in Myanmar.[95] Similarly, Amnesty International documented the gross human rights violations perpetrated by Myanmar state actors against the Rohingya in early 2018.[96] Like PILPG, Amnesty International emphasized the role of the international community in providing accountability for the Rohingya.[97] Amnesty International and Human Rights Watch (HRW) provided key information regarding the previous waves of violence against the Rohingya, supporting the ICC Chamber's authorization of investigations in the situation of Bangladesh/Myanmar,[98] alongside the findings of PILPG and other reports (see below).[99]

These NGO reports use language about 'justice' and 'accountability', align events with specific international crimes, such as crimes against humanity, in their reports, and identify the ICC as a particular focus for delivering such 'justice'. In this way, they attempt to apply norms of international criminal justice to the situation of the Rohingya. However, they also claim to promote the interests and wishes of victims (what they are said to 'want') drawn from their research, presenting ICC attention as something sought locally, albeit among other needs and TJ options. In addition to the documentation of atrocities and advocacy, it is important to consider how NGOs engage directly with the ICC.

During proceedings

In November 2019, the ICC Pre-Trial Chamber III authorized the Prosecutor to initiate an investigation into the situation of Bangladesh/Myanmar over crimes against humanity, such as deportation or persecution, occurring partly in the territory of a state that is party to the Rome Statute of the ICC—most relevantly Bangladesh.[100] According to the ICC website, the request to initiate investigations was premised on the views of victims, who were assisted and advised by individuals and organizations.[101] Furthermore, it is reported that the victims insisted on the ICC investigation as '[o]nly justice and accountability can ensure that the perceived circle of violence and abuse comes to an end'.[102]

As well as representing unique victims' interests that would otherwise be absent, NGO *amicus curiae* observations and submissions can (in theory) make significant contributions to the quality of decision making at the ICC.[103] Thayninga Institute for Strategic Studies, a think tank of Myanmar NGOs, sought to submit *amicus curiae* observations to counter the narratives of the Rohingya, but their application was not granted since it was filed out of time.[104] Nonetheless, this serves as a reminder that NGOs do not always reflect victims' needs and views. In June 2018, the Bangladeshi Non-Governmental Representatives (BNGR), an informal group of NGOs, submitted *amicus curiae* observations in support of the Prosecution's Request for a ruling on jurisdiction under Article 19(3) of the Rome Statute.[105] Most notably, the submissions provided useful contextual analysis for applying objective territorial jurisdiction in line with Bangladesh law.[106] Similarly, Women's Initiatives for Gender Justice, the European Center for Constitutional and Human Rights, and Naripokkho provided insights linking sexual violence committed against Rohingya to the crime of deportation.[107]

International NGO Global Rights Compliance (GRC) also filed submissions on behalf of over 400 Rohingya victims (Shanti Mohila), supporting the Prosecution's request to exercise jurisdiction over the deportation of the Rohingya from Myanmar to Bangladesh.[108] Similarly, a submission 'on behalf of alleged victims from Tula Toli', was said to be 'based on first-hand discussions with the victims, all of whom are former residents of the village of Tula Toli'.[109] These submissions offered broader historical and factual contexts for the alleged crimes, arguing that they were perpetrated in a setting of long-standing and persistent persecution, arguing in effect that 'the Prosecution's approach to jurisdiction [was] unjustifiably narrow'.[110] This was said 'to be distinguished from positions expressed by or attributed to 'civil society'. While some civil society organisations may be well placed to provide useful input to the Court, their views plainly cannot be equated with those of the victims'.[111] Moreover, the Tula Toli victims argued that 'a distinction must be drawn between hearing the [Office of the Public Counsel for Victims] on the abstract, assumed interests of victims, and hearing from specific victims regarding their actual interests'.[112] In other words, the ICC should seek the views of specific victims, rather than hearing only from an 'in-house lawyer who has never met victims' or treating victims 'as a homogeneous mass',[113] or from NGOs with a similarly distanced approach. In the 2018 decision on the Prosecutor's request for a ruling on jurisdiction,[114] Pre-Trial Chamber III made some reference to the GRC submissions, mostly to support Prosecution arguments and commentary on the nature of the crime of deportation and forcible transfers but made little reference to the Tula Toli victims' brief, except alongside references to other *amici.*

In Pre-Trial Chamber III's subsequent decision to authorize an investigation, one important NGO intervention that was reflected in the Chamber's interpretation and discourse related to the use of the term 'Rohingya'.[115] Due to the contestation surrounding this nomenclature by different ethnic groups, the Chamber employed the term 'Rohingya' to refer to the victims individually and collectively, based on NGO reports on the court record.[116] In particular, the Chamber was guided by reports from the Irish Centre for Human Rights (ICHR), International Crisis Group (ICG), Amnesty International (Amnesty), Public International Law & Policy Group (PILPG), and the United Nations Office of the High Commissioner for Human Rights (OHCHR),[117] as well as some representations by victims.[118]

More broadly, the decision makes significant use of NGO reports that documented violence, including the PILPG, Amnesty, and ICJ reports mentioned, for instance citing an HRW report drawn from interviews with victims from Tula Toli twice as many times as the legal representations made on behalf of 86 individual victims from Tula Toli.[119] On the other hand, the latter representations supported Pre Chamber III's determination that 'the Prosecutor is not restricted to the incidents identified in the Request' in the investigation.[120] This is just an example but suggests that NGOs can play a powerful role in preliminary ICC proceedings by offering reports of documented violence, but that legal submissions by victims groups (specifically) still offer crucial perspectives on how determinations should be made. Further, the preponderance of larger INGO reports has a potential to obscure the pertinent views of affected communities, if not sourced from those communities.

Victim engagement and outreach

Local ownership is emphasized as an imperative aspect of TJ and international criminal justice.[121] It is therefore crucial to examine whether and how NGOs involve the Rohingya in justice and accountability discourses. Of particular importance to issues of justice and accountability is the issue of local outreach. The Centre for Peace and Justice (CPJ) of BRAC University in Bangladesh, and the Asia Foundation have gathered information about the Rohingya's perceptions of justice.[122] As in many other contexts within the global South, the NGO findings illustrate a range of perceptions about justice, including legal accountability, freedom of movement, and restitution.[123] However, the ICC's role and activities are far from clear to many Rohingya refugees. Indeed, an ICC personnel (victims' representatives and outreach)[124] mission to Bangladesh concluded that 'most of the Rohingya in the camps heard about the ICC investigation being authorized' but 'it was equally clear that there is massive confusion, and that the overwhelming majority of people have very little information and understanding, if any, of these various justice initiatives and, importantly, their different mandates and functions'.[125] The ICC has attempted to develop social media, audiovisual, fact sheet, and other materials working with civil society and media—and 'the Rohingya remained focused and continue to demand information about the developments related to the various justice initiatives'.[126] However, according to the ICC's 'interlocutors on the ground', circulating rumours persisted (exacerbated by the COVID-19 pandemic).[127] Although the identity of the ICC's partners 'on the ground' is redacted, they are likely to be NGOs playing the important role of informing the ICC of the challenges involved in 'localizing' its activities and messages, and influencing the language and methods used in revised efforts to communicate to Rohingya groups.

A common theme of transnational NGO coalitions' activities concerning the Rohingya is a focus on sexual and gender-based (SGV) crimes. This has been reflected in engagement with the ICC. Discussions during a virtual side-event on 'Justice and Accountability for Sexual and Gender-Based Crimes Against the Rohingya', held at the ICC ASP on 11 December 2020 illuminate the NGOs' interest in seeking justice for victims of SGV.[128]

GRC, which represented over 400 Rohingya victims in the submissions mentioned above,[129] also developed 'Basic Investigative Standards for International Crimes' to assist local NGOs in Bangladesh (and elsewhere) in maintaining minimum standards for the investigation of international crimes, including those against the Rohingya.[130] It can be argued that the empowerment of local NGOs to investigate international crimes can facilitate the localization of TJ, since, by adapting international 'minimum standards' for use by local NGOs and including a function to contact GRC lawyers,[131] NGOs might be persuaded to shift their activities toward supporting international crimes prosecutions.

Beyond localizing ICC activities for Rohingya audiences, NGOs have also worked toward physically moving the ICC case closer to the affected Rohingya communities and victims. In August 2020, a group of NGOs and Rohingya victims' representatives formally requested the ICC Pre-Trial Chamber III to consider sitting outside The Hague, in order to have reasonable physical proximity to the affected population.[132] Eight NGOs were based in Cox's Bazar: the Arakan Rohingya Society for Peace and Human Rights (ARSPH), Rohingya Women Empowerment and Advocacy Network (RWEAN), Rohingya Refugee Committee (RRC), Rohingya Women for Justice and Peace (RWJP), Voice of Rohingya (VOR), Rohingya Youth for Legal Action (RYLA), Bangladesh Rohingya Student Union (BRSU), and Rohingya Peace Innovation Unity (RPIU). Legal Action Worldwide (LAW) and GRC also represented both male and female victims of SGV in the ICC case. In their request, the NGOs sought 'to close the gap between Cox's Bazar and The Hague', noting that: '[b]oth the benefits of localized justice, and the logistical considerations associated with hearings outside The Hague warrant consideration of this question [the feasibility of court hearings in Bangladesh] at this early stage'.[133] Important insights for victims' justice are illuminated in the submissions:

> The desire to participate and be informed is at the heart of the victims' preference for eventual ICC proceedings to be held locally. Limiting proceedings to The Hague would necessarily limit the potential for victim involvement, whether as participants or observers. Local ICC proceedings are viewed as allowing for greater participation of the victim community as a whole, and as giving more opportunity for their voices to be heard.[134]

This argument illustrates how NGOs promote the physical 'localization' of proceedings in the hope that this might also shape or localize the content and substance of those proceedings—by allowing more 'voices to be heard'. Although the Chamber held that it was premature to consider the request to hold the trial outside The Hague, it noted that the venue of legal proceedings touches upon the victims' interests.[135] This reasoning affirms the need to maintain victims as central actors in the accountability mechanisms. The request by NGOs reflected their crucial role as mediators for the Rohingya victims in presenting their interests to the ICC, but, more than that, NGOs sought to reconstruct ICC processes in response to local perspectives.

NGOs have advocated for international crimes trials, presented victims as desiring of international crimes trials, documented violence that the ICC has relied upon, and attempted to shift ICC procedures. In addition to individual criminal responsibility at the ICC, NGO coalitions also emphasize the pursuit of universal jurisdiction and state responsibility at the ICJ.[136]

Transnational coalitions: Protagonists for justice at the ICJ

There are fewer formal avenues for NGO engagement with ICJ proceedings than at the ICC, partly because the ICJ has not formally accepted NGO *amicus curiae* briefs, despite receiving many communications, particularly in

Advisory Opinion proceedings.[137] Furthermore, state parties[138] and judges occasionally refer to NGO reports or opinions[139] in or annexed to their own submissions or decisions.

In November 2019, The Gambia filed a case against Myanmar before the ICJ, on the grounds of violations of the 1948 Genocide Convention following the crimes against the Rohingya.[140] The aim was to:

> establish Myanmar's responsibility for violations of the Genocide Convention, to hold it fully accountable under international law for its genocidal acts against the Rohingya group, and to have recourse to th[e] Court to ensure the fullest possible protection for those who remain at grave risk from future acts of genocide.[141]

This wording suggested that there is a possibility for justice for the Rohingya at the ICJ, that is, that state responsibility might contribute to TJ. The case is also regarded by NGOs as a 'significant step towards accountability for the Rohingya atrocities on an international level'.[142]

One month before The Gambia filed its case, GRC and LAW convened a session titled 'Myanmar/Burma: Accountability Strategy Meeting to formulate an accountability strategy (both criminal and civil) for the Rohingya through utilizing both domestic and international mechanisms'.[143] As the title suggests, the strategy was to utilize both domestic and international mechanisms to achieve both individual and state accountability. Param-Preet Singh, the associate director of Human Rights Watch's international justice programme, notes that: 'We reached out to countries that had ratified the Genocide Convention in Europe, Africa, Asia and the Americas … Then, out of nowhere, the West African nation of The Gambia made public their intention to move ahead'.[144] The Gambia's Justice Minister, Abubacarr Tambadou, had experience as a prosecutor at the International Criminal Tribunal for Rwanda and joined an Organization of Islamic Cooperation delegation to Cox's Bazar, where victims told him of horrendous crimes.[145] These narratives illustrate links between the global transnational advocacy networks, the existing justice mechanisms for the Rohingya, and victims' accounts of their experiences.

NGOs then supported Rohingya activists to engage with ICJ proceedings. For instance, for the ICJ hearings on provisional measures in December 2019, LAW supported three Rohingya victims from Cox's Bazar to travel to The Hague.[146] The strategy for this intervention is reflected in the press statement:

> LAW considers the Rohingya presence in the court and the continued engagement by The Gambia legal team with LAW's clients an acknowledgement of great importance of these proceedings to the Rohingya community.[147]

NGOs also worked in Bangladesh to publicize the ICJ's attention toward the Rohingya, organizing for television broadcasts of the ICJ's ruling that Myanmar needed to undertake provisional measures during the remaining proceedings. This made the vice president of the NGO the Arakan Rohingya Society for Peace and Human Rights 'hopeful about our desired repatriation, repatriation with safety and dignity, to Arakan [Rakhine]', even though this would be beyond the scope of the ICJ's activities.[148] Later, in 2020, videos dubbed into the Rohingya language reportedly continued to play a legal aid NGO's summaries of the ICJ's determination at a Cox's Bazar health centre (organized by a different NGO).[149]

There are many NGOs working in Cox's Bazar, and communications about the ICC and ICJ are, as the ICC Registry concluded, confusing but do represent attempts to translate and localize international justice proceedings for local audiences. NGOs attempt to inform communities in modified language and formats, to 'simplify', or even to be 'purposely vague' in order to *not* inflate expectations.[150] This is partly because many victims want to return safely to Rakhine State,[151] something that the ICC and ICJ do not have the power to achieve. In doing so, NGOs may adapt their messages for communities in response to the limitations of international justice processes and the desires of victims but are wary of exacerbating confusion in doing so, preferring an increased presence from the international justice institutions themselves.[152] Yet, for all the limitations of the ICC's outreach (which has also been affected by COVID-19), the ICJ Registry lacks a comparable institutional capability, leaving NGOs with the task of communicating its proceedings, without a commensurate ability to engage with the ICJ process.

Still, an important intervention of NGOs in the ICJ case relates to the issue of compliance by the Myanmar government. The Asia Justice Coalition—a network of organizations working on international justice and accountability in Asia, has engaged the international community to try and persuade Myanmar to comply with the ICJ provisional measures.[153] Similarly, Rohingya NGOs emphasized the need for the ICJ to make Myanmar's confidential reports public.[154] The Rohingya Legal Forum (RLF), a Special Initiative of Newlines Institute chaired by Rohingya activist Dr. Azeem Ibrahim Rohingya, argued that:

> Given the failure of the Court's provisional measures to have an impact on the Srebrenica genocide, the Court's enforcement of the Convention's obligations and the rationale of protective measures risks being viewed by endangered and vulnerable populations as mere words on paper that do not offer a meaningful avenue for justice from genocide or effective protection in the face of a serious risk of a genocide (re)occurring.[155]

In addition to empowering the Rohingya to be active participants in the justice process, RLF advocates for a closer link between the ICJ and the victims, arguing that: 'Now the Court needs to act in a way not disconnected with the victims and their right to exist—the meat of the case—along with the victims' human rights to know, to truth.'[156] This discourse attempts to localize TJ by constructing the TJ norm as being responsive to the views of affected communities and victims. Not only does the NGO advocacy keep the ICJ work visible, but it also mitigates the challenges of proximity and distance in TJ, while seeking greater engagement from the ICJ in doing so.

NGO networks also play an active role in convincing states to support the existing justice mechanisms for the Rohingya. The European Rohingya Council and Free Rohingya Coalition have urged states to intervene in the matter of The Gambia v. Myanmar at the ICJ.[157] In September 2020, Canada and the Netherlands formally announced plans to intervene in the case.[158] In a detailed statement, 36 Rohingya NGOs argued that more international engagement with the Rohingya ICJ case 'would substantially add pressure on the Myanmar government, help ensure accountability, and prevent new crimes in Myanmar'.[159]

Representational practices of victims are also embedded within NGO's views regarding the efficacy of the existing justice and accountability mechanisms. ICG's note on the impact of the ICJ on the international perceptions of Myanmar presents another articulation of victims' justice, noting; 'Anyone can also read about the Rohingya, who continue to live in precarious circumstances at home. Myanmar could lose in the court of international public opinion well before the ICJ makes any legal ruling'.[160] No Peace Without Justice (NPWJ), a partner NGO of the CICC, notes that:

> [C]urrent developments in both Courts [ICC and ICJ] are highly significant, especially for their symbolic force. There is hope that cases at the ICJ and ICC and elsewhere will finally result in justice for the Rohingya, ensuring accountability for perpetrators and redress for victims.[161]

NGOs therefore advocated for the ICJ case and have pursued avenues to identify and highlight victims' perspectives at the Court, including by organizing travel and engaging with states. However, the ICJ's relative lack of external civil society engagement capacity,[162] particularly outside The Hague, limits its ability to respond to the interests of victims and communities, or to clarify its own work for the Rohingya without the assistance of NGOs.

Conclusion

The chapter has aimed to explore the role of NGOs in the existing international TJ mechanisms for the Rohingya. NGOs are shown to be vital stakeholders in the design and implementation of TJ in general, as they articulate a range of beliefs about justice and accountability norms, including those purportedly drawn from victim and affected community groups.

The chapter has drawn on the concept of localization to analyze the role of NGOs in the ICC and ICJ cases, although these represent only a subset of potential TJ responses. In theory, localization applies in the way NGOs have responded to and adapted The Hague-based norms. First, NGOs work to promote and translate the activities of the ICC and ICJ for Rohingya communities, including via producing audio-visual and language-translated information, albeit in a simplified manner that may aim to manage expectations and reduce confusion (even if not always successfully). This linkage underlines the important role of NGOs in TJ, and their potential involvement in the (de)legitimation of The Hague-based institutions. Without an active 'on the ground' presence for either the ICC or ICJ, even internet-based communications respond to the insights of NGOs working with Rohingya communities.

Second, NGO documentation and discourses on justice for the victims have opened up spaces for revealing their experiences, including by securing ICC and ICJ attention through advocacy with states and communications sent to the ICC Prosecutor. NGO reports and analysis of alleged crimes have contributed to legal determinations at the early stages of these proceedings, sometimes even more evidently than the direct submissions of victims. An analysis of NGO submissions and reports also illustrates efforts to communicate the views of affected communities in Bangladesh for reception by the accountability mechanisms, including by publishing demands for 'justice' and presenting events with legal analysis to argue that they do amount to international crimes. Transnational NGO networks have also supported Rohingya activists in engaging with important stakeholders, including states, in the pursuit of justice in The Hague. The discussions have also highlighted measures intended for the Rohingya to participate in The Hague-based processes, through legal representatives and physical visits, as well as the limitations of those options. Attempts to move proceedings toward victims present one way of trying to 'localize' the ICC, but there are few avenues for genuine local ownership, whether via victims or NGOs, in designing these justice processes—while the representativeness of NGOs or how much their reports reflect heterogeneous victim needs is not necessarily clear. There is also a potential for larger, international NGOs to be perceived as intermediaries of Western hegemony, from those critical of The Hague justice mechanisms, in favour of more localized approaches.

Perceptions of justice among victims are not uniform; thus there is a need for more nuanced approaches in TJ. As earlier observed, a 'grounded decentralization' approach allows for the consideration of victims' own conceptions of justice.[163] Against this background, we should not underestimate the work of NGOs in gathering the views of Rohingya about justice—especially given the limited capacities for travel (driven by COVID-19). What is needed is for NGOs to maintain close proximity with the victims in order to achieve the best possible modes of justice and accountability, as the ICC and ICJ cases progress. This should entail continued, but careful and critical, engagement with NGOs and victims' groups through targeted multi-directional communication avenues.

Notes

1 Roger Duthie and Paul Seils (eds), *Justice Mosaics: How Context Shapes Transitional Justice in Fractured Societies* (International Center for Transitional Justice 2017).

2 Emma Palmer, *Adapting International Criminal Justice in Southeast Asia: Beyond the International Criminal Court* (Cambridge University Press 2020) 8.

3 Laurel E Fletcher and Harvey M Weinstein, 'Violence and Social Repair: Rethinking the Contribution of Justice to Reconciliation' (2002) 24 Human Rights Quarterly 573; Paul Gready and Simon Robins, 'From Transitional to Transformative Justice: A New Agenda for Practice' (2014) 8 International Journal of Transitional Justice 339; Roger Duthie and Paul Seils (n 1) 17–26.

4 Tonny R Kirabira, 'Establishing Accountability for Gross Human Rights Violations: An Analysis of the Rohingya Conflict' (2020) 3 Journal of International Law of Peace and Armed Conflict 141.

5 Frederic Megret, 'The Anxieties of International Criminal Justice' (2016) 29 Leiden Journal of International Law 197.

6 Leila Ullrich, 'Beyond the "Global–Local Divide": Local Intermediaries, Victims and the Justice Contestations of the International Criminal Court' (2016) 14 Journal of International Criminal Justice 543.

7 Emily Haslam and Rod Edmunds, 'Managing a New "Partnership": "Professionalization", Intermediaries and the International Criminal Court' (2013) 24 Criminal Law Forum 49.

8 Florian Jessberger and Julia Geneuss, '"Litigating Universal Jurisdiction"—Introduction' (2015) 13 Journal of International Criminal Justice 205.

9 Heidi Nichols Haddad, 'After the Norm Cascade: NGO Mission Expansion and the Coalition for the International Criminal Court' (2013) 19 Global Governance 187; Heidi Nichols Haddad, *The Hidden Hands of Justice NGOs, Human Rights, and International Courts* (Cambridge University Press 2018).

10 Jasmina Brankovic and Hugo van der Merwe (eds), *Advocating Transitional Justice in Africa: The Role of Civil Society* (Springer, Cham 2018); Math Noortmann, 'NGOs in International Law: Reconsidering Personality and Participation (Again)' in Thomas Davies (ed), *Routledge Handbook of NGOs and International Relations* (1st edn, Routledge 2019); Noam Schimmel, 'International Human Rights Law Responsibilities of Non-Governmental Organizations: Respecting and Fulfilling the Right to Reparative Justice in Rwanda and Beyond' (2019) 8 Cambridge International Law Journal 104.

11 Eva Brems, Giselle Corradi and Martien Schotsmans, *International Actors and Traditional Justice in Sub-Saharan Africa: Policies and Interventions in Transitional Justice and Justice Sector Aid* (1st edn, Intersentia 2015).

12 Thomas Risse, Stephen C Ropp and Kathryn Sikkink (eds), *The Power of Human Rights: International Norms and Domestic Change* (Cambridge University Press 1999); Michael Bluman Schroeder and Alana Tiemessen, 'Transnational Advocacy and Accountability: From Declarations of Anti-Impunity to Implementing the Rome Statute' in Alexander Betts and Phil Orchard (eds), *Implementation and World Politics: How International Norms Change Practice* (Oxford Scholarship Online 2014); Margaret E Keck and Kathryn Sikkink, *Activists Beyond Borders: Advocacy Networks in International Politics* (Cornell University Press 2014).

13 Amitav Acharya, 'How Ideas Spread: Whose Norms Matter? Norm Localization and Institutional Change in Asian Regionalism' (2004) 54 International Organization 239; Sally E Merry, *Human rights and gender violence: translating international law into local justice* (University of Chicago Press 2006); Lisbeth Zimmerman, *Global Norms with a Local Face* (Cambridge University Press 2017).

14 Emma Palmer (n 2).

15 Ruth G Teitel, *Globalizing Transitional Justice. Contemporary Essays* (Oxford University Press 2014); Zinaida Miller, 'Embedded Ambivalence: Ungoverning Global Justice' (2020) 11 Transnational Legal Theory 353.

16 E.g., Kachin Women's Association of Thailand.

17 Emma Palmer (n 2).

18 ibid; E.g., The Arakan Project, 'Submission to the UN Universal Periodic Review 10th Session of the UPR Working Group, January 2011' (5 July 2010) <https://lib.ohchr.org/HRBodies/UPR/Documents/Session10/MM/AP_ArakanProject_eng.pdf> accessed 23 April 2022; ND-Burma, 'To Recognize and Repair: Unofficial Truth Projects and the Need for Justice in Burma' (11 June 2015) (not focused on the Rohingya) <http://nd-burma.org/to-recognize-and-repair/> accessed 23 April 2022.

19 Konstantina Stavrou, 'Civil Society and the IIMM in the Investigation and Prosecution of the Crimes Committed Against the Rohingya' (2021) 36 Utrecht Journal of International and European Law 95.

20 UNHRC, 'Resolution adopted by the Human Rights Council on 27 September 2018—Situation of human rights of Rohingya Muslims and other minorities in Myanmar' (UN Doc A/HRC/RES/39/2, Resolution 39/2 2018) para 22.

21 Tun Khin, 'Universal Jurisdiction, the International Criminal Court, and the Rohingya Genocide' (OpinioJuris 23 October 2020) <http://opiniojuris.org/2020/10/23/universal-jurisdiction-the-international-criminal-court-and-the-rohingya-genocide/> accessed 23 April 2022.

22 ibid.

23 Florian Jessberger and Julia Geneuss (n 8).

24 Paul R Williams and Jessica Levy, 'Atrocities Documented, Accountability Needed: Finding Justice for the Rohingya through the ICC and Independent Mechanism' [2019] Harvard Human Rights Journal <https://harvardhrj.com/2019/02/atrocities-documented-accountability-needed-finding-justice-for-the-rohingya-through-the-icc-and-independent-mechanism-by-paul-r-williams-jessica-levy/> accessed 14 July 2021.

25 Erla Thrandardottir and Vincent Charles Keating, 'Bridging the Legitimacy Gap: A Proposal for the International Legal Recognition of INGOs' (2018) 55 International Politics 207; Martine Beijerman, 'Conceptual Confusions in Debating the Role of NGOs for the Democratic Legitimacy of International Law' (2018) 9 Transnational Legal Theory 147, Sarah Williams, Hannah Woolaver and Emma Palmer, *The Amicus Curiae in International Criminal Justice* (1st edn, Hart Publishing 2020).

26 Kjersti Lohne, *Advocates of Humanity: Human Rights NGOs in International Criminal Justice* (Oxford University Press 2019).

27 ibid.

28 Amitav Acharya (n 13).

29 Dominik Zaum, 'Legitimacy' in Jacob Katz Cogan, Ian Hurd and Ian Johnstone (eds), *The Oxford Handbook of International Organizations* (Oxford University Press 2016).

30 We use the term 'victims' consistent with ICC and ICJ usage, but also as shorthand for 'victim/survivors' since we acknowledge that some prefer the term 'survivor'.

31 Riva Krut, 'Globalization and Civil Society: NGO Influence in International Decision-Making' (Discussion Paper No. 83, United Nations Research Institute for Social Development 1997). 'Civil society' is a broader term that refers to professional associations, community groups, women's organisations, trade unions, 'humanitarian aid organizations, associations of survivors and family members of victims, human rights and development NGOs, lawyers, academic, mental health and medical associations, and religious organizations'—see Naomi Roht-Arriaza, 'Civil Society in Processes of Accountability' in M. Cherif Bassiouni (ed.), *Post-Conflict Justice* (Transnational Publishers, 2002) 97, 98. In practice, however, NGOs may be aligned with political organisations, the government, religious

groups, and work with particular media platforms, see Renée Jeffery, Lia Kent and Joanne Wallis, 'Reconceiving the Roles of Religious Civil Society Organizations in Transitional Justice: Evidence from the Solomon Islands, Timor-Leste and Bougainville' (2017) 11 International Journal of Transitional Justice 378.

32 Roger Duthie and Paul Seils (n 1).

33 Diane F. Orentlicher, 'Settling Accounts: The Duty To Prosecute Human Rights Violations of a Prior Regime' (1991) 100 Yale Law Journal 2539.

34 Tonny R Kirabira (n 4).

35 Renée Jeffery and Hun Joon Kim, 'Introduction', in *Transitional Justice in the Asia-Pacific* (Cambridge University Press, 2014) 1, 1.

36 Paul Gready and Simon Robins, 'Rethinking Civil Society and Transitional Justice: Lessons from Social Movements and "New" Civil Society' (2017) 21 The International Journal of Human Rights 956.

37 Aaron P Boesenecker and Leslie Vinjamuri, 'Lost in Translation? Civil Society, Faith-Based Organizations and the Negotiation of International Norms' (2011) 5 International Journal of Transitional Justice 345.

38 Hugo van der Merwe and Jasmina Brankovic, 'The Role of African Civil Society in Shaping National Transitional Justice Agendas and Policies' (2016) 1 Acta Juridica 225.

39 See Adam Kochanski, 'The "Local Turn" in Transitional Justice: Curb the Enthusiasm' (2020) 22 International Studies Review 26.

40 Paul Gready and Simon Robins (n 3).

41 E.g., in Myanmar, carried out by ALTSEAN-Burma, see <https://www.altsean.org/training-and-workshops.html> accessed 23 April 2022; or Asia Justice and Rights (AJAR), see <https://asia-ajar.org/myanmar-burma/> accessed 23 April 2022. For an overview of earlier initiatives, see Patrick Pierce and Caitlin Reiger, 'Navigating Paths to Justice in Myanmar's Transition' (International Centre for Transitional Justice June 2014) <https://www.ictj.org/sites/default/files/ICTJ-Myanmar-Development-Report-2014.pdf> accessed 23 April 2022.

42 Valérie Arnould, 'Reflections on a Decentralized Approach to Transitional Justice in the DR Congo' (2021) 33 Africa Policy Brief 1.

43 ibid 7.

44 Lydiah Kemunto Bosire and Gabrielle Lynch, 'Kenya's Search for Truth and Justice: The Role of Civil Society' (2014) 8 International Journal of Transitional Justice 256; Christoph Sperfeldt, 'The Trial against Hissène Habré: Networked Justice and Reparations at the Extraordinary African Chambers' (2017) 21 The International Journal of Human Rights 1243.

45 Noha Aboueldahab, 'Transitional Justice Policy in Authoritarian Contexts: The Case of Egypt' (Brookings Doha Center 2017).

46 Marlies Glasius, *The International Criminal Court: A Global Civil Society Achievement* (Routledge 2007); Michael J Struett, *The Politics of Constructing the International Criminal Court: NGOs, Discourse, and Agency* (Palgrave Macmillan 2008); Peter Brett and Line Engbo Gissel, 'Explaining African Participation in International Courts' (2018) 117 African Affairs 195, 206.

47 Sarah Williams, Hannah Woolaver, and Emma Palmer, *The Amicus Curiae in International Criminal Justice* (1st edn, Hart Publishing 2020).

48 Kenneth A Rodman, 'Intervention and the "Justice Cascade": Lessons from the Special Court for Sierra Leone on Prosecution and Civil War' (2015) 16 Human Rights Review 39.

49 Florian Jessberger and Julia Geneuss (n 8).

50 Carsten Stahn, 'Legacy in International Criminal Justice' in Margaret M deGuzman and Diane Marie Amann (eds), *Arcs of Global Justice: Essays in Honour of William A. Schabas* (Oxford University Press 2018).

51 Boesenecker and Vinjamuri (n 37).
52 Jasmina Brankovic and Hugo van der Merwe (n 10).
53 William A Schabas, 'Internationalized Courts and Their Relationship with Alternative Accountability Mechanisms: The Case of Sierra Leone' in Cesare P R Romano, André Nollkaemper and Jann K. Kleffner (eds) *Internationalized Criminal Courts: Sierra Leone, East Timor, Kosovo, and Cambodia* (Oxford University Press 2004).
54 Emma Palmer (n 2).
55 ibid; Laurel E Fletcher and Harvey M Weinstein, 'Writing Transitional Justice: An Empirical Evaluation of Transitional Justice Scholarship in Academic Journals' (2015) 7 Journal of Human Rights Practice 177.
56 David Backer, 'Civil Society and Transitional Justice: Possibilities, Patterns and Prospects' (2003) 2 Journal of Human Rights.
57 Paul Gready and Simon Robins (n 35) 964.
58 ibid; Kochanski (n 39).
59 Susan Harris Rimmer, *Gender and Transitional Justice: The Women of East Timor* (Routledge 2010).
60 Corri Zoli, M. Cherif Bassiouni and Hamid Khan, 'Justice in Post-Conflict Settings: Islamic Law and Muslim Communities as Stakeholders in Transition' (2017) 33 Utrecht Journal of International and European Law 38; Hakeem O. Yusuf, 'Transitional Justice in the Middle East and North Africa: Taking Account of Islam' (2017) 14 Muslim World Journal of Human Rights 145.
61 Elham Kazemi, 'Transitional Justice in Tunisia: When Religion Meets State' (2019) 13 International Journal of Transitional Justice 590.
62 Kimura Ehito, 'The Struggle for Justice and Reconciliation in Post-Suharto Indonesia' (2015) 4 Southeast Asian Studies 73–93.
63 Paul Gready and Simon Robins (n 35) 968. See also Elizabeth F Drexler, 'Fatal Knowledges: The Social and Political Legacies of Collaboration and Betrayal in Timor-Leste' (2013) 7 International Journal of Transitional Justice 74–94.
64 Corri Zoli, M. Cherif Bassiouni and Hamid Khan (n 60).
65 Sara Dezalay, 'The Role of International NGOs in the Emergence of the Field of Transitional Justice: A Case-Study of the International Center for Transitional Justice' in Cheryl Lawther, Luke Moffett and Dov Jacobs (eds) *Research Handbook on Transitional Justice* (Edward Elgar Publishing 2017).
66 Sara Kendall, 'Donors' Justice: Recasting International Criminal Accountability' (2011) 24 Leiden Journal of International Law 585.
67 Alex Jeffrey, Lynn Staeheli and David J Marshall, 'Rethinking the Spaces of Civil Society' (2018) 67 Political Geography 111.
68 Diane F Orentlicher, '"Settling Accounts" Revisited: Reconciling Global Norms with Local Agency' (2007) 1 International Journal of Transitional Justice.
69 Aileen Thomson, 'Prospects for Justice in Myanmar: Does the New Political Reality Offer Opportunities for Addressing Human Rights Violations?' (ICTJ Briefing, International Center for Transitional Justice 2016) <https://www.ictj.org/sites/default/files/ICTJ-Briefing-Myanmar-TJ-2016.pdf> accessed 12 July 2021.
70 ibid.
71 ND-Burma (n 18), 75, emphasis added.
72 ND-Burma, 'You Cannot Ignore Us Victims of human rights violations in Burma' (ND-Burma 2018) 16 <https://nd-burma.org/you-cannot-ignore-us-victims-of-human-rights-violations-in-burma/> accessed 23 April 2022.
73 ibid; Helene Maria Kyed and Ardeth Thawnghmung, 'Trends in Southeast Asia: The Significance of Everyday Access to Justice in Myanmar's Transition to Democracy' (ISEAS Yusof Ishak Institute 2019) 9; 'Searching for Justice in the

Law: Understanding access to justice in Myanmar' (MyJustice 2018) <https://www.myjusticemyanmar.org/sites/default/files/MJS%20Report_FINAL_online.pdf> accessed 23 April 2022.

74 Veronica Collins, 'Opinion: Without justice, the innocent will continue to be killed in Burma' (ND-Burma 3 October 2017) <https://nd-burma.org/opinion-without-justice-the-innocent-will-continue-to-be-killed-in-burma/> accessed 23 April 2022.

75 See ICC, 'Civil society and the ICC', <https://www.icc-cpi.int/get-involved/Pages/ngos.aspx> accessed 23 April 2022; Sarah Williams, Hannah Woolaver and Emma Palmer (n 47).

76 E.g., Betsy Apple, 'School for Rape: The Burmese Military and Sexual Violence' (EarthRights International 1998).

77 E.g., International Federation for Human Rights (FIDH), the Alternative ASEAN Network on Burma (ALTSEAN-Burma), and the Burma Lawyers Council (BLC), 'Burma/Myanmar: International crimes committed in Burma: the urgent need for a Committee of Inquiry' (August 2009) 6 <https://www.fidh.org/IMG/pdf/bu08.pdf> accessed 23 April 2022.

78 Progressive Voice, Rohingya Women Welfare Society and Kachin Women's Association—Thailand, 'UN Security Council Must Act Now and Refer the Situation in Myanmar to the International Criminal Court' (ND-Burma 26 October 2018) <https://nd-burma.org/un-security-council-must-act-now-and-refer-the-situation-in-myanmar-to-the-international-criminal-court/> accessed 23 April 2022.

79 The first Special Rapporteur was appointed in 1992, for reports see OHCHR, 'Special Rapporteur on the situation of human rights in Myanmar' (United Nations) <https://www.ohchr.org/en/hrbodies/sp/countriesmandates/mm/pages/srmyanmar.aspx> accessed 23 April 2023.

80 E.g., Human Rights Watch, '"All You Can Do Is Pray" Crimes Against Humanity and Ethnic Cleansing of Rohingya Muslims in Burma's Arakan State' (22 April 2013) <https://www.hrw.org/report/2013/04/22/all-you-can-do-pray/crimes-against-humanity-and-ethnic-cleansing-rohingya-muslims> accessed 23 April 2022; Amnesty International, 'Myanmar: "We are at breaking point"—Rohingya: persecuted in Myanmar, neglected in Bangladesh' (19 December 2016) <https://www.amnesty.org/en/documents/asa16/5362/2016/en/> accessed 23 April 2022; Human Rights Watch, 'Burma: Rohingya Recount Killings, Rape, and Arson; Video Testimony Matches Satellite Images of Attacks' (21 December 2016) <https://www.hrw.org/news/2016/12/21/burma-rohingya-recount-killings-rape-and-arson> accessed 23 April 2022; Human Rights Watch, 'Crimes against Humanity by Burmese Security Forces Against the Rohingya Muslim Population in Northern Rakhine State since August 25, 2017' (25 September 2017) <https://www.hrw.org/news/2017/09/25/crimes-against-humanity-burmese-security-forces-against-rohingya-muslim-population> accessed 23 April 2022.

81 ICC Prosecutor, 'Request for authorisation of an investigation pursuant to article 15' (ICC-01/19-7 4 July 2019) paras 18, 293–294.

82 ibid.

83 E.g , American Bar Association and FIDH, 'Challenges and Prospects on the ICC's Horizon: Afghanistan, Myanmar and More (6 December 2018) <https://globaljusticecenter.net/press-center/events/1020-challenges-and-prospects-on-the-icc-s-horizon-afghanistan-myanmar-and-more>.

84 E.g , Fortify Rights, 'Policies of Persecution: Ending Abusive State Policies Against Rohingya Muslims in Myanmar' (Fortify Rights 2014) <https://www.fortifyrights.org/downloads/Policies_of_Persecution_Feb_25_Fortify_Rights

.pdf> accessed 23 April 2022; Fortify Rights, 'Myanmar: Cooperate with ICC and Independent Mechanism on Accountability for Atrocities' (Fortify Rights 2019) <https://www.fortifyrights.org/mya-inv-2019-03-18/> accessed 14 July 2021.

85 ibid.

86 Fortify Rights, 'Ending Impunity in Myanmar: Can the National Unity Government of Myanmar Delegate Jurisdiction to the International Criminal Court?' (2021) <https://www.fortifyrights.org/downloads/Ending%20Impunity%20in%20Myanmar%20-%20Fortify%20Rights%20-%20August%202021.pdf> accessed 23 April 2022.

87 PILPG, 'Documenting Atrocity Crimes Committed Against the Rohingya in Myanmar's Rakhine State: Factual Findings Report' (Public International Law & Policy Group 2018).

88 ibid.

89 PILPG, 'Documenting Atrocity Crimes Committed Against the Rohingya in Myanmar's Rakhine State: Factual Findings & Legal Analysis Report' (PILPG Factual Findings & Legal Analysis Report, Public International Law & Policy Group 2018).

90 ibid.

91 ibid.

92 Argelyn Adlawon, 'Documenting Atrocity Crimes Committed Against the Rohingya, Accountability and Next Steps'—An Overview of the Conference Held by the Public International Law and Policy Group (PILPG)' (2019) 11 Amsterdam Law Forum 103.

93 ibid.

94 ibid.

95 ibid.

96 Amnesty International, 'Myanmar Forces Starve, Abduct and Rob Rohingya, as Ethnic Cleansing Continues' (Index number: ASA 16/7835/2018, Amnesty International 2018) <https://www.amnesty.org/download/Documents/ASA1678352018ENGLISH.PDF> accessed 14 July 2021.

97 ibid.

98 Situation in Bangladesh/Myanmar, Decision Pursuant to Article 15 of the Rome Statute (No. ICC-01/19-27 14 November 2019) <https://www.icc-cpi.int/sites/default/files/CourtRecords/CR2019_06955.PDF> accessed 26 April 2022, paras. 15, 68, 81, 91.

99 ibid, para 22.

100 'ICC Judges Authorise Opening of an Investigation into the Situation in Bangladesh/Myanmar' (ICC Website 14 November 2019) <https://www.icc-cpi.int/Pages/item.aspx?name=pr1495> accessed 17 September 2020.

101 ibid.

102 ibid.

103 Sarah Williams, Hannah Woolaver and Emma Palmer (n 47).

104 See 'Transmission of an *Amicus Curiae* Submission from the Thayninga Institute for Strategic Studies' (ICC-RoC46(3)-01/18-34-AnxI 6 August 2018) <https://www.icc-cpi.int/RelatedRecords/CR2018_03979.PDF> accessed 23 April 2022. See also Decision on the Request of the Thayninga Institute for Strategic Studies for Leave to Submit *Amicus Curiae* Observations (ICC-RoC46(3)-01/18, Pre-Trial Chamber I 10 August 2018) <https://www.icc-cpi.int/CourtRecords/CR2018_04009.PDF> accessed 23 April 2022.

105 See *Amicus Curiae* Observations by the Bangladeshi Non-Governmental Representatives (pursuant to Rule 103 of the Rules) on the 'Prosecution's Request for a Ruling on Jurisdiction under Article 19(3) of the Statute' (No.

ICC-RoC46(3)-01/18 18 June 2018) <https://www.icc-cpi.int/CourtRecords/CR2018_03120.PDF> accessed 23 April 2022.

106 ibid para 111.

107 See Decision on the Joint Request for Leave to Submit *Amicus Curiae* Observations pursuant to Rule 103 of the Rules (ICC-RoC46(3)-01/18-15, Pre-Trial Chamber I 11 June 2018); Joint Observations Pursuant to Rule 103 of the Rules (ICC-RoC46(3)-01/18-15, Pre-Trial Chamber I 11 June 2018).

108 'Submissions on Behalf of the Victims Pursuant to Article 19(3) of the Statute' (ICC-RoC46(3)-01/18-9 30 May 2018) (GCR Submissions).

109 'Observations on Behalf of Alleged Victims from Tula Toli' (ICC-RoC46(3)-01/18-26 18 June 2018) (Tula Toli Submissions) para. 10.

110 GCR Submissions (n 108), para. 4.

111 Tula Toli Submissions (n 109), para. 11.

112 ibid, para 80.

113 Ibic para 80.

114 'Decision on the "Prosecution's Request for a Ruling on Jurisdiction under Article 19(3) of the Statute"' (ICC-RoC46(3)-01/18 6 September 2018).

115 'Decision Pursuant to Article 15 of the Rome Statute on the Authorisation of an Investigation into the Situation in the People's Republic of Bangladesh/Republic of the Union of Myanmar ("the situation in Bangladesh/Myanmar") (ICC-01/19, Pre-Trial Chamber III' | Decision 14 November 2019) (Authorisation Decision 2019) para 13.

116 ibid.

117 ibid.

118 ibid para 16.

119 ibid, containing 10 citations of the HRW report, 'Massacre by the River/ Burmese Army Crimes against Humanity in Tula Toli', 2017, compared to five citations of the Representations of Victims of Tula Toli, ICC=01/19-19.

120 Authorization Decision 2019 (n 115), para 126 and see fn 266.

121 Vasuki Nesiah, 'Local Ownership of Global Governance' (2016) 14 Journal of International Criminal Justice 985.

122 Faustina Pereira, Jessica Olney and Azizul Hoque, 'Community Perspectives on Access to Civil Justice after Cross-Border Displacement: The Needs of Rohingya Refugees in Bangladesh' (Policy Brief, Centre for Peace and Justice and The Asia Foundation 2021).

123 ibid.

124 Victims Participation and Reparations Section of the Registry and the Registry's Public Information and Outreach Section.

125 Public redacted version of 'Registry's First Report on Information and Outreach Activities' (ICC-01/19-33, Registry 6 July 2020) para 14.

126 ibid, para 23.

127 ibid, paras 20–23.

128 Virtual side event at the 19th Session of the ICC Assembly of States Parties, convened by No Peace Without Justice (NPWJ). Besides NPWJ, other NGOs included Amnesty International, Asia Justice Coalition, the Association against Impunity, Burma Task Force, International Federation for Human Rights (FIDH), Fortify Rights, Global Centre for the Responsibility to Protect, Global Justice Center, Human Rights Watch, Justice for All, Parliamentarians for Global Action and the Women's Initiatives for Gender Justice.

129 'Submissions on Behalf of the Victims Pursuant to Article 19(3) of the Statute' (ICC-RoC46(3)-01/18-9 30 May 2018).

130 See GRC, Basic Investigative Standards for International Crimes <https://www.globalrightscompliance.com/en/projects/basic-investigative-standards-for-international-crimes-investigations> accessed 23 April 2022.
131 ibid.
132 'Situation in the People's Republic of Bangladesh/Republic of the Union of Myanmar' (Victims' joint request concerning hearings outside the host State) (ICC-01/19, Pre-Trial Chamber III 4 August 2020).
133 ibid para 12.
134 ibid para 53.
135 'Situation in the People's Republic of Bangladesh/Republic of the Union of Myanmar (Decision on Victims' joint request concerning hearings outside the host State) (ICC-01/19, Pre-Trial Chamber III 27 October 2020) para 23.
136 See Asia Justice Coalition, 'Statement on the International Court of Justice Provisional Measures Order in The Gambia v Myanmar' (23 January 2020) <https://2c13781c-c65e-48b5-ac86-efc598a2bd62.filesusr.com/ugd/811bc6_776b99cb2dd04aada7130c57b86e5e62.pdf> accessed 23 April 2022.
137 E.g., 'Advisory Opinion of 8 July 1996 on the Legality of the Threat or Use of Nuclear Weapons', separate opinion of Judge Guillaume, para 2; as opposed to the dissenting opinion of Judge Weeramantry, 438.
138 E.g., in Gabcikovo-Nagymaros (Hungary v Slovakia) 1997 the Natural Heritage Institute prepared a brief which was included as one of the annexes to the Hungary Memorial; *Armed Activities on the Territory of the Congo* (*Congo v Uganda*) 2005, the Uganda memorial included annexes with information from Amnesty International and other non-governmental organizations, see discussion in the dissenting judgment of Judge Kateka, para 27.
139 E.g., Judge Van den Wyngaert in Arrest Warrant of 11 April 2000 (*Congo v Belgium*) 2002, paras 154–155.
140 *Application of the Convention on the Prevention and Punishment of the Crime of Genocide* (*The Gambia v. Myanmar*), The Gambia's Application Instituting Proceedings and Request for Provisional Measures (11 November 2019)
141 ibid para 15.
142 GRC, 'Gambia argues use of forced starvation against the Rohingya in its ICJ submissions' (18 November 2019) <https://starvationaccountability.org/news-and-events/gambia-argues-use-of-forced-starvation-against-the-rohingya-in-its-icj-submissions> accessed 23 April 2022.
143 ibid.
144 Param-Preet Singh and Amy Braunschweiger, 'Interview: Landmark World Court Order Protects Rohingya from Genocide. How a Small African Nation Took on Myanmar's Crisis—and Won' (Human Rights Watch January 27 2020) <https://www.hrw.org/news/2020/01/27/interview-landmark-world-court-order-protects-rohingya-genocide#> accessed 23 April 2022.
145 Aaron Ross, 'With memories of Rwanda: The Gambian minister taking on Suu Kyi' (Reuters 6 December 2019) <https://www.reuters.com/article/us-myanmar-rohingya-world-court-gambia-idUSKBN1Y91HA> accessed 23 April 2022.
146 ibid.
147 Legal Action Worldwide, 'Where we work: Rohingya Crisis' <https://www.legalactionworldwide.org/where-we-work/rohingya-crisis/> accessed 26 April 2022.
148 Radio Free Asia, 'Rohingya Refugees Hail World Court's Ruling in Myanmar Genocide Case' (BenarNews 23 January 2020) <https://www.rfa.org/english/news/myanmar/refugees-01232020155348.html> accessed 23 April 2022.

149 Verena Hölzl, 'Three years after Rohingya exodus, mismatched expectations of justice' (The New Humanitarian 24 August 2020) <https://www.thenewhumanitarian.org/news-feature/2020/08/24/Bangladesh-Myanmar-Rohingya-international-justice> accessed 23 April 2022.
150 ibid.
151 ibid.
152 ibid.
153 See Asia Justice Coalition, 'Statement on the International Court of Justice Provisional Measures Order in The Gambia v Myanmar' (23 January 2020) <https://2c13781c-c65e-48b5-ac86-efc598a2bd62.filesusr.com/ugd/811bc6_776b99cb2dd04aada7130c57b86e5e62.pdf> accessed 23 April 2022.
154 See 'Joint letter to ICJ: Myanmar's obligation to comply with the Provisional Measures' (20 June 2020) <https://freerohingyacoalition.org/en/joint-letter-to-icj-myanmars-obligation-to-comply-with-the-provisional-measures/> accessed 23 April 2022.
155 Erin Farrell Rosenberg, John Packer and Fernand de Varennes, 'Provisional Measures in The Gambia v. Myanmar Case before the ICJ: The Case for Making Myanmar's Report Public' (Newlines Institute for Strategy and Policy 2021) <https://newlinesinstitute.org/wp-content/uploads/20210522-Gambia-v-Myanmar-ICJ-Rohingya-NISAP-1.pdf> accessed 28 July 2021.
156 ibid.
157 Büşra Nur Çakmak, 'Rights groups urge UK to join Rohingya case at ICJ' (Anadolu Agency 12 December 2020) <https://www.aa.com.tr/en/europe/rights-groups-urge-uk-to-join-rohingya-case-at-icj/2074607> accessed 23 April 2022.
158 See 'Joint statement of Canada and the Kingdom of the Netherlands regarding intention to intervene in The Gambia v. Myanmar case at the International Court of Justice' (2 September 2020) <https://www.government.nl/documents/diplomatic-statements/2020/09/02/joint-statement-of-canada-and-the-kingdom-of-the-netherlands-regarding-intention-to-intervene-in-the-gambia-v.-myanmar-case-at-the-international-court-of-justice> accessed 23 April 2022.
159 See 'Joint Statement of 36 Rohingya NGOS, urging the United Kingdom to join the ICJ case' (11 December 2020) <https://burmacampaign.org.uk/36-rohingya-organisations-call-on-uk-government-to-join-icjrohingya-genocide-case-against-myanmar/> accessed 23 April 2022.
160 See ICJ, 'Myanmar at the International Court of Justice' (10 December 2019) <https://www.crisisgroup.org/asia/south-east-asia/myanmar/myanmar-international-court-justice> accessed 23 April 2022.
161 Alison Smith and Francesca Basso, 'Justice for the Rohingya: What has happened and what comes next?' (CICC 13 February 2020) <https://www.coalitionfortheicc.org/news/20200213/justice-rohingya-what-has-happened-and-what-comes-next> accessed 23 April 2022.
162 For a more elaborate analysis, see Saratoon Santivasa, 'The NGOs' Participation in the Proceedings of the International Court of Justice' (2012) 5 Journal of East Asia & International Law 377; Dinah Shelton, 'The International Court of Justice and Nongovernmental Organizations' (2007) 9 International Community Law Review 139.
163 Valérie Arnould (n 42).

10 Re-envisioning the Responsibility to Protect for the Rohingya context

Ahmed Shafquat Hassan

Introduction

Since its development in 2005, the Responsibility to Protect (R2P) has seen varying levels of acceptance, implementation, and development. However, over the years, many scholars have debated at both ends, arguing whether the doctrine was a success or not. In light of the situation in Myanmar and the impacts it has had on a community of people—the Rohingya—it is important to assess whether the principle could be employed to offer protection for the most persecuted community.

This chapter will analyze the principle of R2P. First, it analyzes the existing framework of R2P and argues that the core failure of the existing framework is in its expectation that the political leadership of the world will be able to freely and neutrally employ the principle. In doing so, the analysis posits the necessity for an expansion of the R2P to look beyond simply conceptualizing military-oriented interventions. Second, the chapter analyzes previous instances in which R2P was evoked or where military intervention was sanctioned or assented to by the global leadership. The chapter will then draw parallels between the Rohingya situation and the conditions in Myanmar to argue that R2P could be employed in this case. However, with recognition of political restrictions surrounding the proposition, the chapter will argue for the employment of an altered vision for R2P. Finally, the chapter will explain the necessity for the R2P to be expanded to respond to further developments of similar situations, and why this proposed expansion is likely to be more palatable to the global *body politik* but also to be adequate to meet the immediate necessities to respond to the humanitarian crisis.

Development of R2P

In the post-cold war era of the 1990s, the world saw an increase in UN Charter Chapter VII peacemaking interventions across multiple jurisdictions.[1] However, these interventions largely lacked consistency or a core theory that justified intervention in each case.[2] Considering the commitment of the international political leadership to the principle of sovereignty, the world was faced with a dilemma in reconciling the need to intervene in the face of mass atrocities and the need

DOI: 10.4324/9781003304883-14

to respect the domestic sovereignty of individual nations. In response to the dilemma, the International Commission on Intervention and State Sovereignty (ICISS) published its 2001 report titled, 'The Responsibility to Protect' (R2P).[3] The core tenet of R2P is that sovereignty entails a responsibility on states to protect their citizens; in the event that they are unwilling or unable to do so, the right and the responsibility then fall upon the international community and the state is assumed to have abrogated its sovereignty.[4] A few years of debate later in 2005, at the World Summit, the United Nations General Assembly (UNGA) unanimously committed to the principle by articulating paragraphs 138[5], 139[6], and 140 in the summit's outcome document. The outcome document was subsequently adopted into UNGA resolution 60/1 of 2005.[7] At the time of adoption, R2P received this support as a result of the global community has just witnessed the horrors in Rwanda and Yugoslavia in the 1990s and their commitment to ensuring that the world never again fails to adequately respond to such horrors.

The principle was established on three pillars. First, that every state has the Responsibility to Protect its populations from four mass atrocity crimes: genocide, war crimes, crimes against humanity, and ethnic cleansing; second, that the wider international community has the responsibility to encourage and assist individual states in meeting that responsibility; finally, that if a state is manifestly failing to protect its populations, the international community must be prepared to take appropriate collective action, in a timely and decisive manner and in accordance with the UN Charter.[8] These principles were formally laid out in the UN Secretary-General's 2009 report entitled, 'Implementing the Responsibility to Protect'.[9] Again, in a 2009 General Assembly Debate, a resolution was passed[10] in support of the 2005 principle, taking into account the Secretary-General's report. Since then, the Secretary-General has published numerous reports on the invocation of the R2P—by 2018, records show that the principle had been invoked on around 80 different occasions in the Security Council since its conceptualization.

History of R2P

The principle at this stage was made more comprehensive compared with the generalized vision it was born with.[11] In elaborating R2P, the three-pillar approach was adopted. The first pillar, the nation where a humanitarian catastrophe is about to ensue, is expected to take responsibility for it, enacting appropriate and preventative measures. The second pillar proposes well-targeted assistance in the form of development aid, foreign investment, tactical assistance, and economic incentives, among others, to be taken by the international community. The objective is to capacitate the concerned nations with the tools required to address the impending problem. The third pillar proposes a more coercive set of measures, including international fact-finding, the deployment of peacekeepers, the imposition of arms embargoes and other diplomatic and economic sanctions to address the impending problems. Finally, where these proposed actions prove inadequate, the Security Council could authorise military intervention as a last measure.

In his clarification and elaboration, the Secretary-General of the UN made it clear that R2P only applies to cases of genocide, war crimes, crimes against humanity, and ethnic cleansing, without detracting from existing commitments under international law. Furthermore, the report clarified that, in the case of coercive action, the Security Council would have to assent, and the action would have to be in accordance with Chapter VII of the Charter. It was evident that R2P did not support unilateral military interventions.[12] However, this is not to say that instances of unilateral interventions did not receive retrospective assention.

From 2010 to 2017, the office of the Secretary-General has published yearly reports. These reports serve to document the advances of the principle and its practice. In 2012, the report entitled 'Timely and Decisive Response'[13] illustrated the parameters of the practice of coercive intervention. It also addressed the disagreements over UN-sanctioned NATO interventions in Libya—one of the earlier possible uses of the principle. The report highlighted the need for the principle's uniform application, a need for roles for regional and local actors in developing strategies for responses, and a need for integrating a nuanced understanding of the three pillars—in particular, the fact that pillar three was envisioned with the purpose of reinforcing pillar one. The report also noted the increase in active engagement on the part of the Security Council. More significantly, with regard to the proposition in this chapter, the report highlighted that pillar three interventions did not always necessitate the application of military force. It highlighted a series of other possible sanctions under Article 42 of the UN Charter.[14] In recognition of the fact that most member states had come to the conclusion that non-coercive measures had proved insufficient, the UN Security Council did authorize the actions taken in Libya, despite the contention of a few other members.

The military intervention in Libya in 2011 presented an instance of considerable developments in the R2P principle.[15] The objective of the intervention was the protection of the Libyan people from the oppression of the Gaddafi regime. NATO-led bombardment allowed Libyan rebels to fell the dictatorial regime and return the nation to its people. Despite the military success of the action in Libya, there were many within the UN who saw this as a form of abuse of the Council's mandate. Although Resolution 1973 was passed with the sole intent of civilian protection, and a view of neutrality, the actions of the NATO forces made it evident that the terms of the resolution had been stretched to now engage visible political objectives.[16] What is of note is the fact that, where it was felt necessary, certain members of the UN effectively cited R2P to engage in severe actions that ultimately had significant political implications. However, Libya continues to suffer in terms of its governance, despite the intervention by the 'Western powers'. Even as late as 2017, there have been instances of violent clashes and bombings.[17] Effectively, the Western intervention into Libya was largely focused on military intervention and regime change, without adequate consideration for rebuilding Libya. It can be argued that this so-called success was dubious. Yes, the regime had changed, and, for a while, the transition into a new form of government did bring about an end to the horrors of the previous regime—however, the long-term impact of this change has left Libya scarred.

In 2015, the Secretary-General published his next major report,[18] where he reflected on the first decade of the principle's adoption. In his reflection, the Secretary-General noted that there were significant failures in the attempts to uphold the principle. Mass atrocity crimes persisted across Syria, the Central African Republic, and Yemen, among others. Although the Secretary-General did remark upon certain successes, the overwhelming reality of the first decade was that the implementation of R2P was largely marred by a lack of political will.[19]

As an example, when the Syrian crisis was emerging in 2011, three draft Security Council resolutions recommending different degrees of condemnation and international interventions were vetoed by Russia and China. In 2014, another resolution referring the situation in Syria to the International Criminal Court (ICC) was also vetoed. The argument advanced in these instances was that the international community could not accept a repeat of the Libyan situation. A significant barrier to any R2P intervention in the Syrian case was the fact that the political opposition and the rebel military were visibly divided. The composition of the opposition was entrenched by different military and militia factions and their own agendas—among which was the nature of some military groups being fundamentalist in nature. In no way was any global power willing to back a rebel victory which might have resulted in hard-line Islamist rule.[20] By 2012, newly formed and volatile political groups engaging in Syria also made it difficult for any potential interveners to actively support any leadership in Syria, particularly where a vision of Syria after the Al-Assad regime still seemed largely unclear.[21] Furthermore, Syria's position as a strong trading partner and its outlook as a somewhat stable government in an otherwise volatile region also functioned as a significant disincentive for Security Council action or condemnation as to its state.[22] Additionally, Syria's conflict and the potential intervention could have significant impacts on neighbouring countries. Nations like Lebanon, Iraq, Iran, and Jordan had already taken in large numbers of refugees, and people from these bordering nations had also crossed into Syria to play roles in the conflict as well. In effect, the cross-border movement posed significant political implications in the region, threatening the stability of each of these governments.[23] In 2013, Turkey even made public statements after having received 170,000 refugees about their unwillingness to make concessions on its oppositional stance on Syria.[24] Evidently, however, Russian military, political, and economic interests and investments in Syria proved to be of significant concern. Russia remained staunchly against the possibility of any intervention and had vetoed eight UN Security Council resolutions proposed by France, Britain, and the United States.[25] By 2015, Russia unilaterally deployed its own military forces to fight against the rebel forces—or, as they claim, 'the ISIS threat'.[26] R2P's most belligerent opponent, Russia, had now undertaken the form of intervention that could effectively end the war. This made any possibility of a Security Council intervention near-impossible. What was telling from these events was that, despite numerous lost lives and significant damage to global peace and security, the global political leadership acted with utmost reverence for their own interest and very little concern for the actual loss of lives.[27] This then begs the question—with political will (or lack thereof) being the driving force of significant decisions around R2P, is the doctrine likely to remain a principle and never manifest into material frameworks or action?

As the Syrian situation worsened, in 2013, violent conflicts broke out in South Sudan and the Central African Republic. Crimes against humanity and war crimes were being committed in both countries by numerous actors and with impunity. All conditions were present for UN Security Council's use of the R2P doctrine to intervene. However, the conflict raged on without any major steps being taken by the Security Council to halt the mass atrocities. In South Sudan, the conflict was driven by an undercurrent of tribal affiliation. The clashing sides were the government, led by the President hailing from the Dinka tribe, and the opposition, led by a man hailing from the Nuer tribe.[28] Their clash led to the deaths of more than 50,000 people, the internal displacement of about two million, with another 1.9 million being forced to flee as refugees in 2016. By 2017, six million people were left severely food insecure.[29] Also in 2017, the death toll in the Central African Republic had risen to more than 5,000. There were continuous clashes between communities and militia groups warring over natural resources, attempts to gain territory, inter-religious disputes, and power. Predominantly, the clashes were between the Sleka (a Muslim militia group) and the Anti-Balaka (a Christian militia group). About 500,000 people (mostly Muslim) fled as refugees, and a further 384,000 were internally displaced.[30]

Considering the state of these nations, they would be logical candidates for the application of R2P. Beyond the evidence that emerged early on, depicting the commission of large-scale atrocities, both states had also effectively failed to exercise their responsibility to protect their population. Under the framing of R2P, where sovereignty is seen as a responsibility, the nations' inability or unwillingness would effectively allow the international community to intervene and in lieu of the states themselves, assume the responsibility. Additionally, neither of these states had any significant political or strategic ties. That is to say, that intervention in any case would not result in a political imbalance in the region to a scale that would have deep entrenching effects. Also, none of the members of the Security Council at the time had any military or political interest in these states that would bear significant consequences. Furthermore, in both cases, the nations lacked the political and institutional infrastructure or resources to assume control of the situation or resist any intervention—economic or military. Despite these facts, Security Council's intervention in these situations remained absent for years while conditions worsened.

Almost unnoticeable factors had built up over the period to contribute to this situation. First, the situation in Central Africa was too distant from the major powers for them to pay political or diplomatic attention. This was partially due to other politically significant concerns, and partially due to simple apathy due to no direct impact. This was depicted in interviews with diplomats in UN headquarters in New York—many individuals were incapable of even recognising the region on a map.[31] Second, the logistical and political barriers in the deployment of resources and peacekeepers became overwhelming. With dwindling support from typically well-equipped countries, UN peacekeeping forces had to be called in from Bangladesh, Ghana, Kenya, etc. This led to difficulties in organizing and managing resources effectively to reach the needed objectives at the time, which in turn led to delays. For example, the UN Security Council authorized the establishment of a peacekeeping force in Sudan in 2014, but the complement took more than 12 months to arrive. The dwindling support for these causes was mostly perpetuated by the fact that they seemed ultimately more costly than the benefits these nations would otherwise gain on an individual level.[32] Finally, there were considerable disputes surrounding the rules of engagement with regard to the authorization of peacekeeping missions. Whereas nations like Britain and France were in favour of more assertive framing to authorize the use of force, nations like Russia and China preferred a more politically sensitive approach.[33] This led to UN forces being deployed for the sole protection of UN missions and to protect civilians in UN facilities. An example of this form of protection led to UN peacekeepers standing by as 300 people were killed in Pibor County in South Sudan. With the UN Security Council being divided on such issues, negotiations of peacekeeping mandates were likely to be protracted and were likely to continue to pose a danger of political complications and contentious deliberations getting in the way of decisive action where it might otherwise be required.[34] Assuming that these concerns and systematic problems remain entrenched, it can be surmised that mandates on R2P are likely to continue to be complex and take incredibly long times, resulting in inadequacy. This points to the fact that, despite the framing of R2P, the contentions around sovereignty and humanitarian responses will continue to plague the global political leadership. Basically, this points to R2P being largely inadequate, as it is consistently marred by a series of other barriers, making the principle difficult to implement in reality.

The Myanmar nexus

The situation in Myanmar erupted in 2017, with over 700,000 Rohingya individuals being subjected to mass atrocities at the hands of the Myanmar military, forcing them to flee to Bangladesh. Since then, the Rohingya refugees have been placed in camps strewn across Bangladesh. Although Bangladesh's response to the eruption of the situation has been deservingly applauded, the conditions in which the Rohingya refugees now find themselves is less than adequate to sustain the population. Dwindling aid and support from the international community has placed significant burdens on an economy that had been stretched even before the influx. The Rohingya have expressed a desire to be able to return home, and diplomatic efforts to make that possible have thus far met with failure. This was further exacerbated by the military coup in Myanmar in 2021, resulting in a stalemate across numerous diplomatic tables, leaving the Rohingya people with little hope of being able to return safely and with full access to their rights.

The Rohingya in Myanmar have been suffering apartheid-like conditions since the 1940s. The hatred of the Rohingyas in Myanmar was triggered by their allegiances during World War II. Whereas the majority Buddhist population of Myanmar predominantly sided with the Japanese forces, the Rohingyas sided with the British allied forces. After the war, while the Rohingya were hoping for independence, the British colonial powers, wanting to appease the Buddhist majority, decided that the Rohingya-populated areas would become part of Myanmar (then Burma). This started a series of decisions by the government of Myanmar, slowly stripping the Rohingyas of all civil and political rights.[35] In 1962, the coup in Myanmar led to the establishment of Ne Win as the new dictator. Under his leadership, Myanmar adopted a new constitution in 1974.[36] The new constitution effectively allowed the government at the time to strip individuals of fundamental rights. Additionally, the constitution now provided recognition to certain ethnicities while effectively leaving out others.[37] On this basis, the Ne Win government launched operation 'Naga Min'—designed to weed out 'illegal migrants' and distinguish them from 'genuine citizens'. The process resulted in widescale attacks on many Rohingyas—arbitrary arrests, rape, pillage, and destruction of territory were among a series of other decisions and actions that threatened the safety of all Rohingya. While many suffered, around 250,000 Rohingya were forced to flee to Bangladesh at the time.[38] However, the military junta was later compelled to accept the repatriation of about 200,000 Rohingya in 1978.[39] Later, in 1982, the Ne Win government decided to solidify their pursuits of exclusion by drafting a citizenship law which listed 135 ethnic groups but excluded the Rohingya.[40] Under the new laws, the Rohingya did not have citizenship in Myanmar, and, to add further to their troubles, they were unable to apply for associate citizenship. To make matters even worse, many Rohingya people lost numerous documents pertaining to their rights to citizenship as a result of multiple military operations.[41] This depicts a long-standing practice of otherization of the Rohingya people in Myanmar. Not only were the Rohingya subject to atrocities and violence locally, but they were also systematically deprived as a part of state policy. Both of these factors constitute elements of crimes against humanity, per the Rome Statute.[42]

After the uprising of 1988 the Shwe government undertook an enormous militarization project in Rakhine 1991–1992, inflicting terrible violence, forced labour, and forcibly displacing 250,000 Rohingyas from their homes, and pushing them into Bangladesh.[43] These Rohingyas were placed in camps strewn across Bangladesh's Cox's Bazar region. Pursuant to an agreement between the Bangladeshi and Myanmar governments, brokered by China at the time, about 180,000 Rohingya were repatriated back to Myanmar. However, the conditions of that repatriation agreement were still largely dubious and did not provide adequate safety assurances for the Rohingya.[44] Later in 2012, communal violence broke out in Myanmar, forcing thousands of Rohingya out of the country and many more into Internally Displaced People camps in Rakhine State.[45] Furthermore, by 2014, President Thein Sien's regime had adopted a series of laws that discriminated against Rohingya cultural practices, limiting the ability of Rohingya individuals to integrate into the general Myanmar population. To add to the woes, the same government registered the Rohingya as 'Bengali' in the 2014 UN-funded census in an attempt to appease Burmese ultra-nationalists.

By 2017, Aung San Suu Kyi had promised to uphold the recommendations made by the former UN Secretary General Kofi Annan, which cited 88 recommendations to address long-standing human rights concerns, and a need to review the 1982 citizenship laws.[46] On 24 August 2017, after the release of the report, clashes broke out. The government deployed about 35,000 soldiers tasked with carrying out clearance operations.[47] Thousands of Rohingya were killed in the operation, and 354 villages were destroyed, with nearly 800,000 Rohingyas fleeing to Bangladesh for fear of their lives.[48]

While conflicts raged on in Myanmar and the Rakhine region, with hundreds of thousands of deaths on both sides and policies being specifically crafted to limit the rights of the Rohingya people, the situation had not improved in any way for Rohingya people. Nearly 600,000 Rohingya still remain in Rakhine State, many of whom are forced to live behind barbed wire with no political representation or any access to citizenship rights, and very little freedom of movement.[49]

Historically, a vast majority of the atrocities committed against the Rohingya people have been perpetuated by the military. Following the coup in 2021, the hopes of safe repatriation for the Rohingya in Bangladesh and the hopes of political representation and safety have been stymied.[50] Since then, conditions have hardly improved or moved towards any promises of safe repatriation. Multiple diplomatic efforts towards resolutions on the crisis have also failed. With dwindling support for the Rohingya refugees living in Bangladesh and limited access to international support for those in Myanmar, it is imperative to consider whether R2P principles should be invoked to take more concrete actions to respond to the situations in Myanmar.

In effect, it would seem that Myanmar's actions towards the Rohingya population show a clear lack of willingness or an inability on behalf of the Myanmar government or military to protect the Rohingya from any of the harm discussed above. In particular, the curious question is whether the lack of citizenship (formally speaking) should have any impact on the implications of R2P on the Myanmar government—considering that the first pillar places a responsibility on the sovereign state to maintain its sovereignty by protecting its citizens. However, an obvious response to this should be that citizenship should only be a secondary concern where human lives are clearly in danger.

R2P in light of the coup

The international response to the military coup in Myanmar, led by the Tatmadaw, has been abysmally minimal. While hundreds were dying[51] the UN Security Council was unable to unite behind a single statement of condemnation of the coup, let alone being able to pass an actual resolution. At a regional level, the response was even more muted, with nations like Thailand, Vietnam, and Cambodia refusing to condemn the coup, calling it an internal matter.[52] This depicted an evident reluctance among the international community to consider

R2P in response to the Myanmar situation, almost like a repeat of the conditions in Syria where political and economic interests of local actors led to an inertia in response. It took almost two months for the UN Office on Genocide Prevention and the Responsibility to Protect to issue a public statement, reminding the international community about the importance of R2P in such circumstances.[53] This was despite the fact that the military coup in Myanmar is a strong indicator of increased risk according to the UN Framework of Analysis of Atrocity Crimes.[54] Indeed, it was the Tatmadaw that forced its way back into power, and has been the historic perpetrators of violence against various ethnic groups, including the Rohingya.

It is important to note a few things at this juncture. First, the situation in Myanmar at this stage had reached a point where it was evident that atrocity crimes were being committed against a population of civilians and that such actions were being propagated by the very entity that was now in control of the state apparatus, meaning that the state was in large part both unwilling and incapable of protecting the Rohingya people. Second, the international community was altogether too slow to respond or to even craft an adequate response. It had been about four years since the exodus in 2017, and the world had been attempting diplomatic talks to try and help achieve the hopes of the Rohingya people—safe repatriation. Considering that this had not happened as of this point, it was even more unlikely to happen now, until some form of intervention took place. Third, the attitude of the Tatmadaw towards international obligations revealed a trend of further non-compliance. It therefore begs the question of whether R2P is likely to be effective in this scenario under its current framework, or whether it is likely to be invoked at all. To this effect, it is important at this stage for the international community to begin considering R2P from the lens of atrocity prevention and the protection of human lives, as opposed to focusing efforts to try and restore the former democratic government. The focus on atrocity prevention makes the issue more of an international concern and less of an internal matter, as it reframes the situation in Myanmar as a matter of urgency. In fact, under the current framing of R2P, it is astounding coming to the realization that, while hundreds and thousands were being forced out of their homes, the focus of the Western international powers was geared towards demanding the release of State Counsellor, Aung San Suu Kyi.[55]

Structural failures of R2P

The Rohingya situation is one of the greatest failures of the international community to apply R2P. Despite the universal consensus to make use of the doctrine,[56] most international actors avoided political conflict with Myanmar on the Rohingya issue. In fact, the conviction of the international community that a Chinese and Russian veto would arise on the matter of intervention on the Rohingya issue is likely to have emboldened the Tatmadaw's handling of the Rohingya situation.[57] Effectively, there was minimal effort to employ R2P at any level or across all three pillars of the doctrine.

Evidenced by history, the Rohingya's status as an extremely vulnerable group in Myanmar only worsened over the years leading to 2017. The Rohingya became victims of mass atrocities and found no protection under Burmese security forces—who were, in many instances, complicit in the crimes. In the 2015 elections, their loss of political rights and the anti-Muslim campaigns against the Rohingya became even more visible. At this stage, external actors should have employed R2P under the second pillar of the doctrine to address the growing risks of atrocity crimes and crimes against humanity against the Rohingya. However, as a result of its existing structure, countries focused more on democratization, economic development, and political access over a human rights-based approach to R2P. Furthermore, the employment of R2P under the second pillar requires the consent of the state in question—the objective has always been, in this case, to empower the state to protect its own citizens. However, in the Myanmar situation, this was impossible, considering the government of Myanmar's denial of the Rohingya's rights within the country.[58]

Although, at this point, logic dictates that the protection of the Rohingya through the third pillar of R2P, the most decisive measures, such as referral to the ICC or an intervention by force, seem highly unlikely. The use of any pillar three measure requires Security Council authorization, which is likely to be met by a veto by China, based on their recent commitment to the Myanmar government. Furthermore, regional actors also seem resistant to the idea of any form of intervention.[59] These structural barriers led to the focus shifting towards humanitarian efforts for the survivors of the atrocity crimes and post-fact accountability efforts. This meant that discussions surrounding the possibility of any form of intervention, including the possibility of embargos on arms sales, were effectively stymied .

This supports the observation that R2P is inherently structurally limited in its reliance on the Security Council for its implementation. Hence, as with other instances, like Syria, or the Uyghurs in China, R2P, in its current form, is highly unlikely to be implementable for the protection of the Rohingya. It will inevitably be met with political resistance at diplomatic tables as a result of certain permanent members of the Security Council, their relationship with Myanmar's government, and the Myanmar government's attitudes towards the Rohingya people. It is therefore imperative to consider whether an expansion of the R2P principle, to include alternative measures geared towards human protection, should be developed.

Expanding R2P

Considering these barriers, the R2P has previously been discarded as a failure.[60] This led to the states committed to R2P to devise alternative mechanisms for its employment outside of the regular R2P norms. In 2018, considering that the UN Security Council was likely to be blocked, the UN Human Rights Council established an independent international mechanism to advance the issue of accountability for the crimes committed against the Rohingya. These measures were modelled after the UN General Assembly mechanisms employed as a response to the situation in Syria. Although the Myanmar mechanisms could not prosecute those responsible for atrocities under these measures, they were tasked with gathering and documenting evidence should prosecution become feasible in the future.[61] These investigative mechanisms included new potential atrocity crimes in light of the military coup.[62]

These mechanisms technically do not fall under the second pillar but rather fall under a softer iteration of the third pillar. This is owing to the fact that the second pillar typically requires the concerned state to develop its own structures to respond to these atrocities. However, as it stands, Myanmar has vehemently opposed receiving any assistance in this regard. Instead, these mechanisms have started to assist national trials in third states through the principle of universal jurisdiction,[63] although, unlike the binding effect of a UN Security Council resolution, these measures lack any binding impact. However, they benefit from and contribute to international efforts to provide support towards accountability measures. Additionally, these measures are less likely to be blocked by political complexities, as they can function without Security Council approval or the consent of the target nation's governments. However, the employment of these measures does not contribute to the international community's responsibility towards the R2P principle. This illustrates a need to rethink the application of R2P in situations like Myanmar and Syria, given the political circumstances.[64]

Conclusion

Considering the discussions above the expansion of the R2P principle is not only a necessity in the *status quo* but is also not impossible. Refocusing R2P towards the prevention of atrocities and the protection of human rights is likely to assist in yielding better results. Although the current framework focuses on developing capacity of target nations, respecting the principle of sovereignty, and, in the event of non-compliance, requiring Security Council approval to engage in intervention, a focus on human rights is likely to allow R2P framing to consider alternative forms of interventions. This proposition does not eliminate the need for the first two pillars but instead proposes alternative pillar three interventions.

R2P has currently proven to be largely inadequate. This is predominantly a result of global political incentive structures preventing actionable decisions. States tend to be averse to the idea of intervention depending on how it is framed. In particular, this is true of militaristic interventions in individual states. Additionally, considering the fate of Libya, interventions of such styles have typically themselves been driven by the interests of the intervener and have not adequately addressed the needs of the target nation. Hence, interventions have been mostly undesirable. Furthermore, interventions of capacity building to develop states to a point of being able to address the commission of atrocity crimes on their own requires the consent of the target states. Considering the unique situation where states are unwilling to entertain such efforts, it begs the question of what else is possible in such scenarios. In the case of the Rohingya, not only has there been no willingness nor any evidence of ability on behalf of the Tatmadaw-led government to ensure protection for the Rohingya people, but also Myanmar's position in the Asian region and its political ties with the global leadership make it highly unlikely that Security Council approval in favour of strong interventions would be achieved.

R2P principles thus need to incorporate greater support for Rohingya refugees through protection mechanisms. These mechanisms ought to be crafted with the intent of ensuring the protection of lives above all else. This could be achieved by policies that are contingent on the willingness of nations committed to the principle, without requiring their interaction on a political scale with any other nation. By way of example, nations committed to R2P could incorporate policies that take on responsibility sharing. For the Rohingya, currently facing persecution, and being forcibly displaced, R2P could incorporate policies that offer physical safe havens being offered to Rohingya refugees fleeing persecution in Myanmar. Not only does this ensure greater protection for a greater number of refugees, but it also alleviates logistical pressure from nations like Bangladesh, which is currently hosting Rohingya refugees at great costs to itself at a social and economic level. Furthermore, this incentivizes more nations to act in favour of resolving the Rohingya situation faster. In the absence of concrete measures of accountability, these policies are an effective stop gap that ensures human protection. Additionally, because these policies only require the willingness of individual nations, they are unlikely to be blocked by international political machinations. Considering the universal consensus towards R2P and considering that a majority of its concerns for implementation was driven by potential blocks at the Security Council level, this expansion provides a palatable alternative that is not only sustainable but is also likely to be effective at ensuring that human lives are protected. Furthermore, this allows the opportunity for the international community to assist the Rohingya in galvanizing activities and advocate for their demands. By first ensuring their physical safety, global actors in this field are then able to move towards capacity building for the victims of such crimes to push towards policy changes that protect them.

Another proposition that is reasonable at this stage is the empowerment of regional bodies. In the evidence that there is sufficient political will to respond to a crisis, often the response is stymied as a result of a logistical bottleneck or a lack of a nuanced understanding of the local complexity of the problem. It is therefore argued that regional organizations or *ad-hoc* coalitions made up of local actors might be able to respond faster than most UN organizations.[65] Whereas it is true that such actions are likely to attract less legitimacy from the wider global community, it is also argued that this form of action is likely to be more precise and still carry enough support within the region to legitimize the action by virtue of those acting. Ultimately, it is likely for the same constraints to appear at both international and regional stages. However, it is more likely that the constraints are easier dealt with at the regional level.[66]

Although no one should be under the illusion that this is likely to happen immediately, it is worthy of consideration that, in the absence of any active efforts towards resolving the situation, and with building pressures on Bangladesh—currently hosting over a million refugees, often in camps which offer very little freedoms—it is imperative that the R2P doctrine starts incorporating a vision that actively redistributes that pressure in order to optimise the protection of the Rohingya. These alternative mechanisms to R2P implementation are assessable through the quantification of resources deployed to that effect and hence offer a more comprehensive determination of each nation's commitment to the doctrine. But above all, it attempts to respond to the greatest concern of such situations—protection of vulnerable groups.

Notes

1 See, e.g., S.C. Res. 788, U.N. Doc. S/RES/788 (Nov. 19, 1992); S.C. Res. 929, 3, U.N. Doc. S/RES/929 (June 2, 1994); S.C. Res. 940, 4, U.N. Doc. S/RES/940 (July 31, 1994); S.C. Res. 1181, U.N. Doc. S/RES/1181 (July 13, 1998); S.C. Res. 1244, 9, U.N. Doc. S/RES/1244 (June 10, 1999).

2 Francis Kofi Abiew, *The Evolution of the Doctrine and Practice of Humanitarian Intervention* (1st edn, Springer 1999) 16–17

3 Int'l Comm'n on Intervention and State Sovereignty (ICISS), The Responsibility to Protect: Report of the International Commission on Intervention and State Sovereignty (Dec. 2001). The Commission members were Gareth Evans (Australia), Mohamed Sahnoun (Algeria), Gisele Cote-Harper (Canada), Lee Hamilton (United States), Michael Ignatieff (Canada), Vladimir Lukin (Russia), Klaus Naumann (Germany), Cyril Ramaphosa (South Africa), Fidel V. Ramos (Philippines), Cornelio Summaruga (Switzerland), Eduardo Stein Barillus (Guatemala) and Ramesh Thakur (India).

4 Ibid; Francis M. Deng and others, *Sovereignty as Responsibility: Conflict Management in Africa* (The Brookings Institution 1996)

5 United Nations General Assembly, 'Resolution adopted by the General Assembly on 16 September 2005' (2005) A/RES/60/1 <www.un.org/en/development/desa/population/migration/generalassembly/docs/globalcompact/A_RES_60_1.pdf> accessed 25 April 2022; Paragraph 138, UN World Summit Outcome Document, 'Each individual State has the responsibility to protect its populations from genocide, war crimes, ethnic cleansing, and crimes against humanity. This responsibility entails the prevention of such crimes, including their incitement, through appropriate and necessary means. We accept that responsibility and will act in accordance with it. The international community should, as appropriate, encourage and help States to exercise this responsibility and support the United Nations in establishing an early warning capability'.

6 Ibid; Paragraph 139, UN World Summit Outcome Document, 'The international community, through the United Nations, also has the responsibility to use appropriate diplomatic, humanitarian, and other peaceful means, in accordance with Chapters VI and VIII of the Charter, to help to protect populations from genocide, war crimes, ethnic cleansing and crimes against humanity. In this context, we are prepared to take collective action, in a timely and decisive manner, through the Security Council, in accordance with the Charter, including Chapter VII, on a case-by-case basis and in cooperation with relevant regional organizations as appropriate, should peaceful means be inadequate and national authorities are manifestly failing to protect their populations from genocide, war crimes, ethnic cleansing, and crimes against humanity. We stress the need for the General

Assembly to continue consideration of the responsibility to protect populations from genocide, war crimes, ethnic cleansing, and crimes against humanity and its implications, bearing in mind the principles of the Charter and international law. We also intend to commit ourselves, as necessary and appropriate, to helping States build capacity to protect their populations from genocide, war crimes, ethnic cleansing, and crimes against humanity and to assisting those which are under stress before crises and conflicts break out'.

7 United Nations General Assembly, 'Resolution adopted by the General Assembly on 16 September 2005' (2005) A/RES/60/1 <www.un.org/en/development/desa/population/migration/generalassembly/docs/globalcompact/A_RES_60_1.pdf> accessed 25 April 2022

8 Jennifer M Welsh, 'Norm Robustness and the Responsibility to Protect' (2019) 4 (1) Journal of Global Security Studies <https://academic.oup.com/jogss/article/4/1/53/5347912> accessed 25 April 2022

9 Implementing the Responsibility to Protect, Report of the Secretary-General, UNGA, A/63/677, 12 January 2009

10 UNGA Resolution, A/RES/63/308 <https://undocs.org/Home/Mobile?FinalSymbol=A%2FRES%2F63%2F308&Language=E&DeviceType=Desktop&LangRequested=False> accessed 25 April 2022

11 Implementing the Responsibility to Protect, Report of the Secretary-General, UNGA, A/63/677, 12 January 2009

12 Ibid

13 Responsibility to Protect: Time and Decisive Response, Report of the UN Secretary-General, UN DOC A66/874

14 Charter of the United Nations 1945, Article 42

15 SC Res 1973 (17th March 2011) <www.un.org/securitycouncil/s/res/1973-%282011%29> accessed 25 April 2022

16 Paul D Williams and Alex J Bellamy, 'Libya' in S von Einseidel, D Malone, and B Stagno Ugarte, *The UN Security Council in the 21st Century* (Lynne Renner Publishers)

17 Human Rights Watch, 'Libya: Events of 2016' (Human Rights Watch, 2017) <www.hrw.org/world-report/2017/country-chapters/libya> accessed 25 April 2022

18 Responsibility to Protect: A Vital and Enduring Commitment: Implementing the Responsibility to Protect, Report of the Secretary General, UN Doc A/69/981 (13 July, 2015) <https://digitallibrary.un.org/record/798795?ln=en> accessed 25 April 2022

19 Ibid

20 Spencer Zifcak, 'The Responsibility to Protect' in Malcon D Evans (ed) *International Law* (5th edn, Oxford University Press) 503

21 Ramzy Mardini, 'After Assad, Chaos?' *The New York Times* (Amman, 3 February 2013) <www.nytimes.com/2013/02/04/opinion/after-assad-chaos.html> accessed 25 April 2022

22 Cf Zifcak n (20)

23 Roula Khalaf, 'Lebanon's Complex Part in Syrian Conflict' *Financial Times* (29 October 2011) <www.ft.com/content/a14d8a1c-21ba-11e2-9cb4-00144feabdc0> accessed 25 April 2022; Nicholas Pelham, 'Jordan Starts to Shake' *The New York Review of Books* (8 December 2011) <www.nybooks.com/articles/2011/12/08/jordan-starts-shake/> accessed 25 April 2022.

24 Ibid

25 Dergham R, 'Commentary: The Council's Failure on Syria', in Sebastian von Einsiedel, David M Malone, and Bruno Stagno Ugarte (eds), *The UN Security Council in the 21st Century* (Lynne Rienner Publishers 2016).

26 'Russia joins in War in Syria: Five Key Points' *BBC* (1 October 2015) <www.bbc.com/news/world-middle-east-34416519> accessed 25 April 2022.

27 Charles Glass, 'In the Horrorscape of Aleppo' *The New York Review* (25 May 2017) <www.nybooks.com/articles/2017/05/25/syria-horrorscape-aleppo/> accessed 25 April 2022.

28 'Two Elephants Trample the Grass' *The Economist* (Nairobi, 21 December 2013) <www.economist.com/middle-east-and-africa/2013/12/21/two-elephants-trample-the-grass> accessed 25 April 2022.

29 Report of the Panel of Experts on South Sudan established pursuant to UN Security Council Resolution 2206 (2015), UN Doc S/2016/793, 19 September 2016 <https://digitallibrary.un.org/record/842365?ln=en> accessed 25 April 2022

30 Report of the Secretary General on Central African Republic, UN SCOR UN Doc S/2013/677 <www.un.org/sites/un2.un.org/files/s68.pdf> accessed 25 April 2022

31 Interview with European Ambassador to the United Nations (New York, May 2014).

32 Ramesh Thakur, 'R2P and the protection of civilians in armed conflict', in Ramesh Thakur, *The Responsibility to Protect: Norms, Laws and the Use of Force in International Politics* (1st edn, Routledge 2011)

33 UN Office of Oversight Services, Evaluation of the Implementation and Results of Protection of Civilians Mandates in United Nations Peacekeeping Operations, UN Doc A/68/787 (7 March 2014) <https://digitallibrary.un.org/record/767929?ln=en> accessed 25 April 2022

34 Report of the Secretary-General on Protection of Civilians in Armed Conflict, UN SCOR, UN Doc S2013/689 (22nd November 2013) <https://digitallibrary.un.org/record/761321> accessed 25 April 2022

35 Harrison Akins, 'The Two Faces of Democratization in Myanmar: A Case Study of the Rohingya and Burmese Nationalism' (2018) Journal of Muslim Minority Affairs 38:2, 229–245.

36 K S Devi, 'Myanmar under the Military Rule 1962–1988' (2014) International Research Journal of Social Sciences 3:10, 46–50.

37 Archana Parashar and Jobair Alam, 'The National Laws of Myanmar: Making of Statelessness for the Rohingya' (2019) International Migration 57:1, 94–108.

38 Zoltan Barany, 'The Rohingya Predicament.: Why Myanmar's Army Gets Away with Ethnic Cleansing' (Istituto Affari Internazionali (IAI), 7 March 2019) <www.jstor.org/stable/resrep19683?seq=1> accessed 24 April 2022; Morten B. Pedersen, 'The Roots of the Rohingya Refugee Crisis' (2018) Human Rights Defender 27:2, 16–20.

39 Mark Cutts, *The State of the World's Refugees, 2000: Fifty Years of Humanitarian Action* (Oxford University Press 2000).

40 Cf Barany (n 38); Andrew T H Tan (ed), *A Handbook of Terrorism and Insurgency in Southeast Asia* (Edward Elgar Publishing Ltd 2007)

41 Syeda Naushin Parnini, 'The Crisis of the Rohingya as a Muslim Minority in Myanmar and Bilateral Relations with Bangladesh' (2013) Journal of Muslim Minority Affairs, 33:2, 281–297

42 Rome Statute of the International Criminal Court 2002, Article 7

43 Nyi Nyi Kyaw, 'Unpacking the Presumed Statelessness of Rohingyas' (2017) Journal of Immigrant & Refugee Studies 15:3, 269–286

44 AKM Ahsan Ullah, 'Rohingya Refugees to Bangladesh: Historical Exclusions and Contemporary Marginalization' (2011) Journal of Immigrant & Refugee Studies 9:2, 139–161

45 Andrew Selth, 'Myanmar's Armed Forces and the Rohingya Crisis', Working Paper 140, Asia Center at the United States Institute of Peace, Washington DC,

2018 <https://archivefda.dlib.nyu.edu/bitstream/2451/61001/2/pw140-myanmars-armed-forces-and-the-rohingya-crisis.pdf> accessed 14 April 2022

46 Murray Hiebert, 'Whither U.S. Myanmar Policy after the Rohingya Crisis?' Center for Strategic & International Studies, Washington DC, 2018. <https://www.csis.org/analysis/whither-us-myanmar-policy-after-rohingya-crisis> (accessed 15th April 2022)

47 Michael F. Martin, 'Burma's Brutal Campaign against the Rohingya' (US House of Representatives Congressional Research Service, 2017) <www.congress.gov/115/meeting/house/106434/witnesses/HHRG-115-FA05-Wstate-MartinM-20170927.pdf> accessed 25 April 2022

48 UNHCR, 'Rohingya Emergency' (UNHCR 2019) <www.unhcr.org/rohingyaemergency.html> accessed 15 April 2022

49 Adam Simpson, Nicholas Farrelly, Ian Holliday, 'Myanmar Futures' in Adam Simpson, Nicholas Farrelly, Ian Holliday, *Routledge Handbook of Contemporary Myanmar* (Routledge)

50 Jessica Olney and Shabbir Ahmad, 'Beyond the Coup in Myanmar: The Views of Rohingya Refugees in Bangladesh' (Just Security, 10 June 2021) <www.justsecurity.org/76857/beyond-the-coup-in-myanmar-the-views-of-rohingya-refugees-in-bangladesh/> accessed 17 April 2022

51 International Crisis Group, 'Responding to the Myanmar Coup' Briefing No. 166, 16 February 2021 <www.crisisgroup.org/asia/south-east-asia/myanmar/b166-responding-myanmar-coup> accessed 16 April 2022

52 'ASEAN Urges Peaceful Solution to Myanmar Coup Standoff' (VOA News, 2 March 2021) <www.voanews.com/a/east-asia-pacific_asean-urges-peaceful-solution-myanmar-coup-standoff/6202775.html> accessed 25 April 2022

53 Joint Statement by UN Special Adviser on the Prevention of Genocide and the UN High Commissioner for Human Rights on Myanmar (28 March 2021) <www.un.org/sg/ en/content/note-correspondents-joint-statement-un-special-adviser-the-prevention-of- genocide-and-un-high-commissioner-for-human-rights-myanmar> accessed 17 April 2022

54 United Nations, 'Framework of Analysis for Atrocity Crimes: A Tool for Prevention' (United Nations, 2014) <www.un.org/en/genocideprevention/documents/atrocity-crimes/Doc.49_Framework%20of%20Analysis%20for%20Atrocity%20Crimes_EN.pdf> accessed 16 April 2022

55 By way of example, see an overview of the responses by the Nordic states in Mette Larsen, 'Myanmar Military Coup: Nordic and Asian Reactions' (ScandAsia, 2 February 2021) <https:// scandasia.com/myanmar-military-coup-nordic-and-asian-reactions/> accessed 16 April 2022.

56 See the lists of resolutions provided by the Global Centre for Responsibility to Protect (4 January 2021) <www.globalr2p.org/resources/un-security-council-resolutions-and-presidential- statements-referencing-r2p/≥ and (14 September 2020) <www.globalr2p.org/resources/ un-human-rights-council-resolutions-referencing-r2p/≥ accessed 18 April 2021.

57 Ivan Šimonović, 'Why "Never Again" and R2P Did Not Work in Myanmar' (2021) Global Responsibility to Protect 13 (2–3), 387–391

58 Pedersen, M B 'The Rohingya Crisis, Myanmar, and R2P 'Black Holes'' (2021) Global Responsibility to Protect 13 (2–3), 349–378.

59 Claire Q. Smith and Susannah G. Williams, 'Why Indonesia Adopted 'Quiet Diplomacy' over R2P in the Rohingya Crisis: The Roles of Islamic Humanitarianism, Civil–Military Relations, and ASEAN' (2021) Global Responsibility to Protect <https://brill.com/view/journals/gr2p/13/2-3/article-p158_158.xml> accessed 25 April 2022

60 David Rieff, 'R2P, R.I.P.' *New York Times* (Paris, 7 November 2011) <www.nytimes.com/2011/11/08/opinion/r2p-rip.html> accessed 25 April 2022

61 'Mandate of the Independent Investigative Mechanism for Myanmar' <https://iimm.un.org/> accessed 18 April 2022

62 UN, 'IIMM: Recipients of illegal orders should contact us' (UN, 17 March 2021) <https://iimm.un.org/iimm-recipients-of-illegal-orders-should-contact-us/> accessed 25 April 2022

63 Trial International, 'Universal Jurisdiction Case in Argentina: An Important Decision for the Rohingyas (Trial International, 12 August 2021) <https://trial-international.org/latest-post/universal-jurisdiction-case-in-argentina-an-important-decision-for-the-rohingyas/> accessed 19 April 2021

64 Mennecke, M, and Stensrud, E E, 'The Failure of the International Community to Apply R2P and Atrocity Prevention in Myanmar' (2021) Global Responsibility to Protect 13(2–3), 111–130

65 Nilsson, Desirée (2008). 'Partial Peace: Rebel Groups Inside and Outside of Civil War Settlements', Journal of Peace Research 45(4): 479–95

66 Syed Mansoob Murshed, *Explaining Civil War: A Rational Choice Approach*, Edward Elgar Publishing Limited, 2010

Index